ROBERT GORDON'S LEGACY

A History of Robert Gordon's Hospital and College

ROBERT GORDON'S LEGACY

A History of Robert Gordon's Hospital and College

Brian R.W. Lockhart

BLACK & WHITE PUBLISHING

First published 2007
by Black & White Publishing Ltd
99 Giles Street, Edinburgh EH6 6BZ

ISBN 13: 978 1 84502 157 3
ISBN 10: 1 84502 157 6

A CIP catalogue record for this book is available from the British Library.

Typeset by Ellipsis Books Limited, Glasgow
Printed and bound by MPG Books Ltd

CONTENTS

ACKNOWLEDGEMENTS

When I was Headmaster of Robert Gordon's College I was aware that there had been no history of the School written since the late 19th century. Unfortunately, plans for a major work to coincide with the 250th Anniversary of the Opening of the Hospital, in 2000, did not come to fruition. Thankfully, two members of staff came to our rescue. Phil Skingley produced *Div ye myn Lang Tam?* and Rod Richmond compiled *A Pictorial History*. These added greatly to our knowledge and the College Board of Governors approached Jack Webster in spring 2003 to ask him to produce a 'popular' history. The result, *The Auld Hoose,* published in 2005, was exactly what was wanted – a work with its emphasis very much on the modern period, balancing up the earlier histories, and on the people 'who brought life and fascination to the story'.

On my retiral, the Governors, knowing my interest in Hospital foundations, (having already written a book on Heriot's, the first of the Scottish Hospital schools), asked me to review the documentary material available to establish whether another book would be justified. The result is a work aimed at complementing the recent contributions. Indeed it specifically plays down, or even omits, matters dealt with recently elsewhere unless they are essential in explaining the development of Robert Gordon's Legacy over the past, almost three, centuries. As an institutional history it is essentially 'top-down' and it deals only with the Technical College and its successors as they relate to the College.

I owe many personal debts of gratitude to those who have helped and encouraged me in this work. Specifically I wish to thank the Governors, especially the former Chairman, Sir Graeme Catto, who commissioned the book, and Bob Leggate, the Bursar, who made the practical arrangements with the publisher; the staff of the University of Aberdeen's Special Libraries and Archives at King's College, especially Michelle Gait and June Ellner; the staff of the Archive Department of the Town House, Judith Cripps, Gwen McGinty and Fiona Musk; the Old Aberdeen Archive staff especially Eleanor Rowe; Jim Fiddes of the Robert Gordon University Library; Sheila Dunn of New College

Library, Edinburgh; staff at the Royal Commision on the Ancient and Historical Monuments in Edinburgh and Neil Cameron in particular for access to the Schools' Project material; Arthur McCombie who has shared with me his considerable insight into the relationships between the College and the Grammar School; Reverend James Stewart who did likewise with relationships between the College and the Aberdeen Endowments Trust; Neil Curtis of Marischal Museum, who arranged for Donal Bateson of Glasgow University to give his expert opinion on Robert Gordon's coin collection; and Dr Trevor Chalmers who came to my aid with transcriptions of 17th-century documents.

The first chapter of the book was a particular challenge given the almost complete lack of knowledge about Robert Gordon's stay in Danzig. Dr Paul Dukes initially gave help, and Dr Robert Frost and Dr Karin Friedrich (all of Aberdeen University) went to great lengths to make a trip to Gdansk possible for me. There Professor Edmund Kizik of the University of Gdansk helped me spend my time fruitfully in the State Archives.

I would also like to acknowledge the work of all those at Black & White Publishing who have been involved in the production of this book, and the technical help of my daughter, Joanne.

Finally, my profound thanks to all my former colleagues at Gordon's for their contributions, knowing or unknowing. In particular, former Heads of the College, George Allan and the late Jack Marshall, taught me to appreciate the special nature of the College. Penny Hartley has improved my understanding of many aspects of the College's history by her painstaking research. She read and commented on an early draft, and also helped greatly with the images reproduced in the book. Gordon Millar, of the Fachhochschule of Central Switzerland, did much to improve a later draft and gave me invaluable advice. I am pleased to acknowledge their contribution but take personal responsibility for the final contents. As a relative newcomer I hope I have done justice to a great Scottish school.

I dedicate this work to my wife,
Fiona,
for her support
and encouragement
during the writing.

1

ROBERT GORDON

The 'Grave Gordons'[1]

Robert Gordon was born into an established family in Aberdeen in 1668 and 'enjoyed the impress of a cultured home and the traditions of his branch of the great house of Gordon'.[2] He belonged to the Pitlurg family, which was descended from John Gordon of Auchleuchries,[3] third son of John Gordon of Scurdargue,[4] a first cousin of Elizabeth, the Gordon heiress whose marriage to Sir Alexander Seton founded the line of the Earls and Marquesses of Huntly, later Dukes of Gordon. John Gordon of Scurdargue and his brother Thomas of Ruthven,[5] commonly known as Jock and Tam, were the last male representatives of the original stock of de Gordun (or Gordon), of that Ilk, who owned lands in Berwickshire,[6] and later the domain of Strathbogie[7] in Aberdeenshire.

His great-grandfather, John,[8] was an infant when he succeeded to his properties of Pitlurg,[9] Botarie[10] and Kinmundy[11] and between 1579 and 1586 he was frequently mentioned in the records of the Privy Council, which was trying to settle ongoing feuds between the Gordons and Forbeses. For the next decade he was much in favour with James VI and was knighted by him on the occasion of Prince Henry's baptism in late August 1594.[12] He became the member of the Scottish Parliament for Aberdeenshire.[13] He married Isobel, daughter of William, Lord Forbes, and died in September 1600, being buried at Cairnie,[14] leaving two sons and a daughter.

The younger of these sons was Robert of Straloch, known as 'The Great Straloch' for his literary abilities[15] and his work in surveying and mapping the northern parts of Scotland. He was born at Kinmundy[16] in September 1580 and studied humanity, mathematics and philosophy at Marischal College[17] where he was reported to be its first Master of Arts (A.M.) graduate in 1597.[18] He went on to study at the University of Paris between 1598 and 1600 and was much influenced by his time there, which was shortened when he was called home on the death of his father. However, he continued his studies and produced (Latin) epigrams, epitaphs and emblems[19] for his family as practical devices to teach the force and elegance of the Latin language. As a result his children became excellent classical scholars. He purchased Straloch[20] in 1608 from his elder brother, to whom it had been disponed two years earlier.[21] However, Robert continued to live at Kinmundy for another ten years, while improving the Straloch property and restoring its manor house. He bought Fechil[22] before 1618, leaving it to his second son, and succeeded to Pitlurg and other family properties in 1619 on the death without issue of his elder brother, John.

During the Civil Wars Straloch endeavoured to reconcile the differences between the two sides and was frequently consulted by the second Marquis of Huntly and his son – though his advice was not always taken![23] He is remembered chiefly as a cartographer. In October 1641 Charles I asked him to 'reveis the saidis cairtiss' of various shires of Scotland. The maps, drawn by Timothy Pont,[24] had been sent to Joan Blaeu for inclusion in his Atlas.[25] Probably Straloch was not expected to revise plates already engraved but to fill gaps in the coverage of Scotland. However, he seems to have set about depicting Scotland quite independently of Blaeu.[26] In this work he was assisted by his son, James of Rothiemay, and Straloch was given immunity from all quartering of soldiers and public burdens in 1646 to complete it. He remained free during Cromwell's administration to engage on his work and appears to have retained the respect of both sides in an increasingly bitter period.

Straloch is now regarded more for his chorography than his cartography[27] although Blaeu himself gave credit to the Gordons for their 'finishing touches'.[28] Although best known for his contribution to Blaeu's Atlas, that was only a small part of his scholastic pursuits. His contact with Pont's work came relatively late in his career, in consequence of his reputation and not the cause of it. His magnificent astrolabe, dated 1597, and typical of the European version of this ancient Eastern instrument for solving problems relating to time and the position of the sun and stars in the sky, is still extant.[29] Straloch lived to see the Restoration of Charles II, dying in August 1661,[30] and he was buried in the kirkyard of Newmachar church.[31] Shortly after his death he was described as 'one of the most worthy and learned Gentlemen of our nation'.[32]

Straloch had played his part in ensuring that Scotland became one of the best-mapped countries in the world.[33] On his death the manuscript maps passed to James who treasured the collection containing his father's work.[34]

Among the other bequests in Straloch's Will was one of 200 merks to the poor of Newmachar, especially householders burdened with young children[35] – a bequest which Robert Gordon, founder of Gordon's Hospital,[36] knew about and was to repeat on a far grander scale some three-quarters of a century later.

Robert of Straloch had married Katherine, daughter of Sir Alexander Irvine of Lenturk, a cadet of the Drum family, in 1608 and the union produced seventeen children.[37] The oldest son, Robert, 6th of Pitlurg, (1609–81) spent some time on the continent on military service, which was regarded as a necessary part of a Scottish gentleman's education, joining the Swedish army fighting in the Thirty Years' War under Gustavus Adolphus.[38] On the latter's death in 1632, a number close to the late king and some high-ranking army officers were awarded the 'Order of Gustavus Aldophus' – a rarely awarded medal in gold and enamel.[39] Robert was included in that number.

Straloch's fifth son and seventh child, James, was born at Kinmundy in May 1617. He graduated from King's College in 1636[40] and became Parson of Rothiemay, Banffshire, in May 1641.[41] Following in his father's scholarly pursuits he was trained in cartographic description and in 1642 was involved in compiling maps of Fife and Kinross. The former surpassed Pont's original map, which had already been engraved, and so it was added by Blaeu to his Atlas. The latter survives in manuscript form.[42] His next cartographic project took him in 1646–7 to Edinburgh, where he drafted the most detailed bird's-eye view of the town in its entire history. It became the standard map or view of Edinburgh for nearly a century. In addition to paying him 500 merks for his labours, Edinburgh Town Council elected him a burgess and guild brother as a token of their appreciation.[43] Despite clear skills as a surveyor and draughtsman he waited some years before receiving his next and final major commission – to map his home town of Aberdeen. On 16 October 1661 he delivered a plan of Aberdeen, new and old, with prospects of each, and wrote a flattering textual description of the city, which was not superseded until the mid 18th century. He was rewarded by the Town Council with a silver cup, a silk hat and, for his wife, a silk gown.[44] On the literary side his best known work was his[45] 'History of Scots Affairs'[46] covering the years 1637–41.[47] He died in 1686.

The eleventh son, Lewis[48] (1631–1704), became a burgess of Aberdeen in 1663 and spent his working life as a physician in the town. He did not marry and left his property to his nephew, Robert Gordon, Founder of the Hospital.[49]

The ninth son (and thirteenth child), Arthur, was born at Straloch on 5 April 1625 and graduated from King's College in 1648.[50] He followed the pursuit of several of his older brothers and studied law. He practised in Edinburgh and in 1655 'under ye usurpers' he was admitted to the Faculty of Advocates in the capital.[51] His membership was annulled soon afterwards although probably he continued chamber work while not practising before the courts. All advocates were readmitted to the Faculty in 1661 and appearances before the Supreme Court suggest a successful career. He was much involved in family matters, witnessing the marriage contract of his brother, James, to Margaret Menzies of Pitfodels[52] in July 1643 and being, along with his mother and brothers, Alexander and Lewis, an executor of his father's will. He kept up his Aberdeen connections and was admitted as an honorary burgess of the city on 6 November 1661,[53] payment of the usual composition fees being dispensed with.[54] He married Isobell Menzies from a prominent Roman Catholic family,[55] the contract signed at Buckie and dated 16 April 1663.[56] Although the marriage was frowned upon by the Scottish Kirk, as it was a period when stringent measures were being taken against Catholicism, and there were presbytery discussions about Arthur being 'married by a priest with a papist womane',[57] it prospered. At a relatively young age Arthur felt able to retire to Aberdeen.[58] The family took up residence in the then fashionable Huxter Row[59] at the northern Broad Street corner of the Row.[60] Arthur became an assessor to his old university in 1674 and died, leaving a young family, on 31 March 1680. Four children had been born in Aberdeen to Arthur and Isobell – Robert, founder of Gordon's Hospital, baptised on 18 August 1668;[61] Anna baptised on 27 August 1669; Mary baptised on 1 June 1671 and John baptised on 28 March 1673.[62]

Robert Gordon's family lineage has been termed 'the Grave Gordons', stressing its domination by serious-minded individuals and intellectuals rather than those of a more frivolous nature – the 'Gay Gordons'. The Pitlurg Gordons, as a younger branch, had to struggle hard, especially after the main estate was inherited by the Huntly Setons. They had to make their own way in the world, foraging for themselves rather than living off their lands.

The Early Years

Robert Gordon was brought up in a privileged home and was educated by private tutors, probably including members of his immediate family.[63] Unfortunately, his father had died when he was only eleven, and, as his heir,

Robert inherited the 'heritable' estate which appears to have been worth 20,000 merks,[64] a small fortune for the time.[65] He went abroad to the Continent probably in August 1682 when he ended his 'pupillage'[66] and seems to have spent much of his legacy beginning what was to become a lifetime's collection of engravings, coins and books.[67] He also benefited from broadening his knowledge and experience and was able to size up the prospects of economic advancement in various parts of Europe. His itinerary would probably have begun with the Low Countries[68] and included France, Germany and Italy. Moreover, he began thinking of a future livelihood and career for he became a burgess of guild on 25 April 1684, still aged only fifteen.[69] His admission was recorded in the Burgess Registers[70] and as a result he gained access to full trading privileges and acknowledged his belief that commerce was an honourable calling.[71] Robert Gordon was to remain a staunch supporter of the burgess system throughout his life.

Following his grandfather, Straloch, rather than his father, Robert attended Marischal College from 1685.[72] Of the two colleges Marischal had been founded a century after King's as a distinctively Protestant college in New Aberdeen[73] and offered an emphasis on the liberal arts. Perhaps Robert Gordon had a utilitarian motive when making his choice as to which to attend: a practical grounding in such a liberal curriculum would benefit someone destined to spend his life trading on the Continent. He took with him to Marischal his personal servant, Robert Blinshell. Although such an arrangement was not unique[74] it was unusual and marked Robert Gordon out from the other students. Both Roberts studied for an Arts degree, which they both received as magistrands on 23 May 1689.[75]

Without his father's influence Robert had to decide on his own profession. His early admission to the guild showed he was contemplating a commercial career rather than the path laid down by his father and uncles.[76] He would have been helped in his decision by Baillie Alexander Skene's 'Memorialls',[77] a personal copy of which Robert signed and dated (1690) at the bottom of the frontispiece.[78] Skene was writing specifically to be useful to young men and discussed the ways the prosperity of a burgh like Aberdeen could be developed. Prominent among these were 'trade and merchandise' and 'education'. In the former Skene pinpointed Aberdeen's staple commodities[79] and referred to a merchant who sent to Danzig on the Baltic 30,000 lamb-skins in one year;[80] in the latter Skene commended the erection and maintenance of 'Schools of Learning', where boys' education should be geared to developing 'naturall Genius and Disposition' and ensuring that they be employed accordingly.[81] Robert Gordon was inspired by Skene's book not just in his own youth but also in his later life when he finalised plans for his Bequest. Skene had urged tender care of the poor and encouraged the support of 'hospitals' – schools where young boys and girls should learn according to their 'Capabilities and Inclinations'.[82] However, parents should not keep children at school or university when 'their Talent and Inclination are not in that Channell . . . The sooner ye betake your selves to your Callings, the better'.[83] Sometimes parents purchased estates from their success at trade, and their children became too proud and vain and refused to follow their parents' example. The result was idleness and a lack of calling which in turn led to a decline in fortunes. Robert Gordon could not have listened to better or more opportune advice: fortunately he followed it.

The Years Abroad 1690–1720

Having decided on a trading career Robert Gordon chose about 1690[84] to go to Poland with Danzig[85] as his base. There were good historic reasons for doing so. Trade between the Scots and the Baltic dated from the late 13th century and prospered despite the vain attempts of the English to hinder its development. Generally, Poland offered great opportunities for trade, so much so that significant numbers of Scots in Poland-Lithuania were involved with commerce, from wealthy merchants to the many pedlars who ensured that the term 'szot' in the Polish language ('Scot') denoted not only the origin of those named but became synonymous with 'trader'.[86] The pedlars carried their wares in baskets and traded in iron goods and tin utensils (scissors and knives), woollens (Scottish) and linen kerchiefs while a number of traders and merchants had shops or booths at fairs. Although not popular given their trading practices and competition, the Scottish pedlars were important. They managed to bring the goods of Scottish peasants to market, and moreover were intermediaries between those involved in cottage industries and the wealthier Scottish merchants both at home and abroad. They in turn were employed by the merchants to take more refined goods back into the countryside or wherever they could best be traded. With the profits gained, the merchants could build enough capital to move further afield.[87]

The numbers of Scots were bolstered by constant emigration from Scotland as a result of periodic periods of distress,[88] the religious and political wars[89] and the law of primogeniture which forced many younger sons to go abroad to seek their fortunes. Impoverished Scottish soldiers of fortune from 1577 joined in defending Danzig from the attack of the Polish king Stefan Batory and gained a reputation as the best of fighters.[90] With immigration from Scotland reaching a peak in Poland-Lithuania between 1590 and 1630,[91] its economy flourished on the back of a growing population, both within its own borders and from abroad, for grain and for naval stores.

By the early 17th century the Scots population in the region was considerable and may have been as many as 40,000.[92]

Although Scots were throughout the area, Danzig had been their first settlement. Around 1380 a Scots' colony was founded in a suburb of the town and called 'Alt Schottland'.[93] Beginning as small peasant-proprietors they soon progressed into trade-workers as weavers and trimmers dealing primarily in Scottish linen. As early as 1433 'Alt Schottland' was well-established enough to have been burned by the Hussites,[94] and a Scottish factor or 'resident' was introduced to look after their interests. For Aberdonians, in particular, this proved a convenient starting point and many lived and worked firstly there and then further afield. Scottish pedlars, apprentices and merchants were attracted to Danzig and other towns by the presence of their countrymen and the favourable conditions which awaited them.[95] They branched into the leather trade and to brewing and distilling.[96] Soon they occupied positions of trust in Poland and Germany, and even served the state in various capacities.[97] Andreas Aidie was Headmaster of the High School in Danzig while Gilbert Waugh (Wachius) became pro-rector of the Sts Peter and Paul church. Many Scots were anxious to conform and Germanised their names – both Christian and surname – to make integration easier.[98]

In the early 17th century, although an economic downturn affected trade, Danzig remained a popular destination as it proved a relatively safe haven during the Thirty Years' War (1618–48), which affected much of Europe.[99] However, in the aftermath of the wars of 1648–60 the trade of Scottish pedlars was significantly limited, although a number of relatively affluent merchants continued to do business in Poland. Robert Porteous from Krosno (died 1661) amassed a great fortune by acquiring the virtual monopoly of trade in Hungarian wine, the favourite drink of the Polish nobility. He rebuilt the local Roman Catholic church and in his will left money for large local improvements. He was unusual in leaving his fortune to the Poles, for most Scots retained their 'clannishness' and made major bequests to other Scots and Scottish institutions. Given the general level of prosperity it was no surprise that, when the exiled Stuarts sought funds after 1649, they appealed to what was considered one of the largest and wealthiest Scots exile communities.[100]

All Europe was well informed about the fate of Scots in Poland. Personal correspondence of the period was inundated with references to the area.[101] Robert Gordon must have been impressed by the success of members of his own class, who had gone before him to the Baltic.[102] He would also have approved of their commitment to the two German Presbyterian churches in Danzig – the church of Saints Peter and Paul and the Church of St Elisabeth – evident in a number of significant bequests left to them and other charitable causes by the Scottish community of the town.[103] He would also know that in the former the Scots had created a church within the church, attending divine services in German but having their own officials conducting baptisms and burials.[104]

By Robert Gordon's time in the late 17th century Danzig trade was dominated by foreign entrepreneurs: some 50 Dutch firms maintained resident agents, while there were about 20 British agents, mainly Scots. Acting on commission for partners spread throughout Europe, they dominated banking and credit operations as well as normal commercial transactions. With greater capital resources, more ships and continental contacts at their command, they gradually squeezed their local competitors until something approaching a foreign monopoly had been established.[105] Yet, despite the volume of the Vistula grain trade remaining substantial through the 17th and 18th centuries, a 'graceful'[106] decline had set in. Nonetheless, grain continued to flow and every day in Danzig up to about 400–500 vessels would be moored, about half running eastward within the Baltic, bound for Lubeck, Copenhagen, Stockholm, Libau, Riga or Vyborg, while the other half sailed through the Sound. The longer Mediterranean trips were giving way to shorter runs to Holland, Portugal, France or Britain.[107]

The decline of the grain trade (and also the herring trade) hit the dominant Dutch, whose share in Baltic trade declined and opened the way for other European merchants. The percentage of vessels from Holland passing through the Sound eastwards declined from 55% (in the early 17th century) to 42% (in the early 18th century), while that coming from England and Scotland increased from 10% to 18% in the same period.[108] More opportunities for entrepreneurs like Robert Gordon presented themselves as Amsterdam's dominance was weakened and trade became increasingly diversified in terms of both geography and product.

Cargoes of grain going westward were complemented with wool, shipbuilding materials, flax, hemp, iron and copper,[109] and from Russia, hides, skins, leather and tallow. The inward journey involved bringing in salt, herring, coal, industrial products such as textiles, and luxury goods such as wine and colonial products.[110] In the mid 17th century in terms of value, corn made up over 70% of exported goods, with metals/minerals at 11% and other agricultural produce 8%: with regard to imports manufactured goods stood at 41%, colonial products 21%, fuels/coal 11%, fish and fish-oil 10%, and alcohol/wines/spirits also at 10%. During this era Danzig handled some three-quarters of the total foreign trade of Poland-Lithuania.[111]

Trade in the region was badly affected by the Great Northern War between Sweden on the one hand and Russia and Poland (and from 1710 Denmark-Norway) on the other between 1700 and 1721, particularly the crisis years of 1715-20 when Sweden moved against British interests in the Baltic,[112] and the civil wars in Poland-Lithuania which disrupted the commercial life of the interior, with external demand also much reduced. Swedish troops appeared in front of Danzig in 1703 and 1704 and the city was forced to make huge payments and recognise Stanislas Leszezynski, the king enthroned by the Swedish Charles XII. Then, when Sweden was defeated at Poltava in 1709 and Danzig was relieved of the Swedish menace, the plague, which had previous struck the region in 1655, returned in 1710 and 1721 and the population fell from 77,000 in 1650 to 48,000 in 1730.

The situation in January 1716 was described in a memorandum produced by a group of British merchants in Danzig and forwarded to the Commission of Trade in London by George I's ambassador to Poland-Saxony, Richard Vernon. They claimed that trade had been decaying for twenty years not just because of war and famine, but also because of cloth competition from Silesia and Holland, and tobacco rivalry from Holland and Germany. Other parts of their trade were in decline as a result of the 'miserable poverty' in Poland, and given a recent tax on soap, reliance was placed on linen, wood and potash.[113]

Robert Gordon joined the Scottish community in Danzig about 1690. If he followed the pattern of other successful merchants it is likely that he completed some form of apprenticeship and/or some journeyman time before being allowed to trade.[114] Moreover, he would have needed to hone his language skills to deal with the intricacies of trading in a foreign country with complicated legal and commercial practices. Perhaps he did these simultaneously by training in a merchant's office. No matter his preparation, it would still have required much business acumen given the determination of local traders not to allow foreigners, and Scots in particular, any undue advantage, particularly at a time when the days of heady Polish economic growth were over.[115]

One of his early decisions was not to become a Polish citizen, which brought benefits but responsibilities as well, suggesting that from the beginning Robert Gordon had determined that his stay would not be permanent.[116] As a non-citizen he was prevented from buying a property in Danzig and rented a room from another Scot, William Thomson, in Frauengasse near the banks of the river Motlawa. However, as he showed later in his life, he was not too concerned about his living conditions but more preoccupied with being successful financially.

His commercial strategy was based on the grain trade. Several navigable tributaries of the Vistula flowed through Poland,[117] so Danzig's site at the mouth of the river[118] was ideal for shipping grain from manorial farms in the south,[119] and equally good for its subsequent export to Western Europe, especially England and Scotland. In fact, grain was rafted to Danzig cheaply and relatively securely. Robert Gordon could expect to do well as the price of surplus grain in the south and east of Poland was only half of its price in the Baltic ports and in Western Europe the price was twice as high again.[120] On the return voyages a variety of refined and luxury goods[121] could be imported.

Unfortunately, disaster almost overtook him for, in November 1696, he was accused by Alexander Ross, the factor of the Polish prince, Hieronim August Lubomirski,[122] of various 'excesses' perpetrated against the state-regulated system of customs duties.[123] Ross demanded the seizure of all Gordon's goods in Poland, claiming the disputed total debt at 6615 tymfy (zloty) excluding duties.[124] Facing ruin, Gordon turned for help to his friends in the Scottish community.

Until the later 17th century in Danzig there were several levels of citizinship rights.[125] Merchants enjoyed the 'great right', most craftsmen the 'small right', while others belonged to their respective guilds. A third category existed for those who could not pay to join a guild of a lesser craftsman and included municipal clerks and others employed by the town administration. By the 1690s a group of four Scotsmen who had been granted the 'great right' had become the dominant Scottish shipowners of Danzig – Daniel Davidson,[126] Peter Forbes,[127] William Brown[128] and Thomas Gellenty.[129] Gordon asked for the help of Davidson and Forbes, who immediately agreed to give their 'caution'[130] of 10,000 florin (Danzig zloty). They did so in the belief that Gordon had fallen foul of complex Polish regulations and had made an honest mistake.

Their prompt action saved Gordon and his reputation. The surety ensured that his grain was freed from confiscation and enabled him to trade and do business again. Although the case dragged on for some months it ended with Gordon being found guilty and fined.[131] One assumes that Gordon paid back the caution in due course and no doubt he appreciated the value of his powerful Scottish friends. He would not make such a blunder in future.[132]

The intervention of the Scottish community in Danzig to help Gordon was the result of a long-standing code of propriety which had been developed. It came from standards set out by Scotland's royal burghs which ensured that trade and mercantile activities were seen as respectable even to landowning families. When the influence of the royal burghs in public affairs declined, the code lived on and enclaves of Scots abroad continued to draw on responsible norms of conduct when running their affairs. Throughout the 17th century in Danzig the leading Scots attempted to sanction incoming countrymen if they were deemed idle or immoral or given to improper business tactics or indeed did anything to discredit the Scots nation.[133] The corollary of this was a willingness to support and co-operate with their fellow Scots when in trouble or in need. Robert Gordon was a thankful beneficiary of this networking.

Of Gordon's later trading career in Danzig little is known. Unlike many Scots he did not integrate fully into Polish society, probably by design rather than accident. Tradition has it that he moved to rooms in the large seven-storeyed 'Englische Haus' at the river end of the Brotbanken Gasse, the street parallel to his previous residence. It was the first multi-storey building in Danzig, built by Johann Kramer for the patrician, Dirk Lilie, in 1570. When the latter hit hard times the house was inhabited by a number of affluent families but by Robert Gordon's time it was the base for London cloth merchants.[134] There he associated with other merchants, making frequent business trips to Warsaw and other Polish commercial centres. He worked hard and made money. However, he was also fortunate to trade in a time before conditions changed dramatically and demand fell substantially. Large tracts of the Netherlands, France and East Anglia were soon to be drained and turned over to cereal production. The growth of France and England led to new preferences and new routes. As markets and price differentials shifted, there was no longer to be the same strong incentive for entrepreneurs to send their ships to Danzig, particularly with its increased tolls. Other towns such as Hamburg began to develop but it was Königsberg which would take over Danzig's supremacy, and the economic decline and decay which set in made Poland a helpless victim only half a century after Robert Gordon's departure.

Given his remarkable success, clearly Robert Gordon kept abreast of economic trends by meticulous attention to detail and a high degree of commercial instinct. He realised early on in his Danzig career that restricting his activities to trade with Scotland would limit opportunities for wealth creation. This realisation paid dividends in 1698 when Danzig, as well as Scotland, had a corn crisis and closed its port to corn exports.[135] Instead he used the Scottish network when necessary and helpful, while simultaneously taking advantage of more international connections. It seems likely that Robert Gordon did business with his namesake, the British factor in Bordeaux, whose brother served as factor in La Rochelle, and whose kinsman, William Gordon, worked in a similar capacity in Paris, while James Gordon completed the kin network in Edinburgh.[136]

With regard to business practices, Robert Gordon chose those which minimised risk. When he had to accept unasked-for return cargoes in lieu of payment for goods delivered he added interest for the time it took not just to sell cargoes but also for the time delay before payment. Moreover, the canny Scot probably only paid for the cargoes when he finally sold them. By such means he made profits when others failed to do so. Trade was a high-risk venture: warehouses had to be paid for, insurance and taxes had to be paid, and embezzlement proved a constant hazard. Gradually Robert Gordon built up his reputation for being trustworthy and a good judge of character. He proved a master at recognising and overcoming the dangers in every transaction.

Like other Scots in Poland, Robert Gordon engaged not only in trade but in financial operations as well, for ships' masters rarely carried sufficient cash to pay for the cargo they took home. Eventually it was paid for by bills of exchange drawn up at Amsterdam or Rotterdam. It seems likely that he became involved in international bill-broking, not only on his own account but also for other merchants with less capital.[137] As he began to accumulate capital he loaned it out to those in need of ready money. Probably this involved between two-thirds to three-quarters of his total capital. It was his success in these transactions that was to give him the confidence to do the same in Scotland when circumstances there improved. Meantime he kept an active interest in matters back in Aberdeen. On 25 October 1693 he petitioned the local magistrates regarding a dispute with neighbours over a property of his.[138] His interests took him to the burgh sasine court on 23 March 1694, 28 April 1694, 15 December 1694 and, probably immediately after his permanent return, on 11 August 1720.[139] His absence from this court between 1694 and 1720 confirms that he had sold off any property he had before going abroad and this is supported by his inclusion in the Poll Tax returns in 1695/6 as a 'gentleman, no wife, child or servant'.[140] He accepted this description and its financial repercussions (tax at the equivalent of holding land of valued rent of 200 pounds Scots) and admitted no property or stock to his name.

Surviving correspondence and accounts from the period[141] suggest he was involved in a business partnership with John Rickart of Auchnacant in the salmon trade in 1700–3. It seems that Gordon and Rickart were good friends: they were close in age (Rickart being three years younger); both were bachelors living in rented accommodation (Rickart married Marjory, daughter of John Gordon of Fechil, a cousin of Robert, in October 1704); both had spent time on the Continent (Rickart arriving back in 1692 on the death of his father); and both were frugal and cautious in their business dealings. At this time Robert Gordon left money for Rickart to continue their joint activities while he was abroad in Poland and Rickart paid a rent for Robert's chambers.[142] Further transactions took place between them on 2 February 1705 when they jointly took legal action against the lands of Blaremormon,[143] while in 1718 Rickart transferred his salmon rights on the Midchingle to Gordon, who presumably was preparing to return permanently.[144]

His time abroad coincided with a time of 'hammer blows'[145] for which Scotland was ill prepared. Four factors in the 1690s tipped her into an economic abyss: a series of harvest failures (King William's 'Ill Years'); the deleterious loss of markets during the war with France (1689–97); the introduction of tariffs which blocked Scottish exports; and the fall-out from Darien, Scotland's greatly ambitious scheme to found a colony on the Isthmus of Panama to trade with the Pacific and Atlantic simultaneously. Its failure proved a disaster for noblemen, lairds and merchants at a time when many landowners were already suffering from a collapse of rental income as a result of the calamitous harvest failures.[146]

Although the worst of the crisis was over by 1700, the legacy of the 1690s was long-lasting. It took a half-century before the population of Scotland began to rise above its 1690 level. Economically, Scotland remained in the doldrums until the 1730s with frequent complaints of shortage of money and tightness of credit. Commercial transactions virtually ended in December 1704 when the Bank of Scotland[147] suspended cash payments, bill discounting and lending. Although business resumed in April 1705 lending on bonds was halted for a further eighteen months.

Given this situation at home the cautious Robert Gordon waited until the passage of the Act of Union of the Parliaments had been achieved in March 1707 before beginning to invest in Scotland. On 17 November 1708 he lent 1073 pounds, six shillings and eight pence Scots to the town of Aberdeen.[148] Gradually he felt increasingly comfortable, even from the distance of Danzig, to take bonds on the landed property of lairds who were desperately short of the working capital needed to improve their land and increase its value. In doing so, Robert Gordon consistently built up his own wealth, although not all deals went smoothly. However, his reputation for financial astuteness grew, as he usually seemed to know when to make the best of things and when to accept an offered composition of a bad debt.[149] Before he returned home Robert Gordon had been involved in over twenty transactions with local north-east lairds and had lent out over £2000 sterling.

Robert Gordon had yet to establish himself in Poland when the Principal of Marischal College, Robert Paterson, and the Professors appealed for financial support to build a new edifice. The Danzig community generally were supportive and help came from a number including Patrick Forbes, John Turner and Alexander Aedie. Finally in 1692 Robert Gordon's namesake, Robert Gordon of Tillielt, gifted £112. Tillielt had settled in Warsaw in the early 1680s and supplied the Court and nobility with tea and other luxury items.[150]

However, the situation was somewhat different by the time of the next Marischal College appeal in June 1699 'to all our Generous and Charitable within the Cityes of Dantzick and Königsberg and the Kingdom of Poland'. According to William Miller of Königsberg, who replied to the Principal, contributions were difficult because 'tymes are so very hard in this country and so little trade'.[151] But for Robert Gordon, with his fortunes now improving, it was an opportunity to show how far he had come. He wrote personally to the Principal from his temporary base in Warsaw on 23 August 1700 promising financial help and future support if needed.[152] Later that year he donated 60 daler (168 pounds Scots).

Robert Gordon was not only a benefactor of his university but also of his church. Alexander Burnett was still taking services in his home in Frauengasse until the successful appeal of Dr John Robinson in 1706 for funds to enable a permanent church to be erected 'for procuring a decent place for the worship of God'. Robert Gordon was among the subscribers who were able to buy and adapt premises at 80 Heilige Geist Gasse. Burnett, who had studied at the University of Aberdeen and been a minister at Crichton near Edinburgh, was the first minister of this 'British Chapel',[153] bringing Scots and English together at the time of the Union of the Parliaments.[154]

Perhaps, as he approached old age, Robert Gordon was nostalgic for his homeland, where there were signs that the Union was beginning to bring positive results; perhaps he was concerned about his declining profit margins in Danzig and worried about the risks he continued to take; even the end of war in 1720 did not signal a quick return to normal trading levels, for the spread of pestilence followed;[155] perhaps he was not attracted by the Polish tax laws. The 'jus caducorum'[156] held that the property of a man dying childless reverted to the Crown if not claimed within a certain time: the 'quarta detractus' ensured that if the wealth was to go out of Poland the Crown could claim 25% of it.[157] And considerable wealth he had made, for he had accumulated an estate comparable to that of the most successful of entrepreneurs of his age.[158] Whatever the reason or reasons, in 1720, at the age of 52, Robert Gordon determined to return to Aberdeen to make plans for another great venture.

The Bequest

Robert Gordon probably took longer than expected to settle back in Aberdeen. In personal appearance he appears to have been tall and straight, always wearing a long coat and invariably carrying white gloves.[159] He must have become a well-known figure in Aberdeen for he walked regularly round the town, and made no secret of his vision to found a hospital[160] for boys. He liked to stroll with his friends upon the very place on which he wished to see it built. However, having been abroad for some thirty years his German accent and mannerisms made him an unusual figure and one easy to make fun of. Although his wealth gave him entry to Aberdeen society, and he appears to have been accepted into the gentry class, his lack of contribution to civic life in his retirement years suggests an unwillingness or an inability to fit back in to an expected role. It seems that he was even a virtual stranger in the household of his surviving sister, Mary. If this relationship languished it may have been for good reason for the available evidence does not sustain the charge of a Robert Gordon lacking in family feeling.[161]

As well as wealth Robert brought home with him books, pictures, etchings and coins. He had inherited a love of the arts and literature, collecting good books and manuscripts, which, like Baillie Skene's work, were important to him. Unfortunately on his death the Governors of his Hospital decided that, as he left no specific instructions regarding his library, his books should be subject to inventory, 'rouped and sold',[162] and the proceeds added to the 'Stock of the Mortification'. Fortunately some idea of the sort of books he cherished can be glimpsed for, before the sale, the Governors gave over two 'ancient manuscripts' to the Library of Marischal College, probably following permission of the Principal and Professors for Gordon's body to lie in state in the College prior to his public funeral.[163]

The first is a manuscript of the Bible (consisting of 375 folios) beginning at the Second Book of Samuel chapter XIII, from the early 14th century. Although incomplete it has a number of coloured rubrics.[164] The second appears to have been acquired by Robert Gordon in 1697 (according to the date beneath his signature). It is a beautiful, illuminated book of prose and verse containing Cato's 'Morals' and Boethius' 'De Consolatione Philosophiae'.[165] It was bound by John Reyes in London in the early 16th century with two metal locks.[166]

In recent times two of Robert Gordon's other books have surfaced in the New College Library, Edinburgh. One is a copy of Hector Boece's 'Scotorum Historiae', published in Paris in 1575.[167] It has Robert Gordon's signature on the frontispiece. The other is a copy of 'Basilikon doron' or 'his Maiesties instructions to his dearest sonne, Henry the Prince' by James VI and I printed in London in 1603. This, too, has Robert's signature. The work expounds the Divine Right of Kings but has been described by one of James's biographers as 'entertaining and readable'.[168]

During his student days when visiting London on 13 March 1687 Robert bought a folio edition[169] of Robert Burton's 'Anatomy of Melancholy' for four pounds Scots,[170] which he presented to Marischal College in 1705.[171] Burton's writing impressed many at this time and Robert must have been struck in particular with his views on charity. For Burton, true charity was rare and should not be tainted by base motivations such as concern for one's soul or a desire to impress posterity. Later in his life this was an issue with which Robert Gordon himself grappled.

Another book survived and was returned to Robert Gordon's College. 'Apologie' by Pierre de Moulin printed in La Rochelle in 1607 was signed on the frontispiece by Robert Gordon of Straloch. Moulin[172] was a pastor in the French Reformed Church and although his writings had limited circulation in France he was able to produce works of scholarship, skill and humour. It is not difficult to see why Robert Gordon would admire him and treasure his grandfather's book.

It is probable that Gordon was an ardent and discriminating collector of books and his collection would have included the classics, works on piety and religion, the chronicles of Scotland, England and France and books on the countries he had visited, as well as books on numismatics and on art. Works of his grandfather, Straloch, and his uncle, the Pastor of Rothiemay, would be part of his collection, as would some volumes handed down from their libraries.[173]

There is no accurate account of the size of Robert Gordon's Library, which sold at auction in December 1738 for £345/13/-.[174] By examining book traders' testaments at this time in Scotland some estimate can be made. Assuming Robert's Library followed their pattern it would total 662 volumes. However, this may underestimate the number for if we based the calculation on that of the only book trader in Aberdeen, James Nicol,[175] the count of the Library would reach 1771 books.[176] On another basis it would have reached over 2000 volumes.[177] Whatever the size of his Library its sale was a great loss. Fortunately in his Mortification he left specific instructions on maintaining his engravings and coins. About 750 of the former were gathered in eleven volumes and remain housed in the College. They are part of a family collection typical of the period. It included items inherited from his father and many he obtained when on the Continent or in London. A significant number reflect Robert Gordon's trading activities in North Europe with Flemish and Dutch works being particularly prominent.

Robert's taste in etchings and engravings was eclectic, the range of subject material being remarkably diverse: scenes of wildlife, country estates, royal and noble portraits, battles, mythological, classical and Biblical events are all included. However, throughout the collection quality shines through, for he acquired the work of the best contemporary engravers, Sebastian Le Clerc[178] – the influential French engraver, particularly in the use of small images in book illustrations – and Gerard Audran,[179] Louis XIV's engraver – being well represented.[180] It seems likely that he also inherited prints from his grandfather, Straloch,[181] for included in his collection were the masters of a previous period: the series of impressions by Jacques Callot (1592–1635), the Lorraine artist, which stemmed from involvement in fetes and pageants in Florence,[182] and a significant number of engravings of Dutch origin from Amsterdam. The most important were seven large prints by Jan Pietersz Saenredam (d. 1607), engravings of Cornelius Bloemaert (1540–93) and his son, Abraham (1566–1651), and the engraved Passion cycle by the printmaker and artist, Hendrick Goltzius (1558–1617), who became Europe's pre-eminent graphic artist before becoming the most important and influential painter of the Harlem 'Academy' at the beginning of the 17th century.[183]

Bound among the engravings in Book 10 is a manuscript containing a compliment in verse 'apparently from a fond relative'[184] addressed to Robert Gordon:

Right hopeful youth: your waxing wit
O for brave actions will you fit
Birth you have from Straloch's clan
Ey [Aye] it is hoped you'll prove a man
Religion, learned, good and wise
Then honour great shall be your prize.
Go on in learning's course and run
Only pains that prize does win.
Read, recollect, improve your time.
Do not give way to any crime.
One day the sweetness you will find,
None more. Then virtue will prove kind
and all your friends rejoycing be
in learning's progress you to see.
Then you'll be fit for actions great
either in the Church or State.

The acrostic spelling of the Founder's name from the beginning letters of each line is less important than the fact that he kept the poem among his most treasured possessions. This suggests a pride in his family and its traditions of public service going back through the centuries, and perhaps a determination on his part to do something special with his life to enhance the reputation of the Gordons.

Robert Gordon's coin collection was, on his death, handed over to his executors who deposited it in the town's Charter Chest. It was discussed when his books were sold but it took till 20 August 1753, after the Hospital had opened, for the decision to be taken to move it to the Charter Room of the Hospital. This was done in 1756 when Baillie Gordon and Master Abercrombie inspected the collection and called for an inventory to be completed and the prints to be bound together in book form. The latter was carried out but the inventory was only of a general nature. The Governors again discussed the matter on 20 May 1833 when it was suggested that the collection be opened up for inspection. Despite the then Head's[185] commitment to arrange this, nothing resulted and the collection remained locked away until 1892, when a number of the coins were placed in a glass case in the Governors' Room of the College and were accessible 'to those desirous of inspecting the same', and a competently compiled catalogue was published.[186]

Robert Gordon's coin collection was one of the earliest recorded coin collections in Scotland[187] and he added to it almost up to his death. It consisted of 168 Scottish coins, 132 English, 83 European, 52 Roman, 25 British medals and 15 European medals. The Scottish collection was thus the main element, accounting for 35% of all the coins. It was reasonably representative of the Scottish coinage in gold, silver and base metal running from Alexander II (1214–49) to the last pre-Union issues of Queen Anne (1702–14). The English coins started with Henry II (1154–89) and ended with three half-pennies of 1729 [George II (1727–60)]. Among these are seven pieces of Irish gunmoney collected by Gordon after 1690. The European coins, up to crown-sized silver, came from about a dozen countries and probably represent his travels and contacts as a merchant.

The medals also comprised a very early collection and their number and scope suggest they were put together with some thought. The British medals consisted of coronation medals from Charles II (crowned in 1651 in Scotland) to George II (in 1727), as well as a small number of early Jacobite medals, and a few specimens of the commemorative series of Queen Anne's reign. Together with the coins they made up a collection unusual for a merchant of his time and still important today, having survived intact for so long.[188]

Soon after his final return to Aberdeen in 1720 it seems Robert Gordon acquired the croft or house of Silverton (Sillerton).[189] Certainly, in particular between 1720 and 1723, he was referred to in numerous legal documents as 'Silverton' or 'of Silverton',[190] and he and the property were so closely linked that in Paterson's 1746 Map of Aberdeen the completed, but unopened, Hospital was designated 'Silverton Hospital'.[191] James Ray in his 'History of the Rebellion' of 1750 held that 'there is at the End of Aberdeen a stately House with Gardens etc., called Silerton's Warke' which the Duke of Cumberland 'fortified' in 1746.[192] This explains why from the beginning of the Hospital its boys were known in the town as 'Sillerton loons'. Robert Gordon, however, could not have lived in the property for long, for towards the end of his life he rented chambers owned by Jean Ross, widow of the deceased Baillie, James Robertson. His rooms, which must have been spacious to house his considerable effects, cost 20 pounds Scots annually.[193]

Throughout the 1720s Robert Gordon continued lending money to local lairds and by the time of his death he had completed another fifty transactions involving around £7,500 sterling. He even lent money to the head of his own line – Alexander Gordon, who in 1724 had to sell his ancestral estate of Pitlurg. The wealth Robert Gordon accumulated (at 5% per annum) enabled him to begin making exciting plans for the future.

Robert Gordon's way of life in his last decade has led to recurrent claims that he was a miser. However, there was no contemporary account of this. Nonetheless, in 1782, over half a century after his Gordon's death, Francis Douglas[194] wrote of an oral tradition which had been handed down concerning Robert Gordon's 'sordid economy'.[195] He detailed stories, but held that Gordon's actions were 'a necessary means to the great end he had in view'.[196] Writing in 1811 Walter Thom saw the Founder as a 'humane and amiable' benefactor. For him 'many ridiculous stories have been handed down concerning Mr Gordon's private character, which are extremely improbable, and quite unnatural.' His actions were for the good of posterity and 'if, to accomplish a noble act of beneficence, he should have denied himself those enjoyments of life to which he was so well entitled, it must place him still higher in the scale of philanthropy'.[197] His view was echoed by William Kennedy: 'he [Gordon] denied himself, for many years, the comforts and conveniences of life, at home, that he might provide a fund adequate to the accomplishment of his favourite object; and in this he completely succeeded.'[198] Such was the growing consensus when John Ramsay, who had been on the staff of Gordon's Hospital between 1827 and 1834, produced his devastating critique. Although he claimed he would confine himself to the facts, Ramsay indulged in much fanciful conjecture. His detailed description of Robert Gordon in particular had no factual basis and he went on to accuse Gordon of habits in his later life which were 'parsimonious in the extreme'.[199] Even when Ramsay praised he did so grudgingly – suggesting that the Founder's benevolence was partly based on selfish motives.

Ramsay's comments were more those of a newspaperman (which he had just become)[200] than a schoolmaster. Unfortunately they carried weight because the public believed that Ramsay had insider knowledge about Gordon's character, which he clearly did not. It was left to James Bruce to take subjective criticism to a more virulent level in his 1841 essay[201] in which he set out to expose human nature, with Robert Gordon one of his targets.[202] Following Ramsay, Bruce, too, wove gossip, traditions and legend into his fictional picture. He, in a relatively short article, called Gordon a 'miser' some seven times and accused him of wasting his patrimony on 'riotous living' and, through being jilted, of developing an 'unreasonable hatred' of women.[203] Bruce took Kennedy to task: Gordon would have announced his intention if he had been half-starving himself to provide funds for a Hospital rather than allowing himself to be reviled as a miser. Yet Bruce gave no evidence that Gordon was in fact so reviled and indeed admitted that many of the anecdotes circulating were unlikely to be true as they were identical to those being used against others.

Nonetheless, according to Bruce, Gordon's will, which made no provision for his surviving sister, Mary, and her family, showed how the Founder's avarice had hardened his feelings of natural affection.

For the best part of half a century Robert Gordon's reputation was sullied by the comments of Ramsay and Bruce.[204] Fortunately, more recent histories have been more objective. Alexander Walker did not mention the issue in his 'sketches' printed for private circulation in 1876,[205] and when he came to expand and update his work a decade later he very much played it down.[206] It was left to Robert Anderson in the most comprehensive history to date in 1896 to find the proper balance.[207] He suggested that the miser stories about Robert Gordon should be taken 'with a large pinch of salt'.[208] Gordon's foundation was not built on a decade of penny-pinching but on the results of a lifetime of successful business enterprise. Even on the worst interpretation 'his splendid bequest has made ample atonement for his sordid habits and his squalid life'.[209]

Robert Gordon claimed in his Mortification of 1729 that he had intended and resolved 'for these several years bygone' to leave his wealth for the building of a Hospital. In doing so he was not just following the precedent set in Scotland by George Heriot in his will of 1624, for educational mortification had been becoming more common in Aberdeen, particularly in the early decades of the 17th century when the poorly endowed Marischal College became a favoured cause for the charity-minded.[210]

Between 1593 and 1659 some 22 individuals made endowments in perpetual trust of money and lands for the support of education in Aberdeen burgh.[211] By 1660 the extent of educational mortification was extensive.[212] From the advent of the first bursaries in 1616 until the end of the 17th century 462 individuals were admitted by the Town Council to be supported in some way at school or university by mortification.[213]

These bequests came from 'wandering scholars',[214] who had experience of Continental practice and primarily wanted to improve Aberdeen's educational shortfall, and from the landed gentry who believed they should use their fortunes for the honour and glory of God. The focus of much charity was the Guild Brethren Hospital.[215] Its popularity for donations partly explains the marked lack of mortification for education by merchants in the town. It was only in June 1677 that James Milne made the first merchant mortification – 2500 merks Scots for two bursars at Marischal, being followed by Robert Cuming (July 1677) and John Turner (1688).[216] The last was a successful

Danzig merchant, who gifted 400 merks for the maintenance of four bursars at Marischal and 200 merks for the schooling from nine to fifteen years of age of two children of name Turner, as well as 200 merks to be paid annually[217] to a regent by name Turner should there be one at King's or Marischal.

Aberdeen merchants, concerned with education, instituted a Guild Box in 1600[218] which offered support to children or orphans of poor merchants, who became eligible for educational bursaries. Craftsmen followed suit and in 1633 founded the Trades Hospital, which became the focus for their collective welfare.[219]

So Robert Gordon, when thinking about framing a mortification for educational purposes, did not just want to ensure that Aberdeen should have a similar institution to those developing in Edinburgh and Glasgow.[220] He determined to build on the century-long Aberdeen experience. In deciding, however, on a specifically educational mortification he intended not only to help the decayed and unfortunate. As a devout Calvinist he saw the need for a godly and disciplined vocational education to control vice and encourage diligence and also ensure all in society would fulfil their necessary role.[221]

Robert Gordon wished to found an institution which would cater for a different section of Aberdeen's inhabitants from the Grammar School which still retained its status as the provider of classical education as preparation for university entry. Gordon had no desire to prepare the distressed members of the burgess class [222] for university: in his view there were already too many qualified people in Scotland chasing too few jobs.[223] Instead his Hospital would help cushion burgesses from downward mobility, and perhaps keep them from the indoor relief of the Guild Brethren Hospital or the Trades Hospital. His institution would emphasis a vocational approach which would aim at securing an apprenticeship for all its inmates when they had completed their time there.

The Hospital initiative was not aimed at the common poor who had to wait until 1741 for their Poor Hospital to open.[224] His concern for the corporate poor[225] was also secondary to those with his family names of Gordon and Menzies. In this he again followed the example of other benefactors who gave precedence to their own kin groupings. This 'reasoned compassion'[226] towards his relations was in place of sharing his wealth with them. To do so would have meant dissipating his fortune and making his venture less likely to succeed. He was no revolutionary and was not even attempting to create social mobility for the deprived.[227] However, what was different about Robert Gordon's bequest was its scale and his willingness to share the glory for its development with any future benefactor who donated £2000 sterling to the Hospital.[228]

Robert Gordon entrusted his benefaction to the Town Council probably because no better alternative existed. As in Edinburgh and Glasgow,[229] concerns about the administration of mortifications were common and well-founded, especially the alienation of funds to other purposes.[230] Yet it is perhaps unsurprising that town councils used the ready monies of mortifications in times of financial crises.[231] Robert Gordon knew and accepted this. He also knew that town officials were, for the most part, conscientious and meticulous with the auditing of accounts and believed in their determination to manage the funds as well as circumstances would allow.

A Deed of Mortification was signed by Robert Gordon before witnesses[232] in Aberdeen on 13 December 1729. It was the result of a considerable period of gestation – probably years rather than months. He took Heriot Hospital's 'Statutes' of Rev. Dr Walter Balcanquall, Master of the Savoy,[233] and those of Watson's Hospital,[234] as his starting point. The former because it had been the first and most famous of the Hospitals in Scotland, whose reputation had been enhanced during the worsening economic conditions of the 1690s when it 'without a doubt prevented the early death of many children':[235] the latter because it was the most recent of Hospitals and produced its Statutes at precisely the time Robert Gordon was beginning to formulate his own scheme.

Gordon's Preamble spelled out his intention to leave his 'whole substance and effects . . . towards the building of an Hospital, and for maintenance, aliment, entertainment, and education of young boys,[236] whose parents are poor and indigent, and not able to maintain them at schools, and to put them to trades and employment'. He did so for 'the glory and honour of God', to propagate the Christian religion more effectively in young people and to ensure that 'the knowledge of letters and of lawful employments and callings may flourish and be advanced in all succeeding generations.' He expected his bequest to be £10,000 sterling, which would be left to the Lord Provost, Baillies and Town Council of Aberdeen and the four Church of Scotland ministers of the burgh, and their successors, who were to be the 'sole and only executors'.

His Statutes (or Rules) were twenty in number, and began by asserting that Robert Gordon's Hospital, as it was to be named, was 'for entertaining and educating indigent male children and male grand-children of decayed merchants and brethren of guild of Aberdeen, of the name of Gordon, in the first place, and the name of Menzies, in the second place (the nearest relations of the mortifier, of names Gordon and Menzies, being always preferred to any others), and the male children of any relations of the mortifier, that are of any name, in the third place, to be preferred to others; and then the male children or male grand-children of any other merchants and brethren guild of the said burgh'.[237] The Governors were to determine the Hospital site although Gordon suggested the Blackfriars ground on the north side of Schoolhill. The building was to be kept to a budget of 30,000 merks Scots and it was only to open when the capital sum had been replenished and after the expenses of buying the site and building the Hospital had been settled.[238]

All this was encompassed in Statute I, which was largely taken from the corresponding Rule at Watson's, while Statute II followed Heriot's in the composition of the Governing Body with the Lord Provost as President (Chairman). The oath to be taken by all Governors on appointment was almost word for word that introduced by Balcanquall at Heriot's a century before.

Statute V of the Hospital summarised the important role of the Treasurer in Gordon's institution. He was to be 'a sufficient merchant in Aberdeen', re-elected annually. As well as being in charge of financial affairs, producing accounts annually for the Governors with quarterly accounts being monitored by four auditors, he was to be 'frequently' in the Hospital to observe and superintend the Master, officials and servants and report any neglect of duties. Again Gordon relied heavily on the substance and wording of both the Heriot and Watson models.

Statute IX made provision for the Master, an unmarried man, of good respect, and free of the burden of children,[239] whose principal function was to ensure that the boys and servants were brought up and instructed in the fear of God. For that to be accomplished the Master had to be a man of the 'true Protestant religion' who could teach the catechism and principles of the 'holy Christian religion'.[240] Gordon was as strong on his religious foundation as Heriot and Watson had been before him. The Master was to correct and chastise boys or servants if they were guilty of misdemeanours, and generally supervise all within the Hospital. He had to remain overnight in the Hospital unless he had the Lord Provost's permission to do otherwise. He was also to attend Governors' meeetings but did not have a vote in the proceedings.

In Statute X Robert Gordon provided for one or two celibate Schoolmasters[241] to teach the boys to read English and the Latin tongue 'in so far as the Governors shall think fit they should be taught within the Hospital'. His curriculum emphasised the teaching of writing, arithmetic, bookkeeping and vocal music. Although limited, it bears comparison with that of Heriot's where the Schoolmaster was limited to teaching the boys to read and write Scots distinctly, to cypher and cast all manner of accounts and to give only the rudiments of Latin 'but no further'. At Gordon's the Schoolmasters were expected to correct the faults of the boys, and involve themselves fully in the religious life of the Hospital.[242]

There followed a series of Statutes spelling out the duties of the various officials. The only significant difference from the Statutes of the Edinburgh hospitals was that Heriot's employed six unmarried servant women and Watson's appointed a Mistress to keep the boys clean and take care of them when sick. Gordon had thought that there should no place for women in his Hospital but as he did not specifically rule this out the Governors' first amendment to the Statutes on 19 August 1751 brought Gordon's into line. It seems very unlikely that this would have happened so early in the history of the institution and with seemingly little fuss if the Governors had believed that Robert Gordon would have vehemently opposed it.

The educational aims for the boys were outlined in Statute XV. They would be taken in between the ages of eight and eleven and would remain until the age of fourteen, fifteen or at most sixteen.[243] Thereafter the boys would be put to 'merchandizing, or lawful trades and employments, according as their genius and inclination leads them'. The apprentice fee paid by the Hospital to masters was set at £10 sterling to merchants and £5 sterling to tradesmen.[244] At the conclusion of an apprenticeship, usually of five years, provided a boy had behaved faithfully and diligently he was given 200 pounds Scots if apprenticed to a merchant and 100 pounds Scots if apprenticed to a tradesman.[245]

It was particularly recommended that the Treasurer and auditors be 'at pains to know the capacity and genius of the boys two or three years before they go out of the Hospital, that they may be able to judge what business or trade they will be best fitted for, that so their education in the Hospital may be adapted to their genius, to fit and qualify them for the employments they are to follow'. Such a clause was remarkable, being well ahead of its time.[246]

For Robert Gordon there was no mention of going on to university, unlike Heriot's where provision was made to support 'hopeful scholars' for four years at university and Watson's which similarly did so for those with 'extraordinary genius for letters'.[247] That did not mean that Gordon did not expect Hospital boys to do well financially in life. He believed that a vocational education was exactly what poor boys, and indeed poor Scotland, needed. He expected a number to do well and was the only benefactor who made provision for this eventuality. Boys who did well[248] were 'obliged to pay back to the Hospital, what was laid out and expended on them'.[249] The Governors were to return to this issue at a later stage[250] in an attempt to implement the clause.

Another significant difference from the Statutes of Heriot's and Watson's was Gordon's inclusion in Statute XVII that anyone donating £2000 sterling would be deemed a co-founder 'in [the] name and title of the Hospital'. Given his own contribution which dwarfed this sum this clause gives us further insight into a character willing to share the glory of his institution with others for the good of the recipients of the bequests.[251]

The Statutes were comprehensive and precise and although they borrowed much from others they were original enough to bear the imprint of Robert Gordon. They were to be the yardstick for the successful working of the Hospital for well over a century. That they lasted so long, and were referred to so much, was a testimony to their grounding in practical common sense and to their 'astonishing foresight'.[252] For this specifically Robert Gordon must take the credit for including a vital clause enabling amendment of his Statutes.[253] His document was to be no 'dead hand' holding back the progress of the institution. This alone made his legacy exceptional.

Robert Gordon had diagnosed the needs of Scotland and in his Statutes he had made what he considered to be his contribution to meeting them. He concluded from the failure of the Darien Scheme 'the necessity of training Scottish merchants of juster notions and wider horizons than their predecessors'[254] as it had proved an ill-advised and hasty venture. The initial harmful effects on trade of the Union of Parliaments of Scotland and England in 1707 led him to appreciate that new opportunities were of no avail unless men were trained to utilise them. Thus he saw the need, given Scotland's recent history and for future opportunity, to train for the service of her trade and industry, young men of good character and balanced judgement. He believed culture and industry and commerce were interdependent, for markets and craftsmen would gain from being educated in a liberal tradition.

Gordon's diagnosis was reinforced in 'The Interest of Scotland Considered' written by Patrick Lindesay in 1733. It began 'Idleness is the source of almost every mischief which afflicts human nature' and foremost among its remedies was the training of children for work. Gordon agreed, believing universities had overstocked Scotland with lawyers, doctors and ministers. He wanted to revive the merchant and trading classes that had fallen on hard times. His Hospital was to be restricted to the poor members of that class, as Article XV of his Statutes spelled out.

Aberdeen, proud of its two colleges,[255] saw education primarily in terms of sending boys to university and was startled at Gordon's modern and new-fangled ideas, which were deemed foreign and labelled Anglified.[256] Particularly difficult to accept was Gordon's attempt to produce a true community by introducing the novelty of 'residence' in a charity school intended for future merchants and tradesmen. His critics saw this as a costly and ostentatious luxury which would not work. For his part, Robert Gordon did not underestimate the problems but he was too bold to be deterred. As a result Aberdeen, for a century and a half, was saved from one-sidedness in education.

Two copies of the Mortification were made: one was kept by Gordon and one by Lord Provost William Cruickshank.[257] After all, it was a most generous bequest that, if used properly, could make a significant difference to Aberdeen and could perhaps persuade others to follow his example. The original was registered in Edinburgh.[258] However, before then Robert Gordon had produced an Appendix which was signed on 19 September 1730[259] as 'further fortification and collaboration' of his original Deed. He ensured that any monies over £10,000 sterling should also go to the Hospital. On reflection he decided that in order to erect a 'decent building' the total to be expended should be raised to 36,000 merks Scots.[260] However, he still insisted that the principal bequeathed was to be accrued again before the boys were to be admitted. Although this would mean a delay after the building was complete Gordon was determined that when it did finally open it would have a firm financial base.[261]

On 21 September 1730, two days after he signed the Appendix, Robert Gordon petitioned the Town Council to feu[262] the Black Friars' Manse, with its ground and buildings (some 'earth houses')[263] and gardens belonging to Gavin Harvie, merchant in Aberdeen, and his sub-tenants – all of which yielded a rent of 100 pounds Scots per annum. His application requested that the gardens of the houses, possessed by John Bisset, minister of the West Church, and John Milne, Master of the Grammar School, be disjoined and annexed to the Manse on the site for his planned Hospital. He offered £10 sterling – a fair value. Given his 'pious and laudable design' and 'the great advantage that will redound to the publict and private Interests of the burgh' from his Mortification, the Town Council found the petition 'just and reasonable' and agreed to the feu.[264] In completing this Gordon had acquired the land he had admired for so long as the site for his Hospital and made all the needed arrangements for his Bequest.

Robert Gordon took ill in late April 1731 and his nephew, William Abercrombie, an apprentice to a doctor, bled him. As the situation grew worse his cousin, Dr John Gordon and his doctor son, James, as well as Dr Donaldson all tried in vain to save him.[265] He died on 24 April.[266] No expense was spared on his funeral. A wainscot coffin was made by Robert Law, wright, and it was covered by a black canopy. His body was laid in state in Marischal College where all who wished to see it could do so. At the 'princely burial'[267] on 28 April the church bells were tolled[268] and minute guns were fired, and the cortege wound its way to St Nicholas kirk with two mortcloaths[269] – unusual for the time.[270] The burial cost 40 pounds Scots, more than double the normal cost, presumably for the use of Drum's Aisle.[271] As a large number of citizens were expected to attend William Duncan, baxter, produced 'sugar biscakes, seed-cake and plumb-cake' and Margaret Craig supplied 'fine biscake and confections', while wine was supplied by some five local people. In total some 1,246 pounds Scots was spent on the day,[272] including a sum for Mrs Robertson for attending the death-bed and for allowing use of several of her rooms at the time of the funeral.[273] According to Douglas, it was too late for Robert Gordon to object to such expenditure.[274]

A judicial inventory, of Deeds, Vouchers of Debt, Medals and Money found after Robert Gordon's death, was made up in the presence of Commissary officials on 28 April. An inventory of movable effects included seventeen pictures. Unfortunately it is not known what became of a number of these. Of particular loss is 'one of Pitlurg', the grand-uncle of the Founder and 'one pictur of the Defunct's father'. Robert Gordon's furniture from his chamber and garret included a feather bed, wainscot table, six chairs, armchair, writing desk and various chests of drawers, which in particular contained significant quantities of linen (from Holland and Danzig), muslin and silk. His personal wardrobe included four suits (coat, vest and breeches) of different colour, although two were 'almost worn', and four pairs of shoes – two of which were 'almost new'.[275] He also owned several pistols and an old sword. A supply of peat and coal was extensive enough to be shared between two beneficiaries, and the Governors shared out the furniture, cloth and the best of his clothes to William Pittendreich and his sister, William Menzies and his mother, and Thomas Innes.

In his final years it is clear that Robert Gordon lived modestly but his effects do not suggest a miserly existence. Moreover, 'one point and fifteen Chapin bottles' (one pint and fifteen half-pint bottles of ale) and 'one pair of women's stays' and 'one wheit satin bedgown for a woman' suggest a different Robert Gordon from that usually described.

Robert Gordon was laid to rest in Drum's Aisle in St Nicholas kirk. In the summer of 1734, the Hospital Governors paid the painter, Nicholson, for 'drawing an escutcheon with Robert Gordon's arms and the eight nearest branches of his family' which was to be placed above his grave.[276] However, it appears that this wooden escutcheon deteriorated quickly and as the years passed the precise burial-place was forgotten. A proper tablet was placed on the west wall of the Aisle in 1857. By that time, however, there was no need for such a memorial, for Gordon's Hospital had developed significantly and substantially into a living memorial of Robert Gordon.

2

THE 'AULD HOOSE'

William Adam

The first meeting of the Hospital Governors took place on 17 May 1731 with Lord Provost James Morison Snr[1] in the chair, presumably in the Town House. The Mortification and Appendix (including the Statutes) were produced and accepted without discussion. Following Statute the Governors took their oath and proceeded to appoint office-bearers: James Udny,[2] advocate in Aberdeen, was appointed Clerk at 100 merks Scots salary; Magnus Milne, the Town Sergeant, appointed Officer of the Hospital; and from the Governors three Auditors were chosen. Udny was instructed to compile an Inventory of Robert Gordon's effects,[3] and the Auditors were to audit the accounts.

Later in May, at their second meeting, the Governors chose William Cruden as Treasurer at £15 sterling per annum[4] and, having taken his oath, his first task was to chase up the many debtors of the Founder. Meantime it was announced that after funeral expenses there would be about 124,000 pounds Scots[5] left for the Hospital. The Governors resolved to build the Hospital in spring 1732 and agreed that ships would be sent as soon as possible to Norway for timber.[6]

It was at this stage that the Governors contacted William Adam, Scotland's leading architect, and asked him to design a plan for the Hospital. Adam worked from Edinburgh and his reputation, coupled with his ability to undertake sizeable jobs, made him Scotland's foremost designer of public buildings at this time.[7] By 1730 with Hopetoun House well underway and Mavisbank, the Drum and the greater part of Arniston completed, Adam was first choice,[8] especially as he was personally known to the Governors having already been employed in 1730–1 by Aberdeen Town Council to enlarge the Town House.[9] With the commissioning of Adam the Governors were indicating that what was wanted was a 'good show'.

Lord Provost William Cruickshank[10] chaired the next meeting on 28 June 1731 when more detailed decisions were taken. Francis Ross, wright, was to proceed with Andrew Dyce, shipmaster, to choose 'proper wood and timber'[11] which would be brought from Norway.[12] Adam's plan for the Hospital was submitted to this meeting,[13] but the Governors believed that if followed exactly it would prove too costly. Cruickshank agreed to go to Edinburgh to consult with Adam 'so as to lesen the plane'[14] and ensure the costs were kept within the budget allotted by the Mortification.

By mid-August Cruickshank had conferred with William Baxter,[15] who, as expected, confirmed that Adam's plan would cost £3200 sterling to follow exactly. However, as a way forward, Baxter suggested that by having one room less, making the others smaller in size and doing away with the garden walls the cost could be reduced to the budget figure of £2000 sterling. This good news was reported back immediately to the Governors by Cruickshank, who offered either to complete the building to this revised plan but also add the garden walls for £2000 or to oversee the construction of the building until its completion for £100 sterling.

The Governors rejected Cruickshank's offer to build the Hospital but on 2 September accepted his bid to oversee and manage the building. He was to be paid in two instalments: the first when the mason-work was complete, and the remainder when the Hospital was finished.[16] Within two weeks he had been given the authority to buy materials and organise the workforce. A decision was now needed on finalising the site. As the feu Robert Gordon had been granted in 1730 had not been formally completed, the Council granted to itself, as Governors of Gordon's Hospital, a feu charter of the ground. However, the Governors felt that they needed a further consultation with William Adam before going any further with their arrangements.

On 16 December 1731 Adam produced his detailed proposals and had lengthy discussions with the Governors on the room arrangement and garden layout. The main difference from his original plan was on the first floor, which involved a reduction in the size of the Governors' Hall (the 'Great Room') and the loss of two rooms, leaving five small rooms for the Master, Treasurer and schoolmasters between the Hall (on the west side) and the School room (on the east side), while the middle room over the vestibule would serve as a vaulted Charter Room. The second floor and attic comprised 21 rooms, twin-bedded, but with two boys to each bed some 84 in total would be accommodated. The Dining Hall and offices were housed on the ground floor. As Robert Gordon had envisaged in his Mortification a complement of only 50 boys the Governors were understating the situation when agreeing that 'sufficient' accommodation was being provided.[17]

Having examined the proposed site Adam found it 'too small and too low situate for erecting the Hospital' and gardens.[18] However, he adjudged the rising piece of ground, commonly known as College Croft on the north side of Schoolhill, adjoining the Black Friars' Manse but owned by Marischal College, 'a proper situation' for the Hospital providing a dry position with good air and a beautiful prospect and for making the avenues and gardens large and regular. The Governors immediately approached the Principal of Marischal College, John Osborne, who fortunately agreed to a perpetual feu of the enlarged site, despite it being an alienation of Marischal property and contrary to its Foundation Charter.[19] As an added piece of good news, Adam believed that the total cost of the building would be contained within Robert Gordon's proposed budget of £2,000 sterling. With all seeming in place by 28 February 1732, the Hospital was to be founded as soon as practicable and 'built conforme to Mr Adams Plan'.[20]

By this time considerable preparatory work had already been carried out. John Elmslie, quarrier, had been supplying granite from his recently opened quarry at Loanhead in the Rosemount area,[21] while John Thain and Andrew Edward were cutting the stones and transporting them by horses and carts to the proposed site. Blacksmith James Sangster was employed for ironwork on the carts and saddler Robert Smith to make harnesses for the horses.[22] The stonemasons, William Sangster, John Aikenhead and Alexander Riach, began work on 2 December 1731 and their work intensified once the foundations were completed in the following spring.[23] Three boatfuls of surface stones arrived from Moray[24] and further large timber supplies were brought from Arundall and Mondall in Norway by Andrew Ross,[25] shipmaster, and his son, John.[26]

The building seems to have progressed well, for on 1 September 1732 the Governors decided to send to London for lead for the roof. There the price was deemed most competitive.[27] However, Cruickshank reported that the money set aside to pay the masons had run out, despite the Governors still owing for work that had been done. He convened a special meeting of Governors on 23 October to deal with a growing number of such concerns. On inspection of the Hospital building it was apparent that the pillars could not take more weight, making the erection of a stone cupola impracticable. As winter was approaching the Governors agreed that the middle part of the Hospital had to be roofed immediately. The cupola was so contrived as to allow a seven foot square area to be raised in the spring if Adam was of the opinion that a cupola was needed.[28]

By February 1733 work on the gardens had been advanced and dykes were erected by the masons, who, as a bonus, were to receive a pint of ale every Saturday 'providing they keep sober and be diligent in their work'.[29] However, there were still worries about costs, so on 21 May 1733 Adam produced new designs which the Governors accepted.[30] But there still remained the issue of whether the cupola should be of stone or a cheaper wood version. At first the Governors wanted the more expensive option but when it was realised that this involved strengthening the supporting walls as well, the Governors accepted a wooden cupola covered in lead with the middle walls made of brick. This design, produced by local wright, William Crystal, in July 1733, resulted in a considerable saving.[31]

Now the garden was behind schedule. Eighteen men were engaged to complete laying it out, while money was saved by building the gardener's house with timber already on hand. Adam provided a design but, as it was three storeys, the Governors, on 19 August 1733, agreed to only the ground floor and put off a decision on whether to add any further storeys.

By February 1735 the building and garden were near completion. Trees were ordered from London for the garden. Final bills were settled: William Crystal for roof-work; James Anderson for glazier work;[32] and William Adam himself was given an extra £5 sterling 'for his pains'.[33] Through 1736–7 little more was done other than some paving work on the forecourt and Dining Room in the west end of the Hospital by John Aikenhead[34] and an agreement made to obtain an estimate for a statue of Robert Gordon to place in the niche at the front of the building.[35] In 1737–8 Aikenhead completed the gate and pillars at the front and back of the Hospital entries.[36] The rest was maintenance and during 1739–40 there was no expenditure on the Hospital other than the salaries of the appointed officials. However, following complaints about the state of the garden, Alexander Drysdale returned in December 1740 to keep it and the walks 'in good order'.[37] Drysdale's job was extended in February 1741 to caretaker: he was to keep all the Hospital windows 'whole and entire', keep the upper floors free of dust and rubbish, and if, as a result of storms, water should leak through the roof or windows, he was to clean and dry them within 24 hours.[38]

William Adam, although he designed the Auld Hoose building and indeed chose its specific site, only appears to have visited Aberdeen some five times during 1731–3[39] and then probably on his way to Duff House. Perhaps this explains the wrong assertion by Kennedy that the Aberdonian James Gibbs provided the design,[40] an error repeated by Robert Wilson,[41] James Wilson[42] and Rettie.[43] Adam was very much in demand and was engaged in supervising at least nine other sites at this time,[44] and, as a result, the masons must have had a deal of autonomy. William Crystal complained that during construction 'there were many alterations and additional pieces of work'[45] not on the plans, helping to push the work over-budget. It is said that Adam did not work under contract, the arrangements and details of the building being settled in informal coffee house meetings; this perhaps explains the 'local feeling' of the building being a translation by the local builders of Adam's designs.[46] Unfortunately it is the only one of Adam's public buildings to survive[47] and in unaltered condition, although it has been described as Adam's 'first and perhaps least impressive' public building.[48] To some extent this view, if correct, was a result of the budget parameters.

Adam's original design for the south or show front can been judged from the plan in 'Vitruvius Scoticus',[49] which, in its decorative parts, was lifted from 'A Book of Architecture' (1728) by James Gibbs.[50] This envisaged a pedimented centrepiece carrying a Gibbesian steeple. Adam's major deviations from this involved removing the tower and further reducing the central emphasis by replacing a single pediment by two small pediments over the end bays with the three central bays being recessed. Adam also extended the second storey (first floor) to produce three equal floors and added an attic storey which appeared sandwiched between the cornice and pediments on the end base but expressed only by dormer windows on the centre and end facades. The result was a much squarer aspect than originally envisaged. Changes to the horizontal bands of windows intensified the vertical look, with the projecting end bays taking on an almost tower-like appearance. Adam balanced this by use of a bold cornice below the attic storey. He removed the dado, which formed the sills of the ground floor windows and the window and front door surrounds. The plainness of the building was relieved by the buckle quoins, a decorative way of turning corners on a harled building. The rounded doorway was replaced by a rectangular door with simple mouldings, and between the door and the niche, introduced to accommodate Robert Gordon's statue and returning some importance to the central part of the Auld Hoose, was placed, on a plinth, the inscription – 'Erected 1732'.

The principal or south elevation remains one of great beauty: it is divided into three bays, the centre one being recessed about eighteen inches, while the end bays were carried up to form bell-shaped gables or pediments. It is composed of granite squared rubble, with yellow sandstone dressing for quoins, window and door. The entrance doorway has a moulded surround with a long strip entablature above and then the plinth with its insciption and the niche with engaged columns, quasi-Tuscan capitals, round arch head with floreated voussoirs and foliate keystone, flanked by narrow windows with moulded entablatures (linked to capitals). The mouldings on the jambs and lintels of the windows, and the cornice which runs all round the building, are beautifully profiled.

The rear of the building differs from the front elevation only in the central bay where a double set of windows is set midway between floors lighting the staircase. Two low service-wings existed by 1746. The side elevations have no attic storey. Of particular interest, internally, is the original stone staircase with its peculiar drop arches, keystones and corbel blocks, Doric pilasters and richly carved cornices. It rises the full width to the attic, with elaborate freestone screens at each stair-landing. The Charter Room (first floor, centre of south front) was entered from the main landing and an iron door was specially commissioned.[51] The Governors' Hall is an impressive all-through apartment on the first floor. It measured 33' 9" x 19' 6" x 12' (high in roof) with two fireplaces on the south side, with marble chimneys. It is panelled throughout with dado rail and has a deep plaster cornice. The door from the corridor is six-panelled in lugged architrave with foliate enrichment, carrying enriched arch with foliate and scalloped keystone.

Probably it was this room which was finished by Patrick Barron in 1749–50.[52] It soon contained a George I walnut and parcel gilt elbow chair,[53] and a set of provincial Queen Anne red walnut dining chairs.[54] Later, a set of three George III oak double gate leg tables,[55] a George III mahogany pembroke table[56] and a William IV mahogany pembroke table[57] were added.

Douglas held the Hospital to be an 'elegant, granite building,'[58] a view echoed by Wilson,[59] while Kennedy described the Hospital as 'a very neat building of three stories [sic], with pediments projecting in front, and on each end'.[60] More recently, Simpson believed that its leading characteristic was 'the balanced effect and carefully studied proportions'.[61] This was echoed by Wyness who stressed its 'charming proportions despite its massive severity, each individual feature being carefully studied, so that together they form a complete harmony'.[62] It measured 86' x 34' and stood at the north extremity of an extensive garden ground extending from Schoolhill and the Woolmanhill to the Loch.

The Hospital Accounts detailed the expenditure on the building and garden in pounds Scots and are a good indicator of the pace and pattern of the work.

	Building	Garden	Gardener's House
Apr.–Nov. 1731	2251	–	–
Nov. 1731–1732	17334	–	–
Nov. 1732- 1733	8751	–	–
Nov. 1733- 1734	6984	1099	292
Nov. 1734- 1735	548	438	1846
Nov. 1735- 1736	392	24	68
	36,260	1,561	2,206
In sterling	£3,022	£130	£184

Investment in Land

Two issues other than the building of the Hospital concerned the Governors in the period before it opened. The first involved collecting the debts owed to Robert Gordon's estate. From as early as 26 May 1731 the Governors were taking steps to have outstanding monies repaid.[63] Gradually the financial situation improved as systematically the debts were cleared.[64] There were, however, opportunities to buy land for investment purposes from certain landowners who could not meet their obligations. Usually the Governors took these up provided the price was right, even if it meant that, temporarily at least, they would have to borrow to buy. On 13 June 1733 the Governors agreed to purchase Orchardtown in the parish of Udny from Sir William Seton of Pitmedden. The tradition of giving the disponer's lady money for a gown for her consent to the sale was fulfilled six months' later on 13 December.[65] The Governors paid 36,495 pounds Scots for the land (yearly rent at 23 years' purchase) and Lady Pitmedden's gown cost 441 pounds Scots.[66]

On 18 November 1734 the Governors agreed to purchase the lands of Dumbreck from the Trades of Aberdeen[67] contiguous to the land already bought from Seton and in the first vote of the Governors in their history this was carried 'by a plurality of votes'.[68] Such purchases were to be important in the finances of the Hospital longer term[69] but the immediate result was that Treasurer Cruden needed to borrow 10,000 pounds Scots in the middle of 1735.[70] The lands cost the Governors 26,060 pounds Scots,[71] and a sasine[72] for both Dumbreck and Orchardtown was lodged on 12 April 1737. A further campaign directed at more debt collecting was commenced.

Another major purchase took place on 16 September 1736 when the Governors agreed to pay 42,000 pounds Scots (and 60 guineas for a gown) to Sir Alexander Bannerman of Elsick for the lands of Findon and Crookston.[73] The Governors believed this to be a 'very convenient' purchase.[74] Further debt transactions continued: in late 1738 the debts of Sir Archibald Grant of Monymusk and the Countess of Errol and her husband, Alexander Hay of Delgety were revisited. Throughout 1739 the Governors pressed Kenneth Gordon of Cluny to clear his debt, threatening to have his lands sold to pay it off if he did not settle. However, Cluny was still prevaricating in August 1744 when the Governors took out a 'summons of adjudication' against the Cluny estate.[75]

The next major investment contemplated was in May 1745 when, after a walk round Techmurie, the Governors determined to buy the Kinmundy estate.[76] This, however, fell through and other potentially lucrative land deals – such as that over the Lochlands – failed to materialise, despite the interest of the Governors in buying in October 1799.[77] They also decided not to offer for the lands of Aberdour believing that the price of 64,000 pounds Scots with yearly yield barely 4½% was not attractive enough.[78] Nonetheless, they still looked for good investments and on 19 December 1749 Lord Provost Chalmers attended a roup in Edinburgh and bought the lands of Mid Beltie, part of the Durris estate, for 40,000 pounds Scots (on a 30-year purchase).[79]

The second issue resulted from the petition of Sir James Abercrombie of Birkenbog[80] and his wife, Mary, surviving sibling of Robert Gordon. It reached the Governors on 8 November 1731[81] and was given over to the four City ministers to review. A week later the Governors accepted Abercrombie's appeal on behalf of himself, his wife and their son, William, that they be given a sum to compensate them for attendance at Robert Gordon's funeral and due respect at the 'mournings',[82] in return for renouncing their claims to Robert Gordon's estate. As William had attended Robert Gordon during his last illness, given him medicine, and 'was most carefull both of his person and effects while he was on his deathbed'[83] the Governors decided to give him a 'handsome' honorarium.

The Governors appreciated that any challenge to Robert Gordon's settlement could be costly and also take time to resolve, so their first thought was to give Abercrombie 6,000 merks Scots. However, a further discussion made them rethink – after all it had been Robert Gordon's express wish in his Deed of Mortification that his relatives would not be allowed to share in his estate. As a result the Governors decided to seek legal opinion,[84] which, on 7 February 1732, held that Abercrombie deserved financial consideration because otherwise he could delay the building of the Hospital. It also further advised that the Governors had the power to overturn the Deed. As a result the Governors determined to give Abercrombie the rights over three heritable debts owing to Robert Gordon, amounting to 6000 merks, provided a majority of burgesses of Aberdeen agreed.[85] Abercrombie accepted 'this just and generous resolution' and would pursue these debts. The outstanding accounts for their mourning expenses were also paid.[86] Sir James and (Dame) Mary ratified the Deed on 19 May 1732.[87]

To what extent had the Governors rectified a 'wrong'? Why had Robert Gordon decided that Mary and her husband should not benefit from his fortune? After all Mary had a large family, although at least four of her fifteen children had died young. It seems likely that Robert Gordon, knowing that the Abercrombie's financial affairs were in disorder, was determined that his money would not be frittered away trying to shore up the Abercrombie mess. Significantly, the money problems of the Abercrombies continued even after the Gordon 'windfall' had been received and when Sir James took ill later in 1732 (he died in 1734) his son, Robert, had to come back from India to take charge of matters. Such circumstances perhaps make Robert Gordon's unsympathetic stance more understandable.

The Jacobite Interruption

From the time of the first Governors' meeting in May 1731 until late August 1745 there were 174 such meetings – effectively one per month. However, there was to be no further meeting for the next year until 18 August 1746 because of the 'late unnatural rebellion'.[88] Aberdeen had been under the control of the Jacobites since 25 September 1745 when John Hamilton of Strathbogie led an armed force into the town. They stayed until 23 February 1746 when the Jacobite rear-guard left the town 'in some hurry',[89] two days before the arrival of the first Government troops. On 27 February, the Duke of Cumberland[90] arrived with the rest of his army. He was received in Schoolhill by a deputation of the magistrates, who had served in office previous to the rebellion, and was conducted to his lodgings with crowds of citizens looking on.[91] Although it had been intended that the Duke would lodge in Marischal College the quarters there were found to be too damp and unsuitable and so he was given instead two spacious and secluded mansions within the courtyard of number 45 Guestrow.[92]

Cumberland strengthened his position in Aberdeen and prepared his troops to withstand the Highland charge which would have to be repulsed when the armies met up. The whole town of Aberdeen became a military encampment with reinforcements arriving by sea and the full complement was made up of fifteen regiments. By the time Sempill's Regiment had arrived, billeting was in short supply and so the unoccupied Gordon's Hospital building and nearby Lochermalks Houses were allocated to them. Being garrisoned by regular troops led, in turn, to the fortification of the Hospital to protect the lines of support and Aberdeen from Jacobite encroachments. The Hospital was surrounded by a trench, fifteen feet wide at top, and earthen ramparts; the garden wall was demolished and palisades erected in front of the ramparts. A well was sunk and the Hospital became known as 'Fort Cumberland'.[93] A plan of the fortification[94] included the first dated plan of the Hospital as built. The outline of the north bastion is preserved in the oblique alignment of Crooked Lane. The Fort was garrisoned by two hundred men of the Royal North British Fusiliers under the command of Captain John Crosbie, securing the town against the followers of Gordon of Glenbucket.[95]

Cumberland placed the civil government of Aberdeen under the direction of James Morison Jnr of Elsick, who had previously been Lord Provost[96], and of eleven other citizens, six of them ex-Lord Provosts.[97] The citizens themselves, four hundred in number, enrolled as volunteers to serve as guards in the town in the absence of the King's forces and were regularly trained to arms. This new militia took their duties seriously although they did not have nearly enough firearms to go round.

Cumberland completed his preparations and on 8 April 1746 left Aberdeen. Eight days later he decisively defeated the Jacobite forces at Culloden after which he gained his nickname of 'Butcher'. With the threat over, two days of rejoicing were embarked upon in Aberdeen. Part of the royal army returned to the town, where Fleming's Regiment remained throughout the summer months, relieving the Fusiliers in Fort Cumberland. Periodically there were incidents between soldiers and citizens and the most serious took place on 1 August, the anniversary of the accession to the throne of George I. The order to illuminate windows was not complied with as expected and so a number of windows were broken. The magistrates stood their ground, demanding reparation, and ultimately, after arbitration, some £61 sterling was paid by the officers to the citizens in compensation for the damage caused.

With normality restored Aberdeen elected their magistrates and Town Council on 9 July, ensuring that the Hospital Governors could meet. On 25 August 1746 the new Governors took their oath and they set up a Committee of Four[98] to recommend what action to take over the Hospital 'being turned into a Fort and laid wast'. Despite deciding to take legal opinion[99] this was not done and so the Governors pressed for action.[100] On 16 February 1747 a new Committee was finally formed with a remit to have the Hospital and gardens inspected, the damages estimated and reparation sought.[101] The following day William Crystall, William Green and Patrick Barron, wrights; James Hector and John Rhind, masons; George Crystall, Alexander Stuart and Thomas Midleton, gardeners; and James Mercer, architect, deemed the 'most creditable tradesmen of their respective professions', were authorised to estimate the damage done to the Hospital during its occupation by Government troops.[102]

Within a month the damage estimates had been finalised. The three gardeners had examined trees, bushes, hedges, walks, bowling green and borders and agreed 'in ane voice' that £71 sterling would put the garden to its previous shape.[103] The two masons and architect had inspected damages and agreed also 'in ane voice' that to reinstate mason work would cost £121 sterling.[104] The three wrights detailed the estimate of the expense of repairing wright work, glass windows, locks and ironwork at £23 sterling.[105] Some extras were included in the total damage estimate – planks burned and lead removed from windows and roof (with small amounts included for neighbours for damage to their garden walls) – which amounted in total to £275 sterling.[106]

On 9 April 1747 the magistrates of Aberdeen petitioned the King to recover the costs of arms sent to Edinburgh Castle with Sir John Cope, and the costs of repair to the Hospital during its occupation.[107] The claim for the Hospital was now put at £290 sterling.[108] On 18 May the Governors were informed that their Petition had been delivered by John Maule, M.P. for Aberdeen Burgh, to the Duke of Newcastle, who had laid it before George II and had employed an attorney to manage the matter.[109]

The Government did its own investigation. Lieut. Colonel David Watson, General Hawley's principal aide-de-camp, reported on 21 August 1747.[110] His remit had been to advise whether the Government should meet the demand or whether it should undertake its own repairs. He confirmed that the Hospital had been in good repair when taken over by the troops and that the damage reports were 'fairly stated'. He referred, in particular, to broken steps, staircases and bases of pillars, as well as to missing doors and locks. As a result, Watson was persuaded that the cheaper option was to meet the estimated account.

On 15 October 1747 the Lord Provost William Chalmers[111] announced that the Government had officially given back the Hospital to the Governors[112] and within two weeks a royal warrant for the damage sum had been received. The actual money was paid in a series of instalments during the first half of 1748, and the total received by the Hospital was 3,109 pounds Scots [£259 sterling] – a sum somewhat less than that claimed by the Hospital.[113] The way was now open for the repairs to be progressed and for the internal furnishings to be finalised. The following month the Hospital gardener worked on hedges, sowing grass and laying turf on the bowling green, and early in the new year the Governors sent to Edinburgh for fruit trees – pears, apples and cherries.[114] During 1747–8 the Governors spent 2,475 pounds Scots on the building, in 1748–9 some 678 pounds Scots and in 1749–50 some 3,232 pounds Scots.[115]

Final Arrangements

With the financial position strengthening[116] the Governors began to make final preparations for the opening of the Hospital. A Committee of Seven was formed on 21 November 1748 to equip the Hospital as soon as possible 'so as the boys may be brought in'.[117] A new gardener, John Davidson, was appointed to keep the external features of the Hospital in good order and to provide vegetables for the Hospital kitchen.[118] Moreover, it was ruled that the Hospital boys or apprentices would not be allowed to use the bowling green when gentlemen wanted to play bowls,[119] for even at this time the ground in front of the Hospital was used by the public for recreation and the citizens had priority on the public bowling green.[120]

From the new Treasurer, William Gordon, 'greater application' was expected and as a motivation his basic salary was increased to £20 sterling per annum.[121] The funds were at last deemed 'sufficient' to take in boys[122] and a scheme preparing for this was drawn up on 20 February 1750. In the event the Governors decided to take in fourteen and advertised for them in the 'Aberdeen Journal'.[123]

The Governors, at their meeting on 1 March 1750, agreed to appoint a Master, George Abercrombie, minister at Footdee, at £20 sterling per annum[124] who was not obliged to attend church with the boys because of his commitment to preach at Footdee.[125] A schoolmaster, William Mitchell, son of James, minister of Old Aberdeen, was chosen by a 'great majority'[126] although his salary of £15 sterling per annum was only agreed 'by plurality'[127] to teach English, writing, arithmetic and bookkeeping and to take the boys to church. A steward, Alexander Forbes, was taken on at £8 sterling to keep accounts; a male cook, George Dun, at £5 sterling and one servant, William Bowie, at £3 sterling per annum were also employed. Dr James Gordon, grandson to John, first cousin of the Founder, was appointed Physician, his salary to depend on his services.[128] James Chalmers was 'to teach the Church Tunes' three times a week.[129]

On 3 April the Governors selected the first boys for entry, and they were examined by Dr James Gordon of Pitlurg to ensure that they were free from distemper. Of the fourteen chosen, Thomas Ritchie refused to enter, so when the Hospital opened officially on 10 July 1750 only thirteen were called in,[130] ordered to obey the Rules 'in every thing'[131] and handed over to the Master. Their parents were then summoned and accepted the Rules after they had been read over to them. The Master and schoolmaster also took their oaths that day and Abercrombie produced a scheme of rules for masters, children and servants regarding the government of the Hospital and the teaching syllabus.[132]

The original thirteen boys were joined on 31 July 1750 by Alexander Gordon to make up the full complement. The first on the roll, Gavin Harvie [1][133], son of Gavin, burgess of guild, was born in July 1741 and remained in the Hospital until May 1756 when he was apprenticed to a cooper. William Webster [2], son of Francis, burgess of guild, was born in February 1741 and on departure went to Jamaica. Robert Marr [3], son of William, burgess of guild, was born in September 1740 and left in 1755 to be apprenticed to a writer; he was to become a clerk and emigrated to the West Indies, where he died. Robert Thomson [4], son of James, burgess of guild, was born in April 1740 and died in 1751.[134] James Laslish [5], son of Francis, burgess of guild, was born in December 1739 and left in June 1755 to be apprenticed to a wright; he completed his apprenticeship and died abroad leaving to the Hospital a house in the Broadgate, which was sold for £142. Andrew Donald [6], son of Andrew, burgess of guild, was born in August 1739 and left in June 1755 to become a merchant; he completed his apprenticeship and died in Jamaica. Alexander Gordon [7], the first with the surname Gordon to join the Hospital, son of Francis, burgess of trade, was born in September 1739 and left in June 1755 to complete his apprenticeship as a saddler. His younger brother, James

Gordon [8] was born in December 1740 and left in May 1755 to become a silversmith. William Law [9], son of John, burgess of trade, was born in December 1739 and left in June 1755 to become a wright; he later received an additional £10 from the Governors to study navigation and bookkeeping in Edinburgh. John Bennett [10], son of William, burgess of trade, was born in July 1740 and left the Hospital in June 1755 to become a saddler; he died in Edinburgh. John Sligo [11], son of John, burgess of trade, was born in December 1741 and was apprenticed to a druggist; later he was involved in spirit distillation in Leith and although he left a legacy to the Infirmary in Aberdeen there was nothing forthcoming to the Hospital.[135] James Hardie [12], son of William, burgess of trade, was born in November 1740 and was the first to leave the Hospital in May 1753, going to London to complete his education.[136] John Gordon [13], son of Robert, journeyman wright, was born in August 1740 and completed his apprenticeship as a barber. And Alexander Gordon [14], who joined them three weeks later, was the son of Alexander, journeyman wright, and left in June 1755 to become a wright.

Of the original thirteen boys, four were nine years of age at entry, three were ten years and six were eleven years. Nine completed their apprenticeship and followed their allotted career path: the Governors paid their apprenticeship fee of £8/6/8 and then £5 to the boys when they completed their apprenticeship satisfactorily. Three became wrights, two saddlers and there was also a clerk, merchant, druggist and barber. Robert Gordon would have been pleased that his Hospital was at last open and beginning to fulfil the terms of his Bequest.

3

THE EARLY YEARS OF THE HOSPITAL, 1750–1790

Rev. George Abercrombie

All went smoothly in the opening months. The Governors felt confident to add to the number of boys and on 18 February 1751 agreed to take in a further twelve.[1] To cope with them further staff were appointed including Robert Abercrombie[2] as another schoolmaster. The second tranche of boys was elected on 3 April; seven were sons or grandsons of burgesses of guild and five were sons of burgesses of trade, but only one had a deceased father. They joined three days later and again were mainly ten or eleven years of age. Two of them – John Edward [18] and Roderick Forbes [20] – died in 1756, aged fourteen, and the Governors developed the practice of paying the funeral expenses of boys who died while attending the Hospital.[3]

The Governors rigorously followed the aim of Robert Gordon's Deed to relieve poverty, as spelled out in his Mortification, and took steps to ensure that the boys who were admitted were genuine 'objects' of the Charity and were sons or grandsons of, firstly, burgesses of guild or, secondly, burgesses of trade.[4] This policy was strengthened as early as 3 April 1756: no boy was to be allowed admission unless formal attestation of his background was obtained.[5] Of the 420 boys who attended between 1750 and 1790, some 126 had a burgess of guild background and 272 a burgess of trade qualification.[6] Parental occupations almost exactly mirrored the apprenticeship destinations in the period.[7] However, there was some upward mobility for some boys.[8]

The Governors had the goal of fitting Hospital boys for some useful trade or situation, and this explained their refusal, on 15 February 1755, to let Robert Marr [3] leave to go to the Grammar School to learn Latin when the

Master (Abercrombie), following the Founder's Deed, judged the boy 'to be fit to be put apprentice to a cooper or square wright'.[9] Following this case the boys were to choose their trade a full year before leaving the Hospital so that their education could be adapted to suit their choice.

The Governors also attempted to fulfil the Founder's instruction that preference should be given to boys with the surnames of 'Gordon' or 'Menzies'. Although by 1790 no boys named 'Menzies' had been admitted, those named 'Gordon' admitted numbered sixteen, while in total eighteen gained entry by claiming to be related to Robert Gordon. The Governors also went further and gave employment or help to relatives of the Founder. Dr James Gordon[10] was employed as Physician between 1750 until his death in 1755; Elizabeth Menzies was employed (20 February 1750) 'for making and mending the linen belonging to the Hospital', and in 1755 was given the boys' old clothes;[11] Robert Menzies was given financial help to go to London on 21 May 1750; while William Menzies was helped in 1785,[12] 1790[13] and 1796–7.[14]

Growing in confidence with the Hospital open, the Governors disregarded the enactments in Gordon's Deed against the employment of women. As well as the precedents of Heriot's and Watson's Hospitals in this regard, the saving in expenditure which it entailed was also a powerful inducement. It was made possible by the clause authorising the alteration and improvement of the Statutes, provided the change was agreed to by three-fourths of the whole Governing Body at two meetings held at least a month apart, and provided also that the alteration did not infringe 'the standing fundamental rules'.[15]

So as early as 20 August 1750 the Governors agreed to give 'the woman that comes every morning to comb the boyes heads' eight old pence Scots per week per boy.[16] In February 1751 she was engaged to act as Nurse to attend to any of the boys when sick, for which she was to receive an additional one shilling and six pence (sterling) every week and 'dyet'. This led on 21 May 1751 to the vote by 14–1 to employ women servants, which was confirmed 16–1 on 19 August. At first three women were to be involved in the domestic arrangements, including cooking, washing and dressing of linen and to ensure the cleanliness of the boys. By the end of the year it seemed appropriate to appoint a Housekeeper,[17] Isobell Mark, who was to remain in post for almost forty years. Her job specification was detailed in February 1752. She was to keep and distribute provisions and oversee the diet of the boys; she was to keep a daily ledger and was entrusted with thirty shillings (sterling) for ongoing expenses; she was to keep the fire 'frugal'.[18] The Housekeeper soon won over the boys as well as the Governors who were pleased with her work. In November

1753 her salary was increased as a result of the savings she had made in the Hospital and 'her extraordinary working with her own hands'.[19]

A tradition soon grew up concerning one of the women servants then appointed. The Hospital had not long opened when one Sunday, while all were at church except a servant girl, some thieves broke in and began to seize things of value. The girl bravely resisted this and was murdered in the Governors' Hall. The floor was stained with her blood. Later investigation showed a large triangular-shaped reddish-black stain, about two feet in length. All who attempted to remove the mark only sent it deeper into the floor. The ghost of the murdered girl has been seen by several persons.[20]

The first Master, Rev. George Abercrombie, proved a conscientious and caring person. He was born on 9 January 1713, the seventh son of Baillie Robert Abercrombie, an Aberdeen merchant. He graduated from Marischal College in 1734 and spent the next eleven years teaching and tutoring while awaiting ordination by the Church. He took up his ministry at Footdee in June 1745 and was 37 years old when he took over the Mastership of Robert Gordon's Hospital. He had a genuine concern for, and a keen interest in, his charges and did what he could to soften the strict monasticism of his institution, believing the introduction of women was important in that regard. His Report of August 1754 assessed the progress of the boys as a number readied themselves to leave the Hospital and take up apprenticeships. He held that even those who 'seemed not to have any capacity for several things that were being taught in this House and were therefore losing time and contracting idle habits by being kept at tasks for which they had no genius' were sturdy boys who 'might be capable enough of mechanical employments if proper masters were found for them'.[21] The Governors instructed Abercrombie to take this further: he was to make lists of boys categorising them, finding out their particular genius and what business they might be fit for, in the process consulting with the boys and their parents on their choices.[22] A Committee of Governors was set up to help Abercrombie determine what business boys should go into when they departed the Hospital.

The day-to-day teaching was mainly the responsibility of the schoolmasters, and the Governors recommended that 'as the boyes may come to knowledge and may have a genius for the Mathematicks or Navigatione, both the masters be obliged to teach the boyes in these Sciences as they may be capable.'[23]

From an early date the Governors were anxious to monitor the standards of learning in the Hospital and to that end it was decided that the Lord Provost, senior Baillies and ministers would visit the Hospital every three months.[24] Following one of their early examinations it was noted in January 1753 that the boys 'gave great satisfaction . . . and some small premiums were given to the most deserving'.[25] After other exams several books were given to the boys by the Lord Provost.[26] As a result of the exams held in November 1754 the Master and schoolmasters were commended for their part in the progress of the boys.[27]

Given these advances it was unfortunate for the Hospital that William Mitchell resigned in January 1753 having been called to a ministerial charge. The Governors advertised for a replacement who had to have his moral character attested and who was expected to be able to teach English, writing, arithmetic, bookkeeping, French, Church Music, geography and navigation. He would receive £15 sterling an annum with bed, board and washing, but had to remain overnight in the Hospital except on special occasions and even then only with the Lord Provost's consent. Alexander Rose, a third-year student at Marischal, put himself forward but was rejected by 10–9 on the casting vote of Lord Provost James Morison Jnr:[28] William Duff was interviewed and given the post. He was retained for eighteen months but instability followed as John Middleton, Gavin Mitchell and Charles Copland came and went, although Robert Abercrombie remained in post until his death.

The music teacher James Chalmers also left and he was replaced by Andrew Tait and James Abercrombie, who were appointed in 1752 to 'teach the boys to sing'[29] but on 18 November 1754 Mr Channon, an Englishman, joined the Hospital staff after receiving an invitation to come to Aberdeen to teach Church Music.[30] He, in turn, was replaced, in August 1756, by James Gillet, Precentor of the West Kirk.[31] The boys attended Sunday services there[32] and worship was also conducted daily in the Hospital where the praise was led by two boys selected as precentors.

The Governors returned to the issue of Robert Gordon's statue being situated in the niche above the front door of the Auld Hoose. A metal statue from his picture was discussed in February 1752[33] and, following a visit to London, ex-Lord Provost Alexander Robertson of Glasgowego[34] brought back several plans for a statue.[35] Among those who had been asked to submit a design was John Cheere (1709–87), then Head of the Hyde Park Corner workshop and yard,[36] usually associated with his better-known brother, Sir Henry Cheere (1703–81)[37]. It seems certain that he delegated the work to Louis-Francois Roubiliac (1702–62),[38] who had worked for his brother. The statue he produced was similar to his scheme for Sir Thomas Molyneux at Armagh the previous year. As an idealised and heroic statue of the dead Founder, custom dictated the use of classical dress. The figure of Robert Gordon leans on a plinth on which is a representation of Charity as a woman nursing little children, reflecting the central object of the Founder's benefaction.[39] The scroll he holds is his Deed commemorating the foundation of his Hospital. 'The richness of the treatment is singularly well suited to the plain architectural niche in which the statue stands.'[40] Cheere's account was paid by November 1753 and amounted to 894 pounds Scots (£74 sterling), with the Hospital also paying freight, carriage[41] and erection costs of 57 pounds Scots. It was by far the greatest expenditure of the time.[42] The statue was raised in position by James Wylie, mason in Aberdeen, on Saturday 11 August 1753, where it remains today.[43] Unfortunately the marble was painted early in its history.[44]

The only other major building work in the 1750s involved general maintenance. The windows of the Hospital had to be mended and plated with lead to keep out the rain and Richard Wallace, plumber, was employed for this. Several pieces of the steps of the stone floor had been broken and needed attention. Wooden partitions in the upper floor were to be painted a dark colour to 'conceal a great many ugly writings that had been scribbled upon them while the House was uninhabited'.[45]

The garden was a constant matter of concern for the Governors. The gardener, John Davidson, was producing about £4 sterling worth of roots, kail and herbs annually and the Governors believed they could get better value. In August 1752 it was decided to give over part of the garden for a bleaching field for the Hospital, and to put the remainder (with house and bowling green included) out to tender to the highest bidder. On 20 November 1752 the Governors approved a roup of garden and house to James Clerk for eleven years at £12/10/- per annum.[46] They were also keen to show off the garden and the Auld Hoose and to that end in February 1754 the garden walks were opened up to gentlemen and ladies, but nurses and children were restricted to certain areas.[47] Later that summer four garden seats were introduced. By August 1757 the gardener was being pressed to recommend exclusion for any disorderly person found 'cursing or swearing' in the garden or bowling green.[48]

Finance was always a major worry for the Governors. By April 1755 they were concerned that the income from their yearly rents were not sufficient to maintain their aim of keeping 36 boys in the Hospital and the same number as apprentices. As an economy measure another change was made to the Founder's deed: the level of apprentice fee was reduced to one hundred pounds Scots and all boys were to receive £5 sterling whatever their destination after the completion of their apprenticeship.[49] This alteration was estimated to save 1,400 pounds Scots every year.

Rev. John Hucheon

The loss of both Abercrombies – Robert, the schoolmaster, who died in April 1758, and George, the Master, who left to take up the charge of Forgue in August 1759[50] – left the Hospital in some disarray. The Governors turned to the newly appointed schoolmaster, Rev. John Hucheon, and persuaded him to take on the post of Master while retaining his teaching responsibilities.[51] He was a young man, having been born in 1733, and attended King's College as a bursar, graduating in 1753. Hucheon retained both positions in the Hospital until 26 September 1763.

It was during Hucheon's short period as Master that the Governors decided to complete the spire and cupola of the Auld Hoose. William Littlejohn was employed for this operation during the late summer of 1760, while Richard Wallace did the lead work.[52] It was built on the flat roof of the building on an octagonal leaded base from which arose the shaft or windowed position, consisting of eight semi-circular leaded windows divided into small well-proportioned panes. Above a shallow cornice the tapering lead spire rose and was decorated with small fleur-de-lys and lead imitation rolls. About halfway up the spire was a moulded collar. The completion of the fleche gave the building a striking and distinctive appearance and was similar to the Tolbooth spire of a century earlier.

The Governors then commissioned William Mosman (c1700–71)[53] to paint a full-length portrait of the Founder and this was completed in 1761 and placed in the Governors' Hall. They were pleased with the work and Mosman, who ran a Drawing Academy in Aberdeen, was employed as a teacher of painting and drawing in the Hospital between 1762 and 1769.[54]

On Wednesday 25 May 1763 John Wesley visited the Hospital during his tour of Scotland. In his Journal he gave details of how he found the building:

> About noon I went to Gordon's Hospital, built near the town, for poor children. It is an exceedingly handsome building and (what is not common) kept exceedingly clean. The gardens are pleasant, well laid out, and in extremely good order; but the old bachelor who founded it has expressly provided that no woman should ever be there.[55]

James Anderson

On Hucheon's resignation[56] James Anderson, who had taken up the post of schoolmaster in 1762, was made Master. He was only twenty and had just graduated some months before from King's College. His lack of teaching experience led to a failure to keep the interest of the boys and it was not long before the discipline of the House deteriorated markedly. Although he survived in post until 1790, Anderson's time was a difficult period for the Hospital and problems with the boys surfaced periodically. The situation worsened after the appointment of Thomas Dyce as a master in 1777.

On 3 October 1780 the Governors received a Petition from James Robertson, weaver burgess, on behalf of his son, James [244], complaining that his ear had been hurt by Dyce. Dr Livingstone[57] was asked to examine the boy and Dyce was requested to reply to the complaint.[58] Meantime the boys' parents had taken their son out of the Hospital without permission and Anderson had reacted by suspending him. A Committee of Three Governors, Lord Provost James Jopp[59], Dr Campbell and Rev. George Abercrombie, was set up to enquire into the circumstances.[60] On 19 February 1781 the Governors examined the Committee's report, which relied on evidence from Livingstone, Dyce and the Housekeeper, Mrs Mark. They held that 'all private correction of the boys in the Hospital is improper' and Dyce's correction was 'not a proper mode' of punishment. Dyce and the other masters had been informed of this. However, the Governors also believed that the boy had 'greatly exaggerated'[61] the incident. Unfortunately, Robertson's father had made 'a great noise in the Town' and in so doing he had blackened the name of the Hospital, despite the considerable benefits the family had received from the institution.[62] The Governors supported Anderson's action and confirmed that the boy would remain suspended until the parents publicly acknowledged their faults in writing.[63] A further Petition was deemed unsatisfactory in terms of tone and language by the Governors, and James Robertson was finally excluded on 12 April 1781.[64]

A month later, in early May, Anderson reported to the Governors that six boys had deserted the Hospital to join a Russian ship at Newburgh.[65] When apprehended and interviewed four were allowed to return to face a public whipping in front of all the boys, but the other two had poorer discipline records and were excluded permanently. Such strict treatment did little to stem the spate of desertions. On 30 October another five boys absconded, three of whom were found at Leith trying to board a ship as sailors. The patience of the Governors was exhausted. When another three boys absconded on 5 November and boarded a ship, Captain Roth, the commander, inclined to keep them. The Governors decided to 'take no further concern with them'[66] and decided that they had forfeited their Hospital benefits, refusing to entertain any petitions from them or their relatives.

The Governors were not only concerned with the indiscipline of the boys but also their academic standards. In October 1781 when it was reported that only one boy was fit to leave the Hospital the Governors determined that 'there must be some error in the present mode of education or neglect of discipline'[67] in the House. They set up an immediate inquiry, which was frustrated by the failure to find a set of House Regulations. This situation was deemed to be the root of the problems in the Hospital. It was decided that a comprehensive set of regulations for the government of the Hospital was needed and should be produced as soon as practicable.

The Governors were also anxious to maintain standards of dress and appearance. The Statutes had stipulated that the boys were to be 'decently apparelled in clothes made after the Fashion of the Time, or such Fashion as the Governors would think fit, their clothes being all of one Colour and Fashion'.[68] The result was the introduction of a uniform, consisting of a tailed coat and waistcoat of blue cloth[69] with yellow-metal buttons with Hospital crest, knee breeches,[70] black leather helmets or caps,[71] a stock[72] and black, buckled shoes.

Staffing issues, too, continued to be a priority for the Governors. In May 1782 Anderson was granted eight weeks' leave of absence to visit friends and his work was shared among the other masters. To ensure that he came back at the end of this time the Governors warned him that if he failed to return his post would be held vacant. In October 1783 Anderson informed the Governors that Thomas Dyce had not for the first time failed to return from his leave of absence (which officially ended on 16 September). The Governors took this seriously[73] and Dyce was to be called upon to explain himself on his return. Anderson reported him back on 6 October and at their meeting Dyce proferred an apology which was accepted meantime.[74]

In the interim a Committee of Ten under Lord Provost William Young[75] and including the Treasurer and Clerk, had held 'many meetings'[76] and produced a new set of Regulations which were discussed and unanimously accepted at a Special Meeting of thirteen Governors on 12 April 1784. These spelled out in great detail all aspects of Hospital life and were to remain largely unchanged for the next century.

The 1784 Regulations

A daily timetable was specified. Between 1 March and 1 October a detailed routine was scheduled for the boys from 6am (rise) and 10pm (bed).[77] Essentially the same pattern was laid down for the rest of the year but with a start to the day at 7.30am or 8am. On Saturdays the boys had play in the afternoon or were able to visit friends or relatives until early evening. Sundays were dominated by religious observance. The boys remained in their rooms for devotions, before taking a walk in the garden or courtyard before family worship. After breakfast the boys attended the West Church, a place in the loft being kept for them by the beadle.[78] They followed the Master in good order to and from the church and were allowed to dally in the garden before 'dinner'. Family worship and church were repeated in the afternoon before the boys met in schoolrooms for their Catechism and further family worship. Although there was more 'free' time at the weekends the boys were closely supervised and the gates were locked except at the times of going to and from church. The boys were not allowed out of the grounds without permission and a ticket, which they handed back on their return.

A discipline code defined bounds and spelled out expected behaviour – good manners and avoidance of drink and debauchery, swearing, lying, stealing, quarrelling, fighting, spoiling of clothes or property. The boys would be chastised publicly for misdemeanours and expelled for grosser or repeated faults. Parents had to accept the Regulations and not frequent the Hospital 'as an inspector, nor meddle officiously', nor bring in food. They needed permission before visiting or taking boys out and could give money only after informing the Master.

The curriculum was to be taught in an order laid down – English, writing, arithmetic, Church Music[79] and drawing[80]– and those who 'discovered a genius' for English grammar, bookkeeping, French, elements of geometry, trigonometry, navigation or geography could study them. However, even in the higher classes, there continued daily exercises in reading, writing and arithmetic.

The 'bill of fare' was different for boys and masters. At breakfast the boys were given oatmeal pottage and milk, while the masters received tea and white bread. The main meal of dinner was taken in the middle of the day and varied daily; the boys had the following menu:

Monday	Barley broth and a little beef.
Tuesday	Milk and barley boiled.
Wednesday	Boiled beef and turnip.

Thursday	Brose and kail boiled with beef.
Friday	Milk and barley boiled.
Saturday	Barley broth & sheep heads.
Sunday	Mutton or beef & potatoes.

The schoolmasters had similar food on Monday, Wednesday, Thursday and Sunday, although the quality was better. On Tuesday they had fish, on Friday roast mutton and potatoes and on Saturday barley broth and beef.

In the afternoon while the boys had bread and butter or milk, the masters had tea, while at supper when the boys had barley meal pottage and sweet milk the masters had potatoes, eggs or fish. The normal drink for all was 'small beer' and the normal bread oatmeal.

The duties of the Master, schoolmasters, Treasurer and Clerk were itemised. The Master was to exam the boys publicly every Tuesday and Thursday evening; between 2 and 3pm daily to teach the boys elements of geometry, geography, bookkeeping and French; remain on the premises overnight except with the permission of the Lord Provost; ensure that strangers were ejected and the Hospital locked up by 10pm and keep the keys with him; monitor the health of the boys; make funeral arrangements spending no more than £2 sterling; ensure no gifts were given to the staff by parents or boys; and report quarterly to the Governors.

The schoolmasters had to be on duty at all times on the premises; check every night that all boys were in bed and lights out; visit rooms at noon to see if clean and neat; supervise meals; and attend evening lessons. The Treasurer was to visit the Hospital at least twice every week; supervise officials; ensure the diet of the boys was wholesome and sufficient; inspect Hospital rooms; keep Accounts, detailing all items of £5 sterling or more; assist the Master in finding apprenticeships; and negotiate tacks. The Clerk was to keep all Hospital papers, records and Minutes, registers, land transactions and inventories.[81]

By the next Governors' meeting on 2 August 1784 five hundred copies of the original Statutes and new Regulations had been printed[82]. They contained the Founder's Deed of Mortification and Appendix,[83] Alterations to the original Statutes,[84] Instructions for Parents,[85] General House Regulations,[86] Bill of Fare,[87] Powers of Masters,[88] and ended with the Royal Charter of 1772, which determined that the Governors and successors became 'one corporation and body corporate and politic in deed and in name'.[89] Copies went to all Governors, officials, staff and parents. The boys were called in and informed. The Governors gave the Clerk, Treasurer and Officer a gratuity for their 'extra trouble' over the Regulations.[90] An improvement in all Hospital affairs was now expected.

Discipline Problems – Staff and Pupils

As part of the closer monitoring regime, a Hospital Journal, which would be kept by the Master, was to be produced and perused at Governor meetings.[91] On 16 May 1785 this resulted in surprise at the 'frequent absences of the masters'.[92] A further discussion in August concentrated on the attendance record of Thomas Dyce,[93] which was deemed too irregular. A Committee of Eight under Lord Provost William Cruden[94] determined that in future all occurrences were to be noted daily as they happened in the Journal, which was to be available for inspection at all times.[95] Its examination in August 1786 showed that Dyce had been absent from the Hospital for a single day several times in a few months. The Governors feared that closer scrutiny would find other discipline issues and the Committee of Eight was asked to inquire further.[96]

In August 1787 the Journal showed that Dyce had gone to the country on 15 June without permission and had not returned until 15 July. Moreover, the Treasurer had observed 'great differences and disagreement to subsist between Mr Anderson and Mr Dyce which may be productive of very bad consequences in the Hospital'.[97] This led to a Special Meeting of the Governors on 17 October 1787 during which Dyce claimed he had the Lord Provost's permission for three weeks' absence and his return was delayed by the lack of a horse. He had not informed Anderson because he had been refused permission previously and been treated 'haughtily and insolently'.[98] The Governors held Dyce to be in breach of his duties and he was rebuked by the Lord Provost with regard to his future conduct. They also found the relationship between Anderson and Dyce poor, with both resorting to 'improper and indecent expressions'[99] in front of the boys. Both were warned to conduct themselves better in future. Anderson protested in vain.[100]

In February 1788, in an attempt to defuse matters, the Governors, on advice from Anderson, recommended that each of the masters should be given leave of up to three weeks between 1 June and 1 October, provided that only one was absent at any one time.[101] To appease Anderson, the Governors agreed to cut down on his commitments. He could dispense with his meeting with the boys between 6 and 7pm on four days but he was to continue to examine them on Tuesdays and Thursdays and with Catechism on Sundays. Anderson

The Heritage of the Pitlurg Gordons

Estates bought by Gordon's Hospital

The original Hospital Building – the Auld Hoose

Effigy of Sir John Gordon of Pitlurg in the Boray Aisle, the remains of St Martin's Church at Cairnie

Not much remains of the 16th century Z-plan tower house and courtyard of Pitlurg Castle

Robert Gordon of Straloch (1580–1661) –
grandfather of the Founder

Astrolabe of Robert Gordon of
Straloch (1597)

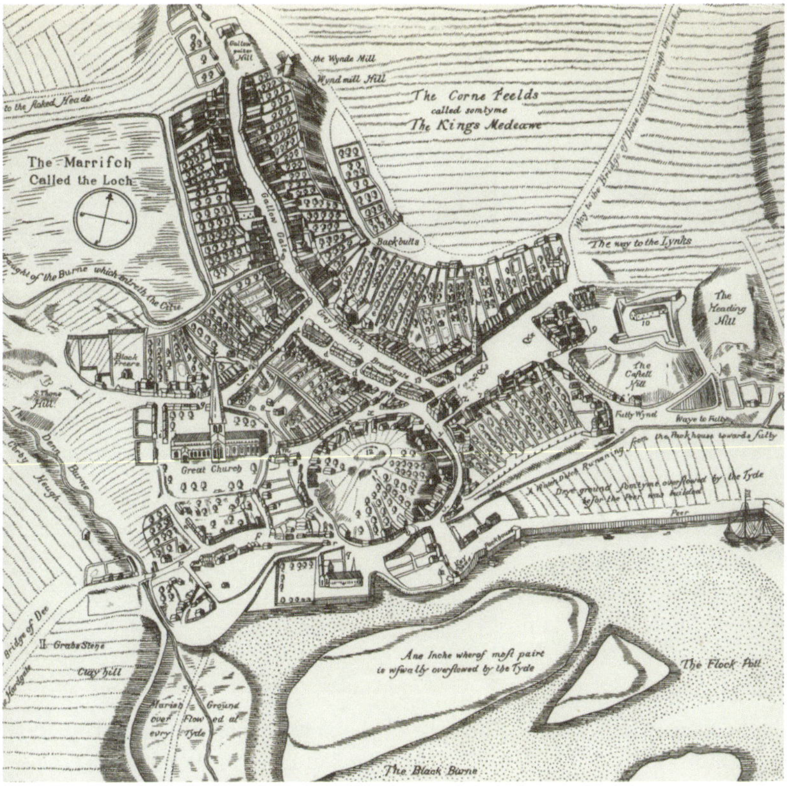

Parson Rothiemay's Map of Aberdeen (1661). His associated description related that only the ruined wall of the Dominican (or Black Friars') house remained

Portrait of the young Robert Gordon, the Founder

Order of Gustavus Adolphus awarded to Robert Gordon of Pitlurg (1632)

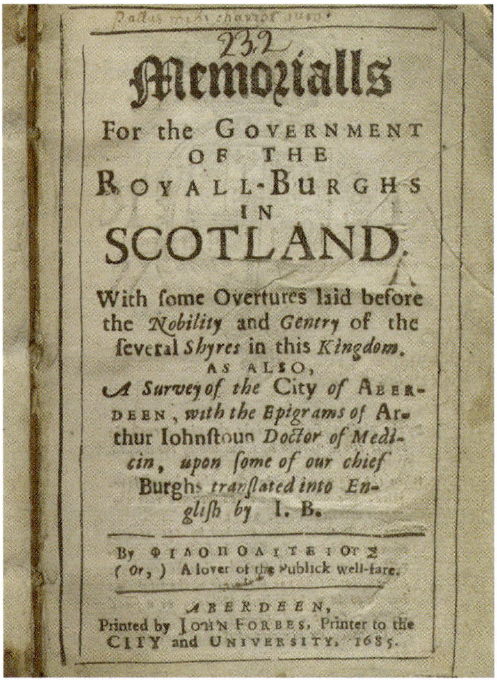

232

Memorialls

For the GOVERNMENT OF THE ROYALL-BURGHS IN SCOTLAND.

With ſome Overtures laid before the *Nobility* and *Gentry* of the ſeveral *Shyres* in this *Kingdom*.

AS ALSO,

A Survey of the City *of* ABERDEEN, *with the Epigrams of* Arthur Iohnſtoun *Doctor of Medicin, upon ſome of our chief* Burghs *tranſlated into Engliſh by* I. B.

By ΦΙΛΟΠΟΛΙΤΕΙΟΣ

(Or,) A lover of the Publick well-fare.

ABERDEEN,

Printed by JOHN FORBES, Printer to the CITY and UNIVERSITY, 1685.

Frontispiece of Baillie Skene's 'Memorialls' (1685)

Portrait of the mature Robert Gordon, painted in the 1720s

An Engraving from Robert Gordon's extensive Collection, now housed in the College

The 'Englische Haus' in Danzig where Robert Gordon lived after 1700. It was ideally situated for trade, close to the banks of the river Motlawa

Looking down Broad Street with Huxter Row (Robert Gordon's birthplace) on the right before its demolition in 1867

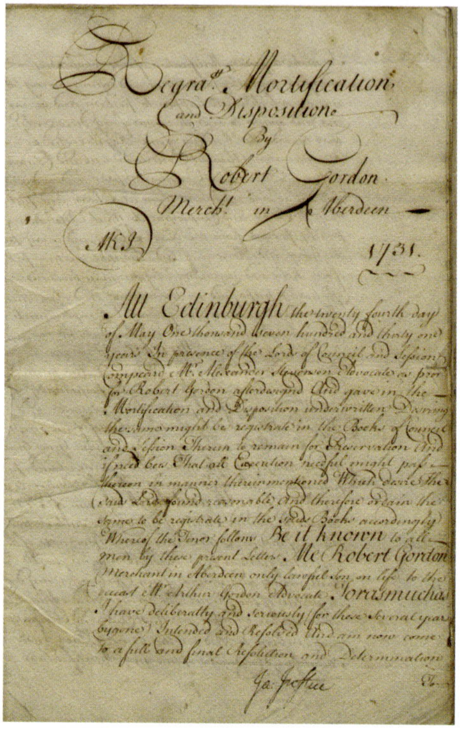

Regra[td] Mortification and Disposition By Robert Gordon Merch[t] in Aberdeen

MKI

1731.

Att Edinburgh the twenty fourth day of May One thousand seven hundred and thirty one years In presence of the Lords of Council and Session Compeared Mr Alexander [illegible] Advocate as pror for Robert Gordon aforesaid And gave in the Mortification and Disposition underwritten Desiring the same might be registrate in the Books of Council and Session Therein to remain for Preservation And if need bee That all Execution needful might pass thereon in manner therein mentioned Which desire the said Lords found reasonable And therefore ordain the same to be registrate in the said Books accordingly Whereof the Tenor follows Be it known to all men by these present Letters Me Robert Gordon Merchant in Aberdeen only lawful son on life to the deceast Mr Arthur Gordon Advocate Forasmuch as I have deliberatly and seriously (for these several years bygone) Intended and Resolved And am now come to a full and final Resolution and Determination

Ja. Justice

Robert Gordon's Deed of Mortification and Disposition (December 1729) was registered in May 1731

Silverton Hospital is shown on this section of Paterson's map

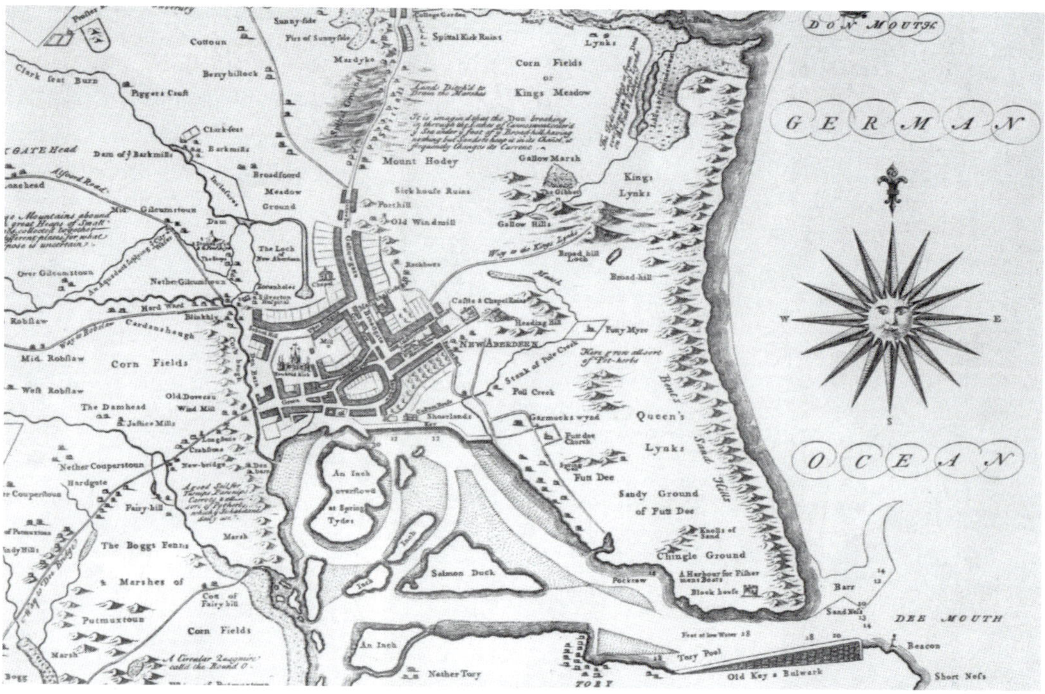

G. and W. Paterson's 1746 Map of Aberdeen

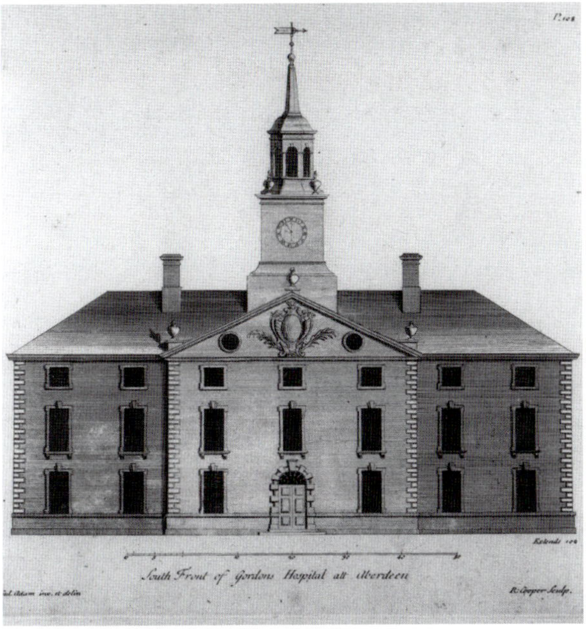

William Adam's original design for the show front of the proposed Hospital (1731)

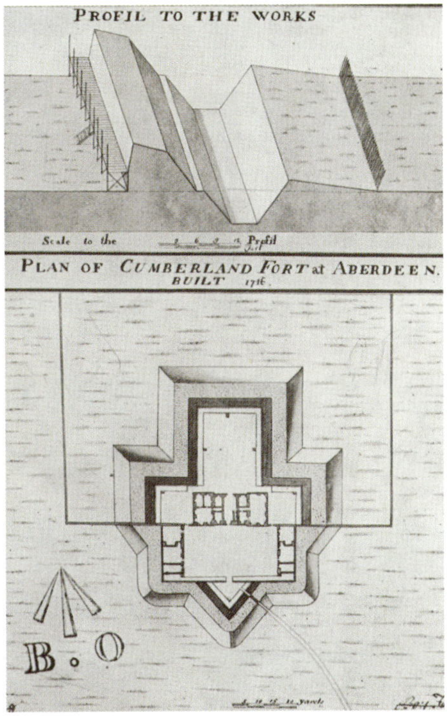

Plan of Fort Cumberland (1746)

The terracotta statuette model of Robert Gordon (1752) is now in the Governors' Room

Robert Gordon's Statue was positioned in its architectural niche in August 1753

The architectural designs produced for the proposed extensions to the Auld Hoose in 1826–27

The grandiose Jacobean plan of William Burn

The design of John Smith, which the Governors ultimately favoured

Archibald Simpson's design lost out in the competition stakes

no longer had to examine every boy but only as many as time permitted. On 19 May 1788, with finances in good shape, Anderson and Mrs Mark were awarded twenty guineas each for their 'long and faithful service'.[102]

Since the introduction of the new Regulations in 1784 there had been fewer instances of indiscipline by the boys, although the problem of boys wetting their beds became a concern at this time.[103] Two, in particular, 'abused' their beds to such a degree that within a few weeks their beds were 'rotten and useless'. The Governors held bed-wetting a nasty habit and the schoolmasters had failed in their extensive efforts to end the 'dirty practice'.[104] It came to the stage where the servants refused to make their beds. On 3 October 1785 the Governors decided to set an example and dismissed the two boys concerned – Alexander [298] and Robert [320] Garvock – publicly announcing this to all the boys and the Lord Provost giving an exhortation to others to avoid such nasty practices. In November 1785 it was decided that from now on any boy seeking admission to the Hospital had to produce a certificate for the Hospital physician holding him to be 'wholesome and sound' in his body.[105] Livingstone was urged to be 'particular in his inspection'.

Unfortunately more discipline problems arose again in February 1790. William Jenkins [359], already seen as incorrigible after numerous corrections and warnings, placed a train of powder on the naked buttocks of James Wilson [401] and then persuaded another boy to set fire to it. He went further and kicked George Martin's [417] 'privy parts'[106] to the imminent danger of his life.[107] Given his verbal attacks on servants, and his dangerous and pernicious effect on others, Jenkins was expelled.

The fact that Jenkins could commit so many offences before being dealt with was bad enough but also worrying was the general belief that the boys 'had not made such progress as might have been expected from the time they have been in the Hospital'.[108] A considerable number read too fast and indistinctly without proper regard to the points, and others in a rambling stammering manner. The Governors examined the boys in their proficiency in writing and arithmetic. Dyce's class was found not to have made the progress expected from his pupils. As a considerable number of them had not been taught any writing at all Dyce was deemed negligent in his teaching. The Lord Provost admonished him and threatened that if he offended again he would be 'deposed'.[109] Donald's class, however, showed considerable proficiency especially given the short time he had been teaching in the Hospital.[110]

Within a week the Governors had interviewed the Treasurer, Anderson and schoolmasters and found that there were 'considerable defects in the education, discipline and economy of the Hospital'.[111] A Committee of Nine plus the Treasurer and Clerk under Lord Provost Cruden was given the task of remedying the grave situation. This was too much for Anderson, who, after 27 years' service, resigned on 15 May 1790.[112] He claimed to be suffering from a 'depression of spirits' which prevented the proper performance of his duties.[113] This probably saved him from dismissal. By 14–6 the Governors voted to give him an annuity of £40 sterling, as a reward for his long and loyal service and in appreciation of the creditable features of his tenure.

One positive feature of Anderson's tenure had been a Governor initiative which resulted in (up to) four Hospital boys being permitted annually to attend the mathematical and natural philosophy classes in the College without payment of fees, in return for a one-off payment of fifty guineas to buy astronomical and other instruments.[114] A Committee of Five under Lord Provost Jopp signed the agreement with Principal Campbell of Marischal on 24 August 1781. Under Anderson, Hospital boys began to attend university classes. The first 'College Boy' in November 1782 was James Finnie [123], who, having left the Hospital in November 1771 to be apprenticed to a wright, desired a 'more general and extensive knowledge of mechanics',[115] and others followed.[116] Although these were other examples of modifying Robert Gordon's original intention it was a logical development from the stated aim of allowing boys to find their particular genius: for a small minority this meant going on to attend university classes.

Finance

The funds of the Hospital seemed increasingly to be in good order as the 1780s progressed, with separate major loans of surplus cash amounting to £2300 sterling being given over to the Town Treasurer and Shoremaster.[117] This was increased in the case of the Town by another £1,200 sterling at 4½% interest in November 1785.[118] These loans, although understandable given the overwhelming preponderance of Town representatives on the Governing Body of the Hospital, were given over at a time of growing concern over the misuse of public funds. In 1784 a Committee of burgesses was set up and, following its demand for openness, its members were allowed to examine the Town's Books. They held that 'the general misfortune, which could have happened to the interest of the citizen, is the facility with which the magistrates have been able to borrow money from the other funds, under the administration of the Council, for the ordinary purposes of the treasury, without consulting the citizens'.[119] It was further suggested that this 'misfortune' had been increased by the practice 'of mingling with the treasury funds every public money transaction and, by some means or other, every other fund has been made to blend its transactions with them'.[120] The total debt of the Town treasury was £12,383 sterling with Gordon's Hospital the main creditor.[121] Unfortunately the warning was not heeded and the Town continued to use funds of other institutions to solve its financial problems and in retrospect it is perhaps surprising that the more independent ministers on Gordon's Governing Body did not protest more vigorously.[122]

By November 1787 the Governors were proclaiming a 'great yearly surplus' of funds[123] and discussion ensued on how best to dispose of it. However, by February 1788 the Governors appeared to be backtracking and were unwilling to overturn the cuts to apprentice fee levels (introduced in 1755) and return them to the original sums in the Mortification.[124]

Lack of funds was not, therefore, the motivation behind the Rev. Dr Duncan Shaw's motion of 20 November 1786. He reminded the Governors that the Deed of Mortification required that if any who had been educated in the Hospital acquired or succeeded to a considerable fortune, he be obliged to pay back to the Hospital what was laid out or expended upon him during the time he was in the Hospital and putting him to trade. As some ex-pupils had recently died in good circumstances Shaw proposed that the Governors 'use their best endeavours to recover the sums expended on these persons'.[125] Further discussions on this issue led the Governors to ask the Clerk to inquire as to the practice of the Edinburgh Hospitals,[126] which found that the Deeds of Heriot and Watson had no such clause. After the Treasurer had written letters to a few ex-pupils with disappointing results the Clerk took legal advice from solicitor Dundas and advocate Charles Hay on whether a legal action would be well founded.[127] Both Dundas and Hay were optimistic in their separate opinions of August 1788[128] and after extended deliberations the Governors decided by 11 votes to 4 in November 1789 to go ahead with a prosecution.[129] However, by April of the following year the Governors were having second thoughts[130] and when a prosecution was deemed 'inexpedient at present' the matter was dropped, at least temporarily.[131]

The Governors also grappled with thorny issues involving the admission rules to the Hospital. Throughout its history there had been disputes as to whether sons or grandsons of butchers, bakers and other tradesmen in Aberdeen, not being members of the Incorporated Trades, were entitled by Robert Gordon's Mortification to be admitted into the Hospital.[132] It was resolved in October 1781 that precedence should be given to those belonging to the Incorporated Trades but those unincorporated trades (litsters, barbers, etc.) should be eligible immediately after them and before residents in general. In October 1786 it was found that the father of one of the applicants for admission, Francis Clerihew (son also called Francis) had been admitted to trade burgess status in August 1785 and the suspicion was that this was for the sole purpose of gaining admittance to Gordon's. The Governors saw this as 'highly improper'[133] and on 19 February 1787 unanimously decided that boys would only be elected if fathers/grandfathers had been burgesses for five years.[134]

The Hospital saw some internal and external improvements in this period and the buoyant funds meant the work done was to a high specification and quality. In May 1785 the Governors were persuaded that the boys' bedrooms were overcrowded with resulting bad air. They decided to create two large wards, on either end of the attic storey, each containing twelve beds (two boys to a bed). New oak beds were made with dimensions three and one half foot wide and five and one half foot in length.[135] Many of the Hospital windows had decayed, especially those in the east wing and roof, and the rain came in constantly. Expert opinion advised replacement rather than repair and the new windows, when completed in 1787–8, were made of the best red fir and painted with three coats of white lead and oil, prior to being glazed.[136] In May 1790 the Governors noticed that part of the great stair, which was built of freestone, was so worn as to be dangerous. It was replaced in granite.[137] Later that summer the porch of the Hospital was rebuilt 'in a neat manner'.[138] It became stilted and segmented with five bays formed by plain granite monoliths, carrying large ogee cornice and parapet. Four bays contained doors (three of them were panelled dummies) with plain square-pane fanlights above. The bell was remounted and the Back Gate was renewed.[139] The Governors also closely monitored the garden and bowling green, conscious of the need to present the citizens with a pleasing prospect at all times.[140]

By 1790 the immediate surroundings of the Hospital grounds had been greatly altered especially by the feuing of the Lochlands on the north and north-east. The new streets created were to be called George Street, Crooked Lane, Hospital Row (later part of St Andrew's Street), Charlotte Street, St Andrew's Street and John Street.[141] It was not until just prior to 1812 that Blackfriars' Street, to the west of the Hospital grounds, was opened by the Governors and brought about improvements in that area. However, a good part of the old wall which separated the Hospital from the Lochlands remained, and still remains, and the back entrance gateway, with its V-jointed granite piers, cornice and finely moulded coping, is still in use.

Fate of the Hospital Boys

The harsh monastic regime had produced a number of casualties by 1790 in terms of those who were dismissed, those who deserted and those who died. Dismissal was either because of ill-health (ten cases in the period) or specifically for having scrofulous tumours (two cases)[142] or for behavioural problems (fifteen cases). John Smith [90] was dismissed for 'improper' conduct in February 1764; Alexander Low [148] and James Gillet [160] were expelled 'for some faults' in July 1772, while Donaldson Milne [151] was dismissed for 'six misdemeanours'. Samuel Duncan [156] was discharged in November 1777 for 'indecent behaviour' and Alexander Garvock [298] was expelled for 'nasty practices'.[143] In the same period some nineteen boys deserted the Hospital, usually running off to sea. Simpson Strachan [94] did so in February 1769 and made a fortune in Grenada, leaving £100 sterling to the Hospital in his will as a repayment for his education.[144] Usually, however, the consequences were not so favourable, many drowning at a young age. With regard to death seventeen boys died while in the Hospital[145] between 1750–90 while another twelve died[146] during their apprenticeship.

Even from its earliest days the Hospital produced a number of boys who did well in later life. Colin Milne [15] became an English clergyman showing that it was possible to benefit from the Hospital education in unexpected ways. James Malcom [33] attended the Hospital between 1752–8 and became a physician in Jamaica; his brother, John [57], who attended 1757–63, became a successful merchant. Alexander Finnie [47] gained a premium for his drawings while attending the Hospital between 1756 and 1764 – he became apprentice to Robert and James Adam in London and was sent to Italy to improve, where he 'acquired great applause'. Unfortunately he died 'much regretted before he completed his studies'.[147] Charles Eglistone [111], who attended between 1765–70, served with the East India Company before joining the Portuguese service and rising to be captain of a man-of-war. George Milne [230], attended 1776–80, became a Procurator before the Sheriff Court of Kincardineshire. Andrew Baxter [256], attended 1778–83, was apprenticed as a ship-carpenter and served on whaling ships before becoming a master of one in 1814. William Adam [284], attended

1780–3, became a surgeon in the navy. Alexander Stewart [312], whose weaver father was deceased, resided in the Hospital between 1782–7 and in time became Baillie Stewart.[148] The Governors could be proud of their early record with regard to the boys and their careers. Significantly, too, it was not just the north-east of Scotland that benefited. Geographical mobility was encouraged. Before 1790 some 31 boys had gone to the West Indies, two to the Carolinas, 21 'abroad' and twelve to London, all with not just the Governors' blessing but with their financial support.

With these kind of successes and a Hospital roll which reached 55 by 1790 the institution had survived despite the lack of strong and consistent leadership. Fortunately this was shortly to be provided.

4

THE ADVANCE OF THE HOSPITAL, 1790–1832

Alexander Thom

Although the Governors were pleased at Anderson's departure there was no reason to suppose that his successor would prove more successful. There was only one candidate for the post of Master, which remained at the same salary of £26 sterling, and indeed was even less attractive given the decision of the Governors to appoint the Master and schoolmasters annually for one year to avoid a repetition of staffing problems.[1] Alexander Thom was in his early thirties and as an Arts graduate of Marischal in 1779 he had become a preacher in Aberdeen. He had already failed in his attempt to become one of the Hospital schoolmasters, when James Donald had been appointed, and being a 'little spare man'[2] did not even look the part. However, a Committee of Four under Lord Provost Cruden examined Thom in reading, writing, arithmetic, bookkeeping and other branches of education and found him sufficiently qualified. He was unanimously elected Master on 28 June 1790.[3]

Immediately Thom had to face the staffing issue which had plagued Anderson: the unreliability and unprofessional attitude of Thomas Dyce. He tackled it head on. At his first Governors' meeting on 16 August Thom held Dyce to have been negligent in his church duties. Dyce was called in before the Governors and warned regarding his future conduct.[4] When it came to his reappointment in November, Dyce was forced to defend himself against accusations of unsatisfactory work.[5] The Governors were dissatisfied with Dyce's replies and voted 12–7 to investigate further. Following further assurances from Dyce the Governors decided against dismissal, instead putting him on trial for a year.[6] Fortunately for all concerned, on 27 October 1791, Dyce left the Hospital, ostensibly called away on business and giving no guarantee as to when he would return.[7] The Governors quickly voted to give him £30 and advertised for a successor.

A period of staff stability followed but it still proved difficult to obtain and retain quality staff. William Maxwell Shaw, the relatively new music teacher, was frequently absent and he was threatened with dismissal in 1798 unless the situation improved.[8] Thom monitored his attendance closely and when he reported to the Governors that Shaw had been 'remiss in his attendance' his contract was not renewed.[9] However, with no suitable replacement at hand, when Shaw apologised, he was taken back on trial.[10]

One way round the staffing selection problems was to appoint insiders whenever possible and Thom resorted to that practice in April 1802 when David Marshall [425], who had attended the Hospital between 1790 and 1796 and had been apprenticed to a house painter, was appointed drawing master as he 'by application to the study of drawing appeared to have sufficiently qualified himself for office'.[11] In November 1806 another ex-Hospital boy, who had attended between 1792 and 1798, Ebenezer Gerrard [454],[12] was appointed to the same post, as was George Smith [621], who attended 1804–8, and set himself up as an architectural drawer, in April 1814.[13]

By this time complaints against staff were unusual and so the Governors felt in a position of some strength when facing criticism made by a parent about the Housekeeper, Mrs Jean More. She had taken over from Mrs Mark in May 1790[14] on a year's trial at £10 sterling, but her 'great diligence' had led to a salary increase to 20 guineas in August 1793.[15] With her work continuing to be commended, her salary rose to £25 in May 1799.[16] It was no surprise then when, after a Committee of Governors had interviewed staff and boys, on 25 May 1811 the charges against her were dismissed as groundless.[17]

The Governors became more professional and open in their approach to appointments in this period. From February 1812 all were advertised in the press and all candidates for posts were examined to enable valid comparisons to be made. Membership of Committees for such examination were also opened up to all Governors who wished to join.[18] Schoolmaster Thomas Roger was the first to be appointed in this more regular manner and the Governors also commented positively on the three unsuccessful candidates for his post.[19] The result of this more rigorous system of examination and interview was appointees better equipped to provide a quality learning experience for the Hospital boys.

There were few curriculum developments under Thom. Throughout his tenure the schoolmasters did not specialise but taught the whole curriculum, with the exceptions of drawing, which the Governors wished to include for its architectural content, and Church Music. When a Committee of Five, after consultation with Thom, took 'trials of the boys' knowledge and proficiency' in music and found them disappointing, the music master, Chalmers, was dismissed and John Ross, organist, was employed to raise standards.[20] This was adjudged a success, and on 30 June 1797 the matter was given over to Thom, who was instructed to call in proper help and maintain the improvement. To do so he appointed William Maxwell Shaw as music master and he persuaded the Governors in 1806 to buy the organ being sold by the Episcopalian Trinity Qualified Chapel.[21] Being placed in the Hall it seems to have helped progress music under Knott,[22] who taught in the Hospital from 1811 to 1824.[23] With the visiting music masters invariably precentors of the West Kirk it was natural that its choir was recruited from the Hospital boys. On 'Farmer George's[24] Jubilee' in 1810 the boys were specially drilled to sing an anthem in the church in the King's honour, their enthusiastic performance being much praised.

Out of the classroom the favourite pastime of the boys was football and the tradition had already developed that the outgoing boys on their departure presented a football to the others.[25] The ball was constructed by running out the worsted from the legs of old stockings and having it bound in thick leather by a saddler. Games were spirited, with twenty boys playing on each side. Kite flying was next in importance;[26] the kites were the envy of the Town's boys and this led to battles between them and the Hospital boys. The battlefield was the large space between Sim's Square and Charlotte Street – then unbuilt. Such fights were difficult to prevent as Thom had only the Town Sergeant, Robert Cantley,[27] to help keep the peace.

In the playground there was a slight incline towards one of its corners to carry off surface water. The boys blocked the drain and used the resulting water to sail their model-ships. When the water turned to ice, sliding and skating became the order of the day. Thom believed that the boys lacked 'proper amusement during the long winter evenings',[28] so the Governors bought books and geography maps for them, although the boys much preferred their own more physical pursuits. Problems arose in July 1797 when a lady, walking in the Hospital gardens, was seriously hurt when hit on the head by a stone thrown from the playground. A Committee of Six Governors looked into how the boys conducted themselves and what rules were needed to prevent accidents to themselves or others.[29] On 3 October 1797 it was decided that Thom should appoint at least two of the 'most prudent boys' as Censors to supervise the others in the playground.[30]

Thom went to great lengths to deal sympathetically with the intermittent problem of bed-wetting. John Simpson [400],[31] in April 1791, and Alexander Gordon [477], in February 1796,[32] proved immune from his every effort and were deemed medically incurable. Although they were dismissed Thom persuaded the Governors to give financial support to them both.

Thom's regime was also humanised by the caring attitude to the boys characterised by the Housekeepers following Mrs More's death in September 1816. She had been 'more intent on her ducks and hens than on the boys',[33] and her abusive tongue must have made life miserable for many a young loon.[34] From the twelve candidates for the post the Governors selected Mrs Ann Robertson, widow of the late Master at a Lancashire academy. She remained only until December 1817 when she resigned. Fortunately an application was received from Mrs Agnes Keith, Housekeeper in the Infirmary. As she was well known and respected by the Governors they elected her[35] and she proved an able servant to the Hospital until her death in April 1835. In particular she went to 'very great extra trouble' during an outbreak of sickness amongst the boys and, on 21 November 1825, she was given a salary increase by the Governors.[36]

Thom also encouraged the boys to 'let off steam' on occasion and as a result a highlight of the boys' year became their celebrations for George III's birthday on 4 June. In the lead-up the boys cut down whins and other bushes for miles around and trailed them into the Hospital, piling them up for a bonfire in the playground. When the eventful evening arrived the bonfire was lit with much rejoicing. 'Squibs, crackers, pistol firing, and much worse talk and loud profane swearing were abundant.'[37]

Finance

As early as August 1790, following a number of increasing surpluses, a Committee of Nine was set up to examine the funds and it projected future annual surpluses of around £200.[38] It recommended that the Hospital increase its roll to 66 as well as an all-round increase in salaries: Thom to 30 guineas; Donald to 25 guineas and Mrs More to 16 guineas, while the Treasurer was to receive a gratuity of 25 guineas. It was also deemed expedient to buy more land up to a total cost of £15,000.[39] Rev. Hugh Hay dissented on the grounds that the Charter of 1772 debarred Governors from holding more land than would yield £500 per annum. This led to voluminous 'reasons of dissent'[40] from Alexander Duguid, an advanced land reformer. He believed that 'there seems to be a natural inability in corporate bodies for managing territorial property with propriety and effect' and that 'lands held in mortmain i.e. held by church or corporation have always accounted a public evil in every well-governed State'.

Duguid's powerful but lone voice was ignored. He held that despite the inflationary pressures of the time apprenticeship fees had been neglected,[41] and consequently Robert Gordon's vision of benefiting industry was being forgotten.[42] As a new Governor, Duguid's influence was limited and the Governors proceeded to obtain an amended Charter on 16 May 1792, extending their holding of lands to an amount yielding an annual rent of £1500. With this enhanced power, the Governors were able to make an agreement with the Managers of the Infirmary to buy together the lands of Towie-Barclay[43] from the Commissioners of the Earl of Findlater and Seafield for £20,000. The Hospital was to take two-thirds of the land and pay the same proportion, while the Infirmary took the remaining third.[44]

It was suggested in October 1796 that the time was propitious to sell certain feu-duties and with the capital released purchase other land capable of sustaining an increase in rents. As the Governors depended on the level of the latter for ongoing income this was a way of increasing the number of boys in the Hospital. At this time, money was raised by accepting offers for the feu-duties of the lands of Mid Beltie from James Dyce of Bishopton and George Auldjo of Portlethen.[45] In total the Governors realised £10,329 and with the funds 'very flourishing'[46] another four boys were to be taken in to the Hospital.[47]

The Governors continued their active land policy and developed a 'heritage' in Aberdeen. They bought the house of Christian Shewan, lying between the west garden of the Hospital and Woolmanhill, for £101 in June 1804;[48] bought property from Gordon's Mills Friendly Society near Woolmanhill for £123 in June 1805;[49] sold off the Towie superiorities in five lots for £1060 in November 1806;[50] and they purchased five houses from Andrew Robertson, advocate, in Woolmanhill for £107 in April 1809.[51] These transactions led to the decision of 18 February 1811 to take in another eight boys, making the Hospital total 78.[52] Lord Provost Hadden was particularly pleased that such additions did not need additional building although it was clear that the Hospital was nearing capacity and further accommodation would be needed if a further expansion in numbers was contemplated.[53]

In August 1811 the salaries of the Master and schoolmaster were increased again to 40 and 50 guineas respectively.[54] At the same time the Governors resolved to feu the back Hospital garden by removing the existing tenants, and another Committee took a detailed look at the future financial prospects of the Hospital. It was optimistic; more revenue could be expected from feuing around the Hospital and the forthcoming expiry of a number of other leases. The Governors decided to add a further ten boys (making 88) although they appreciated that the schoolroom would be 'considerably crowded'.[55] To that end it was recommended that two new schoolrooms be built, turning the existing schoolroom into a dormitory.

Significantly, the Committee held that as a substantial proportion of Hospital property was rented out at a very low rate, a regulation should be introduced to ensure that in future Hospital property would be sold, feued or leased by public roup or sealed offers after due advertisement. The Governors accepted this and the other recommendations: articles of consumption in the Hospital (milk, beef, clothes, shoes) were to be obtained by contract after public advertisement; and an annual statement of funds was to be published giving clear details to all Governors.[56] These fundamental changes which affected the operation of the Hospital's domestic arrangements took time to introduce but by 1816 they were well on the way to implementation.[57] The Governors were keen to press on and take more boys (aiming to reach a roll of 94) and asked George Smith, drawing master, to produce designs for the two school rooms.[58] However, when the Town was unable to pay back the £7,700 owed to the Hospital it was decided to delay the construction.[59]

On 2 December 1820 Baillie John Shepherd resigned as Treasurer given his 'age and infirmities'[60] despite having been re-elected the previous month. The Clerk, Robert Morice, took over the duties until a successor could be appointed. The auditors announced that they had found errors in the Hospital Accounts of the previous years, and as their inquiry progressed held that Shepherd had a 'considerable deficiency to answer for'.[61] By March 1821 this had been calculated at £740[62] and was put down to mismanagement and misjudgement. The Governors believed that the system of bookkeeping operating before 1811 should be re-introduced deeming it better suited than the existing method to check for errors.[63] Shepherd accepted responsibility but as he had not received the salary increase agreed by the Governors in 1812 asked that this be subtracted from the sum his Cautioners[64] were being pressed to pay on his behalf. The Governors, appreciating the increasing complexities involved in managing the Hospital lands, decided that in future the Treasurer's duties – which Robert

Gordon's Deed had stipulated should be in the hands of a 'merchant in Aberdeen' – would be separated from those of managing the lands, which would be given over to a qualified land Factor.[65] This division was clarified in May 1821 and the Governors unanimously elected Charles Walker as Treasurer and Robert Morice as Factor (previously Clerk).[66]

The Governors turned their attention to Shepherd's Cautioners, William Young and George More, who were given until 1 October to settle under threat of legal action.[67] However, when the date for settlement passed, the Governors, anxious to avoid judicial expense and delay, agreed to take the matter to arbitration.[68] On 19 August 1822 they reluctantly accepted the arbitrators'[69] compromise figure of £262, concerned at the significant loss of revenue by the Hospital.[70]

The confidence of the Governors was eroded by their failure to monitor Shepherd effectively. They had gone to great lengths to build up systems and procedures to ensure strict financial accountability. Indeed the time and effort spent on finance far outweighed that spent on all other Hospital matters. A complacency, however, had set in. This had been bred by the growth in Hospital funds, which were increasingly in good shape. For some of the Governing Body the Hospital was doing almost too well, especially given the contemporaneous financial difficulties of the Town.

By the time of the 1820s, the need for accommodation in the Hospital was acute. The ground floor rooms to the west were used as a parlour for receiving guests at the front, with a pantry to the rear.[71] Further west was the open dining room.[72] The area east of the opening vestibule had a large kitchen in the north-east corner with a larder west of it and the Housekeeper's rooms to the front.[73] The first floor west of the landing had the servants' bedroom at the front, and the Treasurer's room at the back.[74] At the west end was the Governors' Hall[75] while the Charter Room was entered from the main landing.[76] East of the landing was housed the 'public school', running from front to rear of the building, where all the classes would take place.[77]

On the second floor the front room was a 'sleeping room',[78] while the room to the west of the stair was the 'counting room'.[79] At the west end there were two adjoining rooms for masters at the front and a classroom to the back.[80] East of the stair was situated in the front the sickroom[81] and at the back the 'taylor's room'[82]. At the east end was to be found a corridor and four masters' rooms (two adjoining at the front and two at the rear).[83] The attic contained three large sleeping rooms at the front at the east and west ends, with quarters for masters just to the east and west of the stairs.[84] Space was clearly increasingly at a premium.

Alexander Simpson of Collyhill

Alleviation of the problem came from an unexpected source. Alexander Simpson of Collyhill[85] had succeeded to an extensive fortune on the death of his successful merchant father – Andrew Simpson, in September 1809 – and elder brother – John, in August 1811. On his return from continental travel on 16 April 1816 he, conscious of having no surviving siblings, executed a Deed by which the Principal and Professors of Marischal College and the four Presbyterian ministers of Aberdeen became trustees of his lands and estates of Barrack, in the parish of New Deer, and of Crichie, Annochie and Elrick, in Old Deer, in Aberdeenshire, to the benefit of the Hospital. The rents were for 'entertaining and educating' in the Hospital, or in additional buildings built, an additional number of 'indigent male children and male grandchildren of decayed Merchants and Brethern of Guild of the burgh of Aberdeen', failing them sons or grandsons of residents of Aberdeen 'who are indigent and cannot maintain themselves'.

Tragically, Simpson was killed in a game shooting accident on 12 August 1816.[86] The properties produced rents of upwards of £700 annually and these were to accrue to the Hospital on the death of Simpson's mother, Helen Rhind Simpson. In June 1821 she approached the appointed Trustees and offered to give up some of her life-rent to enable more boys to enter the Hospital sooner. In turn the Trustees approached the Governors who were keen to accept the extra funds although there were some concerns expressed that the Collyhill Trust could conflict with the Hospital procedures.[87]

Significantly, although Simpson ensured an overlap of membership of his Trustees with the Hospital in the shape of the local ministers, he stipulated that the Town Council were to have no rights regarding his Trust.[88] Presumably he was unimpressed with their financial acumen. However, potential future difficulties were discounted and the Governors accepted the Articles of Agreement in November 1822.[89] With significant finance promised the question was not whether the Hospital would grow in numbers but when it would happen – before or after new accommodation was planned and built.[90]

Nearing retirement, Thom's reputation was at its highest. His 'exemplary good conduct' during his long term as Master was reflected in the 'good behaviour of the boys and others under him in the Hospital' and the 'high character' of apprentices and the eagerness to join the Hospital.[91] On 25 March 1825 the Governors presented him with a gold watch:[92] Lord Provost Gavin Hadden's[93] address and Thom's reply were inserted in the Governors' Minutes and published in the *Aberdeen Journal*.

On 19 September 1826 Thom resigned his post after 36 years' service having been accepted as minister of Nigg.[94] The Governors warmly congratulated Thom and believed his legacy of order and discipline would live on in the Hospital. On this festive occasion[95] he was presented with a service of Plate.[96] Despite his unobtrusive manner he had been a success perhaps without ever being fully at ease. He enjoyed best escaping to his room and getting away from the hubbub of school life. He was now able to do so permanently.[97]

Fate of the Hospital Boys

Thom's tenure as Master (1790–1826) was a period of strong discipline. Despite his strictness he was held in high esteem by the boys, who 'could have gone through fire and water for him'.[98] Of the 564 boys who entered under Thom some sixteen deserted, a number running off to sea; twenty-one died – eighteen of them in the Hospital, the other three during their apprenticeship; and only five were dismissed. The backgrounds of the boys followed the pattern of the previous period[99] and as before there was some mobility upwards.[100] Geographical mobility was even more marked than before.[101]

The boys, as well as their masters, valued the education given in the Hospital. Indeed, the boys considered themselves second only to the Grammar School for learning and general intelligence.[102] Boys were sent to Marischal College more regularly: Alexander Scott [261] in August 1798,[103] James Thom [502] in October 1799,[104] Andrew Milne [509] in October 1800,[105] William Lawrie [505] and Alexander Coutts [526] in October 1801,[106] and Alexander Grant [613] in October 1817.[107]

The education imparted continued to result in qualified boys entering into all areas of life and a number were successful in different fields. David Laing [423], who attended between 1790–6, proved a great success in business as a painter and glazier in London; John Chisholm [430], who attended between 1790–5, attained eminence in architecture and engineering and superintended public works in Carlisle and on his death in 1808 he was 'universally esteemed and respected'.[108] Adam Mellis [461], attended 1793–8, entered the army and became a captain in May 1808. Charles Downie [579], attended 1801–7, retired from business 'immensely rich'; he bought an estate at Fochabers and married well.[109] George Tytler [591], attended 1802–6, became designer and artist to HRH Duke of Gloucester.[110] John Simpson [624], attended 1804–10, emigrated to Canada and became the first Mayor of Fredericton, New Brunswick, the editor of St John's *Royal Gazette*, director of two banks and chief magistrate of the town before his death in 1863. William Morison [627], attended 1804–10, became a Baptist minister in America in the 1840s. Peter Williamson [630], attended 1805–9, proved a generous benefactor to the Hospital in the 1840s when he was a Baillie of Aberdeen. John Smith [645], attended 1806–10, became a banker in Leeds and presented one of the new bells to the city in 1857. James Grant [677], attended 1808–14, taught at Donaldson's Hospital in the 1840s in Edinburgh. Frederick Cruickshank [699], attended 1809–15, became a distinguished miniature painter. Alexander Gellan [722], attended 1810–5, became precentor in the North Church. Peter Gray [822], attended 1816–22, was apprenticed to an advocate and chartered accountant and a result of his progress he attended classes at Marischal. He is remembered for compiling tables deduced from mortality rates issued by the Institute of Actuaries, of which he became an honorary member. He also became a Fellow of the Royal Astronomical and Royal Microscopical Societies, gaining distinction for his work in optics and applied mathematics. He was included in the Dictionary of National Biography, along with John Gray [818], who attended 1816–21, and became Solicitor to the Treasury.[111] Alexander Gordon [840], attended 1817–23, was known as the 'Aberdeen poet',[112] while William Ritchie [886], attended 1820–6, captained *The Falcon* schooner. Robert Cruickshank [911], attended 1822–7, became a Councillor and Governor of the Hospital in the 1850s.

Given the background of many of the Hospital boys, altogether this is an impressive record for the Hospital, which was to continue and improve as the 19th century developed. There were, inevitably, failures too. A small number of boys became notorious rather than distinguished and these included James Bryce [885A], attended 1820–6, who was transported for forgery, and Peter Nicol [949], attended 1824–9, who was similarly transported.

Robert Simpson

Francis Muil, one of the long-serving schoolmasters, was supported by a number of his ex-pupils in his application for the position of Master. However, the Governors, after advertising in Aberdeen and Edinburgh newspapers, unanimously elected Robert Simpson at an increased salary of £75 (from 50 guineas) with his promise that he would devote all of his time to the Hospital and have no other charge (including Sundays).[113]

Robert Simpson was born in Brechin in 1791, the son of a linen manufacturer, and had been educated at King's College, graduating with an Arts degree in 1815. He intended to become a clergyman and was an assistant for some years before his appointment in the Hospital. Unfortunately Simpson stayed under three years as Master and they were unhappy for him personally and the Hospital. Fortunately there was at least some progress on buildings during his time.

Following the Alexander Simpson of Collyhill bequest the Governors, on 3 December 1825, had asked John Smith[114] to provide a plan[115] for an extension to the Auld Hoose to cope with 200 boys. On further reflection in February 1826 it was thought sensible to have another scheme on hand to make a comparison and Archibald Simpson[116] was asked to provide this. By October extension plans from both Smith and Simpson had been received and although no immediate decision was made about the precise way forward the Governors expressed their earnest wish that progress be made quickly.[117]

On 15 January 1827 a Committee of Seven (the Building Committee) under Lord Provost Alexander Brown[118] unanimously decided that John Smith's plan with 'some little alterations' be accepted for the Hospital extension.[119] Given the expectation of finances being available, the Committee recommended immediate building with a target date for opening in October 1829. However, when the whole Governing Body discussed the matter further it was agreed that, as the building would be 'a matter of some magnitude', it was necessary to obtain plans from one or other of the eminent architects in Edinburgh. On the prompting of James Skene of Rubislaw,[120] William Burn[121] was persuaded to forward plans, which was done by early March. Smith, appreciating the sensitivities, concurred with this decision and with his local knowledge tactfully suggested some minor improvements to Burn's designs.[122] The Building Committee recommended their adoption although understood that as Burn did not know the ground there might be further changes forthcoming. Meantime, given more time, Simpson had produced a new plan for consideration. So, effectively at this juncture there were four different designs lying on the table for the Governing Body to peruse.

The Governors requested that Burn visit Aberdeen, examine the site and make any necessary alterations to his plan so that they could then make a speedy decision on their preference, intending to adopt his plan if it could be afforded. Burn complied and on 28 March 1827 reported that he could make changes, in particular, to the north-east quarter of his design, so moving the sickroom from its position near a public street,[123] and also modify the front elevation so that its shape was more acceptable to the views of the Governors. He agreed to send on the changes at the first opportunity.[124] On 27 July the Governors examined Burn's grandiose Jacobean scheme and, given his assurance that it could be executed within the proposed budget of £10,000, unanimously approved it. Arrangements were made to get the working plans from Burn and advertise for contractors.[125]

All seemed well. The Collyhill Trustees approved the plans, and John Smith and Archibald Simpson were thanked for their contributions and given thirty guineas each for the time and attention they had expended on their rejected proposals.[126] John Smith was even asked to go to Edinburgh on behalf of the Governors to clarify a few matters.[127] The blow fell when the Governors, following advertisements, examined the lowest tenders and found the cost of the building work totalled £14,102 sterling.[128] This figure was significantly over the set budget. At first the Governors looked to make savings and substituted freestone for granite for the fronts and dispensed with bored timber. After more extensive adverts in Aberdeen, Edinburgh and Glasgow further tenders produced savings of £1966 sterling.[129] However, to a great extent this was balanced by the insistence of the Governors that a new enclosing wall was needed for the back and west of the Hospital,[130] which ensured the total cost remained around £13,000, still 'considerably above'[131] what could be justified.

The Governors turned to John Smith in May 1828 and requested that he revisit his own designs and produce proposals within the budget figure. It was now Burn's turn to receive payment for preparing his Plans and Specifications.[132]

In his letter to the Governors dated 15 November 1828 Smith produced two sketches of the ground and first floors of the Hospital showing his new proposals: four classrooms for 240 boys (instead of six in previous designs). These were situated on the ground floor west wing along with the Public School, and, above, four sleeping wards; on the east wing a public dining room, and, above, a fever ward, sick rooms and laundry. Round the interior of the front quadrangle he had placed a colonnade. There was to be little alteration to the Auld Hoose and the total budget was between £9500 and £10,000.[133]

The Governors were delighted and immediately committed themselves to take Smith's plans forward. The change from Burn to Smith as architect was based on purely financial grounds although in retrospect it seems clear that the right architectural decision was made. The style of Burn's plans would not have harmonised as well with the Auld Hoose as Smith's plans would.

James Robertson

It was at this juncture on 16 February 1829 that the Governors set up a Committee of Five to inquire into the internal management of the Hospital following public disclosures of a breakdown in relationships between the Master and his schoolmasters, and a growing belief that discipline in the institution was breaking down. By May a detailed report was submitted to the Governors and it told a sorry story. Simpson was deemed to be too cavalier in his approach to the boys and a number of Regulations were being ignored. The Censor system had deteriorated – the strong rather than the prudent were being used with worrying consequences. Many boys – estimated up to 25% of the total number – were out of the Hospital without permission at any one time: 'an inveterate custom'.[134] Generally, the schoolmasters, Physician and Housekeeper were all doing their jobs but the situation would be improved by 'proper exertion and firmness' on the part of Simpson.[135] Unsurprisingly, Simpson viewed the report as a personal criticism of himself and his leadership and offered his resignation, which the Governors accepted on 12 June 1829.[136]

The Governors adjusted the job specification of the Master: he was to teach the older boys one hour each weekday of geography, geometry and astronomy;[137] he would need special permission to take a service outwith the Hospital; he was to visit classrooms at least once a day and report any transgressions to the Governors. The post was advertised in the *Aberdeen Journal* and *Edinburgh Advertiser* and with three candidates it was decided on 10 July by 13 votes to 4 to select James Robertson, parish schoolmaster of Pitsligo.[138]

Robertson was born in 1803 in Ardlaw, Pitsligo, the son of a farmer. He graduated in Arts from Marischal in 1820 having won the prestigious Gray mathematical bursary and enrolled in Divinity classes. In April 1825 he became schoolmaster at Pitsligo and spent four years there before becoming Master at Gordon's. Although in a letter he described his new post as 'very agreeable'[139] he found the Hospital in 'an unsatisfactory state. The discipline was much relaxed, the morals and the habits of the boys were in great need of amendment, and the system of education was imperfect and faulty'.[140] Robertson determined to take on what he considered the evils of the Hospital System: pacts of secrecy, the bullying, the lying.[141] The result was the introduction of stern and severe discipline which ensured that he soon established his supremacy in the Hospital and won over the Governors at the same time.[142]

Robertson found that a number of the Hospital boys were being admitted without the 'slightest elementary education in reading'[143] and persuaded the Governors that the Master should examine boys resident in Aberdeen before allowing entry to ensure that they had received the level of education expected from boys of their age.[144] Non-residents of the Town were to produce certification to prove that at least they could read an ordinary chapter in the Bible.

In his campaign to improve educational standards in the Hospital Robertson noted with approval the success in Heriot's Hospital of a system of division of labour, which had introduced teacher specialisation there in 1809.[145] On his suggestion in May 1831 his Governors agreed to divide education into separate departments: reading, English and French; writing, arithmetic and bookkeeping; and mathematics, with an increased salary to the schoolmasters of fifty guineas. The Governors took advice from senior academic staff at Marischal College who recommended John Ogilvie as a future advanced mathematical teacher. In the meantime Robertson himself taught the higher mathematics class of more than thirty boys. When Ogilvie did take over he found the pupils 'advanced to a degree which, although using all his efforts, he could never afterwards reach'.[146] Like Thom, Robertson was willing to fill in for absent teaching colleagues and proved an able and efficient substitute.

Robertson's success as Master ensured a steady stream of applicants for admission and encouraged the Governors to press ahead with the proposed extension.[147] The lowest tenders for Smith's revised plans came within budget and were accepted by the Building Committee under Lord Provost Gavin Hadden on 8 December 1829.[148] The contracts were placed and work was scheduled to begin 'as soon as the season would permit'.[149] John Smith was appointed Surveyor and Superintendent of Works.[150] Lord Provost Hadden laid the foundations of the new buildings on the south-west corner of the west wing. Beneath the foundation stone was placed a glass vessel sealed up and enclosing an Aberdeen Almanack for 1830, the *Aberdeen Journal* of 16 December

1829 which carried an account of the celebration of the Centenary Anniversary, the two last published numbers of the three Aberdeen newspapers and specimens of each of the coins of George IV's reign – and this was covered with a Plate with an inscription detailing the occasion.[151] By November 1830 it was reported that the west wing had been completed and the extension would be ready to use by early summer 1831.[152] Smith was paid £150 for his plans and for supervising the work in February 1831.[153] The Governors felt able, having consulted Robertson, to add six more boys to the Hospital roll: ninety was the target for April 1831.[154]

Finances remained buoyant. The Collyhill bequest had been followed by another from George Hogg of Shannaburn, who left £2000 to the Hospital in January 1827.[155] However, his Trustees insisted that his name be co-joined with that of Robert Gordon in the title of the Hospital following the instructions in the original deed. The Governors took legal advice from the Lord Advocate and Solicitor General, who held that this could only happen with a new Charter which would be costly to achieve. The Governors agreed to proceed with an application provided the Hogg Trustees pay the extensive costs involved (thus keeping the bequest at the level of £2000 to fulfil the terms of the Deed).[156] The Trustees decided not to take the matter further and the money came to the Hospital.[157]

Fortunately the Town was able to repay all bonds and bills outstanding to the Hospital in December 1824 but offered an interest of 4% if the money was left invested. The Governors left £8400 invested – another example of the councillors lending Hospital money to themselves.[158] This was ultimately repaid in December 1829 but this time the Governors decided to reinvest with the Harbour Trustees – who were the councillors again with another hat on![159] There was no opposition from the ministers on the Governing Body – perhaps they were keen to strengthen their numbers.

Consequent on the rearrangement and increase in the city parishes in March 1828 to six, the ministers pressed for all six of their number to be given representation on the Gordon's Board. To clarify the issue it was decided that an action should be raised in the Court of Session. The President and Governors of Robert Gordon's Hospital versus the Ministers of Aberdeen was heard before the First Division on 15 June 1831. In his Deed Robert Gordon had specifically referred to all the Town Council and four ministers of Aberdeen on a number of separate occasions in his Introduction and Statutes 1 and 2. With a quorum of 11 under Statute 4 the legal representatives of the Town Council held that the intention of the Founder was to create a 'mercantile academy' by taking in the sons and grandsons of decayed merchants and brethren of guild, the very class from which the Town Council was almost exclusively drawn. As the Town Council was best equipped to judge the education needed for its own class Robert Gordon deliberately ensured that the Town Council would always be in the majority. In doing so Robert Gordon was rejecting the model of George Heriot who provided for all of Edinburgh's ministers and any being added in the expansion of its royalty to be members of the Governing Body of his Hospital.[160] Why? Gordon believed that Heriot's was catering for the sons of freemen, a much more numerous and less respectable class than being catered for in Aberdeen. These arguments swayed the Court, which determined on 4 July that only four ministers were entitled to act as Governors of Gordon's Hospital.[161]

Robertson had proved a hard taskmaster, especially to himself, producing Nineteen Resolutions on 2 January 1831 at the age of 28 as the 'invariable' rules of his future life. He had been less than three years as Master but had made a great impression on all members of the Gordon's community. His personal strengths – particularly his seeming incapacity for bitterness, and stress on harmony – made him popular with boys and staff. As Master he was a 'rugged edition' of Dr Arnold of Rugby (his contemporary): he inculcated the same principles and appealed to the same motives – manliness, honesty, humour and Christian uprightness.[162]

He had, however, an ambition to aspire to the ministry and with the support of the Duke of Gordon he gained an appointment to the church in Ellon. He resigned from his post at the Hospital on 13 July 1832 in typically graceful manner in a letter expressing how grateful he was over the attention and kindnesses of the Governors. He gave his best wishes 'for the continued welfare and prosperity of the valuable institution which, under your judicious management, has already reached so high a degree of respectability and usefulness'.[163] In turn he received the unanimous and cordial thanks of the Governors for 'his excellent and exemplary conduct' while Master.[164]

The Governors decided that the salary of the Master (£75 per annum) should be increased to attract quality applicants (especially given the increased number of boys in the Hospital) and it was set at £100.[165] This, along with the growing reputation of the Hospital under Robertson, led to ten applicants. On 3 September, from a short-leet of four, George Melvin, who had been an unsuccessful candidate when Robertson had been appointed, was elected with 12 votes (the others mustered 8 between them).

Melvin took office after a period of growth and development for the Hospital. Thom and Robertson, in particular, had provided good leadership and the Governors had responded by rising above local considerations and recognising their national profile. Aware of the critical situation in November 1794 the Governors volunteered to join the Home Guard. On 19 February 1798, following the intervention of enemies intending to invade Britain, the Governors agreed to contribute 200 guineas to the Fund being raised for National Defence.[166] When Sir William Seton of Pitmedden appealed for funds in Udny to raise volunteers for an Army of Reserve again the Governors contributed.[167] They continued to allow the Hospital grounds to be used for military training and parades throughout the French Revolutionary and Napoleonic Wars (1793–1815). This period was also a time of distress for many and the Governors were always ready to meet their obligations. An example of this occurred in January 1801 when they supported the poor in the parishes on their land believing that 'scarcely any article of life can be purchased by them without charitable assistance'.[168] Another example was seen in 1812 when the public soup kitchen enjoyed the proceeds from charges levied on spectators witnessing the launch of a hot-air balloon from the grounds of the Hospital.[169]

Sunday 13 December 1829 was the centenary anniversary of the Hospital foundation and it was arranged that on the following day at 5pm all the Governors would assemble in the Hall to celebrate and recall the memory of the Founder, and 'the benefit which has been derived, and is continuing to follow from his charitable bequest, and from the judicious administration of it by those whom he had entrusted with its arrangement'.[170] Two former Masters, Thom and Simpson, attended. It was a low-key affair but significant nonetheless.[171] A Robert Gordon's Hospital Club had been formed by old boys educated in the Hospital and they began to meet annually to commemorate the institution and their connection with it.[172] The foundation in its first hundred years had survived then prospered. It seemed to be gradually winning respect and affection but such optimism was soon to prove somewhat misplaced.

5

FAILURE AND SUCCESS, 1832–49

Extension to the Auld Hoose

Born about 1797 George Melvin was the younger son of an Aberdeen merchant[1] and graduated with an Arts degree in 1817. He was inducted into his post at Gordon's on 10 September 1832, inheriting an institution apparently in good shape with high morale. However, one of the unsuccessful candidates for his position, Francis Muil, was very disappointed, given his 25 years service as schoolmaster in the Hospital. Appreciating this and respecting his 'zeal and assuidity' the Governors added ten guineas to his salary.[2] Unfortunately this action was not enough to satisfy Muil and it was not very long before the honeymoon period for Melvin was well and truly ended.

Melvin took office as the extension to the Auld Hoose was nearing completion. The architect, John Smith, was very much in control of the building development and in stages persuaded the Governors to make a number of changes to the plans, despite the extra cost involved. They agreed to improve the building by introducing granite in place of freestone in the entablature of the colonnade, along the interior fronts of the wings.[3] Robertson Gilchrist, plumber, was contracted to introduce gas to light the new buildings.[4]

By August 1832 Smith had moved from getting estimates for enclosing and levelling the proposed playground to producing a plan for laying out the front garden and grounds of the Hospital and considering where to locate the proposed Porter's lodge.[5] On 23 October the Building Committee accepted the estimate of £79 from Alexander Mackintosh for playground work. Smith was instructed to procure estimates for his plans for 'privies' and an enclosing wall (with the colonnade on the west wing leading to the privies),[6] and also to obtain the estimates for pick-dressing the front of the old building to make it conform better to the new building.[7] In January 1833 the Governors accepted Smith's plans for laying out the front garden and the grounds,[8] showing some signs of impatience at the process, as the matter had been 'frequently under discussion'.[9] They also pressed the Building Committee to act speedily 'without loss of time'[10] to bring work to a conclusion. When Smith produced his plans and elevation for a new gateway and wings with a Porter's lodge they were put out for immediate tender.[11] On 20 March 1833 the contracts were signed.

Exactly two months later the Building Committee finalised the shrubs for the front garden, accepted Smith's recommendations for additional work and, with work almost complete,[12] detailed the job description of the Porter. He was expected to be of good moral and religious character, and of regular, sober, clean habits. He could not be beyond middle age, but should be married (his wife to act as his substitute when he was away) with no young children. His main duties were to keep the school, playground and privies clean, the grass cut, and the gate attended[13] to keep out beggars and vagrants and control the traffic of boys and visitors.[14]

On 18 November 1833 the Building Committee reported that the new buildings were complete and the grounds laid out in a 'creditable' manner. There was general satisfaction among the Governors at the extension and no mention made about the budget overspend. The total cost of £13,255 sterling[15] was a third over estimate but the Governors could look forward to an expansion in numbers as compensation. John Smith was paid £370 'for making designs, sections, elevations, working plans and specifications' of the exterior and interior, and 'superintending' the construction.[16]

The wings built by Smith were of two storeys and made up of three bays; the central block running perpendicular to the old building with pavilions at each end. These pavilions made a great visual impact as the central portions of the wing were considerably recessed. Moreover, on the entrance front, a colonnade linked them to the Auld Hoose – the painted columns, with no base, supporting an entablature with moulded cornice. By marking the central portions the pavilions were given something of an independent look. The elevations of the wings were relatively severe, a trait of the Greek revival in Aberdeen, which suited the local granite. The windows were surrounded by the simplest of mouldings which provided the only decorative features in the otherwise plain ashlar walls.

The pavilions to the south, the front of which were divided into four unequal bays, with two central windows close-set, had their centres ennobled by the use of giant panelled pilasters. These supported a block pediment – a device commonly used by Smith – with the area above the pilasters decorated with bronze laurel wreaths flanked by palmettes. The pavilions were divided horizontally by a string course, a continuation of the cornice on the colonnade, which formed the sills of the upper windows.

Smith made some changes to the old building. Internally these involved the formation of broad corridors on the ground and first floors to provide communication with the new wings. Externally the changes were not extensive but nonetheless made a significant visual impact. Adam's building had bell-shaped pediments with two low windows on each of the end bays and three dormers at the centre with the chimney stacks on the pediments. Smith retained the low end windows but introduced more conventional triangular pediments above, which terminated in double chimney stacks. In the centre, Smith introduced a plain frieze and parapet wall with moulded cornice and a central panel flanked by large palmettos. The result was the creation of a stylistic continuity throughout the building[17] and a 'far more effective intermarriage between new and old'.[18]

The new west wing was devoted to classrooms, with the broad corridors forming a wet-weather exercise area. The east wing contained the Master's house and kitchens. Finally, Smith's lodge – to house a Porter – was created to stand at the main entrance at Schoolhill. It was built by William Leslie, mason, for £213[19] and maintained the standard of work of the rest of the building, retaining the theme of pavilions.[20]

The prospect of new accommodation had already led to additional boys being elected to the Hospital. In October 1831 an extra six were taken in making the total 96[21] and it was recommended that future Governors continue to take an additional six boys regularly to maximise what the Governors could afford to maintain. In April 1832 a further six were elected,[22] which meant that Melvin inherited an institution with 102 boys. In October 1832 a further six increased the roll to 108,[23] while in April 1833 the Governors introduced only an extra four boys.[24] However, by October 1833 a further eight boys were elected to bring the Governors back on schedule with a roll of 120.[25] Then the numbers remained settled with no further increase in the following eighteen months. But given the expected revenue increases from the rents of Towie the Governors determined on 5 June 1835 to increase the numbers to 126,[26] which took effect that October.

The numbers situation changed dramatically in April 1838 when the Governors confirmed the agreement between themselves and the Trustees of Simpson of Collyhill. The Trustees agreed to support a further 26 boys, to be added in stages, while the Governors would increase their total to 140. Within the month the first four from the Collyhill Bequest were elected, and this addition of four boys in April and October became the pattern for the next few years.[27] By May 1844 there were 155 boys in the Hospital.

George Melvin

Unlike previous Masters Melvin was not a Churchman, which was a 'judicious innovation',[28] but brought his experience as a teacher in Aberdeen to his new post. Perhaps this explains his early assessment of conditions in the Hospital which he laid before the Governors. On 22 January 1833 Melvin reported that 'some laxity of good behaviour and discipline seems for some time to have prevailed'.[29] Although something of a surprise, the Governors might have explained these comments away by putting them down to temporary disorder created by the building programme if they had not also received 'Suggestions' from the retiring Master, Robertson. These had been put aside until the new Master was able to digest properly their contents.[30]

Robertson put forward ideas for curriculum continuity in a school career of five years ending at fifteen, the age he considered most suitable for beginning an apprenticeship. Under his scheme, in the first three years the boys would be equally divided between the schoolmasters in 'junior class', and taught branches of English reading, writing, English grammar, arithmetic and commercial (including bookkeeping); if able, progression would follow into the 'higher class' for two years to study Euclid and algebra, plane trigonometry and quadratic equations, building up to astronomy and the mathematical parts of Natural Philosophy in their final months. The higher class would also have two hours a day of English, geography and French.

It seemed appropriate for the Governors to deal with both Melvin's and Robertson's comments simultaneously and they set up a Committee of Eight (on Education and Discipline) under Lord Provost Gavin Hadden to consider the existing plan of study and details of teaching and determine the improvements needed to ensure good behaviour and proper discipline.[31]

Within the week the Committee was recommending that efforts should be made to raise standards of cleanliness in person and dress, the Clerk being requested to spell out what was expected to the staff in front of the Committee.[32] In the next few weeks the Committee questioned the Master and teachers and deemed the Regulations 'amply sufficient' for the maintenance of discipline provided they were enforced.[33] The masters agreed to do so 'with the utmost strictness' and would also ensure that the master-on-duty would be with the boys at all times, including in the playground. With so many boys, the school-masters also agreed to help the Master on Saturday mornings and Sunday evenings with the Catechism and religious instruction.[34]

The Committee decided to formulate new Regulations[35] and these were adopted by the Governors on 4 April 1833. They incorporated a number of Robertson's 'Suggestions', amended after discussion, as well as including the recent changes agreed by the staff. No boy was to be admitted to the Hospital if unable to read a 'plain passage of Scripture with tolerable ease and propriety'[36] and spell the more common words contained in it. On entry all boys would join the 'junior school', and would be taught English reading and grammar, writing and arithmetic and 'such as manifest the requisite turn of mind',[37] the elements of French. Before transfer to 'senior school' boys must have mastered arithmetic (fractions, vulgar and decimal), the extraction of roots and be able to parse a piece of English with accuracy. In senior school, mathematics, theoretical and practical, and writing with occasional revision of arithmetic, and a course of bookkeeping, were to be taught. The Master would daily examine the boys in the senior school in English and writing with dictation, also French for those who studied it, and in the evenings he was expected to hold a regular class in geography and astronomy. Those with the necessary aptitude would be taught Church Music and drawing by 'out masters'. With this comprehensive programme of education confirmed in May 1833 it was expected that the Hospital would settle into disciplined order. Peace, however, lasted only six months.

Insubordination

Aberdeen had experienced large-scale agitation for Parliamentary Reform in 1831–2[38] and November 1833 saw the first elections for municipal bodies under the Burgh Reform Act. The franchise was limited to burgesses, so the electorate in Aberdeen numbered only 1,627,[39] less than 5% of the adult population. These measures had their effect on the Hospital boys – the future members of the burgess class – many of them believing that 'liberty' was at hand.

On 12 November 1833 it was reported that a 'spirit of insubordination was alive in the Hospital' and the previous day about sixty boys 'had resorted to the most unwarranted act of marching from the Hospital in a body'[40] and remained absent without permission for much of the evening. They took their grievances – many of them trifling – to the home of one of the Reform Councillors, McKinnon, who listened patiently before escorting the boys back to the Hospital.[41] Lord Provost James Blaikie[42] addressed the boys; he warned them about their conduct and demanded observance of Hospital Regulations.[43]

At their next meeting on 18 November a Committee of Seven under Blaikie was set up to investigate into the happenings of six days earlier. The Committee reported to the Governors on 3 December that the causes of the insubordination were 'deep-rooted and of long-standing'.[44] In an extensive inquiry the Committee had interviewed staff, boys and the three Masters before Melvin – Thom, Simpson and Robertson. It was concluded that there had existed for many years 'a want of cordiality and unanimity amongst the masters' – a failure to support each other – which the Governors believed was at the root of the indiscipline and riotous behaviour exhibited by the boys. Francis Muil, schoolmaster, had never worked well with the Masters, on occasions completely disregarding their directions and even acting disrespectfully to them in front of the boys.[45] The dismissal of Muil was the Committee's first recommendation.

The Committee was unable to discover whether the actions of the boys on 11 November were premeditated, but they seemed spontaneous and aimless. The most serious grievance appeared to be against Melvin's mode of punishment – correction by cane after the boys had gone to bed and locking boys in a dark closet. The Governors recommended all punishments be administered openly in front of all the boys: but agreed that the use of a closet was a 'very proper and salutary mode of coercion',[46] and having inspected it believed the closet suited the purpose and should continue to be used.

During the investigation, on 24 November, five Hospital boys scaled the walls, followed by three others a few hours later. Of the five, two returned later in the day, the three others went as far as Laurencekirk; the other three went north. All eventually returned. At first the Committee was inclined to expel but rejected that option believing it would 'ruin' the boys and fall on the parents too. It decided that the three ringleaders of 11 November[47] and the eight deserters of Sunday 24 November should be punished in front of all the boys. It was spelled out to the boys that future misconduct would result in expulsion. Melvin carried out the beatings on 27 November.

The Committee found a 'system of tyranny and terror' existing in the Hospital.[48] Fear of the consequences from companions had led to the truth being concealed, and to deception and lying. The Committee expected Melvin and the schoolmasters to remedy 'an evil of such magnitude'.[49] The Governors approved the Committee Report. Muil was dismissed[50] and Melvin took charge of his class temporarily.

Despite these actions another sixteen Hospital boys deserted the Hospital at different times. In December 1833, given their warnings, the Governors proceeded to expel the nine boys considered most guilty;[51] the other seven were deemed to have been led astray and, with previous good records, were allowed back to be punished by Melvin.[52]

Melvin's Achievements

A Vacancy Committee of Seven was set up to find a suitable replacement for Muil. On 14 January it went beyond its brief and recommended following through the arrangements based on division of labour, which had been accepted by the Governors in May 1831 but not put into effect. With an enlarged Hospital it was seen as an appropriate time to innovate, especially as the change was supported by Melvin and the schoolmasters. The three teachers should be assigned to English, arithmetic and mathematics: a writing master would be appointed for three hours a day (five days a week); a drawing master would attend two hours all year (instead of three hours for six months); French would be offered to senior boys by one of the teachers;[53] Melvin was to instruct senior boys in geography and astronomy, and latin to those boys with some aptitude for it.[54] 'The infinitely important tenets of Religion'[55] were to be imparted. To ensure that the new arrangements worked properly a timetable for masters and boys was issued.[56]

With John Ogilvie opting for mathematics, and Arthur Simpson for arithmetic, the Governors looked for a good English master. From the seven applicants the Vacancy Committee elected Alexander Gerard in January 1834 and, having examined specimens of writing, the penmanship post was filled by Alexander Stuart. Fully staffed it was hoped that the Hospital could now progress peacefully. By February 1834 the Governors were, perhaps prematurely, talking of the beneficial effects of the new system.

The Governors turned their attention to other issues. A Committee of

Four examined the Hospital sleeping arrangements and found them satisfactory, the boys being housed in large, clean, well-aired and comfortable rooms.[57] It went on to make some diet improvements – rice was substituted for barley, beef added more often, and potatoes introduced instead of bread.[58] A Committee of Seven investigated whether the Hospital boys needed some form of exercise aimed at promoting health and producing graceful and easy carriage of the body.[59] This resulted, on 19 May 1834, in the employment of a drill master for six hours a week for six months,[60] although the Governors also saw him as important in helping with discipline and appearance.

Melvin himself was busy on several matters. In an effort to encourage the boys to use the Hospital Library he produced, in March 1835, a catalogue of books and a list of proposed additions. The Education Committee agreed to spend £10, and give a grant of £5 annually;[61] having visited the Library it was judged well suited and ample in size. Melvin began to draw up rules for its use. He was also instrumental in introducing small cash prizes to the boys who did well in school examinations,[62] and an extra prize, not more than half a guinea, which was to be awarded half-yearly to one of boys leaving the Hospital for 'general good conduct'.[63] The method used – it was awarded by those remaining in the Hospital – was radical for its time. From May 1835 this 'Out-going Prize' was regularly awarded: the first recipient, James Will, [1057] had shown 'good conduct and kindly behaviour' and was voted the prize by his companions. However, as Robert Davidson, [1035] who left the Hospital at the same time, came a close second in votes Lord Provost James Blaikie gave him an additional prize paid for from his own pocket.[64] In January 1840 the Education Committee, clearly happy with the principle of cash incentives, recommended that sums of one shilling per week should be used to encourage boys in each class.[65]

During Melvin's period as Master there were also efforts to strengthen the non-teaching staff of the Hospital. The Clerk's salary had been static at twenty guineas for a long period and it was increased to £50.[66] When Robert Morice, Clerk and Factor, died in May 1834 the Governors reviewed the job specifications of both Clerk and Treasurer.[67] It was decided that the Treasurer should attend the Hospital between 11am and 1pm every working day, have a room in the Hospital for his business and be expected to visit every apartment in the Hospital once a week.[68] Alexander Stronach, advocate in Aberdeen, was appointed Clerk and Factor in November 1834, while William Reid became the new Treasurer in September 1836.[69]

On 24 March 1835 the Hospital Physician, Dr Dyce, died. He had done his duty loyally but quietly and had not pressed vigorously for medical improvements. From nine applicants, his son, Robert Dyce, was narrowly elected,[70] and almost immediately he recommended the appointment of a Sick Nurse.[71] The Governors asked advice from Melvin, who held that although the maximum number ill at one time had been seven there was always someone sick. The Governors decided to appoint an extra servant to take charge of the sickroom.[72]

Only two weeks after Dyce's death the Housekeeper, Mrs Keith, died. She was a hard act to follow. Her headstone in St Nicholas churchyard was erected by Thom, Simpson and Robertson 'in testimony of their regard for her work and character and Christian virtues'.[73] The advertisement for her successor looked for an unmarried or widowed lady without family of between thirty and forty-five years of age. The Governors agreed that she should not be away from the Hospital overnight.[74] Catherine Rose, of Blackfriars Street, aged 42, was elected by a 'considerable majority'.[75]

Given so many changes in personnel and procedures the Governors took stock and reported on the duties of office-bearers in November 1838. Dr Dyce was asked to investigate the ventilation of the Hospital sleeping apartments; the music master was to take forward flute instruction; the drawing master was to develop mechanical and architectural drawing and teach the use of theodolite for surveying; the writing master was encouraged to instruct in ornamental penmanship; following a number of complaints the drill master's duties and salary were cut; the schoolmasters' salary was in future to be linked to their length of service and efficiency; and the Master, Housekeeper and Porter were to focus on following the Hospital Regulations to the letter.[76]

During the later 1830s arrangements between the Governors and the Trustees of Simpson of Collyhill were advanced. The first stage was to value the Hospital's assets – buildings, grounds and furniture – before working out the proportion to be paid by the Trustees for the extra boys they were electing to the Hospital. The Trustees appointed Archibald Simpson as their representative, while the Governors chose John Smith. Both parties accepted the King's Architect in Scotland as the 'Oversman'.[77] By February 1838 both sides had accepted the value agreed by Simpson and Smith[78] and, following on from the agreement for the extra boys, the Trustees' proportion of the buildings' value – £2923 sterling – was paid over to the Governors.[79]

Had Melvin resigned at this point his reputation would have been secured. His 'kind and genial nature'[80] made him generally popular with the boys who enjoyed his use of visual aids to attract and retain interest during his classes.[81]

With an attractive personality he was a character – he was given permission by the Governors to erect a stable for his pony in the back court of the Hospital[82] – and seems genuinely to have wished to improve the quality of life for the Hospital boys. He allowed the boys to have pets – rabbits, pigeons and crows.[83] He supported giving them better facilities in the form of a shed in the playground and more use of the garden and Library for them[84] so combating the 'confined and prison-like appearance of the playground'.[85] He persuaded the Governors to allow the boys a day's relaxation in the country in May 1838.[86] However, periodically Melvin was faced with outbreaks of indiscipline and insubordination and these were to be his undoing.[87]

Insubordination Again

In February 1837 Alexander Sheriffs [1112] and John Sim [1140] were expelled for misconduct as an example which the Governors wanted to be 'as impressive as possible'[88] and Melvin was also to punish severely three other boys in public. The Governors were beginning to think that Melvin was not being rigorous enough in his discipline and the events of July 1839 strengthened this impression. Melvin reported that Hugh Morven [1155] had drowned while bathing at sea and it seemed that the tragedy would have been much more serious if it had not been for the actions of the Porter, James Hughes, who saved two others. The Governors did not blame Melvin openly but immediately introduced new swimming regulations to avoid a similar incident in future.[89]

One incident seemed to follow another. In September 1839 after a series of desertions the Governors interviewed a number of boys and were dismayed at the extent of lying that went on in an attempt to cover for the deserters. Given this obvious 'great disregard' for the truth, Baillie Forbes wanted an inquiry into the general discipline in the Hospital.[90] In a further discussion on 3 October Forbes criticised Melvin's leadership and when this was printed in local newspapers Melvin reacted by attacking Forbes's motives for unsubstantiated comments and for charges that Melvin held discredited the Hospital.[91] The Governors were in a quandary and believed Melvin had aggravated the situation. After a 'protracted' debate they backed Forbes, claiming he had acted for the best of motives, and set up a Committee of Six under Baillie Simpson to investigate further.[92]

The Committee met 'repeatedly' and interviewed teaching staff. Its Report of 18 November 1839 was a qualified vote of confidence in Melvin. The Hospital was found generally 'in a good state of discipline'[93] and relationships were deemed satisfactory given the number of boys in the Hospital. However, the Committee made a significant reservation, holding that 'there is perhaps some want of that emulation which is desirable among the boys in the class-rooms, and which the reporters believe is not uncommon in similar institutions'.[94] The teachers believed drill was beneficial but recommended a workshop and printing press for use of the boys at play[95] and it was contended that Melvin should supervise the boys more closely during play. Yet, the Master and Housekeeper discharged their duties 'in a very satisfactory manner'[96] although ominously it was believed that occasionally there was 'some appearance of the want of a proper understanding between them'.[97] Nonetheless the Hospital had not suffered as a result. The Governors were pleased with the schoolmasters who completed their duties in a 'very efficient and satisfactory manner',[98] glossing over complaints by the Visiting Committee about their dress and appearance, which set a poor example to the boys. The matter was closed; there would not need to be another such inquiry for a long time to come. Such a statement was made in hope rather than expectation.

In early May 1841 the Visiting Committee of Governors[99] raised the issue of Hospital discipline again and reported an incident where the schoolmasters refused to accompany the Governors into the Matron's parlour. This occurrence was 'strongly indicative of the bad feeling' between the teachers and Miss Rose,[100] and Lord Provost Thomas Blaikie[101] took the view that it was 'subversive of the proper discipline' of the Hospital.[102] A Committee of Seven under Blaikie launched what was to become an extensive investigation. Melvin reacted badly to this; he believed that the Governors did not appreciate how much he had improved the Hospital. In a letter to the Governors, dated 20 May, he went further and claimed the boys' interests were never neglected and that the Hospital was in 'a state of the highest efficiency'.[103] Melvin wanted to defend himself against alleged charges but the Lord Provost thought this unnecessary as no charges had been brought.

The Committee took three months to interview all staff, teaching and non-teaching, and a number of boys. Blaikie gave his detailed 'Observations' on 2 August. For a considerable period the resident masters and the Matron had 'lived on the most unfriendly and uncomfortable terms'.[104] Melvin and Rose were constantly quarelling and exchanging unacceptable personal remarks often in front of teachers, servants and boys. The situation had deteriorated to an extent which affected the whole Hospital. Blaikie recommended that nothing short of the dismissal of Melvin, Rose and two of the resident teachers would solve the problem, and even the Treasurer would need to commit himself to rigorous enforcement of the Regulations in future if he wished to remain.[105]

Blaikie blamed some of the Hospital's problems on the celibacy rule. He saw 'no good reason' for this continuing. He recommended that all new appointments be allowed to live out of the Hospital, believing that a reduction in the domestic establishment would improve matters. A married Master would mean his wife as Matron. Significantly Blaikie thought that the Master should be a gentleman of education and experience: one who had mixed in good society and whose manners and personal appearance commanded respect. He should be seen as the head of the Hospital family, looked up to for counsel and direction, and whose orders were followed and obeyed. The implication was clear – Melvin fell short in a number of crucial regards. The Matron also should have experience of managing a family. Only Ogilvie, given his long service, good character and capability, seemed safe from Blaikie's devastating critique of the Hospital staff.[106]

The following week on 9 August the Governors, at a Special Meeting, requested a formal report from the Committee of Seven, perhaps hoping that Blaikie's 'Observations' would be watered down. If so, they were to be disappointed; the Committee met on 12 August and endorsed Blaikie's comments regarding dismissals. There had been frequent 'scences of quarelling, discord and recrimination', often in front of boys and staff. As a result the Master and Housekeeper were 'not competent to rule affairs from their want of temper and prudence'.[107] The evidence collated by the Committee ran to a massive 160 pages; the Governors accepted its conclusions on 16 August.[108] The dismissals of Melvin, Rose and Douglas were to be final in November.

A sub-committee of three ministers (Reverends Murray, Foote and Gordon) were charged with visiting Heriot's and Watson's Hospitals in Edinburgh, which they did and reported back on 30 August. At Heriot's they had talked with newly appointed Headmaster William Steven about its non-residence arrangements, which had been operating for fifteen months.[109] Steven believed that their introduction had led to refreshed teachers and his own role with the boys had developed into that of 'parental superintendence'.[110] Heriot's general view was that harmony had increased at no extra expense. Although the Aberdeen ministers were sceptical at first, having seen the new system in operation they were of the opinion that it might be tried with some success at Gordon's. For them the all-important issue was the quality of the new Master; to get the right person they suggested an increased salary.

Melvin and Douglas did not accept their dismissals. Both protested by letter.[111] Melvin, on 23 August, claimed himself innocent of remiss, scandal or crime and was not prepared 'to acquiesce in your resolution'.[112] The Governors, however, reaffirmed that they could dispense with services for any cause 'that might appear to them sufficient'.[113] Melvin's response, along with Douglas, was to go to law and the Governors received Suspension and Interdict on 4 October.[114]

The Governors chose Rutherford as senior counsel and Moncrieff as junior counsel to represent the Hospital before Lord Ivory in the Second Division of the Court of Session. The decision on 8 December confirmed that the Governors had full powers to dismiss the Master and teachers and they did not need to give reasons for their actions. Fortunately for Melvin the Governors did not press for their legal costs[115] and expenses, which they would no doubt have won. This enabled the losers to move on without great financial burdens to bear.[116]

To what extent was Melvin unjustly treated? If he was judged solely on the Rose affair then the Governors had glossed over problems in 1839 caused by Rose, and Melvin had made the mistake of being persuaded to let bygones be bygones. However, from the Governors' perspective Melvin had failed to deal well with indiscipline in 1831–2, 1839 and again in 1841. It is true that he had advanced the Hospital in significant terms in his ten years as Master. He also had a strong claim to be regarded as a man of 'character, courage and honesty'.[117] Unfortunately he took over Gordon's when it was already clear that beneath the surface were deep-rooted problems which needing tackling. He either never showed an appreciation or understanding of the evils of the Hospital System or preferred to ignore them. Whichever, the result was that he himself failed and suffered the ignominy of being the only Head to be dismissed in the history of the Hospital.

Before the election of the new Headmaster (the change in title was significant in emphasising his authority over the other masters) the Governors asked Rutherford for his legal opinion. He advised that they were entitled to change the Statutes on celibacy and residency. On 15 December 1841, the Governors settled on salaries of £210 for Headmaster (with apartments), £100 to teachers and £40 to the Housekeeper and instructions that the teachers were to take a weekly turn of being on duty, with all three teachers on duty at church on Sundays with the boys. The 9th and 10th Statutes were formally amended on 17 January 1842 and a century of celibacy and staff residence was ended.

Andrew Findlater

There were thirteen applications for the Headmaster post. Andrew Findlater was chosen after a tied vote (11–11) on the second ballot was broken by the casting vote of Lord Provost Blaikie.[118] In the next few days a number of other appointments were made including Hugh Martin (arithmetic), James Hay (English) and Miss Jamieson (Housekeeper).

Andrew Findlater was born in December 1810, the son of a stonemason who farmed a small croft at Aberdour in Aberdeenshire. Educated in the local parish school he entered Marischal College in 1828 where he gained a number of prizes. He graduated Master of Arts four years later with honorable mention as the most distinguished graduate of the year and the award of the Gray Bursary in Mathematics. He afterwards studied divinity and was licensed as a preacher, but a change of mind decided him against a career in the Church and he gave up the title of 'Reverend'. Instead he became a teacher in the 'side' (additional) parochial school at Tillydesk, Ellon in 1835, moving on to Merchiston Academy in the following year. After only a short time there he went to Canada as an employee of the Colonial Office to superintend the Government Normal School in Montreal and help establish other schools.[119] On his return he was appointed to Gordon's Hospital, an appointment which owed something to his friendship with the ex-Master, Robertson, as well as his own attributes.

Architect John Smith produced plans for some internal changes in the Hospital – the creation of apartments for the Headmaster in the south-east wing of the building; a new washroom for the boys and the construction of an area for cleaning shoes.[120] Findlater brought with him a varied programme of ideas, the majority aimed at improving discipline. He reorganised the rooms in an attempt to cut down on unnecessary traffic around the building and to monitor the boys in their play areas. The parlour, occupied by Melvin, became the museum.[121] He pressed for the appointment of a House Steward to live in but accepted meantime a modification in the Porter's duties.[122] Having examined the Heriot's Hospital Regulations he found boys there entering at age seven to ten (and leaving at age fourteen), while at Gordon's the age of admission had risen to between nine and twelve (from between eight and eleven), which Findlater believed was too old. It was among the senior boys that he found 'a few sour discontented spirits . . . sufficient to poison the whole establishment'.[123] These boys were 'doing little good owing to their incapacity or want of application' and Findlater was determined to eradicate this troublesome element.

From the beginning of his Headmastership Findlater had no illusions about the Hospital System and knew its problems. He was therefore better prepared than a number of his predecessors to deal with its difficulties. He had taken time to study Heriot's Hospital and stressed to his own Governors the need to learn from its experiences. He also had ideas to tighten up entry into the Hospital, to improve conditions in the institution and for the Governors to be more involved with the boys after they had left the Hospital.

As an educationalist, Findlater supported the concept of ensuring that the boys had a certain level of literacy before being admitted to the Hospital. This had been enacted by the Governors in April 1833; however, it had been diluted on 3 October 1839 when the Governors agreed to admit any boy who might not have the educational qualification set out if it seemed appropriate to do so.[124] For some Governors poverty was the crucial criterion for entry but Findlater appreciated that this resulted in the very indiscipline problems which the Governors wished to avoid.[125]

Findlater changed the timetable,[126] with classes starting at 9am (instead of 10am) to cut down on wasted time in the morning[127] and introduced new textbooks for English and history.[128] Following Heriot's he pressed for the creation of a Special Committee of Governors to look after boys when they left the Hospital. He suggested linking apprenticeship allowances to the conduct exhibited in the Hospital. He wanted the Governors to issue separate questionnaires to boys, parents and their masters[129] with the threat of withdrawal of allowances if they were not completed.

Findlater's programme of reform stimulated debate among the Governors on issues fundamental to the future development of the Hospital. While Baillie Forbes moved for a reduction in the apprentice fee to £5 (from £8/6/8),[130] Reverend Murray proposed reducing the age of admission to eight but Councillor Williamson, an ex-pupil, believed that education was more important than maintenance, and opposed the change as it increased the period of the latter.

The new mood in the Hospital encouraged the staff to suggest improvements. Dr Dyce informed the Governors that the boys were well-fed, indeed better fed than they would be if at home, and yet a number suffered from trivial ailments.[131] He suggested diet changes – three meals a day rather than four;[132] lightening the diet also by introducing fish, cutting beef to once a week, replacing potatoes with vegetables regularly and having coarse wheaten bread as a substitute for oatcakes. Moreover, he wanted more emphasis on cleanliness in the Hospital – changing linens more often and having boys take a weekly bath.[133] The Governors agreed to a three-month trial of these changes. Miss Jamieson, Housekeeper, was also keen to institute advances. Her first acts were to ensure each boy had a comb and that the Hospital cleaning was done more regularly.[134] By August 1842 Jamieson's efficiency had led to dispensing with the services of one servant.

Findlater, like his predecessors, had issues of indiscipline to deal with but the Governors felt confident that he was always in control of himself and the Hospital. Fed up with the misbehaviour of ex-inmates during return visits to the Hospital, Findlater, in April 1843, was given authority to determine who could visit the Hospital. When faced with a persistent bully, as in the case of Robert Brown [1426] in March 1845, he persuaded the Governors to expel him in front of the whole Hospital. Deserters, who repeated the offence, also suffered the same fate – James Dunn [1486] was expelled in October 1848. As a result overt disobedience occurred only infrequently, but Findlater knew that although he kept a strict discipline in the Hospital there was a 'conspiracy working in secret against me'.[135] The Hospital System facilitated 'tyranny and combinations': the tyranny of the strong over the weak and combinations to resist inquiry as to the prepretrators of mischief. All hospitals had a 'secret club or union' to prevent divulging anything of harm to another boy, which Findlater deemed 'a very sad feature'.[136]

Despite his misgivings about the Hospital System, and indeed some particular policies of the Governors, Findlater did much to improve the quality of life for the boys, taking an active interest in them both during and outside school hours. To increase their time with their families from 1843 on the boys were given four weeks' (instead of three) summer vacation.[137] He introduced in 1844 the Manual (or 'Pack' as it was called by the boys) – a miscellaneous compendium to be used by the boys.[138] In September 1845 the Education Committee approved of Findlater's proposal to procure a printing press,[139] garden tools and a circular swing with upright posts and cross-bars for gymnastic exercises.[140] He had the annual £5 laid aside for flute (since 1838) transferred to promote the School Band.[141] He allowed Isaac Pitman to send his two brothers, Ben and Henry, to teach shorthand to sixty boys in September 1845.[142] A successful excursion to Kintore was undertaken in the summer of 1845.[143] He reorganised the school exams to make them 'more impressive and complete' and invited parents to attend singing and drill exams and prize-giving.

Fate of the Hospital Boys

Between 1832–49 some 543 boys entered the Hospital. Their backgrounds were not dissimilar to previous generations[144] and their choice of apprenticeships also followed previous patterns.[145] There continued a degree of upward occupational mobility[146] and a number of ex-inmates also continued to go abroad – America, Australia and South Africa now being the dominant destinations.

A considerable number of ex-residents did well in their careers. James Matthews [1021], attended 1829–34, was apprenticed to Archibald Simpson before spending five years in London working for Sir Gilbert Scott. He returned to Aberdeen and his architectural designs included St Nicholas Poor House, Grammar School, Town and Country Bank, Concert Hall in the Music Hall, Rubislaw Terrace, Art Gallery and Ardoe House.[147] Andrew Fleming [1053], attended 1831–5, became a Roman Catholic priest at Blair's College. John Cook [1062], attended 1831–6, and Joseph Wood [1335], attended 1840–5, became shipowners. Robert Kerr [1084], attended 1832–7, also was a distinguished architect who was apprenticed to John Smith and later set up business in London. George Nicol [1365], who attended 1841–6, became a Baillie in 1890–2. Alexander Ellis [1404], attended 1841–6, was also an architect and set up the business of Ellis and Wilson. George Robb [1397], attended 1842–8, became Deputy Town Clerk. George Lyell [1480], attended 1844–9, became a Sheriff's Officer. Peter Leys [1508], attended 1845–50, went to New York and in 1863 was assistant surgeon in the Federal Army of the USA. His exact contemporary, Samuel Smith [1513], also became a surgeon, in Australia. Alexander Machray [1546], attended 1846–51, became a chartered accountant. James Anderson [1647], attended 1849–53, became a physician, while George Neilson [1656], who was at the Hospital between 1849–55, became an executive with the Great North of Scotland Railway.

Findlater's relationships with his staff were good. When Hugh Martin resigned in November 1843[148] he stressed the 'happy harmony' which uniformly prevailed in the Hospital.[149] When the Porter, John Hughes, left in February 1844 Findlater had his way and the Governors appointed David Gray as House Steward with his sister taking over the post of Gatekeeper.[150] James Hay left in August 1845 to take up a ministerial post locally and was confident enough to suggest that the Hospital boys should have some industrial occupation out of school to help them with later employment.[151] This was in line with Findlater's own plans, for already, on 1 June, he had been given permission by the Governors to take seven to ten days' leave of absence to visit some English public educational institutions where 'principles of combining manual industry with ordinary instruction is systematically acted upon'.[152] Findlater reported back after his visits on 18 August[153] and he was granted £25 to fit up a workshop.[154]

Findlater's Legacy

Although there was much progress under Findlater he was frustrated by the failure of the Governors to grasp the nettle of reform of the Hospital System. They had been half-hearted in their attempt to re-introduce the educational qualification of April 1833 and were split in October 1846 on the issue of boys sleeping out of the Hospital, which Findlater supported.[155] Therefore, his resignation in April 1849 should perhaps have not been the shock that it undoubtedly was.[156] Lord Provost George Thompson Jnr[157] and two other Governors were instructed to confer with Findlater in an attempt to get him to change his mind. Findlater, however, was not to be dissuaded, believing he would be 'more useful in some other sphere'.[158]

Later, one of his pupils, John Lyell [1429], who attended the Hospital between 1842–6, remembered Findlater as a man respected by the boys as 'he showed no needless severity'. He also used to read to the boys from Chambers' Miscellany on Sunday afternoons; a great treat on 'fearfully dull Sabbaths'.[159]

He can also be deemed to have been an intellectual, being a close friend of Alexander Bain, assistant to the Professor of Moral Philosophy at Marischal College, George Glennie. Bain 'frequently visited' Findlater in his residence at the Hospital and 'found him highly sympathetic' to his views on philosophy and education.[160]

On 21 May 1849 the Governors recorded their sense of loss at the departure of Findlater. He had carried out his duties in a 'faithful, assiduous and conscientious manner', leaving the Hospital in a 'highly satisfactory state'.[161] The Governors were effusive in their praise of the departing Headmaster[162] and had already asked for, and been given, a report by Findlater on Hospital matters.

Findlater's report, tabled on 18 May, held that the scheme of education operating in the Hospital was sufficiently extensive but its execution was not as thorough as desired. The boys did not exhibit the facility and accuracy expected given the time expended on their studies. This was partly a result of the 'undeniable want of intellectual activity which characterizes [sic] Hospitals'[163] but he believed this could be overcome with special effort, more by narrowing the ground for a time until the standard of accuracy was raised. He recommended more stress on English language, and suggested dropping French at least in the meantime. The Headmaster needed to spend time with English composition and history, while the other teachers could use the time saved on these by concentrating even more on basic English language skills. The writing master should emphasise accuracy as much as style.[164] 'One great obstacle in the way of great advancement and proficiency in a Hospital is the insuperable difficulty of getting lessons prepared out of school, there being little room for retirement or quiet during play hours, even where there is a disposition to study, and then the temptations to romp and play, where so many boys are together, are irresistible. The boy who tries to study is laughed at and even persecuted.'[165]

The Governors responded by confirming that the new Headmaster would teach for two hours daily, and the duty master would supervise an hour of preparation every evening. But they missed the point and it was not long before decisions were being taken which explained the resignation of Findlater.

Three days after Findlater's report, Councillor John Urquhart moved consideration of boys sleeping out of the Hospital. His motion was defeated 14–8 and further discussion on the issue was defeated 13–9.[166] On 25 June the salary of the Headmaster was reduced from £210 to £180[167] – a number of Governors even wished the salary to be lowered further to £160. In this instance the Governors went against the Heriot's model, for ten years earlier in 1839 the Heriot Governors had raised the salary of their Head to £315 (and apartments) in a successful attempt to raise the quality and status of their Headmaster.[168] In not following suit the Governors underrated the importance of leadership. They would not do that again.

6

LIMITED PROGRESS, 1849–81

Rev. William D. Strahan

It was not until 20 August 1849 that Rev. William Dovertie Strahan was appointed Headmaster. Findlater had resigned in April but a delay in filling his post resulted from the Education Committee discussing the proposed rearrangement of the duties and emoluments of the office and a suggestion that the number of teachers should be reduced.[1] Alexander Gerard had applied for the post and although short-leeted he was unsuccessful.

A native of Forfarshire, Strahan was born in 1805 and educated at the Grammar School, Brechin, and afterwards at King's College, where, after having been the second bursar in 1822, he graduated in Arts in March 1826, having completed his fourth or magistrand year at Marischal College. As he aspired to the Church, he then studied divinity and began his career as private tutor in several leading families before his appointment as schoolmaster at Rathven, a post he held for eleven years. From there he went to Rose Street, Aberdeen to be the chaplain to the Bridewell there.[2]

Robert Anderson, who attended the Hospital between 1857 and 1862,[3] later gave the following personal sketch of Strahan. He remembered him as a 'rather portly, well-favoured, benevolent-looking, elderly gentleman; slightly punctilious in his dress, to all appearances, and a trifle ceremonious in manner; and carrying himself with a certain dignity, partly innate, and partly, perhaps, acquired from long dominance over boys'. He conducted the religious services – morning and evening – drilled a number of boys in the Shorter Catechism on Saturday afternoons, and taught the Latin and geography classes. On the whole Anderson judged him 'a kindly man, of tolerably equable temperament; he maintained – at least in my time – a fairly firm discipline, not marked (as far as I can remember) by any excessive or unjust severity'.[4]

When Strahan arrived at the Hospital he found the Governors divided on the issue of greater freedom for the boys on Sunday afternoons. A report had been accepted on 20 August deploring the conduct of boys on Sabbaths.[5] The Committee decided by 11–8 that boys should attend the West Church, as usual, on Sunday mornings and then be allowed to spend the afternoon with parents or friends between 2 and 7pm provided they had written permission. The thinking was that those boys remaining would be more manageable. When all came back together in the evening the Headmaster would address all the boys on moral and religious subjects, with the Governors in attendance to give support and encouragement.

At the next meeting of Governors on 4 October, Rev. Dr Forsyth produced a printed Protest outlining his reasons for dissent against the August decision, which he believed went against Robert Gordon's wishes as set out in his Deed of Mortification. He was supported by two of the other three clerics on the Board – Rev. John Wilson and Rev. Thomas Dewar. A week later the Education Committee chaired by Baillie Ross and including the Rev. Dr Mackintosh (the fourth cleric) produced a detailed eleven-page stinging rebuttal of Forsyth's arguments and language. However, this was only carried 11–10 by the whole Governors, and Wilson gave notice of intention to raise a motion rescinding this decision at the next meeting. Fortunately two ways were found to break the impasse on 19 November. Firstly, the Governors decided to revise the Rules and Regulations of the Hospital and to involve Strahan by having him visit Heriot's Hospital and similar institutions to bring back information on how they were managed.[6] Secondly, 'for the satisfaction of all parties' it was decided to ask the opinion of counsel on whether the Governors could decide on the issue of the boys going out on Sundays, as well as on Wednesdays and Saturdays in summer.[7] Despite Councillor Torrie's attempt to block this it was passed 11–3 with five abstentions.

Quiet Progress

Strahan returned from Edinburgh with the recently published set of Regulations of Heriot's Hospital (1849) and reported to a Committee of Six under Councillor Macallan on 14 December. One of the immediate results of the visit was the reactivating of the Clothing Committee,[8] which, on 18 February 1850, organised two boys to be introduced to the Governors' meeting, one dressed in the costume worn at Heriot's and the other in the Gordon's costume with a jacket in place of the old-fashioned cut-away (or tail) coat. The Governors agreed that for appearance and economic reasons a change should be effected. Within the year the Hospital boys were wearing blue jackets with brass buttons, corduroy trousers and Glengarry caps.[9]

It seems likely that the widening of the Hospital curriculum owes something to the Heriot example. Rev. Dr Mackintosh moved that some boys be taught Latin; at Heriot's all boys were drilled in the subject and its Classical Department included French, time for which was increased there in 1849.[10] In the event, however, the Education Committee did not take forward the proposal for Latin; instead, on 4 October 1852, the Governors accepted its recommendation for a regular French class, with John Jadzowski appointed its teacher at £20 per annum.[11]

The admission rules of Heriot's Hospital were also influential in persuading the Governors to take boys into the Hospital between the ages of eight and eleven (instead of between nine and twelve) and keep them until the maximum age of fifteen. They also returned to their previous policy of 1833, deciding not to admit a boy unless he was able to read correctly a plain portion of Scripture. This was introduced on the understanding that more knowledge was required from an eleven year old than younger candidates. Shortly afterwards this was clarified: all applicants above nine years of age had to produce a certificate verifying two years at school, or being able to write a plain text hand and work the first four rules of arithmetic. The Governors also tightened up the regulations on admission with even renewed applications needing a fresh schedule[12] to ensure that the Governors could determine the most necessitous cases for admission.[13]

Another idea from Heriot's was the Education Committee recommendation of 18 June 1851 of a railway excursion for boys who remained in the Hospital during the summer vacation.[14] This had evolved from a general discussion about recreation for the boys and led in August 1851 to Sir James Carnegie of Montrose showing the boys through his grounds. The following year Strahan took the boys and his staff, and three clerical Governors, on their 'annual trip'[15] to Brechin and Arbroath. They were received well especially in Arbroath 'where the Provost showed them every possible attention',[16] and kindness was also shown by Dowager Lady Panmure. Later in the decade more holiday trips to venues such as Hazlehead and Fyvie Castle occurred.[17]

The measures introduced owed much to the reforms which had been carried out at Heriot's. One issue, however, which was temporarily put on hold, was that of allowing the boys out on Sundays. The joint opinion of the Dean of Faculty McNeill and advocate Cowan was that the resolution was not contrary to the fundamental articles of the Hospital and only lapsed because it did not achieve the necessary three-quarters majority. By this time, over 80 parents/guardians had applied to take their boys out, and a number of Governors still pressed for change. On 17 February 1851 Councillor Macallan put forward the motion, which was carried but only by 11–9.[18] Another legal opinion was sought on the details but again this advised no action given the smallness of the majority. Finally, on 11 June 1851 the Governors accepted this and an opportunity to improve the Hospital System was defeated.

Nonetheless the Governors had at least finalised and agreed the new Rules and Regulations for the Hospital on 19 August 1850. They showed, however, on close scrutiny, how little the Hospital had actually progressed since the last edition of Rules had been published in 1823. The end of celibacy in 1842 had ensured that a married man like Strahan could take office but there were no obvious changes in the Hospital other than the creation of family apartments on the upper floor of the east wing in late 1849.[19] The length of the working week and the need for attendance in the evenings and weekends by the teachers meant that their non-resident status had little impact on the day-to-day running of the Hospital.[20] For the boys their routine and education were much as they had been. Findlater's ambitious curricular programme outlined in May 1849 had been shelved, and the opportunity to reform the 'evils' of the Hospital System was lost, at least meantime.

Since the centenary celebrations of the foundation of the Hospital in 1829 there had been no further occasions to remember the Founder.[21] The Governors, nonetheless, appreciated the significance of the year 1850 – the centenary of the opening of the Hospital. Following a day devoted to the boys marching through the town led by the Sillerton Band, they decided that they would dine at 4.30pm on Wednesday 10 July[22] with the Hospital boys and the Collyhill Trustees. A Committee was set up to discuss a monument to Robert Gordon and it recommended a marble tablet with suitable inscription being placed in Drum's Aisle of the East Church of St Nicholas where the Founder was thought to have been buried. It was also agreed to place an inscription on the front of the Hospital immediately under his statue.[23] However, the driving force behind this measure, Dean of Guild Bothwell, demitted office and the issue languished until 1852 when the Rev. Dr Mackintosh, minister of the East Church, took over the Convenership. Unfortunately he was to die in February 1853 and this slowed matters down again. Finally the tablet on the west wall of Drum's Aisle was erected in 1857. It was surmounted by the Hospital coat of arms, a pelican plucking its own breast to feed its young, with the motto – 'Imperat hoc natura potens'.[24]

After a century of operation the Governors believed that the Hospital was in 'flourishing condition'.[25] There seemed much, from their viewpoint, to be pleased about. The Hospital had never been in greater demand: in April 1851 there were 59 applications for the seventeen vacancies. The Governors also had confidence in Strahan and his staff. When the Headmaster suggested in October 1851 that parents and friends of the boys should be admitted once a month to hear classes being examined on Sabbath evenings, the Governors agreed, deciding with Strahan that it would be a stimulus to the boys.[26] When Strahan wanted to spend a couple of hours weekly visiting boys who had left the Hospital at their places of work to see how they were faring and to encourage them, the Governors 'highly approved' and thanked him for the 'great interest he took in the boys'.[27] Even on the delicate issue of discipline the Governors felt comfortable in involving Strahan more. In February 1854 when reporting a case of desertion 'not of an aggravated character' the Governors recommended that discretionary power be given to the Headmaster in cases of minor offences or where deserters had no family or friends to take charge of them at home. In these cases Strahan should readmit them to the Hospital at once and either deal with the offender himself or confine him in the Hospital apart from the other boys until a meeting of the Governors could be held.[28] By February 1857 the Governors were suggesting even further discretionary power for Strahan in diet and exercise areas.[29] This not only showed their confidence in Strahan's judgement; it was also eminently sensible for the Governors to keep out, as far as possible, of the daily routine of the Hospital.[30]

Improving Academic Standards

Keen to encourage boys with their classwork Strahan suggested the introduction of a Silver Medal each half-year to be awarded to the boy 'who chiefly distinguished himself by his merits during the whole of his Hospital course'.[31] This was taken up by the Master of the Guild Brethren's Hospital, George Bothwell, who gained the approval of the Governors for the innovation on 21 May 1855.[32] Book prizes were also introduced, and on 20 August 1860, under the will of Baillie James Williamson [463], an old boy, the Hospital received £200 to provide prizes 'to encourage scholarship and good conduct'.[33] In a number of other ways too Strahan tried to stimulate the interest of the boys in learning. In November 1856 the Governors agreed to allow twenty of their number, and staff, to attend a class of 'Popular Lectures in Chemistry' at Marischal College given by James Brazier.[34] For ten years (until 1864) Brazier delivered these classes on behalf of the Mechanics' Institution; as there was insufficient time between the afternoon lecture (to the university students) and the evening lecture for the apparatus to be dismantled and fresh experiments set up, the evening classes followed very closely the subject matter of earlier in the day. The success of these led the Governors to introduce chemistry into the Hospital curriculum and soon after his arrival Dale gave a series of classes on elementary chemistry and prepared some experiments.[35] The following year, in February 1861, some 35 boys attended the classes which were a significant curricular development.

Strahan, along with the Education Committee, was committed to raising academic standards and to this end Dr Edward Woodford, HMI for Schools in Scotland[36], was invited into the Hospital to examine the classes in January 1857.[37] His visit was deemed a success but his delay in producing a written report disappointed the Governors. Nonetheless they were resolved to continue with the practice annually of having an external examination of the boys and early in 1858 HMI David Middleton visited and both his and Woodford's report arrived; they were critical of the Hospital teachers, who defended themselves especially against Woodford who had not taken into account the fact that he had inspected during an epidemic which had disrupted teaching and discipline.[38] Yet matters improved and within a few years the Governors were hailing HMI reports as 'highly satisfactory'.[39] They resulted in the introduction of map-reading in geography and the adoption of suggestions for improvements in English reading. Also accepted was Middleton's plan that more attention should be given to French, with a view of enabling boys engaged in the subject to read the language readily before leaving the Hospital. An extra half hour twice a week was allocated from October 1862. Natural history also claimed the attention of the Governors following the successful motion of Robert Cruickshank at the meeting of 3 October 1859 that the Hospital set up a museum for the 'instruction and amusement of the boys'.[40] After organising a lecture by Rev. Dr J. C. Brown to stimulate interest, the Governors decided to concentrate on exhibits of specimens of rocks and minerals, and British birds in the first instance.[41]

The improving academic record of the Hospital owed much to its staff. One of the stalwarts, Dr John Ogilvie, resigned his teaching post in June 1859 after 28 years' service, owing to failing eyesight and declining health.[42] All the Governors spoke highly of him and determined to give him a retiring allowance of £60 p.a. during their pleasure. The boys presented him with a handsome walking stick, a gesture that touched him deeply.[43]

In February 1863 Drill Sergeant Jamieson resigned his post after 29 years' service owing to increasing age and infirmity. Strahan contacted Bedford at Heriot's and found that there in addition to drill, the boys were instructed in gymnastics and dancing. The Governors decided to follow suit although the gymnastics did not take place.[44] John Balfour was appointed dancing master and in order that parents and friends should see the extent of the boys' accomplishments he organised social gatherings in the dining room. The first 'Soiree' was held on 2 March 1865 and its success ensured that it became an annual event.[45] Sergeant 'Billy' Coombs was employed as drill and music master, with forty boys getting dancing lessons for six months for two hours every week.

As well as the good HMI reports and an increasingly diversified curriculum under Strahan there was other evidence that attainment in the Hospital was improving. The number of boys going on to university was five in 1857 – one more than usual – and the following session another five did so.[46] Moreover, the first successes at university were noted in April 1858 when James Forbes [1728] won first prize in the mathematical class and fifth prize in Natural Philosophy, while James Tytler [1734] gained eighth prize in the mathematical class and was in the order of merit for Natural Philosophy.[47]

The union between King's and Marischal had been a strong recommendation of a Royal Commission on Universities which reported in 1830; soon various proposals were put forward and the Universities (Scotland) Act of 1858 paved the way for the fusion, which took effect on 15 September 1860.[48] The Governors were concerned that their special agreement with Marischal, dating from 1781, would cease as the Arts classes in Marischal were being abolished. They consulted with the University Commissioners as to the continuance of the privilege.[49]

The bad news arrived in October 1862 when the Hospital Education Committee under Baillie Urquhart was informed that the Secretary of the Commissioners had decided that the 1781 arrangement was beyond Marischal College's powers and was not binding on the University of Aberdeen. Although regretting this, the Governors determined to go ahead with the presentation of the usual number of boys in future but would pay the ordinary fees for them.[50]

Discipline

Like previous holders of his post, Strahan spent much of his time on discipline. As always there were a large number of low-level offences which usually resulted in detention of varying length on Wednesdays and Saturdays. One of the major problems for the staff was the lack of a systematic policy involving graduations of punishments, so that in practice the boys were punished in the same way for a great variety of misdemeanours. Lateness for class generally was a major problem.[51] Idleness was a great issue, neglect of lessons, fighting, throwing stones, spitting, swearing, practical jokes, smoking, telling lies, stealing, malicious damage to property and deficiency in dress and appearance were all regular offences which meant that detention was always crowded. Some serious or potentially serious incidents also ended in detention. James Gall [1576] and William Proctor [1591] were detained for 'bringing fireworks into the Hospital and firing them',[52] while John Webster [1699], Henry Callander [1650], Alexander Gray [1694], George Neilson [1656], John Gall [1688] and William Robertson [1648] were treated likewise for 'being concerned in firing a cannon'.[53] In February 1858 the same punishment was meted out to James Glegg [1771], who brought a pistol and gunpowder into the Hospital and accidentally shot Richard Chesser [1868]. Bed-wetting was dealt with in different ways at different times but detention was resorted to on occasion and eight bed-wetters was the average in detention in December 1857.

Discipline was also an issue for some teachers in some classes. The French teacher, Jadzowski,[54] seemed to find it difficult to control his classes. He reacted by putting large numbers of boys in detention[55] and the ill-feeling engendered resulted, on one occasion, in his desk being broken into.[56] Flogging was used but probably not as much as might be expected. Bullying in the Hospital System was rife but seldom was the Headmaster in a position to apprehend culprits. When he did so, flogging or whipping was the usual punishment. In February 1856 John Shand [1711], Alexander McQuillan [1726] and Andrew Fraser [1782] were flogged 'for being tyrants'.[57] Expulsion was comparatively rare and usually for incorrigible boys. In October 1858, Lachlan Gregg [1909] and George Duncan [1837] were expelled – even then the vote for doing so was only 9–5, a group of Governors wishing to give them another chance. The boys had, on two occasions, broken into teachers' desks and stolen materials. Gregg appeared to be the instigator but Dr Ogilvie held Duncan to be 'tricky and mischevious', indeed 'the worst boy who ever came under his observation'.[58]

Strahan tried to deal with the perennial problem of bed-wetting by various means, often more carrot than stick. Even before Strahan's time, Dr Dyce, in April 1838, had recommended that nine boys have separate beds, and he had attended at night and in the early morning in an effort to ameliorate bed-wetting. As a result two were cured and some others improved.[59] However, it needed constant attention and by September 1839 things were as bad as ever. The Governors were always looking for new ways to deal with the issue, and on Strahan's visit to Heriot's in 1850 he discovered that there the situation had been tackled with some success by substituting bread for porridge at supper time and using water-proof cloth on beds.[60] At Gordon's the Governors considered sending bed-wetters home at night and by June 1855 they were prohibited from having liquids at night.[61] By February 1857 it was ruled that no boys with a bed-wetting habit would be taken into the Hospital and if discovered once he had been admitted the boy concerned would be sent home at once.[62]

Three months later the Governors employed a wardsman to stay overnight with the boys and raise the bed-wetters frequently and this did reduce the problem.[63] By December, however, matters deteriorated again, with some 21 boys involved in the 'odious' practice. When they were warned that they would lose an hour of holidays on Saturdays for every night they wet their bed the incidence fell away but recurred periodically; in September 1864 with a wardsman being employed again and in May 1874 when it reached an 'alarming level'. At that point the Governors decided if bed-wetting continued the boys would be sent home and would not be readmitted until cured.

Health of the Boys

Under Strahan the Hospital continued to deal well with epidemics that affected Aberdeen and its locality. However, institutions like Hospitals were also prone to particular contagious infections and in October 1856 Gordon's was faced with an outbreak of Itch. Baillie McHardy moved that a Special Committee be set up in an effort to find the cause of the prevalence of the disease and the best remedy 'for checking and removing a disease which has occasioned considerable alarm and discontent among the parents of the boys'.[64] On investigation the Committee found 72 boys in the specially appointed Itch room, but within ten days all had moved into convalescence wards. Having examined the boys Dr Dyce advised that the disease 'was in great measure checked',[65] and would soon be entirely removed. He explained to the Governors that the disease was probably brought into the Hospital from those living in poor and unclean circumstances and soon spread via clothes and bedding to other boys. Although there had been some success with the use of sulphur smoke the outbreak intensified. In future, Dyce recommended the continuation of the weekly bath and that it be closely supervised to ensure that hair and body were effectively washed. He suggested the extension of supervision to daily washing of hands and faces, and combing of hair, which was also to be cut and kept shorter. He wanted all boys returning to the Hospital from vacation or even a short visit to have a bath and be examined, and if necessary treated. When this regime was imposed Dyce reported in August 1857 that three boys had returned from holidays suffering from Itch and all the others 'were more or less filthy'.[66]

Although clothes were not the cause of the epidemic Dyce persuaded the Governors that the boys should be supplied with under-flannels, which also added to comfort in the winter. Some short-term diet changes were introduced too. Moreover, Dyce was concerned at the 'indulgence' of frequent visiting days, and suggested an alternative of a short excursion or walk, combined with amusement. He suggested using the links nearby for cricket or preparing a ball court in the backyard, both of which would provide exercise.[67]

McHardy's Committee took on board Dyce's recommendations. It also held that the Visitation Committee attended the Hospital too infrequently 'to be of any practical benefit'[68] and needed to visit at least once a fortnight. Only such a commitment would have made the Governors aware earlier of the last outbreak and resulted in earlier steps to deal with it. The Governors also expected that Headmaster Strahan should occasionally participate in the supervision of the washing as an example to the other staff. On 24 November 1856 Dyce was requested to attend the Hospital twice a week[69] and within a couple of months was reporting that six boys were in the Itch room but 27 were affected by ringworm.[70] Nonetheless there were long-term improvements effected from this time. The Governors ensured all boys had separate beds and the mattresses were filled with more expensive coconut fibre rather than chaff. Ventilation of the dormitories was improved and discussions over giving the boys adequate living space led to a reorganisation of the sleeping arrangements.[71]

These important developments helped ensure that most of the illnesses experienced by the boys were minor: colds, bronchial problems, coughs, toothache, gumboils, ophthalmia, diarrhoea, measles, chicken pox and fractures were the most common maladies. When more serious illnesses occurred – influenza (September 1858), mumps (November 1859), scarlatina (February 1860), smallpox (April 1860), scarlet fever (December 1860), typhoid (November

1873) – fortunately they tended to be isolated. Throughout this period indeed there is much evidence to show how effective the Hospital Physician was.

Special Events

Being Headmaster over such a long period Strahan presided over a number of events, some important to the Hospital and others of more local or national significance. The centenary celebrations of 1850 and the tablet in Drums' Aisle in 1857 had come in his first decade of office and arrangements were very much in the hands of the Governors. However, as the royal wedding of the Prince of Wales, planned for 10 March 1863, approached, Strahan was asked to organise a special day for the boys. His programme involved the boys leaving the Hospital at 11.30am in procession with rosettes in their jackets, headed by the Hospital band, and returning for a special lunch of roast beef and plum pudding in the Hospital. The boys would then be allowed home to see friends and family for the day, returning to the Hospital at 9.30pm having seen the special fireworks display in the Town. The success of this day led to a similar plan of Strahan when celebrating the marriage of Princess Louise in early 1871.

Under Strahan, as previously, the lads from 'Gordon's' always seemed to be in the forefront when the town was celebrating, and the building and its surrounds were also seen as important to the Town. A pair of Russian guns captured at Sebastopol during the Crimean War (1854–6) were sent to Aberdeen in June 1857 as a measure of Britain's success. They were 36-pounders and, with their carriages, weighed nearly seven tons. At first, it was proposed that the cannon should be placed on display in the grounds of the Hospital but they were sited instead in the Castlegate and remained there until 1874. However, when British relations with Russia improved and the Duke of Edinburgh[72] came on an official visit to Aberdeen, it was decided to remove the guns to a less prominent site, within the Hospital grounds, where they remained until September 1940. Then they were finally removed as part of the Second World War scrap metal salvage campaign.

Throughout his time as Headmaster Strahan continued to work hard to humanise the Hospital. The Governors 'highly approved'[73] plans to resurrect the bowling green, now aimed primarily at recreation for the boys. It was ready for use by May 1859 but proper balls were not available in Aberdeen. The Governors sent to Liverpool for four pairs of balls with jacks. Baillie Fraser obtained a book of instructions on the game which he gave to the House

Steward to guide the boys in their playing.[74] Baillie Adamson persuaded the other Governors to allow cricket to be played on the front lawn and he provided appropriate equipment. It was reported that 'Lily' beat 'Heatherbell' (a team from the Hospital) by 47 runs.[75] However, generally 'Heatherbell' did well, as it was labelled 'ever successful'.[76] The Hospital team even won their first match against the Grammar School (their second XI) by scoring 96 runs against only 12 in 1879.[77] Strahan himself arranged with the Directors of Aberdeen Public Baths, in February 1870, for the Hospital boys to use them on regular basis in order that they could all learn to swim.[78]

Strahan was successful in introducing a reading room in 1857 but unfortunately no catalogue of books has survived. However, from the writings of some of the Auld Lads[79] it can be concluded that history proved of interest among the boys, especially the works of William H. Prescott.[80] Stories of the sea were very popular and of particular interest were tales from Captain Frederick Marryat,[81] an actual 19th-century British naval hero. There was also much demand for the 'blood and thunder' stories of Mayne Reid.[82] A copy of the *Aberdeen Journal* was supplied weekly on Wednesdays to keep the boys up to date with 'current affairs'.

The issue of ex-pupils repaying the cost of their education if they prospered in later life was raised again in February 1861.[83] Since its last review of the position[84] some five old boys had repaid, and a Committee was set up to take this forward.[85] The Clerk drew up a list of those considered able to contribute to the Hospital funds and it was made up of 42 names.[86] The Governors, however, hesitated, and Councillor George Brown was persuaded not to press further, at least meantime. He reluctantly agreed to a delay, and then again, in April 1865, to a further delay of six months.[87] The matter remained in abeyance, the Governors believing that a regular airing of the topic would be the reminder needed to prompt ex-pupils to act. When Dean of Guild George Jamieson raised it again in December 1868 the Governors agreed to keep it 'in view'.[88]

One ex-pupil who did repay his education (valued at £105) was James Matthews [1021], whose contribution in May 1861 was stimulated by his desire to open up the Hospital grounds on removal of the Grammar School to its new site and the vacating of its Schoolhill building.[89] The Governors met on 29 July 1864 to decide whether to buy the Old Grammar School building,[90] believing that it would be prejudical to the Hospital if it was bought by others. In the event, given that there were no offers at the sale, the Hospital Factor did not offer the upset price of £1200[91] but bought it privately afterwards in mid-August for £1000.[92] By the October of the same year it had been leased out to Messrs A. and H. Gray, general merchants, at £63 per annum.[93]

As Strahan grew older he increasingly struggled to cope. His discipline was breaking down. In February 1871, following the expulsion of William Stott [2249], the Clerk wrote to the parents of nine other boys giving them a final warning, as their sons already had three offences against their names. Another ten boys were also warned about their future conduct following an outbreak of stone-throwing over the Hospital walls which had resulted in considerable damage to the neighbouring properties.[94] However, by May, matters had escalated out of hand again. Repeated desertions led to expulsions, and another eight boys broke windows in an uncontrolled rampage. The guilty boys were made to pay for the damage and confined to the Hospital for a month. The Governors threatened to bring in the police if faced with further problems.[95] Although things quietened for a while, by August 1872 Strahan needed to call on the help of the Drill Sergeant to whip four boys for climbing on the walls and roof of the nearby vestry of Blackfriars' Street Chapel and breaking a number of slates.[96]

The reports of HMI Kerr in November 1870 and May 1871 were also evidence of a deteriorating situation. He was more critical of Hospital staff and their procedures and this led the Governors to introduce a number of changes. Wednesday was made a full working day and Saturday (till 8pm) was made a full holiday; Dale replaced the House Steward in assisting boys with their learning in private; 'Hooker' Stuart, who had been deemed 'too feeble to teach or manage a class full of unruly boys',[97] was to be retired after 37 years' service as writing master[98]; French was to be the only modern foreign language taught in the Hospital (although Jadzowski was proving increasingly incapable);[99] Strahan was to teach the Latin and English advanced classes and Scott was to teach Latin to juniors; and any boy showing special aptitude for Latin was to be prepared for the Bursary Competition and be sent to the Grammar School for further instruction.[100]

It was clearly time for Strahan to retire. On 11 September 1872 he resigned after 23 years' service, aged 67. He had presided over an era of quiet progress and consolidation and of happy relationships within the Hospital. In accepting his resignation, Lord Provost William Leslie,[101] on behalf of the Governors, spoke of Strahan's 'long, faithful and successful services' to the Hospital. He was granted a generous retiral pension of £100 per annum.[102]

How far the Hospital had progressed was reflected in the wide interest in the vacant post of Headmaster. There were ninety expressions of interest and of these 54 provided testimonials. At a large meeting of 26 Governors, on 15 October 1872, a leet of seven was chosen: it included parish schoolmasters from Alyth, Forfar, Fraserburgh and Monymusk, the Classical Master of the Grammar School, and Headmasters from Wick and Woodside. At an even fuller meeting of 28 Governors[103] four days later, following three votes, Rev. Alexander Ogilvie[104] was elected as the clear winner with a majority over all the others put together. The Governors decided to accept him unanimously.[105]

Rev. Alexander Ogilvie

Alexander Ogilvie was born in November 1830 on his father's tenant-farm of Ternemny, Rothiemay. His father was the brother of Dr John Ogilvie, while his mother was the sister of John Cruickshank, Professor of Mathematics at Marischal College.[106] He was educated at the local school before going on to Fordyce Academy in 1844. Four years later he won a bursary to King's College where he graduated AM in 1852. Subsequently he took the divinity course and became a licentiate of the Church of Scotland. For a short time he was schoolmaster at Strichen, succeeding his eldest brother, William, and, in 1854, he moved to the parish school of Monymusk, where he taught for eighteen years and conducted a boarding establishment before his move to the Hospital. It was, however, at Monymusk that he laid the foundations of his reputation as an educationalist. In the reports of the Dick and Milne Bequests and of the Endowed Schools Commissioners, there is evidence of his ability as a teacher and of the high level of efficiency which Monymusk School attained under him.

Ogilvie was inducted into his post as Headmaster of Gordon's by the Education Committee on 12 November 1872;[107] his salary was fixed at £260 p.a. with free unfurnished house.[108] He had a number of advantages – especially a knowledge of Gordon's obtained from his uncle, and a knowledge of the Hospital System gained from his older brother, George, who had became Headmaster of Stewart's Hospital in Edinburgh in 1856 and then Watson's Hospital when it changed into a day school in 1870. He also knew much about education generally, with his eldest brother, William, Rector of Morrison's Academy in Crieff, and younger brothers, Joseph, Headmaster at Keith,[109] and Robert, Rector of Milne's Institution, before becoming an HMI.[110] With such a pedigree it was not a surprise that he proved a natural teacher. His enthusiasm and dynamism brought new purpose to the Hospital.[111]

Ogilvie lost no time in visiting classrooms and reported his findings to the Governors on 17 February 1873.[112] Within the month the Education Committee had discussed his contention that the education in the Hospital 'was in many respects not so thorough as it ought to be'.[113] Ogilvie recommended the appointment of an Assistant Teacher (or House Tutor) to reside in and whose main functions would be to superintend the preparation of lessons and to 'associate with the boys out of school [i.e. classrooms] with a view to elevate their moral tone'.[114] The Committee accepted Ogilvie's suggestion and Alexander 'Chappie' Lobban[115] was appointed.

Another area which attracted Ogilvie's attention was the curriculum. In his earliest years as Headmaster he was constrained by his elderly staff yet he still managed to introduce elementary science and developed evening classes which followed the syllabus laid down by the Department of Art and Science in London. He also contributed to the 'Interim Scheme of Improvement' introduced in early 1876 for improving the Hospital System. Lord Provost George Jamieson[116] had moved that, although five years would be the ordinary period of education in the Hospital, those with the capacity for a more advanced course would be maintained for a further two years for technical or classical education, admission to the class being by competition. Ogilvie persuaded the Governors to change the emphasis by substituting 'scientific and classical education' and introducing an examination to determine who would be admitted.[117] To that end the Governors accepted the need to appoint a well-qualified teacher to take forward this 'advanced' class in science and classics.

Within a few years Ogilvie had the opportunity to select an almost completely new staff for the Hospital and as a result his later years proved 'years of vigour such as had never been witnessed in the institution'.[118] In June 1877 John Scott died and Dr Alexander Gerard retired, owing to ill-health, a few months later.[119] With the departure of these two, the old order passed away.[120] Gerard had spent 42 years teaching at Gordon's, gained the degree of LL.D. in April 1875 as a 'deserving and accomplished teacher'[121] and on his retiral was presented with his portrait by a number of his old pupils and personal friends.[122] He was seen as a distinct personality and a loveable character.[123]

On 18 March 1878 the Governors appointed Alexander Lobban as Teacher of English (previously Assistant Teacher)[124]; Basil S. McLellan as Teacher of Mathematics (from Glasgow Academy) and John McKenzie to the new post of Teacher of Classics and Science (also from Glasgow Academy).[125] Thus, of the seven teachers in the Hospital only James Dale (English),[126] appointed 1859, and Samuel Pope (writing and drawing), appointed in 1871, remained in post. Almost immediately the new team were being praised for raising academic standards. Certainly Latin, Greek and mathematics were now taught on modern lines and in 1879 a record six boys attended university.[127]

The Fate of the Boys

The Hospital continued to produce pupils who did well in later life. Examples included Archibald David Reid [1805], attended 1854–9, who became an outstanding painter in oil and watercolour, exhibiting in the Royal Academy from 1872. Alexander Anderson [1943], attended 1858–66, after university, successfully competed for a place in the Indian Civil Service. Walter Reid [2318], attended 1870–5, became a chartered accountant and actuary and was to play an important part in the College's history. Alexander Munro [2403], attended 1871–7, was to become Aberdeen City Chamberlain (1905–11) and wrote extensively about the town's history. (Sir) George Alexander Troup [2432], attended 1873–9, was to become an architect and Mayor of Wellington, the capital of New Zealand. Charles Duguid [2452], attended 1873–8, became Managing Director of the Great Publicity Agency in London. William A. Reid [2493], who attended 1874–81, became minister of West Maybole Church. John Duncan [2592], attended 1879–84, became a physician in Birmingham. John A. Third [2665], attended 1878–81, became the first Director of Education for Ayrshire. James Dean [2675], attended 1879–84, became Convener of the Incorporated Trades of Aberdeen. James Duncan [2748], attended 1881–6, became a Free Church minister in Dumfries. George Hall [2764], attended 1881–5, became a member of the Scottish Fishery Board. All of these and many more made up a class of citizens who played a full and varied part in the life of Aberdeen and far beyond.

A Changing Institution

Like his immediate predecessor, Ogilvie found himself in the middle of debates on the Hospital, its procedures and future. In September 1873 the Education Committee had debated whether the boys should be allowed to spend Sunday afternoons with their parents.[128] It was early in his tenure and Ogilvie feared alienating either side in what was a long-standing and increasingly emotive issue.

He, therefore, declined to vote, and proposer Esslemont carried the day against clerical opposition.[129] When the matter went before the Governing Body in November[130] the difference of opinion revolved round different interpretations of Robert Gordon's Deed and it was decided to seek legal advice. However, by this time the Governors were embroiled in debate over the successor to Rev. Wilson on the Governing Body, which also had to go for legal opinion before it could be resolved in December 1873,[131] and the development of different schemes for remodelling the Hospital.

Radical changes were expected but Ogilvie had inherited an already changing institution. In October 1872 the first boys from the wider admission policy of the Governors were taken into the Hospital and in August 1876 under the 'Interim Scheme' the first day scholars, with allowances given to their parents for boarding, had been introduced. The original 25 'out-resident' boys had increased to 39 by the end of session 1876–7 and continued to grow thereafter.[132] The popularity of the new arrangements were seen by the fact that by the time the system ended in November 1881 there were some 121 out-resident boys, whose parents/guardians were receiving quarterly payments for their maintenance at home.

Ogilvie clearly approved of the moves to reform the Hospital, as his evidence in April 1880 to the Commissioners on Endowed Institutions showed. However, it is too much to claim that the opening up of the Hospital was his work and that since his appointment in 1872 he had worked to achieve it 'with a singleness of purpose'.[133] Changes were underway before Ogilvie arrived and, although his role in them was important, he was still very much the employee of the Governors, as the debate over the Headmaster's power in the lead-up to the 1881 Provisional Order was to prove. As Baillie Donald perceived in his remarks on 30 July 1881 to the last meeting of the Hospital Governors, it was Lord Provost Peter Esslemont[134] who was the driving force behind Hospital reform and the change to a College.[135]

As the days of the Hospital came to an end it was fitting that in November 1876 the terracotta model statue of the Founder, which had long lain in Marischal College, was presented to the Governors by the University Senatus. The statue was placed in the Governors' Hall with an inscription fixed underneath. Referring to Robert Gordon it held 'He being dead yet speaketh'.[136] His Hospital was about to end but a new and vibrant institution was to rise up to ensure that Robert Gordon's Legacy lived on.

7

THE END OF THE HOSPITAL

The 'Hospital System'

All Scottish Hospitals, including Gordon's, were influenced to a greater or lesser extent by events at Heriot's, the oldest and most important Hospital. As early as April 1845 the Governors of Heriot's Hospital in Edinburgh had produced a report, the central theme of which was a devastating critique of the 'Hospital System'. They held that it ensured a large number of young persons were 'educated in a state of comparative isolation from the world under a nearly total privation of the proper home influences and of the cultivation and exercise of domestic and social affection'. The result was that hospital boys were 'sullen and reserved', lacked self-dependence, exhibited ignorance of the outside world, proved awkward in manner and had an inferiority complex. Boys protected fellow offenders by a preconcerted system of falsehood and hospitals were a hotbed of pernicious and degrading practices.[1] At Heriot's, the days of the Hospital System were numbered, as its Governors sought to replace it with the 'industrial school system' where children stayed overnight with their parents.

In Aberdeen, a debate followed the appointment of a Committee, chaired by Francis Cochran, set up on 24 August 1853, to which Rev. Dr Robert Lee, given his seven years' service as Convener of the Education Committee at Heriot's, provided important written evidence. His opinion was forthright: 'I do not know of a single person, whose judgment is of any value, who approves the Hospital System, and those who have been brought up in it . . . least of all'.[2] Others giving such evidence were generally critical and supported reform.[3] The oral evidence taken in May 1854 was also not supportive of hospitals, which were viewed as extravagant.[4] Headmaster Strahan of Gordon's was more judicious in his oral contribution, and probably felt the need to justify his own record. Of the 150 boys who had left during his time[5] Strahan believed that only seven or eight had conducted themselves badly. The Hospital did have success stories and boys who became successful in later life. He accepted that employers complained that Hospital boys were 'dogged, stiff and obstinate' but, with the lowering of the leaving age from sixteen to fifteen, he expected this problem to diminish.[6] He agreed that it would be better if boys had respectable parents so that they could be sent home overnight but this could not be done as there were so few such parents. Thus there was no alternative to the Hospital System.[7]

If Strahan was conservative in his view (at least at this stage in his career), a very different judgement was given by John Ogilvie, the long-serving master at Gordon's for 23 years. He spelled out the evils of the Hospital System: falsehood, fraud, deceit, indiscipline. The weak followed the strong and preferred to do so rather than obey teachers, who faced passive resistance and hurdles placed in their way. The result was limited academic development and the determination of many boys not to send their own children to Hospitals for education.

Given these contrasting views reflecting different perspectives on life at Gordon's Hospital, it is that of Ogilvie which rings truer. As his tenure as Headmaster went on, even Strahan was to become less favourably disposed to the Hospital System, which survived but was defended only when vicious parents were encountered. Cochran's Committee of 1854 ducked the issue. It decided not to recommend going ahead with reform, partly from fear of parental reprisals and partly because of the lack of mechanisms to select appropriate persons and inspect them continuously. By seven votes to one the Committee supported day schools for those whose parents were deemed fit to take children overnight, with only one member holding the Hospital System useful.[8]

Early Attempt at Reform

This unsatisfactory state of affairs could not continue and led to the first major attempt to end the Hospital System at Gordon's. On 4 October 1855 Councillor Henry C. Oswald pressed for a report on 'whether, and how far, it would be beneficial to relax the system which presently obtains in this institution, known as the "Hospital System", and to adopt in its place the Free Day School System of Education or a modification thereof with due regard to the rights of Burgesses, and others, entitled to preference by the Founder's Deed'.[9] At the next Governors' meeting on 18 February 1856 the motion was seconded by the Master of Guild Brethren's Hospital, George Bothwell. The clerical Governors led the opposition:

Rev. Dr Forsyth held it 'inexpedient for the Governors to entertain this motion' and he was supported by Rev. Wilson. However, after 'considerable discussion', the motion passed 9–5 and was remitted to an Open Committee chaired by Lord Provost Thomas Blaikie.[10]

The ministers – Forsyth, Wilson and Dewar – produced their 'Reasons of Protest'.[11] It claimed that Oswald's motion would result in 'one of these reckless and sweeping innovations on long-established and well-approved systems and institutions'. Moreover, it was 'unprincipled . . . interference with that right of disposal and destination of property lawfully acquired'. Robert Gordon had set out the building of a Hospital in his Deed of Mortification – the motion would change his property destination from what he manifestly intended. The ministers held there were no precedents for such an action, and the expense of going to Parliament to produce the change would be a waste of Hospital funds. Fundamentally, they defended the Hospital System and did not recognise claims about its evils. Moreover, Aberdeen did not recognise them either, for it was proud of the Hospital which 'has been for so long diffusing quietly and beautifully its inestimable benefits among the class of citizens for whom it is designed'.[12] The clerics promised to obstruct any attempts to bring about change. As a start their 'Protest' was printed and sent to all Governors.

The majority of Governors used their votes to set up a Committee of Five to 'Answer' the ministers' case and its report was minuted on 19 May.[13] Essentially it held that the Hospital System was far from perfect, although the most recent inquiry had brought considerable improvements. Trusts should be changed by legislation when a better way of securing the founder's design was discovered. However, the nine Governors supporting an inquiry did so for differing reasons. Some, like Oswald, believed the Hospital System – separating children from families and home – was 'injurious' to happiness and the improvement of youth, and all the advantages of education and maintenance could be provided for boys of the preferred class without deprivation of family and home. Others, probably a greater number, had not decided against the Hospital System but were open to persuasion, and were aware of the weighty and growing criticisms of Hospitals. Even in Gordon's Hospital they were aware that from time to time certain evils had surfaced, especially the undue influence of some boys over others, the result of their closed community and their seclusion from other, better influences. They, therefore, looked forward to a thorough and honest appraisal of the Hospital System.[14]

The Open Committee met under Sir Thomas Blaikie[15] on 6 March and again on 18 August 1856. At the latter meeting Oswald proposed a list of queries, which was worked on further at meetings on 4 and 29 October.[16] It was then sent to 28 gentlemen for completion and on 7 January 1857 the replies from seventeen of them were scrutinised. The details were forwarded to all Governors following a special meeting of Governors on 30 April chaired by Lord Provost John Webster.[17]

The momentum for change slackened, leaving Baillie Oswald to drum up support among the newly elected Governors of November 1857. Undaunted, he moved on 15 February 1858 that, as it was beneficial to return boys home at night, the Governors should adopt the Free Day School System. A discussion of 'considerable length'[18] followed, without result. At the following meeting, however, on 15 March 1858 Oswald's motion was met with three separate amendments. The first from Councillor Robert Cruickshank holding the motion to be 'incompetent' (seconded by Rev. Dr Forsyth) received only four votes and lost out, as did an amendment by Rev. Lang which received but five votes. Lang had moved that the meeting 'whilst gratefully acknowledging the services of the committee appointed in 1856 and feeling that the evidence obtained in the recent inquiry tends to show that the Hospital System is unnatural and injurious; taking into account the whole circumstances of the case deems the motion introduced by Baillie Oswald inexpedient'. This left the amendment of Councillor William Ross which stated that 'in the opinion of the Governors the evidence obtained in the recent enquiry tends convincingly to show the great advantage that would result if the boys in the Institution were permitted to reside with their parents, relations or guardians or to return to them during the night, and the Governors are also satisfied that public opinion is rapidly coming to the same conclusion; but as they regret to find that the change of system is opposed by some of their number, and as it is most desirable in any endeavour to accomplish it, to carry as much unanimity as possible among all the parties interested, the Meeting does not consider it expedient at present to take the measures requisite for effecting the change referred to'. This cautious amendment easily defeated Oswald's motion 9–3, with four abstentions,[19] and attempts at reform were ended meantime.

Perhaps it was not surprising that the Governors had failed to grasp the nettle as their model, Heriot's, had also failed to do in 1844–6. What was surprising was the fact that in Edinburgh the reformers were supported by the ministers on the Board, especially Rev. Dr Robert Lee, who, in his Founder's Day sermon of June 1846, made a devastating attack on the Hospital System. In Aberdeen the ministers saw things differently and were in the vanguard of those defending the existing arrangements.

The reformers had to content themselves with a more conservative approach to the Hospital System. They set about tackling its worst aspects piecemeal. The Education Committee reported that the new Regulations on admission and departure[20] had not been passed with an adequate majority. In November 1858 the Governors reiterated their support for the minimum age of admission being nine years and departure at fifteen years except in the case of boys attending College.[21] Then in February 1860, in an effort both to open up the Hospital more and to increase numbers,[22] the Governors repealed the bye-law that fathers/grandfathers of admitted boys needed to have been burgesses for ten years.[23]

The Laurie Report

Events in Edinburgh again raised the issue of the Hospital System, for Simon S. Laurie, Inspector of the Dick Bequest Schools and Secretary of the Education Committee of the Church of Scotland, was asked to report on the state of education in the Hospitals under the charge of the Merchant Company there. His Report of July 1868 was critical of the poor educational results of the Hospitals which Laurie blamed on lack of home or family influence and the regimental routine which weakened the faculties of children. It also attacked the high costs which Laurie put down to the highly-paid officials.[24] On 3 October at a Governors' meeting at Gordon's, Lord Provost Alexander Nichol[25] laid a copy of Laurie's Report, which he had received from the Master of the Merchant Maiden Hospital, on the table. Nichol did not propose any immediate action although he informed the Governors of ongoing talks between the Managers of the Edinburgh Hospitals and MPs aimed at reforming the Hospital System. Instead he wished to keep the Governors aware of developments and promised to circulate the Report to them.[26]

Despite his protestation of 'let's wait and see' Nichol immediately agreed that the Headmaster should allow boys home at Christmas, if they wished to go, similar to arrangements in summer.[27] He then pressed the Governors to allow the Headmaster to select twenty boys (who had been at least two years in the Hospital and whose conduct and attainment were most meritorious) to send to the Grammar School for their education in branches most suitable to them, provided their parents consented. The Governors would pay their fees to the Town Council and make an agreement with the teachers in the Grammar School.[28] After years of comparative inactivity on the question of the Hospital System the Governors now seemed in a hurry to reform it.

Meantime, the Merchant Company used its powerful political influence to persuade the Lord Advocate to bring forward the Endowed Hospitals (Scotland) Bill to enable Hospitals to be turned into day schools. On 4 May 1869 a Special Meeting of Governors at Gordon's was called at short notice to deal with the Bill, which was due to have its third reading in the Commons two days later, and the communication from the Secretary of the Merchant Company, Strong, requesting the Governors' support in promoting the objectives of the legislation. 'After due consideration'[29] the Governors approved of the Bill unanimously. Provost Nichol was authorised to sign a Petition to Parliament in favour of the Bill to be forwarded immediately to Colonel Sykes MP[30] with a request to present and support it in the Commons. The Governors also instructed that the Clerk intimate the resolution to Strong by telegram so it would be received before his leaving Edinburgh with a delegation bound for London to wait on the Lord Advocate on the subject.[31]

The promoters of the Bill were successful and it gained royal assent on 26 July. It allowed Governors at a special meeting held with a month's notice to agree a petition by simple majority to send to the Home Secretary outlining plans for better government and administration. The Home Secretary could remit the petition to a sheriff to take evidence. The resulting Provisional Order would become law if unchallenged for forty days. On 16 August 1869 Lord Provost Nichol laid a copy of the new Act on the table, remarking that 'some of its provisions, which were all entirely permissory, might be adopted by Gordon's Hospital with advantage'.[32] The Clerk procured copies and circulated them to the Governors.

The Merchant Company went forward immediately with its radical reforms without opposition. Five large, fee-paying schools were formed from their Hospitals in 1870.[33] Heriot's, however, had their scheme for reform blocked as the Liberal Government had second thoughts about the 1869 Act following complaints from private school teachers, and the surprise at the extensive nature of the Merchant Company scheme.[34] Gordon's was much slower off the mark, but on 3 October 1870 the Governors decided to discuss how the legislation could increase the Hospital's usefulness and efficiency[35] and a special meeting for that purpose was held on 14th of the same month. This resulted in the formation of a Committee of Eleven chaired by Lord Provost Leslie[36] to propose a scheme for a Provisional Order under the 1869 Act. The clerical Governors, however, continued their opposition.

After three meetings in January/February 1871 the Committee had produced a draft Petition which formed the basis of discussion with the

Collyhill Trustees in March.[37] The Committee then swiftly finalised their proposed alterations in the Regulations, and Leslie moved that they be incorporated in a Provisional Order.[38] Dean of Guild Ross, and Revs. Dewar and Brown were the only dissenters. The Committee of Eleven was to take matters forward; Ross resigned from it.[39]

On 13 April Lord Provost Leslie intimated to the Governors that the Home Secretary had rejected Heriot Hospital's proposed Provisional Order following an opinion from the Scotch [sic] Law Officers to the effect that it was incompetent under the 1869 Act for him to grant the powers sought. As Leslie believed that the powers about to be requested by Gordon's were similar to those asked for by Heriot's, their application was likely to meet with the same response. He, therefore, called for a delay while he and several other members of the Town Council travelled to London. Hopefully they would meet Home Secretary Bruce, put the Gordon's case to him and ascertain what answer might be expected on the proposed application. The Governors unanimously agreed.[40]

Leslie and the other Governors went to London and reported back on 15 May. They had been advised to postpone their scheme. Leslie had also contacted the solicitors of both Hutchesons'[41] and Heriot's and heard at first hand of the difficulties thrown in their way. The Governors decided it better to await Government legislation, which would allow them to proceed. However, the Government's Bill was lost in July, being introduced too late in the Parliamentary session, and the Governors had to be satisfied with the promise of another Bill being introduced in the following session.

With this new setback Leslie put forward the options to the Governors on 21 August – wait for the new Act or go ahead with immediate but revised and restricted improvements before the 1869 Act finally expired on 31 July 1872. At this stage there were no fears expressed by any Governor that any new legislation might be compulsory rather than permissive, nor that there might be an attempt by the Government to divert funds from the objectives for which Robert Gordon had left them, nor that the Governing Body might be changed. These were issues in Edinburgh but not in Aberdeen. And so the Governors decided to investigate what changes could be made to extend the efficiency and usefulness of the Hospital, and a new Committee of Seven under Leslie was set up[42] to take the opinion of counsel, if needed. On 31 August a Memorial drawn up by the Clerk was sent to Messrs Watson and Guthrie Smith, advocates in Edinburgh, and they duly gave their opinion, which was produced at a meeting on 3 October. It discouraged reform, stressing that the primary duty of the Governors was the maintenance and education of boys *within* the

Hospital walls, which blocked sending boys to the Grammar School, developing day arrangements and even allowing boys home regularly on Sundays. However, the Governors could enlarge the class of foundationers, and abolish apprentice fees and allowances after apprenticeship.[43]

Baillie Peter Esslemont[44] now took the lead and moved, on 24 July 1872, that all boys residing or having resided in Aberdeen who were indigent or could not be maintained were to be eligible for admission to the Hospital. They would be examined by a Committee of Governors regarding their habits and aptitude for learning.[45] This was carried 15–4.[46] Further, on 19 August 1872, Esslemont put forward another motion to end allowances,[47] adding that, in the case of boys elected from then on, the Governors could give up to £5 to the needy or those whose fathers were deceased, for purchasing tools or fitting them out for their apprenticeship. This was carried 12–6.[48] The appropriate advertisements were placed in the press. There were 31 applications for admission in October 1872 and of these 21 were elected: four from the burgess of guild qualification, three from the burgess of trade and fourteen from residence.

Colebrooke Commission

The Lord Advocate in Gladstone's Liberal Government, George Young, dissatisfied with the progress being made on endowments, decided to set up a Royal Commission to enquire into all endowed institutions in Scotland and the changes needed to increase their usefulness and efficiency. The Colebrooke Commission[49] collated completed schedules from the various hospitals and its secretary, Simon S. Laurie, acknowledged receipt of that from Gordon's in early January 1873.

The Gordon's Schedule gave details of the recent changes driven by Esslemont and the financial position and property evaluation.[50] In the total roll of 176 boys, 70 were fatherless and 106 sons of decayed or needy families. The Governors were satisfied with the space given to each boy in dormitories[51] and the separate beds for all boys,[52] and believed their playground facilities were spacious, and sanitary arrangements excellent.[53] Details of diet and education were given and the Schedule gave an indication of rising academic standards assessed in terms of successful careers of ex-inmates. It concluded with a statement that the Governors had had under consideration a plan for allowing boys to live out of the Hospital but following the advice of counsel it had been decided to await a general Act of Parliament[54]

Following advice from Laurie it was decided that Lord Provost Leslie, Baillie Urquhart (Chair of the Education Committee) and Dean of Guild Smith should give oral evidence on behalf of the Hospital.[55] However, it was ex-Master Findlater who appeared before the Commission first on Monday 20 January. He criticised the Hospital System, stressing its evils – the tyranny of the strong and 'boy society' with its low morals and taste. He favoured replacing it with day schooling and raising standards by ensuring admission on academic grounds. He thought Gordon's Hospital could become a 'very admirable technical school',[56] but had to admit that during his time in Aberdeen there had been no discussion of ending the monastic system.[57]

Lord Provost Leslie was first to give evidence on Saturday 25 January 1873. His vision for the Hospital was as a higher elementary school, but also sending some boys to the Grammar School and higher schools from Hospital funds, and helping them to go to university. He favoured introducing fees but at a level which could be afforded by the very poor. He claimed that the Governors wished to remain independent of the new School Board, believing they could offer a better education.[58]

When the Dean of Guild appeared he was immediately tackled on his predecessor's opposition to the 1871 scheme. Although he did not dispute the advantages of a day school, Smith's only objection was to the diminution of the number of foundationers below what the Hospital could contain. He accepted the right of the Governors to make changes such as ending the apprenticeship allowances but wished them retained for orphans. Essentially Smith was reluctant to see the complete end of the Hospital System: he believed some boys needed the discipline and guidance which only it could provide.

Baillie Urquhart was the last to be cross-examined.[59] He held that there was no absolute claim for admission and the Governors had the right to exclude the son of a decayed burgess if uneducated. The 1872 changes had weakened any preferential claim of burgesses and he suggested that the Governors would be willing to see the end of all mention of preference after a period of seven years.[60]

Colebrooke's recommendations, published in March 1875, were seen as a crushing below to the remaining Hospitals. As expected, the Report dwelt on the negative influences of the system on children, and exposed Hospitals as costly, even extravagant. Average Hospital expenditure was £34 per head per annum, although lower, at just over £23,[61] at Gordon's – these figures were high when cheap, elementary education was within easy reach and parents of about

80% of Hospital children in Scotland came from families where annual wages were under £80 per annum.

Fundamentally, Colebrooke was totally out of sympathy with the free education offered by Hospitals. Orthodox opinion, which Colebrooke followed, held that parents benefiting from free education, when they could afford to pay, lost self-respect. Parents who could work and earn wages should maintain and educate their own children. Charities which took over a parent's role pauperised the community. Even in cases of need, relatives should contribute. As the cost of educating a child was estimated at about £3 per year, and maintenance around £6 per year, an artisan receiving an average wage of £78 per annum with a family of five children could afford to pay a small fee for education. For orthodox Liberals gratuitous education when indiscriminate was pernicious.[62] Even in the 'economically conducted' Robert Gordon's Hospital half the outlay could be saved without any decrease in the number of foundationers.[63]

Colebrooke approved the deviations from the various founders' wills. In fact, the Commissioners found very few examples of endowments of any importance in Scotland whose administration had not departed from the conditions imposed by the founder.[64] Most of those changes proved for the public benefit and the Commission was keen for them to continue to be developed. Any admission restrictions – of name, of class and of locality – were harmful and should be removed given how much improved communication had changed the meaning of birth and residence. These views explain why the Gordon's representatives were questioned so vigorously on the qualifications for admission.

Remodelling the Hospital

The Governors appear to have accepted the Colebrooke recommendations without much discussion. It was different in Edinburgh at Heriot's where all 54 members of its Governing Body rejected the Report. But at Gordon's by August 1875 two rival schemes for popularising the Hospital were put forward – one by Dean of Guild Alexander Walker[65] and the other from Baillie Esslemont.

Walker proposed taking boys at eight years of age for a year's training in the old Grammar School building, keeping them separate from the Hospital boys. They would live with their parents, who would receive an allowance for their board. He suggested allowing a number of foundationers to live with their parents but attend classes and dine[66] in the Hospital daily. He further wanted to provide for an extra year of higher education for those able to benefit. Esslemont, on the other hand, offered a much more comprehensive reform. He proposed to convert the Hospital into a day school for elementary and secondary education, reducing the foundationers to a maximum of 100 and boarding them out with their parents or relations or others, while taking in day scholars who would pay either no fees or a moderate fee, and establishing bursaries and evening classes. It was the skeleton of a significant change.[67]

Both sets of proposals were forwarded by Lord Provost George Jamieson[68] to the Education Committee for it to furnish a scheme for remodelling the Hospital 'likely to meet the altered circumstances of our times and at the same time, as far as possible, be in accordance with the wishes of the benevolent Founder'.[69] However, that laid the way for further variations and there were four schemes before the Governors[70] at their Special Meeting on 23 February.

Following a hearing of Councillor James Aiken Jnr and Councillor William Paul on their schemes, Lord Provost Jamieson tried to find common ground by moving that: (i) the number of the boys in the Hospital be gradually reduced from 180 and in future those admitted be mainly orphans or boys whose father or mother was deceased; (ii) day scholars be introduced and given allowances for boarding maintenance out of the Hospital;[71] (iii) five years would remain the normal length of time for boys to attend the Hospital but those who could benefit from two more years of science/technical or classical education would be chosen by examination; and (iv) boys who gave evidence of superior ability and scholarship would be given assistance from Hospital funds to pursue their education at university.[72] These formed the basis of Resolutions accepted unanimously by the Governors on 3 April 1876.[73] They were to take effect from October 1876 and to be regarded as an Interim Scheme of Improvement.[74]

There were 23 applications by parents and guardians to board their boys at home and the Governors visited them all and agreed on 25 May to a number being boarded out. However, there was also the opportunity under the Scheme to keep able boys on at the Hospital beyond their normal leaving time. Of the eighteen boys due to leave in November 1876 the Governors decided that seven be retained to join the advanced classes.[75]

The Education Committee monitored these developments and, on 26 December 1877, Councillor Aiken requested a review of the boarding arrangements. The Convener of Education, Walker, reported that he personally had visited most of the homes of the 52 boys who were boarding and found them 'generally satisfactory'.[76] It was agreed that in future visitation would be divided amongst members of the Committee and take place once a year. The continuance of boarding was accepted. At the same meeting Councillor William Paul, seconded by Rev. Tulloch, moved that the Hospital go ahead with its previous commitment to increase the numbers from 180 to 200.[77] The Education Committee concurred, seeing no contradiction in supporting this move while keeping in view that the numbers would be reduced if and when the resolutions of 3 April 1876 were introduced.[78]

The issue of the Hospital moving into the area of secondary education by means of funding bursaries for higher education was bound to come to the notice of the School Board, especially its Grammar School Committee. It was naturally very keen for the Hospital to contribute towards the funding of bursaries for pupils in elementary schools to attend the Grammar School. Representatives therefore pressed for a meeting with the Hospital Education Committee, which took place on 26 July 1877. The bad news was the firm declaration by Convener Walker that the funds had to be used for the benefit of the Hospital. Nonetheless, the Governors were in favour of Hospital boys progressing to university by the means of bursaries via the Grammar School and did not rule out the possibility of future funding of Hospital boys, although it seemed that this would best be promoted by applying to Parliament for an extension of the powers and purposes of the Hospital.

It was Dean of Guild Walker who did some serious thinking on how the Hospital could develop secondary education and take the Hospital boys on to university. He had discussed the issue with Dr Frederick Bedford, Headmaster at Heriot's, which had failed in an effort to link its Hospital with university earlier in the decade. Walker, and indeed Bedford, believed that Gordon's could achieve what Heriot's had been unable to do, as all the boys in Edinburgh continued to go into trade apprenticeships. Walker's scheme brought together various strands of previous thinking into a coherent strategy. He proposed that the Hospital elect the twenty boys needed to make the number up to 200 from 'capable' poor boys, thirteen to fourteen years of age, who, if they had had the means, would have proceeded to the Grammar School (and hence to university), but who, because of their poverty, would be obliged to leave school and seek employment. Having already been taught the elements of Latin they would join the existing Hospital class of eight to ten boys immediately. The new class of thirty would be taught by a newly appointed, first-rate, classical master and all would aim for university entrance. If any critics claimed that the Hospital would rival the Grammar School then they could be refuted as the poverty of the boys concerned had prevented them from attending there. The beauty of the plan was that the class would take up where Hospital education usually ended and in this way Hospital boys would be equipped with a ladder through elementary and secondary education to the gates of university.

Walker's programme was favourably received by the Governors, and the Education Committee on 13 February 1878 finalised the main arrangements. The Hospital would take in up to an additional[79] twenty boys aged twelve to fourteen following their performance in an examination. As foundationers they would have their education and maintenance paid for and their course would last for two years. An advertisement was placed in the national press for a teacher of classics and science and John McKenzie from Glasgow Academy was appointed for the advanced class on 18 March.[80]

Disraeli's Conservative Government finally produced its Bill to reform endowed schools and Hospitals on 29 March 1878. Introduced by the Duke of Richmond in the House of Lords it was as expected: it included an Executive Commission, mainly from parties hostile to existing institutions, with wide powers to amend existing endowments and the right of the Home Secretary (Cross) to override governing bodies.[81] The Governors met on 20 May to consider the proposed Bill and accepted Councillor Paul's motion approving generally of its objectives and clauses but opposing any attempt by the Home Secretary or Executive Commission to make radical alterations or amendments to proposed schemes of improvement without the consent of Governing Bodies. With this proviso the Governors agreed to co-operate with other bodies to press the Government to pass the Bill within the parliamentary session. A Committee of Seven under Dean of Guild Walker was set up to petition Parliament and monitor the legislative process.[82]

In the event, Home Secretary Cross resisted attempts to 'strengthen' the Bill and retained its permissive character, withholding from the Commissioners the power of initiating reform. However, he conceded that if the period of grace was not used by the Hospitals to reform, then the Government would move toward compulsory legislation. The Endowed Institutions (Scotland) Act was passed on 8 August 1878 and, like its predecessor of 1869, set up an Executive Commission[83] to end in December 1880. The Governors immediately, on 19 August, consulted the Collyhill Trustees and added more Governors to the Committee under Walker to advise on the changes to be applied for.[84]

The Provisional Order

By November 1878 the Secretary of the Moncrieff Commission had communicated with the Governors directing their attention to certain provisions in the new Act. The Governors agreed that they needed to hold a Special Meeting to decide whether to apply for a Provisional Order.[85] Meeting followed meeting with Baillie Esslemont becoming increasingly frustrated with the lack of progress.[86] It was not until 11 August 1879 that the Governors determined to propose a Provisional Order and the Education Committee was given the remit to consult with the Collyhill Trustees and to produce a detailed plan for the better government and administration of the Hospital.[87]

A draft of powers to be applied for was produced by the Education Committee under Convener Walker on 30 September 1879 without major dissension. At this stage the envisaged Provisional Order would create Robert Gordon's College,[88] made up of a reduced number of foundationers, along with fee-paying scholars, who would be admitted following competitive examination and taught in the Hospital buildings, which would be converted wholly or partly into day schools. A number of bursaries would be available for those entering the College and a number would also be there for some for further study beyond schooling. Evening classes would be instituted.

The Education Committee proceeded to meet representatives of the Collyhill Trust and, after three such meetings, it was decided that the application to the Commissioners should be co-joint. In return, the Education Committee agreed on 26 December to recommend to the Governors that in the proposed Petition provision be made for the admission of the Trustees as members of the new Board of Governors in proportion of one in five.[89] At the Governors' Meeting three days later Lord Provost Jamieson proposed to accept this recommendation, provided all the funds and properties of both Collyhill and the Hospital were invested in the Hospital General Fund, and this was carried 16–6.[90]

On 16 February 1880 the Governors considered clause by clause the proposed Provisional Order for the future administration of the Hospital with little opposition – the greatest being over the inclusion of the Collyhill representatives into the Governing Body, when six Governors opposed.[91] At another meeting on 22 February the Provisional Order was finalised and agreed to – again the only opposition coming from three Governors, who still opposed the incorporation of the Collyhill Trustees into the Governing Body.[92] The Clerk dispatched the Petition to Home Secretary Cross on 26 February, setting in motion the Provisional Order process.[93]

The Secretary of Commissioners on Endowed Institutions replied on 30 March 1880: it was intended to hold a public inquiry on Thursday 15 April at noon in Edinburgh. The Education Committee nominated Lord Provost Jamieson, Baillie Esslemont and Dean of Guild Walker as a Sub-Committee to represent the Hospital, with the Headmaster (Ogilvie) and Clerk (Paul) to give evidence too.[94] When they did so, also present were Baillies Smith and Duffus and Rev. Dr Beveridge, who represented the 'minority' Governors who had opposed the insertion of the Collyhill clause.[95] Professor Dr Christie[96] was there also, representing the Collyhill position and putting forward a plan for a reconstituted Governing Body.[97] In doing so he stressed how unhappy the Trustees were with the 'compulsory amalgamation'.[98] This led to a letter from the Secretary of the Commissioners, G. R. Gillespie, dated 28 April, suggesting that the Governors and Trustees try to get an agreement on the Governors' proposals for the new Governing Body. This led to the meeting of both parties on 17 May when the basis of an agreement was agreed and then formally accepted on 10 June. This was done by leaving the contentious issue of the joint fund to the Commissioners to decide,[99] settling the new Governing Body at seventeen[100] and, under clause 20 of the Order, leaving the outstanding issues to be decided by the Home Secretary or Lord Advocate.[101] It seemed that this compromise would allow the Provisional Order to be presented co-jointly, which had been the original intention – but there were still problems to overcome.

The compromise, which had mollified the Collyhill Trustees, had alienated further the growing number of allies of Baillie Duffus.[102] Some fifteen Governors signed a Memorial, dated 7 June, objecting to the decision taken on the casting vote of the Lord Provost on 19 May and claiming that the majority demanded the amalgamation of the funds.[103] The Commission also received a Memorial from the ministers of Aberdeen, who objected to their reduction to one representative on the proposed Governing Body. These were among the main issues examined by the Commissioners at the second day of oral evidence on Friday 18 June 1880. Lord Provost Jamieson, Baillie Esslemont, Dean of Guild Walker and Clerk William Paul[104] all appeared again, with Baillie Duffus and Rev. Dr Beveridge[105] putting the 'minority' view, Professor Christie[106] giving the Collyhill position and Rev. Charles Macgregor[107] representing the ministers.

The Commissioners reported to the new Liberal Home Secretary, Sir William Harcourt, on 6 August 1880 and their Report was laid on the table by the Clerk of the Governors on 16 August.[108] They approved of the general purpose and tenor of the Provisional Order, holding the Scheme had been 'conceived in a wise and liberal spirit', and if sanctioned believed it could prove 'a great boon to the citizens of Aberdeen'.[109] Specifically, however, they suggested a number of changes. The instruction in the College should be chiefly in subjects likely to be of service in commercial pursuits, so as not to be the same as the Grammar School. Nonetheless, classics was not excluded from the curriculum. No power was given to provide additional schools; the existing buildings and acquisition of property adjoining the grounds were deemed sufficient. Boys belonging to the County and City of Aberdeen could join the foundation, being orphans, or those whose parents were in receipt of weekly wages, or belonging to the labouring classes. The maximum number of resident foundationers was reduced to thirty. Given the other funds available for elementary education, boys at College 'should have already made such progress in their education as to prepare them to proceed to higher education': no education was to be provided below the Fourth Standard. Eligibility for bursaries was to be extended to boys wherever they were being educated, not being restricted to just College boys. Power of appointment and dismissal of staff was to be given to the Headmaster, with the concurrence of the Governing Body. Significantly, provision was made for the amalgamation of the Collyhill Trust with the Robert Gordon's Trust under the name and title of Robert Gordon's College in Aberdeen and the Governing Body was settled at seventeen.[110] The Commissioners believed the balance of the Governing Body correct with the ministers and university representatives supporting the interests of university as opposed to commercial education.

The Governors were generally pleased with the Report but still wanted to be heard on several issues. However, as no further communication was received by mid-October the Governors began to get 'anxious'.[111] The hold-up appeared to be at the Home Office, so Lord Provost Esslemont took the initiative and pressed for a reply, which he finally received on 30 December.[112] The Education Committee, meantime, had gone through the Report on 22 December[113] and the Governors accepted its report by 16–5 on 18 January 1881. There were four issues of difference with the Commissioners and they petitioned them with their reservations on 8 February.[114]

A group of Governors were unhappy with these developments. Led again by Baillie Duffus, they favoured the replacement of the clerical Governors by two Governors from the School Board. They argued that in the present Governors, numbering 29, there were 24 popularly elected; the move to the College should mean an increase in educational representation, but in fact only eleven of the new Governing Body of seventeen were to be popularly elected. They also opposed giving the power to the Headmaster of appointing and dismissing staff. This 'minority' view had seven supporters[115] and they petitioned Lord Advocate McLaren.

The Collyhill Trustees, too, had reservations and wished the name of Simpson to be added to the College title and objected to the Governors sending off their Petition (of 8 February) without their consent or concurrence. They also claimed that it was incompetent to deal with their funds in a Petition presented by the Governors of Robert Gordon's Hospital without their agreement and reserved their legal right to challenge the Provisional Order.[116] On 23 February, W. R. Pirie petitioned the Home Secretary with these points.

The Commissioners refused to accept the Governors' view of restricting the area of selection of foundationers nor that bursaries should be restricted to College boys. However, the Commissioners accepted some modifications in the qualification for entry and accepted day schools provided no children of school age attended. The Commissioners accepted an inclusion confirming the existing powers of the Trustees but rejected adding 'Simpson' to the title. As far as the 'minority' Governors were concerned, both their points were rejected in the belief that disturbing the settlement arrived at with the Collyhill Trustees and majority of Governors would be 'unwise and inexpedient'.[117] The Commissioners agreed that they may not have arrived at the best Governing Body but it was the best and fairest compromise available.

Although there was a considerable amount of coming and going the Governors received a telegram on 10 June informing them that the Home Secretary had signed the Provisional Order.[118] However, the Governors were not out of the woods for the Order had to lie on the table of the House of Commons for forty days and could be challenged during that period. There was talk of such a challenge as a number of Governors were much aggrieved about the constitution of the Governing Body and others about the abolition of the privileges of the burgesses of guild and trade. It was felt that the Dean of Guild, John Sangster, would call a Governors' meeting and the arithmetic suggested a very close vote, perhaps a majority of two for the Order if all attended. But Sangster reluctantly accepted the situation.

Immediately the forty days were up the Clerk, William Paul, prompted by Lord Provost Esslemont, sent a letter to the Governors on 25 July[119] informing them that the Provisional Order had become law and would be put into effect on 1 August. A final meeting of the Hospital Governors would take place on 30 July. It was attended by twenty Governors and dealt mainly with routine business. The Hospital ended after 131 years without ceremony. A meeting of the College Governors was organised for 15 August.

The Hospital Balance-Sheet

During its 131 years of existence the Hospital had educated and maintained some 2,766 boys, before supporting them in their apprenticeships. In doing so the Hospital made a considerable contribution to the economic and social development of Aberdeen, giving about twenty boys a year from the 'decayed' sections of society much needed support. The ideals of Robert Gordon had been fulfilled: poverty had been relieved, boys had been looked after and in some instances their lives had been saved; in others the quality of their life had been much improved.

Even the education offered went beyond the Founder's expectations, going further than the vocational emphasis he wished. To criticise its standard misses the point. The Hospital was not a secondary school, although in its last days it was beginning to develop further in that direction. Nonetheless, despite its inherent limitations, those who attended the Hospital in the mid-19th century, provided they were diligent, were bound to leave it 'with a tolerably good education – at least for those days'. Moreover, if one compared the Hospital's education with the ordinary publicly maintained schools in Aberdeen of the same period prior to 1872[120] it is fair to contend 'that Gordon's Hospital would not suffer in the comparison'.[121]

To judge the success of the Hospital by the subsequent careers of its ex-pupils and their progress or otherwise in life would not be unreasonable, provided some allowance is made for the fact that the vast majority of its boys were drawn from the poorer classes. Background must have influenced destiny to a considerable extent, while the disadvantages of the Hospital System made it ever more difficult for boys of average ability to rise far. Moreover, when Hospital boys did do well, their successes were often not recorded, for the Registers have few details of careers included. Nevertheless, each period produced a considerable number of examples of old boys who did well and prospered.[122]

In financial terms, too, the Hospital can be judged a significant success. The Governors managed the Hospital well and by October 1879 Hospital property was valued at £184,416 sterling.[123] An abstract of the income and expenditure account for the year ending 31 October 1879 showed an excess of the former over the latter of £504.

Despite these positive features the Hospital System in general and that operating in Gordon's in particular had few defenders. The widespread belief was that the age of Hospitals had passed and if Robert Gordon's bequest was to continue it needed reform. The Education Act in Scotland now ensured that a national system would operate and all children up to the age of thirteen would receive an affordable education. To ensure that the Gordon's legacy was productive it would have to offer something more than elementary education to prevent mere duplication. This is what the Provisional Order of 1881 set out to do.

Why then had it taken thirty years to remodel the Hospital, despite the growing consensus on the failure of the Hospital System? Lack of vision and leadership were major reasons for the delay. The Chairmanship of Lord Provosts, who changed regularly, did not produce a consistency of purpose, and Headmaster Strahan lacked the power and the will to pursue reform. Nonetheless, reform had come finally and the Provisional Order of 1881 was to result, in a very short time-frame, in dramatic changes in Robert Gordon's Legacy.[124]

8

1881–1901: A GOLDEN AGE?

The College[1]

The Provisional Order of August 1881 authorised the Governors to convert the Hospital into a College or day school with the curriculum chiefly 'English Language and Literature, History and Geography, Modern Languages, Mathematics, and the elements of Physical and Natural Science'.[2] They were to reduce the number of foundationers[3] from 200 to 120 as soon as practicable, with one-quarter of them[4] to be elected by competitive examinations, open to all boys suitable in terms of age, health and character.[5] Foundationers could be boarded out.[6] The Governors could admit as many day scholars as could be accommodated on payment of fees.[7] All foundationers or day scholars needed to pass an entrance examination the equivalent of the Fourth Standard of the Education (Scotland) Code.[8] A limited number of bursaries would be available to boys residing in Aberdeen and attending not just the College but also other schools in Aberdeen.[9] The Governors could also establish day or evening classes for children and adults in technical education.[10] This latter clause, along with another giving the Governors the power to combine with other similar institutions to promote technical education,[11] was to enable the College to emulate the steps already taken in Edinburgh and Glasgow.[12]

Under the Order the power of the Headmaster was strengthened[13] and Dr Alexander Ogilvie was expected to move seamlessly from being Head of the Hospital to his new role at the College. Indeed he was immediately charged with the extra responsibility of Superintendent of Evening Classes[14] and Robert Gordon's College became one of the three Scottish 'organised science schools' receiving annual grants from the Department of Education.[15] To reflect his increased workload his salary was increased to £500 (with free house).[16] He was to conduct the entrance exam and had the power to reject any who failed.

The bursaries – equal to the level of fees – would be awarded by the Governors' Education Committee, on the advice of Ogilvie. A Curriculum Committee was set up but Ogilvie's blueprint for the College was accepted. His aim was to offer an education suitable for pupils about to enter any career in Aberdeen: this involved a common course up to thirteen/fourteen years of age and then specialisation to accommodate the proposed career.[17]

The Governors followed the Hospital Committee system to a considerable extent after 1881, with Education, Lands, House and Audit Committees all being retained. However, in the case of the first three committees their numbers were reduced from twelve to eight to reflect the decline in numbers of the Governing Body.[18] A new Finance Committee was created (numbering eight). These were appointed at the first meeting of the College Governors on 15 August 1881. The Governors then fixed the highest fee for day scholars at 15/- per session and determined that the class size for those preparing for the university Arts' class would not exceed forty in number.

The Provisional Order had stated that Headmaster, officials and servants would hold office at the pleasure of the Governors but they would only be dismissed with reasonable notice. This was put into effect with the end of boarding when the Matron and female domestic servants were dismissed on 26 May 1882.[19] Six months later the Governors confirmed all other appointments and discontinued the practice of their re-election annually[20] as had been the practice under the Hospital.

With the College now free of resident boarders, the whole premises were available for educational purposes and the roll rose to 282 by the end of the College's first session, 1881–2.[21] Ogilvie introduced his accommodation plan in 1882. The ground floor of the Auld Hoose had six classrooms (five in the west wing and one in the east wing).[22] The Headmaster's house remained in the east wing corner with three specialist rooms – Room 6, a model and apparatus room; Room 7, a lecture room; and Room 8, a laboratory.

The first floor of the Auld Hoose had four classrooms (all in the west wing).[23] The specialist rooms were Room 14, a drawing room; Room 15 for natural science; Rooms 16 and 16a, chemical labs; Room 17, a chemical classroom; and Room 18 for technical drawing. Room 19, the old laundry room under the landing, became a workshop.[24]

The Governors set up a special sub-committee, which met on 28 April 1882, to consider the appropriate seal, Coat of Arms and Motto for the College.[25] Its recommendations were largely accepted by the Governors on

15 May. The Coat of Arms in its first and fourth quarters was to have the arms of the Gordons of Pitlurg; in the second quarter the arms of Simpson of Collyhill and in its third quarter the arms of the City of Aberdeen.[26] The Governors chose a new motto[27] from Virgil – 'Omni nunc arte magistra', translated (oddly) by the Chairman of the Committee, Sir William D. Geddes, Principal of Aberdeen University as 'With every mystery that yieldeth mastery'.[28] The ancient Seal of the Founder and his coins were placed in the College safe. An Inventory[29] was made of the books, title deeds and other documents inherited from the Hospital.

Critics of the College

As the College developed, a number of critics, both external and internal, emerged. The first of these was Aberdeen's School Board which, when it commented on the curriculum of the College on 26 September 1881, disclaimed 'all selfish wishes to promote the interests of one school at the expense of another'.[30] It held that it was keen to advance the interests of the City and not to shield the Grammar School from the rivalry of Gordon's over university bursaries. The School Board claimed that Gordon's curriculum established a 'rival' to the Grammar School.[31] The Provisional Order had contained the 'seeds of opposition' which were liable to increase rather than diminish over time. As the Grammar did not possess the endowments of the College and could not reduce its fees to that proposed at the College without harming its efficiency, the School Board feared for the future of the Grammar School unless harmonious competition on separate lines could be established. For that to happen, the College should follow more closely the aim of the Commissioners and provide for education in technical and trade subjects, as well as modern subjects generally. To this end, for a few years 'the experiment should be made of teaching classics in Gordon's College only up to the point at which bifurcation takes place; and thereafter to promising Foundationers only'.[32]

In case the College rejected the curriculum restrictions proposed, the School Board had a fallback position. It suggested that the fee for the University Arts Course at Gordon's should be halved from the proposed 25/-, which was 'far beyond the means of working men' and fixed at 12/6d. In the event, the Governors agreed to go some way to meet the concerns and the fee was set at 15/-. Nonetheless, the 'feud' between the bodies, and indeed the schools, remained and flared up intermittently.[33]

Another potential external threat appeared in May 1882 when the Governors' Education Committee reported that the Educational Endowment (Scotland) Bill, proposed by Vice-President of the Council Mundella, had been scrutinised by it clause by clause. Whilst it seemed that under the Bill the Commissioners did not intend to revisit schemes already operating, such a possibility was not excluded. Moreover, provision was made for periodic audit of the College accounts. The Governors, therefore, determined to press for the insertion of a clause in the Bill which would ensure that there would be no interference with an existing Provisional Order (under the 1869 and 1878 Acts), unless the Governing Body concerned agreed, or unless the Governing Body, in the opinion of the Commissioners, had failed to give effect to the provisions of the Provisional Order.[34] Such an amendment was proposed by James Campbell, Conservative MP for Aberdeen and Glasgow Universities, but the Government did not accept it, holding that it was unnecessary as the Commissioners had no intention of interfering with existing schemes.

The news that Conservative Lord Balfour of Burleigh was to be the chairman of the new commission (and also that J. C. Campbell would be a member) helped allay anxieties and, on 18 August, the Bill, having passed through both houses, gained royal assent. The Governors were reassured but appreciated that they would still need to justify the College's progress before the Commissioners in due course.

The most important other threat to the College came from those who remained opposed to the 1881 Provisional Order. They were a small group of Governors, but their spokesmen – Rev. C. C. Macdonald, Alexander Duffus and J. C. Thompson – continued their fight at every opportunity. Essentially, they believed that the new system failed to give effect to Robert Gordon's wishes and in particular the quarter of foundationers elected by examination (and competitive bursaries) had resulted in giving benefits to a class for which the founder did not found his Hospital. Moreover, with high fees (at least in the senior classes), working-class children were wrongly being excluded from the benefits which the College should have been giving purely to necessitous children.[35]

The debate over which class was 'entitled' to attend the Hospitals had been most vigorously fought out in Edinburgh over George Heriot's bequest but, as in Aberdeen, the 'reformers' had a complete victory. Ultimately, it was difficult to argue convincingly that Robert Gordon and other Hospital founders wished to restrict their legacies to one particular class: indigent children could come from any background. It was also problematic gaining accurate information on the background of children, particularly with the majority of Governors resisting attempts to publicise the circumstances of those being presented. Vainly Macdonald claimed that his own research showed that 50% of the boys at the College were middle class. He was, however, unsuccessful in his efforts to impose a higher fee for those attending from the 'better class'. His opponents appreciated that increasing popularity of the College depended on attracting the middle class, which raised the tone and influenced the quality of the education on offer.[36]

In June 1883 Ogilvie recommended, from those who had done well in the foundationers' exam, ten boys who were accepted by the Governors for admission to the College: four (for four years) under eleven years of age, the sons of a ship carpenter, joiner, chemist and blacksmith; three (for three years) under twelve years of age, the sons of a commission agent, harbour master and house carpenter; two (for two years) under thirteen years of age, the sons of a farmer and music seller; and one (for one year), under fourteen years of age, the son of a widow. Fifteen further foundationers were elected by presentation following a home visit by the Visiting Committee of Governors – eight were between eight and ten years, and seven were between ten and eleven. The foundationers were expected to conduct themselves in a proper manner, show diligence and attend regularly; they were also examined by the College Physician to ensure that they were in good health.

The issue of Ogilvie conducting the exams remained contentious, as some Governors believed this gave College pupils an unfair advantage over pupils from Board Schools, and the large proportion of foundationers and bursars coming from the College, compared with that from other Aberdeen schools, fuelled the argument. In March 1884 the Education Committee supported Ogilvie's role and the Governing Body backed this 10–3, with Rev. C. Macdonald, Baillie Duffus and Professor Niven dissenting.[37] This group also failed to persuade the Governors to press for repeal of the clause in the Provisional Order that stipulated one-quarter of foundationers were to be elected by competitive examination.[38]

In June 1884, following the examination, Ogilvie recommended ten foundationers, who were admitted by the Governors. Their backgrounds were house carpenter, druggist, stonecutter, baker, commission agent, tailor, shipwright, tinsmith, mason and widow. Seven of the ten already attended the College. Ogilvie also recommended 27 boys who were accepted for bursaries following examination. Their fathers were shipmaster (3), grocer (2), clerk (2), joiner (2), commercial traveller (2), commission agent, printer, stonecutter, combmaker, stationer, teacher, cooper, timekeeper, upholsterer, plumber, secretary, retired civil engineer, shopkeeper, baker, merchant, and police constable. Twenty already attended the College. At the same time the Governors elected 22 foundationers by presentation and their backgrounds were seventeen widows, shore labourer, weaver, saddler, grocer's assistant and labourer. The Governors also elected 31 bursars by presentation and their backgrounds were widow (11), labourer (5), sailmaker (3), shoemaker (2), mason (2), clerk and shopman (2), coachtrimmer, cabinetmaker, stonecutter, police constable and carpenter.

In June 1885 the same pattern emerged: those doing well in the exams for foundations and bursaries came mainly from the College and from more comfortable backgrounds, while the majority being elected were coming from more disadvantaged situations, about a half having no fathers. Although this result was probably inevitable,[39] it strengthened the arguments of those Governors who wished to keep, indeed increase, the presentation element for admission.

Early Success

The College was not only a day school but also an evening school open to adults and girls as well as boys. The latter had two sections – General and Commercial,[40] and Science and Technology.[41] In session 1882–3 the growth area in evening classes was science, with some 381 individuals attending.

Ogilvie persuaded the Education Committee of the College in May 1882 of the need to appoint a Master of Science to take in hand the burgeoning science department. They looked favourably on Ogilvie's son, Francis, who had taken the degree of MA from Aberdeen University before completing a BSc at Edinburgh University. As he was already assisting Professor Niven with science classes at Marischal College and helping deliver courses at the Mechanics' Institute he was appointed immediately.[42]

Francis Ogilvie was a fine staff acquisition. He was reputed to be 'an effective teacher and a clever experimenter'[43] and 'one of the foremost of Scottish educationalists'.[44] The signs of Gordon's growing academic reputation were already there for, a few months after he arrived, the results of the annual Aberdeen University Bursary Competition were published. Boys from Gordon's College were listed for the first time in sizeable numbers.[45] The success of the school meant growing popularity: in August 1882, 360 boys attended, a year later 507, and the figure of 600 was reached by August 1884, with many being refused admission.[46] The College's rapid academic advance was praised as it stood out as a 'model of a secondary school'.[47]

The objects of the College diversified; in addition to educating foundationers, the traditional role of the Hospital, it now aimed to offer a good secondary education at fees low enough to be within the reach of the working class, to help its own scholars and boys leaving Board Schools to gain a knowledge of subjects not otherwise readily attainable, and to furnish instruction in science and technology of a higher grade to the apprentice and artisan. In short, the College aimed at being a complete and efficient secondary school, forming a much-needed and much-desired link between elementary and university education. The Governors rejected the model of an 'apprenticeship school': it was not geared to teaching a trade but instead to laying the foundations of scientific and technical knowledge which was an 'essential concomitant of trade experience and manual dexterity'.[48]

Developments at Schoolhill

The City of Aberdeen was keen to establish an Art Gallery, Industrial Museum and Exhibition Centre and in May 1882 the City Chamberlain wrote to the Governors asking them to contribute financially to this cause, provided they found it proper and expedient to do so.[49] They did so, giving £250, despite Rev. Charles Macdonald believing it was squandering Robert Gordon's money. Encouraged by the support, the Art Gallery Committee Promoters inquired if the Governors would consider selling them land parallel to the front of the College.[50] Following the valuation by William Smith,[51] on 16 September 1882 the Governors agreed 11–2[52] to sell the site for a proposed Art Gallery: it was composed of a block of land of 1988 square yards and measuring 90 feet from the south-west corner of the College property northwards along the west boundary wall, and from there 160 feet eastward, along a line drawn parallel to the front of the College buildings. The Porter's Lodge was to be moved and re-erected at the entrance of the College by the Art Gallery promoters. With entry offered in June 1883 the price was £3250.

With these plans progressing, the Governors, following the lead of Lord Provost Esslemont,[53] decided that, as the paving in Schoolhill was being widened to accommodate the Art Gallery, they should do likewise on the east side by removing the Old Grammar School buildings.[54] This decision encouraged John Gray,[55] head of the firm of William Mackinnon, Engineers and Ironfounders, to write to Esslemont, on 11 October 1883, offering to provide a School of Science and Art for Aberdeen.

Gray contended that the existing accommodation provided in the Mechanics' Institute for a School of Science and Art was very unsuitable and he wanted a new School built in connection with, and in proximity to, the Art Gallery,[56] which was being erected beside the College.[57] He believed that if the Institute was relieved of the School of Science and Art, its building could be converted into a Public Library at comparatively little cost. Moreover, the Institute Directors were ready and willing to hand over the Institute's own library and their building to the Town Council should it agree to adopt the Public Libraries' Act, which would result in a great boon to the working classes of Aberdeen.[58]

Gray's proposals went further. He wished the College Governors to create the new School of Science and Art on the site of the Old Grammar School buildings, east of the College entrance. If the Governors agreed, Gray was willing to pay for the erection of 'Gray's School of Science and Art'. To ensure that the new building would be in harmony with the design of the new Art Gallery, Gray had commissioned such a plan from Matthews and Mackenzie, the Art Gallery's architects. Once the Gray's School building was complete, the Governors would be expected to take over its running as the School was to become self-supporting through fees.[59]

The acceptance of Gray's generous offer was the last official act of Lord Provost Esslemont, as he retired from the Governing Body in November 1883. The Governors were fulsome in their praise of him, believing that he was responsible for guiding them from Hospital to College and making possible the other exciting developments taking place at Schoolhill. His successor, James Matthews,[60] an ex-Hospital boy, whose firm of architects was involved in the building, presided at the opening ceremony of Gray's School on 16 November 1885 with the Earl of Crawford and Balcarres as guest speaker.

To complete the frontage of Schoolhill, John Gray wished the Art Gallery and Art School to be linked together by an artistic archway and gate. The resulting elliptical arch, springing from fluted pilasters, with mouldings and panelleled spandrils, were all of clean-dressed Corrennie granite, the whole being surmounted by a graceful pediment.[61] In October 1886, the Directors of the Mechanics' Institute used part of the residue of their funds to erect the highly ornamental, wrought-iron gates at the entrance to the College. One of the two bronze shields was inscribed to commemorate the transference of the Institution's work and a proportion of its property and funds to Gordon's.[62]

The School of (Science and) Art, as originally constructed, was composed of six classrooms in which day and evening classes were held. It cost £5000 to build.[63] In its first session 1885–6 some 96 enrolled for day classes and 322 for evening classes.[64] Although the Governors and Ogilvie had direct control of the School, between 1885 and 1909 its Master, John P. Fraser, enjoyed a great deal of autonomy.[65]

In August 1887 the Town Clerk informed the Governors that the subscribers to a statue of General Gordon of Khartoum[66] wanted it erected opposite the gateway to the College. A group from the Improvement Committee of the Council proceeded to Schoolhill on 11 April 1888 and selected the precise site for the bronze statue, designed by Stuart Burnett of Edinburgh.[67] The Governors 'acquiesced'[68] in the decision which was to be understandably confusing for citizens in the years following as General Gordon had no connection whatsoever with Robert Gordon or Gordon's Legacy. Nonetheless the statue was placed on a strip of land on Schoolhill which had been given over to the Council by the Governors in 1885 in return for laying down proper footpaths, and it was unveiled by the Marquis of Huntly on 16 June 1888.

Balfour Commission

The arrival of the Balfour Commission on Educational Endowments (Scotland) in Aberdeen in October 1885 gave another opportunity to the supporters and critics of Gordon's College to set out their cases. On Friday 2 October in the Town Hall the Commissioners heard Lord Provost Matthews explain the development of Gordon's from a Hospital of 200 foundationers to a College of 800 – comprising 120 foundationers, 60 bursars[69] and 620 fee-payers – not to mention the evening classes. He believed that in the completeness of its equipment as a great school for elementary and higher education, in the efficiency of its management and in the excellence and success of its teaching, the College invited 'comparison with any other similar institution in the kingdom'.[70]

Alexander Gill, chairman of the College Education Committee, was less effusive and more defensive. He admitted that a number of pupils of well-to-do parents attended the College although 'we do not wish to take them, as we do not want to introduce many of that class into our school'. He claimed that the College had less than 10% of that class and the Governors were unwilling to differentiate fees because 'it would create a bad feeling in the school', as the boys would know who was rich and who was poor. A list of occupations could be made available to the Commissioners but the Governors refused to publish it widely.[71]

The critics of the College had a spokesman in Rev. Charles Macdonald, who, during his three years on the College Governing Body, had consistently fought what he considered was a 'very hopeless battle'.[72] He believed the College had been turned into a 'middle-class institution',[73] which was incompatible with its original foundation for the needy. Professor Minto of the Aberdeen School Board suggested the Commission examine the development of the classical side of the College. He wanted all the boys at Gordon's who were fit for university to be sent to the Grammar School for their classical training otherwise there would remain a duplication and wastage of resources.[74] Rev. J. Myers Danson, chair of the School Board and a Governor of the College, thought the Grammar School had a real grievance, and the fees of the College should be raised to the level of the Grammar School.[75]

James Moir, Rector of the Grammar School since 1881, voiced his concerns.[76] Given that the Grammar had the lowest fees in a public secondary in Scotland he resented a rival with significantly lower fees, especially as it was richly endowed. The College's Provisional Order of 1881 had made no mention, in the curriculum laid down for Gordon's, of Latin and Greek (for the University Bursary competiton) and other subjects necessary for the Law and Medicine Preliminary Exams. If the College wished to give a classical education it should charge the same fee as the Grammar or send the scholars to the Grammar. Moir held that in the past three years some forty to fifty boys had left the Grammar to go to Gordon's because of its lower fees, and the middle class were edging the poor out of their birthright.

The Governors responded, emphasising that the Hospital was originally for the 'decayed' merchant class, and although they did not wish to be swamped by 'well-to-do' parents the introduction of differential fees would be invidious. To keep Latin and Greek subordinate the College had introduced their own rule restricting the number taking the subjects to forty, and the actual number being taught classics was currently 26.[77] The Governors claimed that when they offered to transfer classical scholars to the Grammar in return for the transfer of technical scholars to the College the School Board had rejected the proposal.

Although Moir failed to convince the Commissioners that the College's rivalry and competition were unfair, a number of Governors felt some sympathy for his arguments. Originally their concern had been over the arrangements for foundationers and bursars – the legacy of the Hospital – and in the desire to enable working-class parents to afford the fees they determined to keep the fees as low as possible. As larger numbers of better-off parents began to send their children to the College and seemed to be taking up more and more places it was important to review fee levels.

As a result, in June 1887, a fee differential scheme was introduced for the first time.[78] The fees for orphans, sons and grandsons of decayed burgesses of guild and trade, and boys of the industrial and lower middle class from Board Schools were reduced and ranged from 7/6 to 15/- a quarter. The fees for children from other groups and classes were increased and ranged from 15/- to 35/- a quarter.

The result, however, was a loss of revenue and the College went into the red. In June 1888 the Governors decided 11–2 to introduce three levels of fees: lowest 10/- to 15/-; middle 15/- to 25/-; and highest 25/- to 35/-. This system lasted until 1894 when an even more complex fee arrangement was introduced, with differentials based on locality (Aberdeen City or County and elsewhere) and wages.[79] A breakdown of the statistics of fee payers in 1895–6 confirms the influx of better-paid parents to the College since Hospital days:[80] regarding City parents the middle group comprised 37%, the lowest group 33% and the highest group 30%; regarding County parents the middle group comprised 54%, with both other groups comprising 23% each. By this time the College had 120 foundationers, 116 bursars and 612 fee-payers (total 848).[81]

Before the Balfour Commission produced detailed proposals, the College and its relationship with the Grammar School came under scrutiny again, when the Committee, under Charles S. Parker,[82] appointed to inquire into certain Scottish educational questions looked into secondary education.[83] In Aberdeen the problem, according to Rector Moir, revolved round the lack of resources for the Grammar School, which 'got not one penny from the rates'. Moir again complained that he was losing pupils to Gordon's, which was teaching classics at low fees.[84] However, according to Professor Struthers,[85] the College was attracting parents because 'it is a better school'. Indeed, he described it as 'the best secondary school I know'.[86] Struthers praised the scientific education of Gordon's in particular, comparing its two well-qualified staff with the one less well-qualified Grammar teacher.

The Grammar was defended before the Committee by Dr D. Ross, Rector of Glasgow Normal School, a representative of the main teaching union, the Educational Institute of Scotland (EIS). He claimed the Grammar School was in a better condition than in 1872 (when the School Board took over its running) and cited the most recent Board report which highlighted success in the University Bursary Competition and the satisfaction of HMI.[87] Ross did not mention, however, that there had been some concern about the Grammar and its leadership for some time, which was not shared with the Committee. Moir himself had arrived following an inquiry[88] but as the 1880s progressed increasing parent complaints were to lead to a further inquiry into 'tone and discipline' in a Grammar School where Moir and his staff were increasingly at odds. It seems that the general rowdiness and widespread insubordination within the School were driving parents to Gordon's – the lower fees were but a bonus.[89]

On the tenth day of evidence taking, on Tuesday 31 May 1887, at Marischal College, Headmaster Ogilvie was questioned.[90] He viewed the developments at the College since 1881 as 'an immense gain'[91] especially for the foundationers who now associated with boys of all classes. Following Balfour's recommendations the Governors had just decided, while restricting foundationers to the class which required assistance, that two-thirds of them would be awarded following competitive exam.[92] The Governors had also decided, again following Balfour, that the fees for the 'higher class'[93] were to be raised to the level of the Grammar School[94] as an experiment for one year, although he was concerned about the implications. Ogilvie would try to prevent boys learning what scale of fees they would be on. For Ogilvie, as indeed for educational opinion generally, the change at Gordon's since 1881 had exceeded all expectations.

The Parker Committee sympathised with the plight of the Grammar School. Given that the School Board appeared apathetic toward secondary education, Parker recommended direct grants to aid secondary schools. However, the Committee also gave a ringing endorsement of schools like Gordon's, believing its mixture of classes was one of its best features.[95] Its success was 'conspicuous'. Like George Watson's in Edinburgh, Gordon's College had prospered because of its ample funds, enlightened management and the skilful organisation of its Headmaster. School Boards should follow its example and give full authority to their Heads, for such a concentration of power was deemed a key factor in the success of the College.

The Balfour Commission had been impressed with the development of the College and contented itself with a tidying-up process for the College while recommending a series of measures for the remaining unreformed Hospitals in Aberdeen,[96] which were consolidated and placed under the newly created Aberdeen Educational Trust from November 1888.[97] This body also took under its control MacRa's Trust (created 1763), Thain's Charity (1788), Davidson's

Endowment (1803), Chalmers' Girls' School (1836), Brown's School (1847) and Ross's School, Holburn (1861) and their assets.[98]

Failure of Draft Scheme

The proposals of the Balfour Commissioners for the College were discussed by the Governors on 7, 14 and 16 March 1888. Practically all the clauses were agreed to unanimously except those relating to the issue of Competition versus Patronage. Clause 30 of the Draft Scheme resulted in a two and a half hour debate on 23 March. The Town Treasurer Walker opposed the Commissioners' attempt to end presentation (Patronage) completely, believing that the very poor would lose out. Instead he wanted half of the 120 foundationers, aged between eight and twelve years, to be elected by presentation. He held that under presentation, in 1885, 22 of 31, under the age of eleven years, were orphans and, in 1886, twelve of 21 orphans, while, in 1887, under competition there were none from fourteen.

Baillie Berry supported Walker's proposal to return to admitting boys at eight years of age as stipulated by the Founder's Deed. Between 1750 and 1887 boys had been taken in at that age, and it had only been changed with a narrow majority. In 1881, he claimed 200 poor boys cost £33 p.a. each (with total expenditure £6,600), while in 1887 120 foundationers at £15/12/- maintenance and £3 fee, and 50 Bursaries at £3 each meant a total of only £2382 being spent on the class Robert Gordon specified in his Deed (with £4218 being spent on others). Dean of Guild Stewart feared that the College would become an educational institution based on merit as opposed to the Founder's vision of a kindly, Christian charity. He believed that the Governors could not end education of children below ten years of age without replacing it with the provision of free education at other schools. George Maconnachie thought it a disgrace that wealthy parents sent their children to the College, which was not Robert Gordon's intention.

The Commissioners had rejected presentation, believing it was open to corruption and manipulation, preferring competitive examination. A number of Governors, a slight majority of the total, agreed. Rev. J. M. Danson thought presentation failed to do justice to the poor, as it failed to select the most indigent. For him presentation was 'election by wire-pulling'.[99] It also created two classes of foundationer. He believed competition would raise standards. Principal Geddes stressed how Robert Gordon valued his money. Now with elementary education being provided by the state to all under age ten, the

Governors had to protect the Founder's endowment and not fritter it away. Lord Provost William Henderson[100] saw the new proposed Order as 'a very great improvement' upon the 1881 one. He wanted to leave it to their successors to ensure that only proper children benefited from foundations. He carried the day by 9–8.[101]

Treasurer Walker's fight was not over. At the next Governors' meeting on 28 March he tried to amend Clause 33 by introducing presentation for half of the fifty bursaries being proposed. The voting was exactly the same as five days before: 9–8 for the Lord Provost with no change of mind on either side.[102]

The other clauses proved non-contentious and the Draft Scheme went first to the Commissioners for their comment and amendment before being forwarded to the Scotch Education Department (SED) for its approval. While this was going on Treasurer Walker tried again to overturn previous decisions and, on 2 August, he was ruled out of order by the Chair, Lord Provost Henderson. In response Walker accused Henderson of being 'worse than the Parnellites' in his obstructionism.[103] Although several Governors left the meeting following Henderson's ruling and the lack of a quorum meant the end of the proceedings, Walker appeared to have gained a majority for his view. He, therefore, organised a Memorial to be sent to the SED on Clauses 30 and 33 claiming that the majority of Governors now wanted the age of eight years to be the lower limit of admission to the College.[104]

With a seeming change in the balance in the Governing Body, the dissident Governors pressed to reopen discussion of the issues which had been decided narrowly in March. At the Governors' meeting on 7 September they did so and, without opposition, modified Clauses 30 and 33 of the Draft Scheme. The minority had now become the majority! The date for objections to the Commissioners' proposals had passed but the new changes were nonetheless forwarded with a plea that they be taken into account.

The Conservative Government was in a quandary, being unsympathetic to the new stance of the Governors. It delayed until pressurised to act. The Secretary of State for Scotland, the Marquis of Lothian, finally agreed to hear representations on 14 December 1888 in London. Walker, Stewart and Maconnachie went and set out their case. Independently, another deputation of James Paterson, Convener of Education, and Rev. Gordon Murray also attended and reinforced the stance of March 1888, still supported by eight Governors led by Lord Provost Henderson.[105]

By March 1889, the Governors rescinded previous decisions and the age of admission returned to eight years of age by 10 votes to 6 after a heated meeting. During it Rev. W. D. Scott was anxious about 'the safety of the furniture' on several occasions.[106]

The sorry business ended meantime on 26 November 1889 when the SED, following further communication with the Commissioners, decided that, given the difference in opinion among the Governors and the changed arrangements about to arrive with the Local Government (Scotland) Act of 1889, it was inexpedient to proceed further at this time with the Draft Scheme.[107]

A Golden Age?

If progress was not made in this area it was made on nearly all other fronts. As a Higher-Class School, inspection of Gordon's by the SED[108] was compulsory. Between 25–27 March 1886 Professor John Birrell of the University of St Andrews and Professor Alexander Kennedy of University College, London, visited Schoolhill. They commended the school timetable and the fair assignment of time for the subjects in the curriculum, and in particular justified the propriety of having a classical side.[109] Ogilvie was singled out for especial praise.

The College produced an Annual Prospectus, which in 1886 listed the staff of eighteen experienced teachers under Ogilvie. The Mathematics Department was led by Basil McLellan[110] (appointed in March 1878 from Glasgow Academy) with support from James Dale (a survivor from a different age, having been appointed in July 1859). Science was under John Buchanan[111] (who replaced Francis Ogilvie in June 1886) and William Lowrie,[112] whose appointment developed natural science. Classics was led by George Bruce[113] and then William Riddoch,[114] while English was under Charles Stewart. Each of the full-time staff had charge of a separate class in a separate room and all were under the personal supervision of the Headmaster, whose duty it was to see that each boy was in the class for which his age and abilities best fitted him, and that the pupils' school time was properly distributed over the subjects of study, and, in short, to aid and direct pupils, teachers and parents.[115]

Following a Circular of 15 January 1886, the Secretary of the SED, Henry Craik, moved forward on 14 November 1887 with the proposal for an outgoing Certificate for pupils of Higher-Class Schools by asking for comments. Ogilvie and the Governors' Education Committee supported the plan, and, following endorsement by the Parker Committee, the first Leaving Certificate

Examinations took place nationally in June 1888. Of the 189 certificates applied for by 49 College pupils, some 169 were awarded (including four at Honours and five at First Grade).[116]

The first of a number of annual HMI inspections by T. A. Stewart was carried out in June 1888. He was very impressed with discipline and order at the College which he deemed 'admirable'. The boys exhibited 'concentration, politeness, eagerness and intelligence'. A competent staff – with Riddoch ('able and thorough'), Stewart ('admirable') and McLellan ('a marvel to witness') being worthy of particular mention – worked harmoniously under Ogilvie, who showed 'very rare professional ability'.[117] Stewart had no suggestions for improvement to make until his fourth report in June 1891. Then in an otherwise glowing report he floated the idea of adding a gymnasium to the College. Ogilvie must have been surprised, unused to implied criticism. He reacted badly, at least at first, dismissing the idea. No parent had mentioned the issue to him and his priority was more classroom space for academic subjects.[118]

During the later 1880s the College had consolidated its position in the University Bursary Competition but it is difficult to describe the sensation caused by the publication of the Arts Competition list of 1889, when the College appeared top of the order for the first time and had seven boys in the top ten. Even Ogilvie must have been surprised how, by the early 1890s, Gordon's had come to dominate, as the College gained first bursar in 1889, 1890, 1891 and 1892.[119] In 1890 Gordon's had seventeen boys, compared with twelve from the Grammar School, in the list.[120] Ten years after the end of the Hospital, Gordon's had overtaken its main rival, whose whole rationale had been based on gaining success in this one area.[121] The Town Council showed its appreciation by presenting in July 1892, for the first time, a gold and silver medal to be awarded annually to the Dux of the College's Science (Modern) School and Classical School respectively.[122] In that year, College pupils also gained 309 Leaving Certificates (including 14 at Honours and 72 at Higher).

HMI Stewart produced his usual excellent report in June 1893. The College had 'a strong man as the masterly head, and pillars of strength in charge of the various departments – Messrs Stewart in English, McLellan in Mathematics, Riddoch in Classics,[123] and Buchanan in Science; and a carefully selected phalanx of promising young teachers, of excellent mettle, who are all ambitious to rise higher in their profession'. But Stewart had a surprise and proved he was not one whose ideas could be dismissed easily. Although very efficient the education offered by the College was 'lopsided'. It needed a large hall for exams, exhibitions, concerts and gymnastics; formation of a cricket or football club, or both, and the acquisition of a field; and the introduction of physical drill of all kinds – gun drill (perhaps a germ of a Rifle Corps), dumb bells, Indian clubs and gymnastics generally.

Even in these days a Head needed to follow HMI recommendations! Ogilvie could not ignore such advice. He determined to ensure that Gordon's curriculum and facilities could not be faulted. He persuaded the Governors to buy the Blackfriars' Street Chapel, a transaction completed in February 1895 for £1000.[124] It cost another £2500 for Jenkins and Marr, architects, to make the appropriate alterations and equip the new gym with the latest equipment available. It was opened on 13 November 1896 by Sir Arthur Grant of Monymusk. Ogilvie was pleased when HMI Buckmaster hailed it to be 'equal to that of any school I have ever visited'. This seemed to be borne out by Ogilvie's own reports to his Governors. In 1894–5 he claimed the discipline of the College to be perfect. 'Not one case of flagrant misconduct has been brought under my notice in connection with either Day or Evening Classes.'[125]

Fate of the Boys

Ogilvie was particularly proud of ex-pupil successes at university. In 1895–6 he boasted that for the fifth time in seven years the First bursar in the Arts Faculty Bursary Competition came from Gordon's and that in every university faculty with such a competition – Arts, Divinity, Law and Medicine – the first bursar was from the College. All six 'great' prizes in Arts went to ex-pupils; three former pupils were admitted to the Indian Civil Service; and William G. Fraser (of the 1889 class) had become Senior Wrangler at Cambridge University. In the 1900 Aberdeen University graduation lists some 26 ex-pupils gained Arts degrees (nine with Honours), four in Science[126] and eight in Medicine (three with Honours).

There was also a step-change upwards in the careers of boys after 1881. Gordon's boys began to flood into the ranks of the professions in Aberdeen and far beyond. They were successful in their hundreds. At least nine educated at the College in the last two decades of the 19th century gained knighthoods: an engineer (William Noble), a scientist (Arthur Keith), a financier (John Ferguson,[127]) a soldier (Andrew Skeen), a civil servant (James Donald), an administrator (Alexander Roger), a surgeon (Gordon Gordon-Taylor) and two academics (William Calder and Robert Wallace). Those who probably deserved such an award are too numerous to mention.[128]

Since 1881, too, evening classes had increased significantly in numbers and courses offered. Chemistry and botany classes had been helpful in developing chemists and druggists. In April 1898 the Secretary of the Aberdeen Pharmaceutical Association requested that the College establish a School of Pharmacy to prepare students for the Pharmaceutical Society's examinations. Ogilvie and the Education Committee negotiated an agreement with the local Association, which offered to share the costs of establishing the new School and give over all apparatus, chemicals etc belonging to the Association and used in the work of the classes. The Governors determined to go ahead and in August 1898 Hugh E. Ellis was appointed master and full courses, by day and evening classes, were offered for the qualifying exams of the Pharmaceutical Society of Great Britain. A Prospectus was issued – the subjects included organic and inorganic chemistry, physics, theoretical pharmacy, practical pharmacy and dispensing, botany, materia medica and prescription reading. The School of Pharmacy functioned from the main College building.[129]

Ogilvie's Achievement

With little left to achieve and advancing in years, Ogilvie requested, on 18 March 1901, that he be allowed to retire at the end of session in June. At the Education Committee meeting on 28 March, it was moved that applicants for his post be invited by public advertisement while an attempt to recommend Charles Stewart, Senior English Master at the College, as Headmaster,[130] was lost 7–4. At the Governors' meeting on 3 April, a further effort to appoint Stewart failed by 9 votes to 5. Nonetheless the bandwagon for Stewart was truly underway. The salary for the new Head was fixed at £550 p.a. and a generous annual retiring allowance of £250 was agreed for Ogilvie.[131] The Governors were effusive in their praise for 'the Potter'.[132] 'Essentially his has been the spirit that has animated the whole College . . . He hands over the College in the highest state of efficiency.'[133] The many tributes were well–deserved. Ogilvie had brought the School a long way in a short time. Yet he left a competitive school with no developed school interests besides work.

The Governors scrutinised the applications of the eighteen candidates for the headship on 21 May. Ten were principals or rectors of institutions, six of them working in Scotland. A short-leet of two was agreed upon[134] – John Macdonald, MA, BSc, PhD, Rector of Dunfermline High School, and Charles Stewart, MA. The Governors decided not to interview the candidates formally, which left the supporters of the well-qualified Macdonald angry, as they knew that Stewart would win an immediate vote, which he did by 9–5.[135] He accepted the post in writing the following day and made an early decision to teach ten hours a week of English along with the onerous roles of Headmaster of the College and Superintendent of the Evening Classes.

Ogilvie went into retirement. During his tenure he had 'made his energising force felt throughout the School. He was far from a figurehead, being vigilant and pervasive, less of a Headmaster than an experience to be lived through'.[136] His career had been an outstanding success. As early as 1883 he had been awarded an LL.D. by Aberdeen University for his services to Scottish education and he gave 29 years devoted service to Gordon's.[137] On 30 May 1901 in a tribute HMI G. Macdonald put on record that: 'Aberdeen will regret the loss of one who had rendered such conspicuous service to education in the north . . . He leaves Gordon's College in the very front rank of Scottish secondary schools.'[138]

Paradoxically, that had not been the intention when the Hospital had been reformed in 1881. Following Colebrooke, the Balfour Commission gave Gordon's, like Heriot's in Edinburgh and Allan Glen's in Glasgow, an 'artisan' mission thought appropriate to its charitable origins.[139] Its workshops and laboratories, low fees and numerous bursaries were aimed at offering a practical, modern curriculum.[140] The Provisional Order had hoped to discourage university ambitions and promote technical education, as well as develop a wide social recruitment. However, Ogilvie and the Governors were not immune from a cultural prejudice against practical and utilitarian education. The prestige of classics and the universities meant that socially mobile Scots aimed at the professions rather than commerce or industry, while at lower levels there was a desire to become clerks or white-collar workers rather than get dirty hands in industry.[141] The balance, therefore, had swung away from technical education and it was expected that Stewart would follow the path set out by Ogilvie. It was a surprise, then, to find that Stewart was his own man and he, for one, had not given up on a different vision for Gordon's.

9

1901–20: THE 'CUCKOO IN THE NEST'?

Growing Concerns

Charles Stewart was born on 16 November 1859 in Kirkmichael, Banffshire, into a farming family. He attended the village school at Tomintoul. When he left he worked as a student teacher during the day while he studied at night to gain entry to Aberdeen University, which he did with a bursary in 1879. He graduated MA in 1883, one of the best English scholars of his year, and was appointed to the staff of Gordon's College by Headmaster Ogilvie. He worked hard and gained a reputation as an enthusiastic and inspiring teacher. His discipline and administration were excellent and he was increasingly relied upon by Ogilvie, who viewed Stewart as his right-hand man.

Stewart's appointment as Ogilvie's successor was popular in the College with staff and boys.[1] Despite his desire to continue his teaching he soon had to cut back to five hours a week. This was a great loss, for, with Basil McLellan and George Morrison, he was an important part of the team which was so successful in ensuring success for the boys in the Bursary Competition.[2] However, Stewart was soon engrossed in the problems surrounding the expansion of the nearby Central Public School.

In February 1899 the School Board informed the Governors of their proposal to enlarge and reconstruct the Central School with a view to it being reorganised as a Higher Grade (Science) School.[3] With a new frontage on Schoolhill and Belmont Street the new school would take a further 600 and be connected by corridor to the existing building which would take elementary pupils. It was to cost £22,500 and it would include a hall, gymnasium, workshops, laboratory, art and science rooms, and eleven classrooms. The plans were designed to create 'one of the finest and most complete schools of its kind in the north of Scotland',[4] and were bound to affect existing schools.[5]

In developing a school aimed at pupils considering a trade or some line of business at fifteen or sixteen, the School Board threatened not just Gordon's but also the modern side of the Grammar School. So the Board sensibly determined to review the educational provision city-wide, and in doing so discussed the possibility of effecting a redistribution of the higher education for boys. For it, the ideal would be for Gordon's to be the organised Science School and the Grammar to be the Classical School of Aberdeen. This would end duplication and, given that both schools would be sharing the educational work of the city, both would be equally supported from the rates. Although the Governors would need to give over their educational work to the School Board it would retain management of its own property and administration of its funds. There would also be no interference with the patronage of the College Trust, as the Governors could continue to determine the conditions of foundationers and bursaries, and elect beneficiaries.

The Governors met a delegation from the School Board on 7 March 1899, but any possibility of an agreement was dashed by Ogilvie's devastating Memorandum, which he produced on 21 March. For him the scheme was superfluous as the College already met the wants of the lower middle and working classes. He estimated that if the Central School went ahead the theoretical loss for Gordon's could be 118[6] plus later losses in senior years. If the Governors accepted the redistribution proposals the College would lose its four lowest classes (209 boys), the whole of the classical school (124 boys) and about 125 in the middle divisions whose advanced education would be on classical lines, but would gain 100 Grammar School pupils, so in total the theoretical loss would be 358.

However, for Ogilvie, it was not the hypothetical losses which were crucial but the impracticality of the proposals. He deemed that it was impossible for meaningful decisions to be made between a literary and scientific curriculum at the early age of twelve. Instead he suggested the way to provide for additional pupils, aged from twelve to fifteen, without dislocating existing institutions and without burdening the community with considerable charges, would be to offer them free places at the College and Grammar School. The Governors were persuaded by these arguments and on 27 March they voted 14–2 not to continue discussing the matter unless and until the School Board had more concrete and practical plans.[7]

The School Board did not give up and another deputation met with the Governors again on 16 June. However, the Governors did not move from their previous position and refused to discuss the abolition of the College Trust as an educational body. Nonetheless, they conceded the need to produce an arrangement with the help of the Scottish Education Department (SED) provided it protected the interests of existing institutions.

The SED, under Craik, argued that Aberdeen could not be left out of the new arrangements, for that would mean forfeiting the grants offered, and noted that Ogilvie's proposal would also exclude the Board from an important part of the work carried on elsewhere by School Boards.[8] The SED played down the effect that the proposals would have on the College, despite the insistence of the School Board to continue talks because the plans would 'seriously militate against the interests of the College'.

The Governors argued in a communication to the SED, dated 1 August 1899, that the position of the proposed Higher Grade (Science) School, at the gate of the College, and the free education it offered, would draw a large proportion of lower-middle and working class boys from the College. The continued existence of Gordon's 'School of Science' would be in jeopardy from severe, unfair competition. They asked for a deputation of Governors to be heard before final decisions were made. On 8 August the SED restated its position but held it was anxious to prevent overlapping of educational provision or any undue interference with existing institutions, and was willing to discuss the whole question of school provision.

It took till March 1901 for the School Board to put its formal proposal to the SED. The model being adopted was unusual in Scotland:[9] all 26 elementary schools desirous of instruction beyond Sixth Standard Stage (after Merit Certificate) were to be concentrated in the one school, the Central (Higher Grade) School. It would be the 'natural crown' to the Board's elementary school system and a desirable addition to the educational facilities of Aberdeen.[10] It would cater for a class not able to pay secondary fees and in many cases their attendance would represent the self-denial of parents who would keep children at school when others of their class had already become wage-earners. Thus it would do no injury to the College.

The Governors were quick to point out the inconsistencies between the School Board statements of March 1901 and the remarks made by the Chair of the Board, Rev. Dr Robertson, in March 1899, when he was part of a deputation to the Governors. Then he had claimed that 150–200 were at the College paying fees of between £2 and £7 a quarter for an education that they would be offered free at the Higher Grade School, and it was unlikely that Aberdonians would continue to do this for long. The Governors also claimed that the Board held the school aimed at completing elementary education and so would have no fees, but it was actually beginning secondary education, and as such should charge fees.[11] It was believed that the proposed school would thus place the College in a 'perilous position' and the effect would be 'to deal a fatal blow at the prosperity of the College'.[12]

The School Board's position hardened, given the support of the SED, and it rejected the offer of tripartite discussions. In September 1901, the SED agreed to the Board's application and approved their plans. The matter may have rested there but for Headmaster Stewart, who placed a Memorandum before the Governors in November 1901.[13] He took up an entirely different position from Ogilvie. His view was that there was a need for such a school as was proposed, as the Higher Grade School (Central) and Secondary School (Gordon's), after Sixth Standard, would pursue paths which could be parallel for a year but which diverged increasingly in successive years. Stewart suggested a joint Committee for fixing spheres of work and an allocation of pupils to both schools. Gordon's would take those intending to aim at university, and the others would attend the Central. The Governors saw this as a positive, progressive response and had two meetings with the School Board to work out details. However, talks stalled and no agreement was reached. The arrangement was seen as 'too exclusively' in Gordon's interests by Morland Simpson, Rector of the Grammar School, and Headmaster Wallace of the Central School was a trenchent critic believing that the plan 'absorbed' its potential rival and was one-sided and undesirable.[14]

The Governors returned to the issue in November 1904 when it was discussed privately by them. They still viewed the opening of the Central School, which was planned for June 1905, as a very serious development. By now Stewart had apparently refined his position. Co-ordination of the work of the College and the School Board 'ideally' would lead to the Grammar School devoted to the literary and classical side, the Central School as the chief Higher Grade School and Gordon's College should be converted into a great technical school. Stewart, it seems, was returning to the ideas of Colebrooke in the 1870s, but now as a way of ensuring the survival of the College in a new guise.

Such thinking was advanced by growing concerns over a proposed Scottish Education Bill, which the Lord Advocate introduced in March 1905. It envisaged new district School Boards with sweeping powers to develop education with resources being supplied from the rates. The Governors were anxious about where they could turn to for financial help if they needed such support. By September 1905 Convener Kemp of Finance was pessimistic: unless the finances of the College were augmented, its educational work would need to be curtailed. A deficit was expected in the coming year of £1018 as a result of a proposed reduction in Government grants. The future of the College was 'uncertain, not to say insecure'.[15]

Technical Education

The Conservative Education Bill came to grief when an amendment to retain small School Boards was passed and with the parliamentary session drawing to a close, the Government dropped the Bill.[16] One effect of this was unspent monies, which had been put aside to finance proposals within the Bill, now had to be reallocated. It was decided that significant sums should be given over to technical education.[17] The College Governors acted immediately and on 24 October 1905 proposed a new Technical College in Aberdeen by means of extending the existing Art School and erecting a new building for engineering and building. Struthers[18] of the SED replied on 16 December encouraging the local authority to make proposals based on the needs of the locality. Such a 'favourable opportunity' could not be missed and the Governors lost no time in proposing a Conference, which was held under the chairmanship of Lord Provost Alexander Lyon,[19] also President of the College Governors, on Friday 11 May 1906. The Conference[20] focused public attention on the matter and helped harness the widespread, and growing, support for a Technical College for the north-east of Scotland.

A Sub-Committee of the Conference met on 8 June and discussed the role of the College in technical education and whether its primary and secondary work could be better undertaken by other bodies. Headmaster Stewart and architect Allan of the School Board were asked to draw up a full report with illustrative plans as soon as possible. They visited technical schools in Scotland and England and their exhaustive Report proposed a new building between the College and Art School/Galleries at an estimated cost of £62,000 and a second school, a Nautical College, near the harbour, at £20,000. At Schoolhill they envisaged Schools of Engineering (occupying 36,600 square feet), Architecture (11,676 square feet), Chemistry (8,345 square feet) and Artistic Crafts (11,380 square feet).

By the time of the next Sub-Committee meeting on 16 October 1906, a significant influx of local support had come on board. Stewart's Report was accepted and the scheme for technical education was agreed in principle. The SED was kept informed of developments and the College Governors and Harbour Board were to be approached regarding sites. The Aberdeen newspapers were also supportive but the *Free Press* suggested that if the Governors took over the proposed Technical College then its elementary and secondary education functions should be handed over to the School Board: this would end unfair rivalry with the Grammar School, and set their buildings and revenue free for technical education. Similarly the Aberdeen Educational Trust could lose cooking and laundry classes to the Technical College, and the rest of its educational work given over to the School Board, relieving revenue for a splendid endowment.[21]

The improved relationship between the School Board and the Governors, helped by co-operation on evening classes,[22] led to a conference on 15 November 1906 between them and from this resulted a joint-committee to advance further co-operation in the field of day school work.[23] The Governors encouraged the School Board to produce definite proposals and the SED seemed to be in favour of this. Stewart was authorised by the Governors to proceed to London to discuss the way forward with Struthers. They met at Dover House on 28 November. Struthers believed that as the School Board had been created by Parliament to carry on primary and secondary education for the district then the Governors should audit their activities and retire from any which overlapped with the former's functions. He further recommended that the question of sites for the Technical College should be settled quickly and an appeal to the public for subscriptions should begin.

On 7 December 1906 the School Board Committee produced their proposals for the Governors. As expected, they suggested that the Grammar School and College day classes be placed under the management of the School Board, while the College concentrate on evening classes and those students taking a modern/scientific education. The Governors' Educational Sub-Committee of John Morgan, Professor H. M. Macdonald and Headmaster Stewart responded positively, being 'strongly of the opinion' that the proposed scheme would be 'of the greatest value'.[24] The Financial Sub-Committee of Convener Kemp (of Finance), Convener James Walker (of Lands) and Thomas Fotheringham (Clerk, Treasurer and Factor) estimated that if the College continued to carry on the present work an annual surplus of £200 would be produced, although Headmaster Stewart believed that vital future expenditure would turn this into a deficit of £650; if the College followed the School Board's proposals then an annual surplus of £1150 was forecast.[25]

Armed with these reports, Lord Provost Sir Alexander Lyon[26] was keen to meet Struthers' expectation that the College would retire from the School Board's sphere and he wished to do so quickly, believing speed was of the essence before other cities put in their bids for funding. At the Governors' meeting on 30 January 1907 he pressed for a commitment to the School Board's proposals and to offering a site for the Technical College. However, the consensus was for making no decision meantime. On 6 February the Governors met again, and decided by 10–2 to accept Rev. Dr C. C. Macdonald's motion to delay until a 'scheme for the establishment of a Technical College is definitely shaped'.[27] However, in order to make some progress, it was agreed to 'consider favourably the provision of a site'.[28]

Despite this partial setback Lyon lost none of his enthusiasm for the Technical College, which was increasingly becoming 'his special lobby'.[29] He requested £20,000 from the Town Council[30] to kick-start the project and chaired the meeting of Governors on 22 May when they unanimously agreed in principle to grant a free site to the Technical College and to transfer Gray's School of Art and the College evening classes to the managers of the proposed College.[31] The SED responded with an initial contribution of £40,000 towards the scheme.

On determining the site the Governors insisted that the amenity of the College should be entirely conserved. No building would be allowed to obscure the view of existing buildings from the front entrance and ample space and light was to be ensured for the east and west wings of the Auld Hoose. Subject to these reservations[32] the Governors agreed 7–4 on 19 November 1907 to allocate 4334 square yards on the east and west sides of ground fronting Gordon's College to the Technical College.[33] Lyon then ensured that the Town Council would take responsibility to erect, establish and maintain the Technical College,[34] and chaired a conference of interested parties[35] on the future of secondary and technical education on 24 March 1908. A Committee resulted, with Kemp, Professor Macdonald and James Walker representing the Governors, and it asked, on 10 April, Thomas Hector, Secretary of the School Board, and Headmaster Stewart to confer and report.

The Hector/Stewart Report was published on 27 May 1908. It recommended that the School Board be responsible for all intermediate and secondary education and that the Town Council merge the College and Aberdeen Educational

Trust under the management of the Town Council with surplus revenue to be devoted to the poor and the Technical College. Stewart knew that he was accepting the death-knell of Gordon's; it would continue as a secondary school but under the School Board it would be a different institution from that which had developed since 1881. The Governors fell into line. On 15 June they agreed that the unification of intermediate and secondary education under one authority was 'sound in principle and desirable in itself' and requested the School Board and Governors to formulate a scheme for educational reorganisation. This decision was confirmed in Committee on 12 October by 10–5 but, with the enormity of the decision now weighing heavily, the Minutes were only approved by the Governors on 2 November by 6–5.[36]

The College at Risk

The narrow majority was the result of the stark realisation that the Governors were proposing a 'revolution'[37] greater than that of 1881. Robert Gordon's College would become a technical college. For Headmaster Stewart this was the best way forward. He believed that the fortunes of the College had already been adversely affected by recent educational developments[38] and if it remained an intermediate and secondary school it was further threatened by the large powers being proposed for the School Boards in the Education Bill before Parliament. He saw Gordon's College moving into a new phase of usefulness, and could envisage a scheme for foundationers, apprentices and scholarships which would benefit some 510 and was very much in accordance with the Founder's Will. For him this was a better option than continuing with a situation where those paying the lowest fee had almost disappeared, and, excluding the beneficiaries, the pupils of the College were 'drawn mainly from the wealthier and upper middle and middle classes'.[39] He naturally regretted the end of the College but if it had to go he wanted it replaced by a more beneficent institution which would advance Robert Gordon's noble design – the diffusion of education.[40]

A number of Governors, however, were opposed to the transformation of the College into a Technical College. Even if the College's accommodation was not adequate for the incoming class size regulations, which Stewart claimed, then the remedy was to take appropriate measures as other endowed schools were doing.[41] They did not accept it was good sense to add to rate levels; they objected to Town Council control of the new Technical College[42] and opposed 'destroying' a successful College for an unproved Technical College.[43]

Certain factors came into play at this time which, when taken together, had an important effect on subsequent events. Sir Alexander Lyon retired from his positions as Lord Provost and President of the Governors and his unique contribution was lost at a crucial time. Some members of the School Board began to lose enthusiasm for the scheme, appreciating that the resulting increase in rates would prove unpopular at the forthcoming municipal elections set for April 1909.[44] And finally, Rev. Alexander Ogilvie's daughter, Dr Maria Ogilvie Gordon,[45] decided on a high profile intervention, addressing a meeting of the Aberdeen Educational Institute of Scotland (EIS) on 19 December 1908.[46] She claimed that there was no immediate financial emergency at Gordon's[47] and Headmaster Stewart's future concerns could be met if the Governors ended their annual contribution to evening classes and the School of Art and started charging for the use of their buildings. Moreover, if the College was taken over by the School Board, the salaries of its 35 staff would need to come from the rates, which would cause public disquiet. Further, the proposal would result in a limited curriculum for both the Grammar School and Gordon's when what was needed was two fully equipped schools.[48] She ended by making a plea for the retention of the College, with a new building for the Technical College in its grounds.[49] A campaign to save the College began belatedly to stutter into life.

Meantime the Governors set up a Special Committee under Lord Provost Alexander Wilson,[50] which began a series of meetings with the School Board in early 1909. However, these were soon in trouble. The Governors had retreated from their earlier stance in the Hector/Stewart Report; now the School Board would need to buy the offered site and erect a new school in the vicinity of the College at a significant cost. With Board elections imminent it voted on 2 April by 9–5 to end the talks.

Recriminations followed as both sides blamed each other for the deadlock. The Governors were unimpressed with the School Board's record on secondary education and its desire to retain control over appointment and dismissal of staff, which they argued meant inefficient schools.[51] Lord Provost Wilson believed that for a maximum of two pence on the rates the City of Aberdeen would receive a fully equipped Technical College but that the School Board was jeopardising this goal. On the other hand, the School Board claimed that the failure of talks was a result of the actions of certain Governors, who were insisting on adding extra conditions.

In this situation the Governors appeared to have no alternative but to reaffirm their commitment to continue with their day classes, which would be managed either by the existing Governors or by the Governors of the new

Technical College.[52] However, that did not mean that Lord Provost Wilson had given up on the plan to absorb the College into the Technical College for he, like Stewart, believed that this would be more in line with Robert Gordon's wishes. Others, and they seemed to be increasing in number, like Sir William Ramsay, who chaired a public meeting of 400 supporters on 5 April,[53] favoured the retention of the College.

The Provisional Order

Such divisions did not stop progress altogether, for the Governors requested that the Town Council prepare a draft Provisional Order on the Technical College, suggesting some guidelines for inclusion. A Committee was appointed to safeguard the interests of the Governors as the Order was prepared.[54] The Town Council produced their draft and the Governors responded with a series of amendments.[55] In the debate on these on 8 April Kemp wanted reference to the transfer of education to the School Board eliminated, while Wilson believed the clause should be retained in case the talks resumed and were successful. Kemp persisted holding that the whole issue of talks was unsettling to the College. It took the casting vote of Wilson to defeat Kemp's amendment.

On 12 April 1909 the Town Council approved a draft Provisional Order and the Governors set up a Committee of Eight under Lord Provost Wilson to consider and report on its contents. It did so on 14 May. Generally the Governors were disappointed, even angry, that the Order bore heavily the imprint of the Town Council and in so doing had ignored or put aside the Governors' recommendations. Particularly controversial was the introduction of two Governing Bodies[56] and the role of Wilson in this fundamental change.

Wilson's change of mind on this issue was investigated by the Inquiry into the Provisional Order on Monday 2 August 1909. Then he held that two bodies would not mean increased expenditure.[57] Under cross-examination he admitted that he was Convener of the Town Council Committee on the Technical College which had unanimously decided to support one Governing Body, and Chair of the College Governors when they had decided to do likewise. He admitted that following his change of mind to two bodies there was no discussion with the Governors, who only discussed the matter in June 1909, two months after the Order had been lodged in the Scottish Office.[58] (Kemp held that Wilson did not call a meeting because he knew that his opponents had the majority support among the Governors.)

Meantime, Wilson had chaired the Governors' meeting on 8 April which had voted to maintain support for one body, while on 17 April lodging the draft Order which contained two bodies. Lamely Wilson argued that it did not matter: it needed to be lodged quickly[59] and as it was a draft it could be changed later. However, it was crucial, for it meant that the Governors had not supported transference of their buildings to two bodies.[60] It seems that Wilson was persuaded by Struthers of the SED as early as December 1908 that there was enough work for the College Board and another Board was needed for the charitable work.[61] Unfortunately he still acted after this as if he favoured one Board.

Wilson diverted attention from his duplicity by playing down concerns over the transference of College property to the new Governing Body. The Governors could block this as they had done with the School Board. He feared that the Provisional Order would be lost unless the Governors were willing to accept the Town Council draft. Not surprisingly he lost the vote in Committee 5–2 to the majority who wished to detail their objections and petition the Secretary of State.[62] When discussed at the Governors' meeting on 18 May, Wilson again lost, this time 6–4,[63] and a Committee of Five was set up to open talks with the Town Council with a view to amending the Order. However, despite a series of meetings between the sides in June and July, no progress was made on the central issue, as the Educational Trust was adamant on retaining the two bodies. There seemed no recourse for the Governors other than to oppose the Provisional Order at the Inquiry, chaired by Lord Belhaven in Aberdeen on 2–4 August 1909.

The Inquiry opened with counsel for the Town Council A. H. B. Constable explaining the historical background and the proposals in the Order. The Order proposed transferring primary, intermediate and secondary education to the School Board and Gordon's would concentrate on technical education. Given the lack of agreement with the School Board, 'meantime' the secondary school would continue, but it would be handed over at the first opportunity.

Evidence for the promoters of the Provisional Order was given firstly by Lord Provost Wilson. He justified the two Boards, which would deal with their own functions without being diverted. John Keir followed, representing the School Board, which, after talks with the Town Council, had decided to support two Boards.[64] Keir also stressed that talks between the School Board and the Governors were aimed at the separation of their spheres so that the Governors could concentrate on technical education. Ex-Lord Provost Mearns, Chairman of the Aberdeen Educational Trust since 1903, strongly favoured two Boards, which he argued were needed given the workload involved. Also giving evidence for the Order was a reluctant Headmaster Stewart 'under warrant' of the Commissioners.[65] He was embarrassed to be called to give evidence against the now official policy of his employers. His contribution in 1908 (with Hector) had proved controversial in retrospect and now he would have 'preferred to remain neutral'.[66] Nonetheless he was of the view that the maintenance of a secondary school should fall to the School Board.

Toward the end of day two of the Inquiry, the first of the College opponents of the Order, George Kemp,[67] gave evidence. He went over the sequence of events, explaining that the Governors did not accept two Boards before the Order's publication, and how it was lodged without further consultation or amendment, or indeed without Town Council ratification. He wanted a technical college but objected to the way it had been handled. He believed the Educational Endowment Commission decision of 6 August 1880 amalgamating the Collyhill and College Trustees into one Board had worked admirably and proved to have distinct advantages. He opposed the transfer of the College to the School Board, suggesting that Board Schools did not have the same sentiment behind them. The 1908 Education Act had been amended to prevent interference in schools with endowments worth more than £1000 p.a. but the Order allowed this if, as was likely, the two Governing Bodies wrangled.[68] If the College was given over to the School Board Kemp believed that the poor would suffer.

The following day Rev. Dr Charles C. Macdonald[69] elaborated on the grievance that the Governors were not properly consulted on the Order. He saw the College as a potential feeder to the Technical College, with both under one Governing Body. He contemplated 'with a kind of anguish'[70] the plan to extinguish the College, preferring competition, especially the 'friendly and healthy rivalry'[71] with the Grammar School. He did not believe there was a financial problem: the excess of expenditure over income in 1908 of £3338 was balanced by the £3400 spent on property.[72] He had been astonished when Headmaster Stewart had supported unification of administration because of the School Board's record especially its attempt to 'obliterate' the College by developing the Central School.[73]

A line of other experienced educationalists supported the concept of one Board: Sir James Donaldson, Principal of St Andrews University; Peter Macnaughton, Clerk of George Heriot's Trust since 1893, and his Convener of Education, Alexander Darroch;[74] Dr Ogilvie Gordon, who also opposed the transfer of the College to the School Board; and James Paterson, a Governor between 1878 and 1885 and ex-Convener of the Education Committee, who feared for the future of the College given the 'predatory instincts'[75] of the School Board.

The most telling contribution on the Board issue came from Thomas Fotheringham, Clerk, Treasurer and Factor of the College since 1886.[76] He played down the 'heavy' workload for foundationers and bursaries, which he deemed clerical.[77] Visitation, if it took place, was once a year. Management of estates was factor work and needed overview of a Lands Committee meeting once a month, rarely for more than an hour. He effectively demolished the case for two Boards. Moreover, he had financial concerns over the Order as it only allowed £2025 for maintenance and education while currently the College spent £3000 on these.[78] He feared that if a deficit grew the Technical College Governors would turn the College over to the School Board.

The defence of the College was left to a number of well-known academics. Sir William Ramsay, Professor of Humanity at the University of Aberdeen, described Gordon's as a 'pivotal school' supplying the driving power to other schools.[79] It would be a 'calamity' if it was impeded.[80] John Harrower, Professor of Greek at the University of Aberdeen, gave details of the successes in the Bursary Competition – in the last twenty years, first thirteen times, and twelve times the College had at least five pupils in the top ten places. In the same period 130 ex-pupils had graduated MA (Honours) and gained the chief classical prize eleven times. It was 'a remarkable record for any school in Scotland'.[81] He held that Gordon's achievement was all the more laudable given its inclusion of large numbers of labouring families. The College, he demanded, should be maintained 'at all costs'.[82] Competition with School Board schools was healthy, while putting the College under the School Board would result in a loss of prestige and esprit de corps.[83] John Murray,[84] ex-foundationer and tutor of Christ Church, Oxford, also opposed the transfer of the College. The last opponent was James Walker, ex-Lord Provost, who had been a Governor for 39 years. He pleaded the case for the ministers and the guildry, both of which had been represented on the Board since the founding of the Hospital, to be included on the Governing Body.

Counsel for both sides summed up. Constable, for the Town Council, claimed the issue was not about lack of consultation over how the Order was initiated but about public interest. The new Governors, he argued, being 'practically derived from the same sources as the existing body of Governors'[85] would be no more likely to sacrifice the interests of the College than the existing body would be likely to do. There was no threat to the school. John Wilson, counsel for the College, held the Order to be an ill-considered scheme, with no consultation with the major parties. There was a clear risk to the College, otherwise why include a transfer clause[86] when the Government already had this power under the 1908 Education Act? Why also were there two Boards when the new Technical College Governors could have had control of all the monies and the day school under one Board? Why the need for a second Board of 21 persons for limited clerical work, which could have been done by a single Factor? Wilson suggested that Struthers at the SED had been determined to have the Technical College the one subject of consideration.[87]

Wilson ended his powerfully argued case by playing the card of justice and fairness. The Technical College was to receive the property and funds of the College and in return the College must be secured as the first charge. The College Governors had been the initiators of support for the Technical College and promoted it before the Town Council took over. This in itself should have ensured that the College's benefactions would not be encroached upon.

The College Saved

The Commissioners[88] were impressed with the weight of the College evidence. On the crucial clauses they took the side of the College. The Commissioners stressed that they were 'anxious to do no harm to this school'[89] and insisted that the first charge should be for general rather than technical education.[90] This financial obligation to clear the deficit of the school before financing the Technical College saved the school. Without this clause, which was not in the original draft, the school would have been handed over to the School Board at the first opportunity. However, the price paid for existence was high – for the College Governors gave over their buildings (to the Technical College Governors) and their estates (to the Aberdeen Endowments Trust).

The Commissioners agreed that the transfer clause[91] was a repetition of public statute and thus superfluous. It was deleted, as they had no wish to appear to support a transfer of this 'old school of which every one is so proud'.[92] Instead, a new clause was introduced which stated that 'The Governors may . . . carry on the primary, intermediate and secondary schools as now carried on by the existing Governors at the existing College'.[93] The College had been saved by the skin of its teeth. In the 68 lengthy sections of the Provisional Order the school received these three lines under 'Miscellaneous', and the clause was not even mandatory![94]

On 23 November 1909 details of the amended Provisional Order, due to come into operation on 1 January 1910, were reported to the Governors. A new Governing Body – the Governors of Robert Gordon's Technical College – of thirty persons was set up.[95] To it was transferred the buildings and furnishings of the existing College; the feu-duties of College properties in Schoolhill, Blackfriars Street and Woolmanhill; the land and property in Blackfriars Street; and Gray's School of Art and furnishings. The second body – the Aberdeen Endowments Trust (AET) – of 21 persons was also set up.[96] To it was transferred the existing Robert Gordon's Trust and all other property, funds and estates belonging to the existing College, and the property and functions of Aberdeen Educational Trust (which was also dissolved on 1 January 1910). The latter included its buildings in King Street and all property, funds and estates of the Educational Trust except what was transferred to the Technical College Governors.

The 'new' AET was to give a maximum of £1750[97] towards the maintenance and provision of books and stationery to the 120 Gordon's foundationers[98] and a maximum of £275 for Robert Gordon's bursaries;[99] with a maximum of £1100 for the fees to educate the foundationers and bursars, in order to maintain and manage the primary, intermediate and secondary schools. The balance of the revenue of the AET was to be applied by the College Governors in the first place to meet any deficit in maintaining and carrying on the schools (after taking into account income from fees and grants).[100] Following valuations the AET published an eight-page pamphlet on the general character of its resources and benefactions. The gross value of endowments was over £300,000 with gross annual revenue approaching £14,000.[101]

Was the creation of two Boards in the best interests of the College? At the time the Order reduced three Boards to two there was an argument that the new situation of a Technical College would be better met with separate administration from that of bursaries. Moreover, the two Boards made geographic sense, given that the one body would be Aberdeen-centred while the Technical College was for the whole of the north-east. Probably the workload argument for two Boards can be discounted, although the experience of those in similar situations elsewhere[102] supported the argument that you do not get the right people for Board technical work if you include a charitable function as well. Nonetheless, it is difficult to make sense of the 1909 Order, and the way it was introduced, unless there was an ulterior motive behind the arrangements, viz a new Board identifying completely with the Technical College and the day school seen as a burden to be got rid off as soon as possible. In this context it was not surprising that College Governors and Headmasters resented its imposition and consistently tried to overturn it.

Principal Stewart

Despite Headmaster Stewart's somewhat controversial role in preceding events there were no immediate repercussions. Indeed, with Lord Provost Wilson chairing the Technical College Governors, and with Sir Alexander Lyon involved again, there was no opposition to Wilson's recommendation that Stewart should extend his responsibilities and become Principal of the Technical College. On 7 March 1910 this was formally accepted by the new Governing Body without a vote, and as his first task Stewart was asked to audit staffing. Standing Committees were also agreed at this meeting and while the Technical College Committee would include all thirty Governors, the Secondary School Committee, dealing with College matters and chaired by Rev. Dr C. C. Macdonald, numbered only twelve.[103] It was significant that Stewart assumed the title 'Principal' from the time of the next Governors' meeting on 28 March.

The new Technical College inherited the day school but also a Central Institution, including Gray's School of Art (day and evening classes) and advanced evening classes (all carried on in the Auld Hoose), and a School of Domestic Science, carried on in 352 King Street.[104] The School had a primary department of four classes (admitting boys aged nine or ten),[105] an intermediate department of four years[106] and a secondary department.[107]

The School roll was 907 with 741 boys from Aberdeen. The primary had 164 (class size 41), intermediate 583 (class size 39) which the SED deemed too large,[108] and the secondary 123, with Modern 54 (class size 27) and Classical 69 (class size 23).

Fees remained differentiated depending on means, the level ranging from £2 p.a. for families in Aberdeen with an income lower than £75 p.a., rising in five bands to £7 p.a. for those with income over £250 p.a.[109] In December 1909 some 109 families paid the lowest fees, 263 the middle and 206 the highest. There were 118 foundationers receiving the maintenance allowance of £12/12/- with free education and books (tenable for four to five years); 95 bursars (either restricted with maintenance allowances between £3 and £7 p.a. with free education and books for one to three years, or open with free education for only one year) and 51 free scholars with free education.

The immediate issue before Stewart and the School Committee was how to reduce numbers to fall in line with SED regulations and requirements. Stewart ruled out increased staff and further building on cost grounds. He aimed at cutting the size of the School by 150 by means of discontinuing graduated fee levels, introducing fees of £5 p.a. in primary and £7 p.a. in intermediate and secondary, and ending free places.[110] In doing so Stewart welcomed the opportunity for Gordon's to concentrate on being a 'proper' secondary school – offering five-year courses to boys committed to continuing to the Leaving Certificate – and simultaneously becoming a smaller institution so that teachers and the Head would know every boy well. Robert Gordon's College should not only ensure delivery of knowledge but should also know the character and aptitude of every boy to help decide for what sphere of work he was most fitted.[111] Stewart envisaged little curricular change other than geometry and physical training being added for intermediate boys. After protracted discussions Stewart's proposals were accepted as there seemed no practical alternative.[112]

Dislocations

All other issues were put aside when, in the early hours of Wednesday 8 March 1911, a fire broke out which destroyed the east wing of the Auld Hoose where the mathematics, classics, physics and chemistry departments were situated. It began in Room 30 on the first floor in the extreme south corner of the block and the cause appeared to be a joist in a beam under an open hearth being ignited. The Aberdeen Fire Brigade arrived at 5.20am and tried to confine the flames but that proved impossible given the speed with which the fire spread along the roof and wooden floors and the explosions in the chemical laboratories. When the fire was at its height it presented a great spectacle, the flames mounting high in the air and burning with tremendous ferocity. Within a short period of time the roof of the two-storey building collapsed and practically the entire east wing, save for three rooms on the extreme east side, was gutted. Thankfully, a thick stone wall saved the central block, although a great deal of damage was done by water.[113] Early estimates estimated the cost at £12–15,000, which was covered by insurance. Principal Stewart was soon on the scene and, personally and with assistance, succeeded in ensuring the College's valuable books and documents were saved.[114]

The School did not open the day of the fire[115] but the gym, Art Gallery and Gray's School of Art were requisitioned to provide immediate accommodation. Temporary buildings were organised and erected in time for the new session.

It took till September 1913 for the reconstructed east wing to be built and occupied again by staff and students. The ground floor included three modern physics laboratories, the first floor a large art room (58 feet by 28 feet), which could be divided into two rooms by partitions, and a chemistry laboratory to accommodate 41, preparation room and lecture room.[116] The southern portion of the wing originally had four classrooms (two on each floor) but these were converted into six classrooms (three on each floor) by the Technical College architect, J. A. Ogg Allan. The total cost of the building was £9000.[117]

After the fire, the accommodation problems of the school were aggravated. More problematic, in the longer term, were the proposals being discussed for extending the Technical College buildings and rehousing the Endowments Trust from King Street. These developments led to a conference on the state of the school accommodation on 30 January 1914. It was assumed that every full-time teacher should have their own room suitably equipped for the subject taught. On this basis 37 rooms were required, including twelve specialist areas, while existing rooms numbered 29 (some others in the west temporary buildings would need to be given up to make way for the expanding Technical College).[118] The four rooms in the upper floor of the Auld Hoose were also deemed unsuitable and were earmarked for the growing administration of the Technical College. The architect, therefore, produced plans extending the school buildings eastwards and northwards from the west wing. They included a new gymnasium,[119] leaving all the ground on the line of Blackfriars Street at the disposal of the Governors as a site for new Technical College buildings. These plans, too, were elaborated: the departments of sculpture and architecture were to be erected as an extension of the School of Arts and Crafts on the Harriet Street side of the site and the School of Building on a site facing St Andrew Street and Blackfriars Street, at a cost of £21,000.[120] In the meantime, as a stopgap measure, two large blocks of temporary buildings were to provide accommodation for engineering, chemistry, pharmacy, architecture and building.

The outbreak of the Great War in August 1914 ended all plans for its duration. Some 600 ex-pupils were, by the end of 1914, serving in the armed forces and by then some 150 existing pupils had joined a school corps.[121] Demands for a new gym intensified as the boys, who had been deprived of such a facility since March 1911,[122] needed to be involved in physical exercise and training. As the War continued more and more teaching staff were called up for active duty, beginning with five until the final number totalled fifteen. Sadly three of these were killed – James H. Adams of German, Herbert Murray of mathematics and John McHardy of classics. Emil True, who had given twenty years' service, was dismissed from his post as principal teacher of German for being a German national. Some Governors wished to pay him an extra three months' salary but, as the School Board had not been so generous in a similar situation and the SED opposed the suggestion, the motion to do so was defeated 11–10, on the casting vote of the Lord Provost.[123]

Staffing dislocation inevitably had an effect on the school and any innovation which occurred tended to be linked to wartime conditions. Spanish and Russian were added to the curriculum in 1916. The major plans for development were shelved and it was not until the War ended that minds turned again to them.

Future Options

In a letter dated 14 December 1918 Principal Stewart requested that he be given more time to deal with general administration rather than the details of any particular department. He foresaw a rapid growth in technical education and also forecast an increasing workload in his role as Headmaster given increasing school numbers.[124] He favoured a change in structure for the secondary school and the Governors set up a Committee of Nine under Lord Provost Sir James Taggart[125] to investigate.[126] It met on 9 April 1919 and of the two options discussed it recommended by 3–2 that a new assistant to the Principal be appointed in the Technical College.[127] However, when the issue was discussed at the following Governors' meeting the decision was reversed by 10–8 and it was decided to appoint a new Headmaster to the School.[128]

Given Stewart's earlier commitment to technical education and the Technical College and the status and power of the post of Principal (head of all the Schools of the Technical College and the secondary school) vis-à-vis the Headmastership, it was no surprise that he wanted to continue being Principal and divest himself of the Headmastership. However, certain Governors, with some justification, believed Stewart was better equipped to manage the school than the increasingly specialised Technical College. The outspoken spokesman of this group, John Croll, argued that Stewart was trained as an English teacher and claimed 'there was no confidence in Principal Stewart so far as the work of the Technical College was concerned'. Croll had heard 'many things from old Governors and old pupils' and 'the feeling was distinctly against Principal Stewart as head of the Technical College'.[129] Despite this, the Lord Provost's motion to appoint a new Headmaster was carried albeit narrowly by 10–8, but its execution was delayed given the uncertainty over the relationship with the newly formed Aberdeen Educational Authority (EA), the successor to the School Board which had disappeared under the 1918 Scottish Education Act.

It was natural that with the War ended there would be speculation on the educational options available to the Governors. Pre-war it had been increasingly assumed that the Technical College and School would somehow co-exist on the Schoolhill site and many expected this to continue. In December 1918, a College Memorandum discussed the idea of abandoning secondary education and concentrating exclusively on technical education, but this was dismissed in view of the school's 'splendid traditions and associations'. It ventured instead doing away with the primary and intermediate departments and retaining only the post-intermediate courses, retaining 300–400 boys of fifteen years and over. The advantages of this would be the solving of the School accommodation problem and feeding the Technical College. However, in February 1919 it was suggested in the *Free Press* that the School should be expanded and the Technical College should move to the Gallowgate or to the even larger old Poorhouse site in Nelson Street, with the vacant ground behind it, facing King Street.

On 6 June 1919 a Special Meeting of the Governors was held to confer with representatives of the Aberdeen EA following its letter on the future of the secondary school. Under the new Education Act the educational authorities had to submit a scheme to the SED for the adequate provision of education in its area.[130] George Duncan, Chair of the EA, was keen that the management of the school should be transferred by the Governors to the EA, that the buildings should be acquired by the EA at a price to be agreed,[131] and that the Governors should acquire another site for the Technical College.[132] Following a conference on 6 June the matter was given over by the Governors to their Conveners' Committee.

After seven meetings it produced a Report which opposed any further 'alienation' of the Schoolhill site and held that the Governors should continue to run the secondary school.[133] It stated that the transference to the EA would not improve matters. The School was already full, so no extra places would be gained and there would be difficulty moving much of the Technical College elsewhere. The debate, however, was dominated by Croll, who criticised the Report on the grounds that it was written by Stewart, an 'interested' party rather than by the Committee. Although Croll's personal attack was criticised as 'cowardly' and 'totally uncalled for'[134] and Stewart's record, as an educationalist, was defended, much damage was done and Stewart's critics lost 10–8. It took a Special Meeting on 12 December 1919 to reaffirm their position and to open talks with the EA regarding the role that Gordon's would play in the new circumstances.

The major problem was how to finance the school. In 1919 revenue reached £9737 (from fees, AET and grants) but the deficiency was £11,717 which could only come from the ratepayers, for the first time as a result of the 1918 Act, and the SED. As it was a matter of much public interest the *Aberdeen Daily Journal* produced three long, detailed articles on 'The Future of Robert Gordon's College'.[135] They suggested that although the plan to jettison the School had failed in 1909 it had remained alive. It was now appreciated that the loss of the School to the EA would also mean the loss of the site and the buildings and the need to transfer the Technical College elsewhere. The result had been a fine show of enthusiasm for maintaining the traditions of the School but these were a sham. The name and traditions had been stolen as the Technical College had none of its own! Faced with dependence on the EA for finance, the Governors understood the necessity of giving it more influence in order to keep the Technical College at Schoolhill. The articles, however, held that a better way forward would be to divorce the School from Technical College by moving the latter, otherwise the School would continue to lose out to the Technical College. The interests of the two institutions were different, and the appearance of 'ugly, corrugated iron sheds' and the planned building extension were symptomatic of the downgrading of the School. The use to which surplus endowments had been put also confirmed the priority being given to the Technical College.[136]

Following further talks between the EA and the Governors, an agreement was reached on 23 April 1920. The EA would give financial support to Robert Gordon's College provided the school's accounts were given to the EA to approve; five further members of the EA were co-opted onto the Secondary School Committee[137]; a Headmaster, separate from the Technical College and responsible to the Secondary School Committee, was appointed; and free places were arranged between the Governors and EA. The Governors accepted these terms[138] and immediately advertised for a successor to Principal Stewart as Headmaster of the School.[139]

On 8 June the enlarged Secondary School Committee met under Convener Kilgour to consider the fifteen applications lodged for the post. Eight were

Heads or Principals of institutions, eleven worked in Scotland and two members of the school's teaching staff applied – Malcolm Murray of the French Department and James Thomson of the Mathematics Department. Neither reached the short list of two, made up of George Morrison, ex-member of the Gordon's staff and Rector of Inverness Royal Academy, and John M. Thomson, teacher of classics, history and English at Fettes College in Edinburgh. However, on 18 June, at their next meeting, a letter was read from Thomson withdrawing his application as he had just been appointed Rector of the Grammar School. Nonetheless it was decided to go ahead and interview Morrison. When this was complete the Committee recommended that he be appointed Headmaster at a salary of £1000 p.a. The Governors unanimously approved on 25 June and Morrison took over the running of the School on 1 September 1920.

It was thought that the decision to appoint Morrison would solve the awkward line-management issue. Technically Morrison was responsible to both Stewart, as Principal, and the Secondary Committee, but given that Morrison had been appointed to the School by Stewart and was very much his protege it was understandably felt that Morrison could cope successfully with this situation. However, although Stewart was immediately relieved of some of his heavy workload, in some respects he was left even more exposed, as the most critical problems revolved around the running of the Technical College. Newspapers were soon full of a 'rumpus'[140] which broke out at the Governors' meeting in late August when the outspoken Croll challenged a remark of Stewart on the question of accommodation. Croll held that he did not trust the Principal, refusing to accept a verbal statement and insisting on a written communication. Stewart left the meeting and did not return. His resignation, dated 3 September 1920, followed soon after.

The Gordon's community were shocked by the turn of events and the general feeling as expressed at the Governors' meeting on 15 September[141] was to have him reconsider. However, in the debate some Governors detailed shortcomings of organisation, the loss of good staff and the seeming inability of Stewart to attract quality replacements. Although only Kilgour supported Croll's motion to accept Stewart's resignation, significantly they were joined by five other Governors when they tried to restrict Stewart's tenure to until summer 1921. Others praised Stewart for his zeal, ability and enthusiasm, but even then there was opposition to much of what he had done. Lord Provost William Meff's[142] motion not to accept the resignation was passed 14–7 and a small group of Governors met with Stewart on 21 September in an effort to persuade him to change his mind. Stewart had, by then, received messages of support from former pupils and individuals and, as result of such representation, he decided 'it is my duty to remain at my post'.[143]

The Special Committee, set up to investigate the financial position of the Technical College, produced its Report on 22 November 1920.[144] Although it recommended that the Technical College should carry on regardless and, in the event of a deficit, the Town Council and EA should defray it, George Duncan, Chair of the EA, produced a Memorandum calling for the closing of the Technical College as a separate institution with its duties being devolved on the EA and University. He suggested the Art School, School of Domestic Science, Navigation School and possibly Pharmacy School should become independent bodies.[145] Such an audacious plan was immediately countered by ex-Lord Provost Wilson and other defenders of the Technical College.[146] However, an immediate casualty was Principal Stewart, who wrote to the Governors on 23 November enclosing a medical certificate for a complete rest for four to six weeks. The Governors granted this and wished him a speedy recovery but their decision the same day (26 November), that Headmaster Morrison should no longer report to Stewart, could only have heightened Stewart's stress level.

Contribution of Charles Stewart

Stewart arrived back to work in late January 1921 but was involved in another unfortunate incident at a Governors' meeting, which Meff had to abandon as Croll refused to withdraw an 'extremely offensive remark'.[147] Things did not improve. On 25 February the Governors decided 15–5 to pay £250 to Stewart and his clerk for secondary school work, which was now the complete responsibility of Morrison.[148] Stewart's enemies had another opportunity to attack his position.

Throughout the year the future direction, even existence, of the Technical College was debated and particularly influential articles appeared in the *Aberdeen Daily Journal* of 6 and 7 July. Radical plans, aimed at reversing the policy set out in the Order of 1909 and encompassing the life work of Stewart since then, were increasingly canvassed. Tired and ill, Stewart felt he had no alternative and on 19 October 1921 he resigned. This time his resignation was accepted.[149]

Since his appointment to the College staff in 1883 Stewart had proved himself an outstanding schoolmaster, whose recipe for success was based on stamina and hard work. Moreover, he had the gift of knowing, individually, his pupils and former pupils. He had also been significant in supporting Ogilvie in the elevation of Gordon's to such a prominent national position.[150] One of its most distinguished former pupils, John Murray, who was at the College between 1892–6, believed Stewart would have been successful whatever profession he had pursued for he was 'so versatile, so adventurous, so sturdy and so heroical'.[151] Colleagues also thought highly of him. His successor as Head, Morrison, praised his ability to carry the heavy burden he did which he held was the result of an usual combination of 'a sanguine and enthusiastic temperament with a tremendous power of work'.[152]

In his career at Gordon's Stewart had accomplished much and if in his final years as Principal he found it difficult to cope with the conflicting demands placed upon him the surprise is how he managed to do so for so long. He brought coherence and mutual support to a number of previously isolated institutions and he created new departments in a time of consolidation and progress.[153] His ultimate failure resulted from the work overload involved in being both Principal and Headmaster, and from the tortuous route followed by the Governors between 1909 and 1921. In that period the relationship between the secondary school and the Town Council and School Board (and later the EA) remained confused and although Stewart was clearer than most on educational priorities that confusion lay at the heart of the problems in the period. His vision for the Technical College, as it entailed handing the College over to the School Board, proved a step too far. The resulting compromise – retaining the College while giving priority to a burgeoning Technical College on a crowded site – was to remain the unsatisfactory situation for half a century. It was an irony to some that the late-coming 'cuckoo' was very much in charge of the nest.

Stewart was awarded the OBE for his contribution to Scottish education in 1920. He and his wife retired to Ballater where he was much involved in municipal affairs. He remained a loyal supporter of Gordon's, having spent 38 years on its staff, and his former pupils always had a warm welcome at Glenbardie. He collapsed and died while working in his garden on 22 July 1938. As a remarkable postscript, an anonymous donor presented the 'Charles Stewart Mace' to the College in June 1974.[154] To be remembered so fondly so many years on suggests that Charles Stewart was a special schoolmaster and headmaster.[155]

10

A TIME OF CONSOLIDATION THEN INNOVATION, 1920–43

George A. Morrison

George Alexander Morrison was born in Dufftown on 30 October 1869. He was educated in his parish school and entered Aberdeen University as fifth bursar aged only fifteen, graduating MA with first class honours in classics in 1889, four years later, and winning the Simpson Greek and Liddel Prizes. After six months' teaching at the Gordon Schools, Huntly, he joined the Classical Department staff of Gordon's College. The promotion of Dr Riddoch to the post of Rector of Mackie Academy, Stonehaven, and then the departure of his successor, James Clark, two years later in 1895, resulted in Morrison becoming the Head of Department, a position he held with distinction for fifteen years. In that time the remarkable success of so many Gordon's boys in the University Bursary Competition owed much to him. In 1910 he was appointed Rector of Inverness Royal Academy where under his leadership the roll increased from 352 to 560 and many more pupils were successful in the Leaving and Intermediate Certificates. He was also responsible for the building of a new science/art building in 1914 and significantly improved the school's sporting facilities. His reputation led to him becoming Headmaster of the College, taking up office on 1 September 1920.

Unlike his predecessor, Morrison had the great advantages of being able to focus entirely on the school and having the time to oversee the minutiae which its day-to-day running entailed. He kept a daily log from his first day, which his successors kept up, and this, allied with his monthly reports to the Secondary School Committee of Governors, showed his all-embracing interest in, and influence over, every aspect of school life. He was exact and hard-working, and demanded similar qualities from his classes. A scholar himself, he inspired his pupils, for whom he had high expectations. His quiet and cultured voice belied a firmness and strength of character, and he was widely respected.

Morrison inherited a school of 839 pupils, with 33 in primary, 654 in intermediate and 152 in post-intermediate stages. There was only one primary class with boys aged eleven to over twelve, equivalent to the highest class in an elementary school, and preparing boys for the Qualifying Examination. The intermediate department was in decline as a result of increasing fees and the introduction of further free 'intermediate' schools with more expected in both city and county.[1] However, Leaving Certificates results were good – with mathematics, science, English, French, drawing and Latin the most successful subjects (in that order) with a sprinkling of successes in Greek, Spanish, German and dynamics.

In June 1921 Morrison persuaded the Governors to introduce a second class at the stage a year before the Qualifying class and was rewarded with a good intake. This led to him successfully pressing to extend the School downwards in age. He believed that taking pupils at a younger age would get them used to College ways and more attached to them. In 1923 three more classes were added and the experiment worked partly thanks to the support of the Aberdeen Educational Authority (AEA), which publicised the fact that parents could apply for assistance in sending pupils to the College.[2] Carefully graded schemes of instruction in nature study, French and mathematics were commenced earlier than in other schools, and Morrison introduced eurhythmics with Madame Murray. By 1925 with primary numbers at 88 (in a school of 663) Morrison was authorised to establish a complete Elementary Department so that boys could complete all their education at Gordon's and on 13 April 1926 a new Kindergarten class opened with fourteen pupils under Miss Georgina Clark.[3]

Members of different parts of the Gordon's community wished to remember those who had been lost in the terrible carnage of the Great War and, on 17 September 1920, Lord Provost Meff, on behalf of the Governors, accepted a Memorial Plaque to the three members of the teaching staff killed. It was placed appropriately in a prominent place in the lower corridor of the Auld Hoose. The College Former Pupils (FPs) determined to do likewise and their Memorial Tablet was erected close-by and unveiled, again by Meff, on 29 September 1922. As a further and more practical act of remembrance the FPs decided to raise £1000 and equip a playing-field.[4] This persuaded the Governors to buy 9.817 acres of land behind 'Thorngrove' on Seafield Road from the

Shipmasters' Society for £2550 in October 1922. It had space for two rugby[5]/association football pitches, a hockey pitch,[6] cricket field and tennis courts. To help defray costs it was decided to introduce a Games Fee[7] and Morrison organised a successful bazaar to raise funds. A special edition of the *The Gordonian* in 1923 also was dedicated to the Field.[8]

The Memorial Playing Field and Pavilion were formally opened[9] by Sir Francis Ogilvie on 18 May 1925 and was followed by the annual sports day,[10] which since 1922 had been held at King's College fields. However, it was soon found that the area was not large enough and so in January 1927 two adjoining areas to the north were bought from the Shipmasters' Society for £800 and this allowed two blaes tennis courts and facilities for football and hockey to be added. Despite these additions the fields were still in great demand[11] and Morrison decided that football could not continue as a main sport. From February 1927 rugby became the predominant sport of the College.[12]

Morrison began a campaign, soon after his appointment, for regaining the gymnasium for the school. The Governors were sympathetic, given that the gym had been operating as a classroom since 1911, and decided to move navigation classes to Crooked Lane. Morrison now wanted a full-time physical instructor appointed and his case was strengthened by a statement from Dr Rose, medical officer to the Aberdeen EA, that the physique of Gordon's boys was suffering given the lack of playground space and a gymnasium. Within a month the Governors had decided to appoint a PT instructor who would also be the Games Master and, in July 1921, Theo S. Fairley from Glasgow joined the staff. Consequently all sports flourished.

Music was a special interest of Morrison, who was a gifted musician himself. As early as October 1920 he had conferred with Dr (later Sir) Arthur Somervell, HMI in music, who suggested how to encourage the study of music. Arrangements were made to carry on extra-curricular music, art and literature on Friday evenings and by 1 December George Innes was employed to teach singing at these classes.[13] To promote the spread of music further Morrison secured the part-time services of Arthur Collingwood, organist of the West United Free Church. A School Orchestra was created for the first time in September 1923 and by January 1927 a full Music Hall was entertained by the College Orchestra and choirs at a concert in aid of the General and Athletic Committees' funds.[14] Following high praise for the orchestra[15] the Governors decided, in June 1927, to appoint a full-time music teacher, J. Kimberley Smith,[16] an organist of great ability. Music prospered and in 1929 a Junior

Orchestra was created. Annual Music Hall Concerts became popular until ended by the Second World War in 1941.

Financial Issues

Although Morrison, unlike Stewart, did not have direct responsibility for the Technical College his plans were much affected by the financial deficits in the Accounts.[17] It was important to get both Technical College and School on a sound financial footing otherwise it would be impossible to go forward with building improvements. A Special Committee met ten times between December 1920 and October 1921 on the issue. The situation was not helped by the retreat of the Town Council from their original commitment to maintain the Technical College and the Governors had to spend their capital funds to meet the shortfalls. Temporary help came from the Scottish Education Department (SED) and EA but a permanent solution was needed.

Protracted discussions between the Governors, Town Council and EA led to an agreement in July 1922. The EA offered to wipe out the deficit and make an annual contribution to the maintenance of the Technical College, provided a new Provisional Order united the Boards of Technical College and the Aberdeen Endowments Trust (AET), and the EA gained significant additional representation on the Governing Body. George Duncan, Chair of the EA, argued forcibly for the School to take control of its own endowments (from the AET), and so go ahead with an accommodation programme. However, having fought hard to retain independence in 1909 the AET, at a Special Meeting on 24 October 1922, rejected the unification of Boards,[18] nor was it willing to countenance an agreement to restore matters to the pre-1909 situation.

The Chair of the EA Finance Committee, John Munro, criticised the AET. Its contribution of £1100 p.a. to the School to educate 120 foundationers and 123 bursars was well below the actual cost, which Munro estimated at £5000. Further, its contribution of only £275 to the bursars meant that each individual received a pittance. Yet the AET retained the right to select and send the boys to the College.[19] Munro believed the Governors should manage their own affairs and, as their central problem was lack of money, they should control their own estates and resulting endowments. This would bring substantial administrative savings and had it been done in 1909 would already have resulted in very different, and improved, financial results.[20] The cumbersome means the School had to adopt to raise funding for the playing-fields could not continue for future projects. By any reasoning the 1909 financial scheme had broken down.[21]

The AET defended its record. It had taken over the debt of the College Governors of £16,000 in 1909 and gradually extinguished it by good financial management. It also ensured fairness in the endowment examinations, which could not be relied upon if left to the Governors.[22] It managed ten other charitable trusts, as well as Gordon's, and had to consider their interests. Nonetheless, the AET wished to help financially and produced a scheme which involved reducing the number of open competitive foundations and bursaries. Duncan was furious holding that this would affect the class of boys, which had been the strength of the School since 1881. It was dangerous, Duncan concluded, to leave the endowments of the College in the hands of a body which appeared not to appreciate its history and traditions.[23]

As there was no possibility of agreement on one body but a belief that a new Provisional Order needed the support of both Governors and the AET, a compromise was accepted. The Governors would borrow on the security of AET funds and they would be consulted on aspects of the admission of applicants. Both Governors and AET would have increased representation on each other's bodies.[24] It was a disappointing settlement for the Governors but, having lost out on the issue of the two bodies in 1909, it was difficult to overturn the decision in 1923.[25]

The Governors and AET became joint promoters of the proposed Provisional Order. It was agreed that the Town Council representation on the Governing Body would be reduced from nine to five and on the AET from nine to six. Aberdeen EA was compensated for taking on the deficits by gaining nine representatives on the new Governing Body of 33 (up from three), and five representatives on the AET Governing Body of 21 (up from three). It was also accepted that the Lord Provost did not have time to chair meetings and the Governors would elect their own Chairman from their number.

The Robert Gordon Colleges and AET Order Confirmation Act gained royal assent on 2 August 1923 and the new Governing Body met for the first time on 4 January 1924.[26] Walter A. Reid[27] was elected Chairman.[28] The Secondary School Committee elected John Munro as Convener.[29] The Former Pupils requested, but were denied, separate representation.[30]

Buildings

With finances on a surer footing the Governors turned their attention to their buildings. The temporary blocks had been built in 1911 and extended in 1919 and the new courses on offer needed upgraded accommodation. An overall strategy for the Technical College was accepted by the Chairman's Committee on 30 January 1925. The plans were supplied by architect, R. Leslie Rollo, and envisaged a two-storey building on the east side of the Quadrangle encompassing engineering, chemistry, pharmacy and navigation, with the three-storey art building being extended eastwards. It was to be completed in stages at a total cost of £103,000.[31] As there had been much initial work, progress was swift and the new engineering laboratories were officially opened on 25 September 1925[32] and the new Physics Department opened by Professor G. P. Thomson, Chair of Natural Philosophy at the University of Aberdeen, in mid-October.[33]

For Morrison and the College the priority was a hall. He had mentioned the importance of a hall to school life when speaking at his first Old Boys' Annual Dinner as Headmaster.[34] In January 1925 Lady MacRobert told the Chairman of Governors, Walter Reid, that following the intention of her late husband she would gift £5000 towards the building of a hall.[35] Two sites were examined – the west side of the College avenue and the north-west corner of the playground at the junction of St Andrews Street and Blackfriars Street. It was decided that the former would be better, and should be able to accommodate the whole school (over 800 pupils) at one time. It would be 90 feet. by 45 feet., and was to include a gallery and platform at an estimated cost of £11,000.[36] Unfortunately, the final estimates in August 1928 were about £5000 over the projected budget and the Governors reluctantly took the architect's advice and deferred building until prices were keener.[37]

The delay highlighted, more than ever, a disparity in spending on the Technical College as compared with the School. During 1927–8 engineering, chemistry, pharmacy, metallurgy and physics laboratories had been provided at a cost of £21,922[38] and gradually the temporary buildings began to disappear. Nonetheless, the Secondary School Committee was able to persuade the Governors to complete the west side of the avenue in a manner corresponding to the Technical College building on the east side. As a result Morrison had talks with the architect and HMI and, after spending two weeks visiting schools in England in October/November 1929, was able to influence the details of the building programme.

The foundation stone of the hall was laid[39] on 13 December 1929 – the Bicentenary anniversary – by W. W. McKechnie, Secretary of the SED.[40] The plan was now to build, alongside the Hall, an extended library (with a capacity for 12,000 volumes), a reading room and administrative offices, along with four new classrooms specifically for the school.[41] The cost of these additions was made more manageable by Lady MacRobert raising her contribution for the Hall to £6,500.

It was at this time (September–November 1930) that the School moved into the semi-detached building beside Crooked Lane. It had been reconditioned following the moving of navigation classes and provided four more classrooms.[42] Meantime the new wing on the east side was completed by late September 1930 with the Hall not far behind. The creation of the Hall caused a problem of nomenclature. Since the building of the Auld Hoose in the 18th century the meeting room of the Governors on the first floor had traditionally been called the Governors' Hall. Its name now had to be changed. After some debate the term Governors' Room was chosen to distinguish it from the new Hall whose opening ceremony was carried out by Lady MacRobert unveiling a bronze plaque in the vestibule. It contained the inscription: 'This hall was opened on 19 March 1931 by Rachel Workman, Lady MacRobert of Cawnpore, India, a generous donor towards the cost of its erection.' The Hall had been built in English Renaissance style, accommodated 900 and would be used for assemblies, presentations of prizes, lectures, exhibitions, concerts, meetings and dramatic presentations.

The Governors planned the removal of the remainder of the temporary buildings at the end of session 1930–1 to allow the gardens to be laid out and the avenues completed. Although somewhat inconvenient for the School which used six classrooms there, Morrison agreed to use other buildings until the new buildings were ready.[43] The kindergarten finally moved into the ground floor rooms three weeks into term-time allowing the primary 1 and 2 classes to gain access to the first-floor rooms.[44]

The Bicentenary in 1929 found the school in good order, although it was perhaps not quite reaching the academic heights of its 'golden age' under Ogilvie. Its roll of 849 was the highest since 1910 (with the solitary exception of the abnormal year of 1919) and this included a primary department of 200, showing the wisdom of Morrison's decision to extend the School downwards in age. The number of county pupils had been increasing again, with some 153 coming from Aberdeenshire and Kincardineshire. Annual HMI reports remained highly satisfactory.

Morrison had inherited, in 1920, a strong staff of 48, including six women, who had joined during the First War and stayed on. It had a good balance of youth and experience, from John Mackintosh (aged 24) to Edward Hay (aged 59). The average age was 39. Exceptional loyalty had been shown by James Rennie, Edward Hay, James Thomson, Robert Ogg, John Craig and Herbert Williams.[45] But, with nine staff members in their twenties, the College did not appear to have problems recruiting young, able and well-qualified teachers. Except for the art and woodwork staff, all had degrees (or their equivalent), half of them had honours degrees and indeed seven had first class honours. The strong academic tradition, developed after 1881, was certainly continuing.

As his Inverness staff had included six connected with Gordon's it was no surprise when Morrison appointed insiders to promoted posts and former pupils to assistant positions. His appointments included the promotion of Malcolm Murray to Head of French in 1921 and former pupils George Gibson (classics) in 1925, James Gordon to Head of Science[46] from Madras Academy, and David Donald (mathematics) in November 1931. Other names to become famous in Gordon's history appointed in this period included John Foster (English), Walter Humphries (English and philosophy) and Hector Donaldson (science).

Morrison's Achievements

Pleased with the progress and efficiency of the School, the Governors increased Morrison's salary to £1100 from the beginning of session 1929–30. It was his first salary increase since his appointment in 1920![47] His achievements were also recognised by the University of Aberdeen, which conferred the degree of Doctor of Laws on him in March 1930.[48] He was also elected President of the Educational Institute of Scotland (EIS), the main teaching union in Scotland, and the Governors agreed to James Duthie taking on some extra duties to free up the Headmaster, who needed to be away from school regularly on EIS business.[49] Indeed, during his Presidential year Morrison was away from school on a number of occasions attending EIS meetings in Edinburgh, Glasgow and London. His musical interests also meant involvement with the Music Committee set up by the BBC and this led in turn to a commitment to school broadcasting.

Morrison took the opportunity of the half-century anniversary of the College to reminisce about the open competition foundationer boys, many from poor homes, who had done well in life.[50] He produced an impressive list of distinguished FPs who had reached key positions all over the world, including the principalships of four universities – John Murray at Exeter, Robert Wallace at Sydney, William Urquhart at Calcutta and John McKenzie at Bombay.[51] This was appropriate, as Morrison himself had been an outstanding scholar who would have graced any university and during his time as Headmaster he had done much to consolidate and enhance the School's standing and reputation. He had done so by being the first Headmaster of Gordon's to play a national role in education.[52]

In a number of respects Morrison was unfortunate to be Head at a particularly difficult period. Financial stringency was the order of the day and the SED, constantly and rigorously, scrutinised all expenditure. The national situation impacted on the School at various points, the 10% salary cuts in teachers' salaries in September 1931 being the most significant example. Taking over from the EA the Town Council also continued to look for possible economies, as its contribution in 1931–2 reached £2520 for the School (up £788 on the previous year) and £5062 for the Technical College (up £680).[53]

Morrison was also deeply conscious of the weak and vulnerable position of the School. Its continued existence could not be guaranteed but co-operation and harmony, especially with the Technical College departments, helped foster the perception of the School as an integral part of 'the Colleges'. Chairman Reid also shared this strategy and the idea of a Founder's Day, first floated by him in September 1928, was to celebrate the unity of aim in the management of the Colleges.[54] He looked forward to having a Founder's Day when the Schoolhill site would be 'a place of beauty'[55] and he returned to this theme again in November 1929.[56] This would only be possible when all vestiges of the 'tin palaces' had been removed and the completed buildings of the Technical College were finally opened. This was accomplished by Sir Frank E. Smith on 6 October 1932.[57] But by then it was too late for Morrison. On 11 November 1932 he had intimated his intention to retire at Easter 1933 after twelve and a half years as Headmaster and 43 years as a member of the teaching profession.[58]

Morrison left the College in April 1933 and his departure was felt most by his loyal staff, who respected him as teacher and leader. He had been the strongest scholar ever to be Head and some of his successor's reputation was based on his groundwork. Fortunately, he was not immediately lost to the educational world. In 1934 he was elected Liberal MP for the Scottish Universities[59] while, in addition, he acted as Parliamentary Secretary to the

EIS. He retired finally in 1945, returning to Dufftown where music, languages, golf and fishing were his major relaxations. He died in a Lossiemouth nursing home on 8 September 1956, aged 86.

In January 1933, the 23 candidates for the post of Headmaster were considered by the Secondary School Committee and a short-list of five drawn up – all honours graduates from Scottish universities.[60] Following their interview on 3 February, the Committee unanimously recommended that Ian Graham Andrew be appointed Headmaster at a salary of £900 p.a., rising in increments of £25 to £1,000. A week later this was accepted by the Governors.[61] On 18 April, Andrew was welcomed and introduced at a special School Assembly by John Munro, Walter Reid, Joseph Bissett, President of the FP Association, and J. W. Thomson, Head of the Mathematics Department.

Andrew Takes the Helm

Ian Graham Andrew was born a son of the manse on 6 September 1893 at Barrhill, Ayrshire. Following a solid foundation at the village school he gained a bursary to Ayr Academy in 1906. The Headmaster there, William Maybin, was still attempting to keep 'modern developments' out of education and so his best pupils, who included Andrew, were debarred from taking science. In 1908, Andrew won a bursary to the High School of Glasgow, 'one of our great national schools',[62] continued a classical education under W. King Gillies,[63] and went on to win ninth place in the University of Glasgow Bursary Competition in 1911.[64] Soon after the outbreak of war in September 1914, he responded to Cameron of Lochiel's call for volunteers, and became part of the Glasgow University's Company of the 6th Cameron Highlanders. He was wounded at Loos in September 1915, and again at Arras in the following year. On demobilisation in April 1919 he returned to the University, where in June he was awarded a good War Honours Degree in English Literature and Moral Philosophy, having discarded the classics despite his brilliance in the area.

His first post was as an assistant English teacher at Kelvinside Academy under the headship of Douglas Millar[65] but after only three months teaching there he was persuaded by his old Rector, Dr Peter Pinkerton, of the High School, to join his staff. He did so believing that his chances of promotion would be significantly better if he joined a state school, which the High School was at that time. This proved correct, for he was short-listed for the Rectorship of Forres Academy before being appointed Rector of Elgin Academy at only 28 years of age. He had less than three years of teaching experience when appointed.[66] Despite some initial problems, his decade at Elgin was very successful. He created a sixth form, introduced morning assemblies, prefects, school uniform and, games,[67] and brought in an elementary department – most of these on the High School of Glasgow model – so making a national reputation. He was 'head-hunted' by Dr Walter Reid, who supported his candidature from the beginning and ensured he became Headmaster at Gordon's College.

At Gordon's, Andrew inherited a talented, if ageing, staff from Morrison.[68] Of particular prominence in the very strong cohort of heads of department were the urbane and gentle 'Devil' Thomson (of mathematics), the invigorating James 'Curly' Henderson (of English), Malcolm 'Convict' Murray (of French), whose Leaving Certificate results were outstanding, and the tenacious William Copland (of classics), who was to become a tower of strength as Andrew's unofficial and unpaid deputy head.[69] However, the first real test on staffing for Andrew came almost immediately as Henderson intimated his intention to retire in summer 1933. Andrew decided that Walter Humphries, aged only thirty and the most junior assistant in the English Department, should be promoted to Henderson's post. Such a brave move was complemented by persuading the Governors to create a separate History Department for the heir-apparent in English, John Mackintosh, himself only 37. With both Humphries and Mackintosh satisfied, a difficult problem had been resolved and the staff appreciated the win-win decision.[70]

Andrew made another significant appointment in his first months. A young George Barton, aged 23, was appointed to the Primary Department and its discipline improved almost immediately. Within a year Barton was in charge of the primary and beginning a career which was to affect the lives of many young boys for the next forty years.[71] He began in his first year by introducing extra classes in primary 4 and 5 for 'backward pupils'.[72]

A 'Breath of Fresh Air'

Andrew saw the need to develop a more tangible esprit de corps, introducing the school song 'Out from the vaulted gateway'. He then furthered the community feeling by holding morning assemblies for the School in the MacRobert Hall,[73] where he had erected newly created Dux Boards.[74] He then informed the Governors that he intended to create prefects, up to eight senior boys, who would be involved in supporting the Headmaster and staff. Their first duty, in September 1933, was reading from the Bible at Assembly.[75]

Andrew was quick to advance the concept of a Founder's Day. Although he could not claim to have thought of the idea – most recently it had been advocated by the distinguished FP, Dr John Murray, then Principal of the University College of the South-West of England – Andrew very much moulded the actual occasion. He made it a School event – with no apparent objection from James McKenzie, Secretary of the Governing Body.[76] He then invited dignatories from the Town and the University, who all arrived in their finery on 28 April 1934 and marched in procession with the College staff and pupils to St Nicholas West Kirk for a service. Wreaths were then laid at the Memorial Tablet of the Founder in Drum's Aisle by the School Captain and the President of the Former Pupil Association.[77] Andrew further determined that an Oration should be given by a distinguished FP and he chose as the first Orator, Baillie John D. Munro, Convener of the School Committee. He asked Munro to speak about Robert Gordon and his historical background, setting a precedent for all later Orators to follow.[78] Another tradition also begun was an annual lunch following the service, which involved Governors, guests and heads of departments.[79]

Andrew rounded off a very successful first Founder's Day with a cricket match between the School and Gordonians, and, in the evening, the first production of a chronicle play, 'The Auld Hoose', written jointly by Humphries and Mackintosh with John Foster of the English Department admirably playing the lead role of Robert Gordon.[80] Its success led to further productions of the play in more recent years. The Governors could not have been more pleased.

Morrison had left a full school with a roll of 1009 (285 primary and 724 secondary) at the beginning of session 1933–4. As a classicist, he had supported the value and importance of a classical education, yet he also appreciated that a number of boys found it difficult to cope with its demands. Therefore he allowed the 'weaker' boys to take commercial or technical subjects instead. Andrew went further: following the Founder's wishes he believed that the most able should have the opportunity to choose to study commercial or technical in place of classics. Gordon's College was one of the first schools with a long-standing classical tradition to make such a provision in areas generally considered to be inimical to that tradition.[81] In the event, despite the concerns of Copland, classics did not suffer and the School's results in the Leaving Certificate and University Bursary Competition remained as spectacular as ever.

As important, Andrew had appreciated from the first that Gordon's was not a grammar school, a classical school: it was a School whose activities would be as varied as circumstances dictated for the needs of the pupils.

The widening of the College curriculum led Andrew to consider the issue of guidance in the choice of careers. At this time official careers masters were almost unknown in Scotland, although Heads and their staff gave much informal assistance to pupils who needed it. Andrew, however, believed that up-to-date and accurate information on qualifications and careers could only be given properly by someone who had developed specific expertise. The retiral of John M. Barclay, in 1936, as commercial teacher after 41 years' service, allowed Andrew the opportunity to appoint William Savage[82] as commercial teacher with special responsibility for careers.[83] The quality of his advice and support – he produced a publication 'Careers Open to Boys' – was soon being noticed in schools in Aberdeen and beyond.

Andrew turned his attention to School accommodation and reported to the Secondary Committee on its inadequacies in September 1934. When his observations were confirmed by the annual HMI Report the Governors undertook a comprehensive survey of School facilities. It made grim reading. The School needed four to six additional classrooms, a second gymnasium (principally for the Junior School), cloakrooms, and additional specialist rooms for art and technical drawing. It also suggested the need to consider improving the staff-room and office accommodation, adding another science laboratory, and refurbishment of the Crooked Lane block.[84] J. A. Ogg Allan, architect, was engaged to prepare sketch plans and give an estimate of costs.

Almost simultaneously, in July 1935, the Governors received a letter from a 'Donors' Committee' made up of Walter Reid, William Tawse and James Mackie, proposing plans for a swimming pool on the site of the plumber's workshop and janitor's house, beside the existing gymnasium.[85] The Governors accepted with alacrity the generous offer and planning began for this exciting new project.

It was at this point that the composition of the Governing Body of the Colleges was changed again. The genesis of this development was almost totally the result of external circumstances. Following a Departmental Committee Report on Educational Endowments,[86] chaired by Lord Mackenzie, in August 1927, the Conservative Paymaster-General, the Duke of Sutherland, introduced a Bill into the House of Lords in May 1928 to review, and if necessary reorganise, all Scottish endowments. The 1881 arrangements and the 1909 and

1923 Provisional Orders for the Colleges came under the scope of this legislation, as the Government held that many endowments were not giving value for money. Despite some concerns about increasing disregard for founders' intentions it therefore pressed on and the Bill became law in August 1928 and a Commission under the Earl of Elgin was created on 20 November.

Immediately hopes were raised in some circles that the 'injustice' of 1909 would be rectified. However, the suggestion of Councillor John Clarke, Master of Mortifications, that the Aberdeen Endowments Trust should work as a subcommittee of the Town Council, under the new Local Government Act which was just coming into operation, was rejected by the AET, which pointed out how efficiently its revenues were being applied and how well the status quo was working.[87] Hopes, however, were not completely extinguished, for the First Report of the Commissioners in June 1930 recommended doing away with extra layers of administration to save considerable expenditure.[88]

By January 1933 discussion between the Town Council, AET, Governors of the Colleges and the FP Association had clarified stances. It was agreed that arrangements between the School and Technical College on the site and buildings were so interwoven that it was 'not productive to set up two bodies to govern what is historically and physically one institution'.[89] Co-option of persons with special skills on the Governing Body and on the Committees dealing with the various Schools of the Technical College and the College was working well and should continue. However, it was conceded that the sizes of both the Governing Body and the AET were cumbersome and, given the demands now being made on councillors, there were good reasons to cut total numbers.

The Commissioners met in the Aberdeen Town Hall in early February 1933, with the Colleges the centre of attention on the third day of proceedings. Given the consensus agreed beforehand, the issues for discussion revolved around amalgamation of certain bursaries and representation for Presbytery and the FP Association on Governing Boards. The resulting Draft Scheme produced by the Commissioners proved 'a good deal better than might have been expected'.[90] The strong reputation of the Colleges had led to mere tinkering – the Boards of the Colleges and the AET were cut down, some benefactions were transferred to the Colleges and AET from the Town Council and private trustees, the AET was to spend £1260 annually on poor orphans, Grammar School boys and bursaries, and a new Technical College Committee was to be introduced.[91]

The Commissioners felt that the Governing Bodies had been unhelpful and unwilling to suggest pioneering alternatives for the use of the endowments. They should be used for something beyond the ordinary and not just to relieve the rates. The Governors, however, could not conceive of any purpose which could not be got from rates. The Commissioners felt that since 1881 the original purpose of need had been overlaid by competitive awards, with merit becoming the criterion. The aim here was to encourage secondary education and its status by advancing scholarship. Now the Commissioners wanted to develop a broader system and suggested one way of attracting more pupils would be to increase the inadequate bursary levels.[92]

The changes were incorporated in the Aberdeen Educational Endowments Scheme 1934 which gained royal assent on 15 July 1935. The first meeting of the new Governing Body under these arrangements took place on 14 October 1935 with Lord Provost Henry Alexander (ex-officio) in the chair.[93] With his inclusion there were now 22 Governors (previously 33).[94] The Governors appointed nine Standing Committees: the Secondary School Committee was made up of ten members under Baillie Munro (and, following an Agreement in 1923, included five more co-opted members elected by the Education Committee of the Town Council); the Playing Field Committee (formed in 1922) under Baillie Munro had seven members – the Headmaster, three Governors, two Former Pupils, and one member of the School teaching staff; only the Finance and Buildings Committee and the Chairman's Committee had a locus in the School, the others (Engineering, Chemistry and Pharmacy, Arts and Crafts, Domestic Science and Navigation) were all purely involved in Technical College matters.[95]

If Andrew had any concerns about the composition of the Governing Body or School Committee, within two weeks they had been allayed. Munro had been confirmed immediately as Convener of the School Committee and on 28 October Walter Reid was reappointed Chairman of Governors.[96] It was business as usual.

Further Priorities

Three weeks later at the London Gordonian Dinner Andrew spoke about his three priorities – the building of a swimming pond, the creation of a worthy library (one as good as that of the Grammar School), and the opening of a boarding house.[97] By Founder's Day 1936 he was well on his way to achieving the first of these and the Orator, Principal John Murray, laid its foundation stone. Moreover, although the idea of a boarding house had been suggested as early as June 1932,[98] in his thought-provoking address Murray made an elegant plea for the provision of a boarding house in connection with the School to which Gordonians who had sought their fortunes further afield could send their sons. Within a month, on 26 May, the Governors were informed that the School had been left a substantial legacy by Peter Scatterty, and the way was open for the realisation of all Andrew's ambitions.

Andrew made a point of ensuring that each successive Founder's Day was marked with some significant school development. In 1937 the 'best-equipped school swimming pond in Scotland'[99] was opened by J. W. Peck, Secretary of the SED.[100] It was 75 feet long by 30 feet wide, varying in depth from 3 feet to 7 feet 6 inches, with 11 springboards at the deep end. The pool hall, with terrazzo work on the walls, rose to a curved roof. The building also housed dressing cubicles, showers and footbaths. The three donors continued to insist on anonymity – in public at least – and so the memorial tablet of pinkish Peterhead granite with a symbolic pelican simply stated: 'This tablet records with gratitude the efforts of three devoted sons of Robert Gordon's College through whose exertions and generosity this swimming-pool has been provided. MCMXXXVII.'

Reid had also persuaded the contractors, as Gordonians, to forgo any personal profit in the building as their contribution towards costs. Andrew obtained advice from George Watson's College, which had just completed a swimming pond, which enabled Gordon's to avoid many of the problems which usually plagued such ventures. Much credit was owing to the architect/engineer, Alexander Cruickshank, Head of the Building and Surveying Department of the Technical College. He ensured that although there might be bigger ponds there were none better appointed or equipped.[101]

Andrew was visited at School in 1936 by the brother of Captain Archibald Bissett Smith, who had attended Gordon's between 1893 and 1895. In March 1917 he had been in command of the steamship *Otaki*,[102] which, with one 4.7 gun of the old pattern, fought to a standstill the heavily armed German raider *Moewe*. The German commander later told how, despite German supremacy of six to one, the *Otaki* came close to sinking its enemy. However, Captain Smith ordered his crew to abandon ship but he remained on it as it went down with flying colours.[103] He was awarded a posthumous Victoria Cross – one of only two awarded to the Merchant Service during the First World War.[104]

Bissett Smith's brother presented the School with a Memorial Shield to be awarded annually to the boy who was adjudged pre-eminent in character, athletics and leadership. He also suggested that the NZ Shipping Company, of which he was a Chief Engineer, was keen to be involved in doing something in memory of Captain Smith. Andrew followed this up and the Company generously offered annually to the winner of the Otaki Shield a free return passage to and from New Zealand. On 26 May 1937 W. J. Jordan, the High Commissioner for New Zealand, wrote to Andrew about the 'heroic' fight of the *Otaki* which 'lives in the memory of every New Zealander'. He offered to contact the Prime Minister and 'ask what can be done to help the scholar when in New Zealand'.[105] From that time on the NZ Ceremonial Office has involved itself in the visits making every scholar an official guest of the Government. With School Captain William Anderson began a link which to date has seen over sixty boys from Gordon's proudly call themselves 'Otaki Scholars'.[106]

At the prize-giving in 1936 Andrew was able to announce that under the Will of Peter Scatterty, a native of North Boddam, Insch, who had died in Johannesberg in May, the College was to receive half the residue of his estate after certain bequests.

Scatterty had made his fortune as a mine manager in South Africa but in his late sixties he contracted an incurable disease. As a bachelor, who had done all he intended to do for his relatives, he asked advice about institutions in Aberdeen which he could consider supporting financially. His closest friends were George Harper and his business adviser William Mackenzie – both Gordonians.[107] In the event, Scatterty divided his money between the Infirmary and the College, and, with £47,000 added to the School funds, Andrew could now take forward his ambitious plans.[108]

Andrew was not supported in his plans for a boarding house by Chairman Reid, who saw it as a step back towards 'monasticism'. Andrew, therefore, turned instead to the President of the Former Pupil Association, John N. Milne, who, given his background as a successful businessman, was well suited to raising the £5000 capital in £1 shares for the RGC Boarding House Company. Milne became Chairman of the Company, with Andrew and Munro ex-officio members of the Board of Directors along with three members of the Secondary School Committee and William Tawse.[109] The property chosen was 15 and 16 Albyn Terrace, situated on a tram route within walking distance of the College and about half-way between the College and the Seafield playing-fields. George Barton was made Housemaster – an inspired choice – and the refurbished buildings, named Sillerton House, were opened officially on 30 August 1937 by Sir William McKechnie, former Secretary of the SED. Its success was immediate and the then capacity of 36 was reached by the end of 1938.[110]

Andrew moved on to what for him was probably his most important project – the Library.[111] The large empty room beside the MacRobert Hall had been earmarked for a library for the Colleges together but, with no agreement on how to proceed and no money to embark on a potentially expensive project, there had been no progress. Another hurdle was the insistence of James McKenzie that any project had to include the whole institution. However, Andrew's proposals, presented on 6 June 1936 to the Governors, were accepted. The empty room would become a joint lending library and reading room, serving the needs of the Technical College and School. In time, the School would use the two adjacent classrooms as a separate reading-room but, in the meantime, a Librarian should be appointed to serve the whole institution.[112] Andrew had made significant progress, knowing that the Technical College and Gray's School of Art, with other priorities and no finance, would not involve themselves much in the project. The bonus was that he had obtained a Librarian, which he would not have achieved without agreeing to a joint Library. Andrew involved himself in the furnishings of the Library along with the architect, Ogg Allan, and in stocking it with books. It was opened on Founder's Day 1938 by Chairman Reid. The Peter Scatterty memorial was placed on its north wall and was unveiled by School Captain, Douglas Fox. It consisted of a bronze plaque[113] on an oak panel with the inscription:

This Memorial commemorates the Peter Scatterty Bequest
to Gordon's College.

Peter Scatterty
born Waulkmill, Premnay 20 April 1868
died Johannesberg,
South Africa 6 May 1936

The Scatterty money was also used for a number of other ventures, such as contributing to William Cullen taking fourteen boys to Austria in summer 1937.[114] The staff, too, benefited. The largest classroom in the School was gutted, oak panelled, and furnished in a similar style to the Library, with a large bookcase, becoming the Staff Room (male). The centrepiece was to be a fireplace made of Rhynie stone but this was opposed by McKenzie, who reminded the Governors that when the central heating system had been installed it had been decided that there would be no more open fireplaces on the grounds of economy and safety. Andrew persuaded the Governors to make an exception, something that would not have happened under Morrison.

Andrew was keen to go ahead with further accommodation improvements. The Pavilion was extended and modernised at a cost of £6600, and finally opened on Founder's Day 1939. Next on the list was a second gym mainly for the Junior Department, which the Governors approved in July 1938,[115] and the reconstruction of the Crooked Lane block, which was an eyesore and also caused safety worries. These developments would have swallowed up the remainder of the Scatterty Bequest but contractor William Tawse urged caution: with building costs declining, a wait of a year, he argued, could save at least 10%. Unfortunately, having persuaded the Governors to delay the international situation deteriorated in the next few months and the cost of building rocketed 300%. The opportunity to improve accommodation was lost for a generation.

The Interruption of War

Session 1938–9 was immediately disrupted with the sudden death, on the eve of the beginning of term, of James Thomson, Principal Teacher of Mathematics. He had, along with Morrison, been responsible for creating the School Orchestra and, with 35 years' service, had been a stalwart.[116] Two weeks later, during the Czech crisis of September 1938, Andrew took steps to put the School into a state of defence in case an emergency should arise. Trenches were pegged out on the lawns and the cellars under the east wing and in the Crooked Lane block were adapted to serve as refuges. Arrangements were made for lectures on first aid and anti-gas training to be given to the staff. Thereafter a permanent first aid unit, consisting of sixteen volunteer teachers, was formed and given further training.

A rough estimate was made of the numbers of different sizes of gas masks required for the pupils: the proper fitting, however, was postponed until they had been delivered. All pupils in the senior School visited the Air-Raid Precautions Exhibition at Woolmanhill on 10 and 11 October. From then on close contact was maintained with the ARP authorities but, until a decision was taken on evacuation, no further steps regarding preparation of shelters could be taken.

Session 1939–40 opened on Friday 1 September with the threat of war imminent. Instructions were issued to the pupils not to return to school until further notice should war break out over the weekend. On 3 September Britain went to war but the SED Circular of 7 September intimated that schools in Aberdeen (a 'neutral' area) could reopen on the completion of safety measures. With emergency shelter available, Forms 5 and 6 returned to School on 19 September. A week later all pupils but the Kindergarten returned.[117] A double-shift was introduced so that a maximum of 500 pupils would be on site at one time: the Junior School and Forms 4, 5 and 6 attended from 8.45am to 1pm, while Forms 1, 2 and 3 attended between 1.45pm until 5.30pm.[118] Under the direction of the City Engineer, covered trenches were dug on both sides of the avenue in the front grounds and, with arrangements for protection completed, practice air raid drills were held for both morning and afternoon schools on 9 and 18 October. During these drills the boys were allocated specific areas in the trenches and were evenly distributed throughout. At the next drill, on 27 October, in the morning all were underground in four minutes, while in the afternoon all were under cover in two minutes twenty seconds.

Staffing became increasingly disrupted as the year progressed. Messrs William Savage (commercial subjects), James Cardno (primary) and Henry Shirley (PT) were called up by the Territorial Army in September 1939, while the Principal PT master J. A. K. Hunter left on 8 November to take up a commission in the Royal Navy. The decision of Alexander Booth (geography) to retire in December 1939 was particularly felt as he had been a pupil at the School for seven years and a member of staff for 38 years and had made an extensive commitment to the College both in and out of the classroom.[119]

Despite such difficulties the SED encouraged the resumption of full-time education. Air shelters in the front grounds catered for 560 and in the cellars another 220 were accommodated. The Governors suggested that with appropriate brickwork and reinforced roofing another 100 pupils could be protected in the main corridor and 100 more in the play-shed. As a result of such arrangements a normal timetable was resumed on 8 April 1940. This helped contribute to the 'excellent' HMI report for the session.[120] The pupils were congratulated for having given up so much of their leisure time to assist in such vital war duties as sandbagging, harvesting and forestry. The adaptation of the life of the School to wartime conditions had been accomplished 'smoothly and successfully'.[121] 'That this change has involved neither an appreciable decline in the standard of the work nor the sacrifice of any essential activity is a notable tribute to the efficiency of the staff and the organising ability of the Rector [sic].'[122]

During 1940–1 air-raid drills turned into real alarms, of which some 31 happened during the year, although most were short interruptions of less than an hour.[123] First aid and fire-fighting parties were formed, composed of staff and senior pupils, and they also provided nightly fire-pickets until November 1940 when their place was taken by night watchmen engaged by the Governors. However, no bombs were dropped on or near the College except on 14 February 1941 when four school windows were broken during the bombing of Loch Street.

Following an appeal by the Secretary of State for Air, a College Squadron of the Air Training Corps was formed in March 1941 and within a few months it numbered 130.[124] Such developments continued despite the increasing depletion of staff: John Gilbert (geography) left for the RAF on 6 September 1940 and James Sawers (Junior School) joined the Scots Guards on 16 October. Before the next session had begun they had been joined by Hunter Diack, Henry Dobbins, Arthur Forbes, John M. Taylor and David R. Thorburn, who had all been called up.

At the Governors' meeting on 28 November 1941 it was reported that two Governors had offered to provide, free of cost to the Governors, a granite memorial tablet to Alexander Simpson of Collyhill, to be placed on the east wall of the west wing of the College and to be inscribed:

> In 1816 Alexander Simpson of Collyhill bequeathed his estates of Barrack and Crichie to the Governors of Robert Gordon's Hospital in Trust. The east and west wings were built in 1833 at a cost of £13,255, of which the sum of £4,147 was paid by the Trust. By these generous gifts the educational benefits of the Hospital were greatly extended.

The Governors accepted the offer and Andrew's special event on Founder's Day 1942 was its unveiling by Chairman Reid.[125]

When Reid decided to retire from Chairmanship of the Governors, in October 1942, owing to the state of his health, the Governors placed on record their appreciation of his work as a Governor for 21 years and as Chairman since 1924. He had personally contributed to the MacRobert Hall, Library and swimming pool and had amply fulfilled the express wish of the pious Founder that boys 'pay back to the Hospital what was laid out and expended on them during the time they were in the Hospital and putting them to a trade or otherwise'.[126] Andrew had indeed been fortunate to have him as his Chairman. Reid decided to stay on meantime as a Governor[127] and the whole Gordon's community was pleased that the Governors unanimously decided to appoint Baillie John D. Munro as the new Chairman, while retaining the Convenership of the School Committee.

There were fewer air raids in 1942–3. Ironically, one of the last, during the night of 20/21 April 1943, proved the most damaging. A high-explosive bomb exploded about ten yards from the windows of the Headmaster's room. Although there were no casualties, or indeed structural damage to the Auld Hoose, about a hundred panes of glass were broken, more particularly roof lights.

Much to the disappointment of all connected to the College, Andrew decided to apply for the post of Principal of George Watson's College in Edinburgh vacated by the retirement of his good friend, George Robertson. In February 1943 the Governors heard with mixed feelings about his success. Later, Andrew held that he had always 'cherished a warm admiration' for Watson's, believing it to be 'the greatest school in Scotland'.[128] Such an admission might have motivated others to remain at Gordon's until it could make such a claim. Yet what seems to have been as important in Andrew's decision to move was a determination not to 'run away' from a new challenge. He had done this earlier in his career and this time he was not going to be deflected 'from the course which legitimate professional pride' told him clearly to follow.

His final Founder's Day occasion in April 1943 was therefore tinged with sadness although Andrew still found something extra to celebrate, with Baillie Mackie opening the new Miniature Rifle Range for the Army and Air Corps.[129]

Some 22 applications were received for the Headmastership and the short-list of four was interviewed on 28 April 1943. There were three external candidates – Nathaniel Clapton, Headmaster of Boteler Grammar School, Warrington; John Clarke, Rector of Paisley Grammar School and David E. Collier (aged 45), Rector of Morgan Academy, Dundee. The one internal candidate was the flamboyant Walter R. Humphries, Principal Teacher of English at the College. The School Committee recommended Clapton: he had a double first in mathematics from Oxford University and had good teaching and administrative experience, having taught at Watford Grammar School then at Glasgow Academy as Senior Mathematics Master (1934–40) before taking up his headship. Clapton, however, rejected the post, perhaps on account of the salary offered[130] and David Collier was appointed at a salary of £1150 p.a.[131]

Andrew's Reputation

Throughout his tenure and in the years since, Andrew's reputation as Headmaster of Gordon's has remained high. His predecessors had been successful, but they were 'insiders' and Gordon's needed, as all institutions do, fresh impetus from outwith. Andrew provided this, having had experience of a leading Scottish school (Glasgow High), the best of Scottish teachers (Maybin and W. King Gillies were outstanding scholars) and the opportunity at Elgin to try out his ideas.

At Gordon's Andrew was popular with all sections of the College community. His genuine interest in young people shone through. The School was full at over 1000 boys and demand for secondary places was particularly buoyant. Leaving Certificate results had improved from 37 to 62 annually, and the extra-curricular life had been strengthened with all sports, especially swimming, flourishing.

However, at his formal farewell ceremony in June 1943, Andrew told a story about Napoleon who, before appointing any Marshals, used to ask 'Is he a lucky general?' Andrew appreciated his own good fortune, in particular his partnerships with Walter Reid and John Milne, who were both determined to take Gordon's forward and leave behind dark days when the survival of the school was in doubt, and in the timing of the Scatterty Bequest, which brought considerable benefits.

Andrew knew how important these factors were in making his Headship a success. But the outbreak of the War had slowed down the rate of innovation and Andrew looked elsewhere for a new project. Yet in a number of areas, especially accommodation, much remained to be done at Gordon's. The real challenge in 1943 was to take Gordon's further forward, not to move to another school which, Andrew believed, was already at the top. Andrew left with work undone and was (and remains) the only Headmaster in the history of the College not to have retired from Gordon's.

Andrew was not to repeat his Gordon's success at Watson's. Unlike his predecessor there he did not delegate routine administrative tasks[132] and involved himself in all aspects of school life.[133] By 1946 the pressure of running Watson's led Andrew into a 'state of melancholic apathy',[134] and to treatment with electric shocks. He suffered an even more critical illness two years later before finally recovering and ending his tenure on a happier note before retiring in 1953.[135] Nonetheless, in a remarkable career, he left his indelible mark on three schools. He died in Edinburgh on 22 May 1962.

11

A LULL THEN MODERNISATION, 1943–77

David E. Collier

David E. Collier was born in Edinburgh in 1898 and, after a short spell as a pupil at Watson's College, he attended George Heriot's from the age of seven until he left aged sixteen in 1914. At school he was academically strong and figured regularly in annual prize-lists. Although he began classes at the University of Edinburgh he left to join the Army serving in France, first as a corporal in the Royal Engineers and afterwards as an officer in the Royal Garrison Artillery. He was decorated for his bravery, winning the Military Cross. On demobilisation in 1919 he returned to the University and graduated two years later with First Class Honours in Mathematics and Natural Philosophy, winning the Royal Geographical Medal, the Bruce of Grangehill Research Scholarship and the Lanfine Bursary. In 1922 he graduated BSc. and gained his Diploma in Education. During his university career Collier showed outstanding brilliance, helped by a remarkable memory which nothing ever seemed to escape.

Collier was appointed to the staff of Watson's College, where he taught and was a Housemaster for five years. From 1927 to 1931 he was Deputy Head and Form Master of the Sixth Form of the Central Foundation School,[1] London, and from 1931 to 1934 the successful Headmaster of the Southern Secondary School for Boys in Portsmouth.[2] His Chairman of Education there described him, on his departure, as the most capable headmaster there had been in any local secondary school for many years.

On 31 October 1934 Collier was appointed Rector of Morgan Academy,[3] a large school of 1300 pupils with a strong academic tradition. He followed the gifted Dr Leighton, who proved a hard act to follow. However, Collier appears to have done well and the Lord Provost of Dundee praised him for his 'sound scholarship coupled with mental alertness and the ability to express his thoughts in a clear and convincing fashion, a grasp of the essentials of education and an interest in all its phases, sound judgment and the courage of his convictions'.[4]

On 13 April 1942 Collier and William Carnon, the internal candidate, were interviewed by the Governors of George Heriot's for the post of Headmaster but Collier lost the resulting ballot by 11 votes to 7. He was very disappointed at not being able to return to his old school as its leader, especially as Carnon was already sixty years of age and clearly a 'stop-gap'.[5] Undaunted, he applied for the Headship of Gordon's College, at first unsuccessfully as the post was offered to Nathaniel Clapton, who turned it down.[6] The Governors improved the salary on offer and Collier was appointed as Graham Andrew's successor.[7]

Collier opened Morgan Academy for the new session and then joined the College on 6 September 1943. As Andrew had left on 14 August, William Copland was in charge until he arrived. The new Headmaster was installed in the MacRobert Hall on 28 September by the Lord Provost,[8] Governors, Dr Andrew Fowler representing Former Pupils, William Copland representing staff and School Captain, Gordon Farquharson, representing the pupils.[9]

Collier inherited a full school of 1043 pupils – 791 in secondary and 252 in primary – which was a record enrolment and a rather serious embarrassment in view of the inadequate accommodation available. He was also immediately involved with staffing issues. Dr. Malcolm Murray, Principal Teacher of Modern Languages, resigned for health reasons[10] and was replaced by John B. Hugelshofer.[11] Other staff changes included the retirement of William Cullen,[12] of German, while Emil Lentz, the part-time native teacher of French, was granted leave of absence to join the Armed Forces.[13] Following Copland's work he was officially made Deputy Headmaster of the College from 1 November 1943.[14] James McKenzie, Secretary and Registrar of the Colleges, had effectively been running the Technical College since Stewart's departure in 1921.[15] He announced his decision to retire and the Governors decided that it was time not just to appoint a new Secretary but also to appoint a Director. Increasingly it was felt that the lack of a strategic head had meant that the history of the Technical College between 1921 and 1944 had been characterised by 'a complete lack of imagination and initiative'.[16] On 10 December 1943 the Governors determined that Dr Alexander D. West[17], Principal of Croydon Polytechnic, be appointed to the position of Director, and three weeks later confirmed the decision of the Finance and Buildings Committee that William D. Murdoch be made Clerk and Treasurer.[18] Such changes meant that Collier faced a very different situation at Schoolhill than either Morrison or Andrew.

Style of Leadership

Although Collier was fully conversant with the atmosphere and working of a large boys' day school he did not always find it easy to relate to his charges. He was quiet and reserved by nature but he spoke his mind frankly, sometimes in such blunt terms as to distress boys, and even their parents. He seemed cool and detached, and although his relationships with the Gordonian Association remained cordial he could not empathise with other members of the Gordon's community as Andrew had been able to do. Collier's strengths were in his formidable intellect and memory – speech-making without notes, for example – and in his meticulous organisation. On the opening day of each session he arrived with every timetable, for masters and pupils alike, carefully prepared to the last detail. His administration could not be faulted.

Collier did not come to Gordon's with a preconceived plan or strategy, and although he was aware of accommodation deficiencies he knew, and accepted, perhaps too meekly, that nothing could be done until the Governors were able to complete their 1936 plans. In the meantime there were other matters which commanded his attention.

In December 1943 the Scottish Education Department offered free midday meals by use of equipment operated by the Ministry of Works.[19] Collier consulted with the Director of Education and Organiser of School Meals in the City and it was agreed that, as an experiment, the room on the ground floor of the Blackfriars Street workshops (behind the MacRobert Hall) be fitted out as a dining-room by the Aberdeen Education Committee, whose outlays would be refunded from Government sources.[20] Some 135 pupils indicated a desire to have 'dinners' in the College, which began on 1 February 1944.[21] The experiment was deemed successful and three years later the Governors decided to erect a prefabricated building in the playground to cater for some 576 secondary pupils in two sittings.[22]

Collier was at his best when reorganising the College at the end of the War. This necessitated a considerable rearrangement of timetables as staff returned piecemeal from active service while maintaining the continuity of school work. Collier did this very successfully, in the process displaying a flair for the meticulous. The result was a remarkably smooth transition period and the re-introduction of many pre-war activities. Unfortunately, owing to a change in policy in the national organisation of the Air Training Corps and in the methods of recruitment for the RAF, Collier had, with much regret, to discontinue the College Squadron of the Corps in September 1945 after almost five years of marked success in training boys for the Service. Fortunately he was able to maintain the Army Cadet Force,[23] which he viewed as also significant in contributing to a broader education, and the 19th and 30th Scout groups which remained popular.[24]

Collier appreciated the importance of the extra-curricular activites on offer and encouraged not just the wide sporting calendar – rugby, hockey, association football and swimming – but also the revival of a Dramatic Society, the Junior and Senior Orchestras and a Literary and Dramatic Society, while a Music Club and Science Club were formed. However, these were at all times secondary to the narrowly academic, which for David Collier was the rationale of the College.

Sometimes this emphasis showed him in a poor light. His resistance to giving music more time as a curricular subject in the early years of secondary and his opposition to its development as a certificate subject for senior pupils is best explained by his determination not to 'dilute' the focus on what he deemed the more academic.[25]

His treatment of Ian Black, one of the most outstanding swimmers Britain has produced, damaged his reputation even more. In late summer 1958 Black, still in fifth year, won a Gold and two Silver medals at the British Empire and Commonwealth Games in Cardiff, and then three Golds in the European Championships in Budapest. He was presented with a silver salver by the Governors in a special ceremony.[26] His sights were now on the Olympics in Rome in 1960, but he was denied access to the school pool, which was being renovated. Then his Headmaster, at both Aberdeen and London Association Dinners, declared that he could not help 'deploring the fuss which has been made of him [Black]' while pupils gaining academic success were receiving little recognition. Finally, for a trivial oversight, Collier stripped Black of his prefect's badge so ending the school career of one of Gordon's most successful pupils.[27]

It is not surprising that pupils showed little enthusiasm for Collier's style of leadership. Yet the Headmaster seemed to get on with an older generation of Former Pupils. They respected a man of high ideals, who made crisp judgements and always had the courage of his convictions. As a result ex-pupils supported the College in a number of significant ways.

In January 1946 the Governors accepted, from an anonymous Former Pupil, a decorative panel, carved in oak, which was placed in the West Kirk of St Nicholas, given its long association with the College.[28] Nine months later the Will of John B. Campbell[29] of New York produced a substantial sum which arrived in instalments.[30] The important Mackenzie Travelling Scholarship[31] was also gifted at this time with William 'Buff' Hardie being the first pupil to embark on a three-month trip to South Africa.[32]

By 1950 there was a general appreciation that there was no immediate prospect of creating a special memorial room in the College so the FP Association decided to gift a Compton Electric Organ[33] to the School in memory of the former pupils who gave their lives in the Second World War. The organ was placed in the MacRobert Hall and unveiled and dedicated on 15 October 1951.[34] The Association followed this up by presenting a carved oak memorial plaque to take the place of that presented after the First World War.[35]

Another magnificent gift was given in 1953 when Tom Scott Sutherland, a pupil under Charles Stewart who had gone on to study architecture at the Technical College and then become a most successful entrepreneur, gifted Garthdee House and the surrounding twenty acres to the Governors of the Colleges as a site for a School of Architecture.[36] This was followed in December 1953 by the decision of the FP Association to build a new stand at the Seafield playing-fields. It seated 250 spectators and cost £1000, the Governors enthusiastically contributing £250 towards its erection.[37]

Such contributions made significant differences to the quality of the educational experience on offer at Gordon's College and were particularly important given the political developments in Aberdeen and the precarious financial position of the School. As early as 1947 the Town Council had ended fee-paying in Aberdeen Grammar School and the High School for Girls, the only schools in the state system locally still charging fees, under the provisions of the 1945 Education (Scotland) Act.[38] Initial reservations were gradually overcome[39] and there were few immediate signs that the professional and middle classes had lost confidence in the schools. However, for Gordon's these decisions proved a mixed blessing: its retention of fees would be advantageous only if the fees remained modest and generous bursaries were maintained, while its special status at least was likely to prevent its inclusion in plans for the zoning of catchments and the separation of nursery/primary schools from secondary.[40]

Financial problems

Throughout the 1950s the College was under constant pressure from the Scottish Education Department to restrict expenditure. In response the Governors, in January 1952, conducted a thorough review of the College's financial position, and in order to keep to the SED target of contributing a maximum of 70% of current expenditure (it made no contribution to capital expenditure), they determined to raise fees for the first time since April 1939. Before the end of the decade fees had to increase again so from January 1959 they had tripled in seven years and reached £17 for primary and £27 for secondary pupils.[41]

Despite the financial constraints on the College, Collier and his Chairman, John D. Munro, who retired from the Board in October 1952,[42] were able to take forward a programme of modernisation at Schoolhill which involved the rewiring of the Auld Hoose, the installation of fluorescent lighting in all laboratories and workshops, constant hot-water being made available in all cloakrooms and the acquisition of new desks for six classrooms. However, the major issues regarding the inadequacy of accommodation for art and the poor equipment for the Geography and Technical Departments remained to be tackled.

The new Convener of the Secondary School Committee, John N. Milne, was diverted from these priority issues immediately on taking office. He was involved in defending the College's financial interests before the inquiry of C. W. Graham Guest QC into Educational Endowments in December 1952. However, as on previous occasions, the Governors failed to regain control of their former endowments and were disappointed in their efforts to gain full control over the entry of foundationers and bursars to the College.[43] Indeed, much of the Governors' efforts were concentrated on deflecting the arguments of Baillie MacIver, Convener of the Education Committee, and Frank Scorgie, Aberdeen's Director of Education,[44] who complained that because of bursaries[45] the College took 77 of the top 100 boys into First Year, leaving only eighteen for the Grammar School and five for the Central School. Fortunately, the Commissioner was not persuaded to open AET bursaries to all senior secondary schools,[46] holding that as little money was left from bursaries after books were bought it was not for financial reasons that parents sent their boys to Gordon's.

As the Grammar School had been obtaining most of the 'best' boys pre-war it seems that by the early 1950s the situation had been reversed, presumably because of the attraction of Gordon's as a fee-paying school.[47]

New accommodation plans

In 1954 the accommodation issue came to the forefront again when Aberdeen City produced its Local Development Plan. The Governors took their opportunity and pressed for the inclusion in the Plan of the allocation of an area of ground at Crooked Lane to be used for future extensions to the Secondary School and for additional space.[48] When this was accepted the Governors requested their architects to update the College's pre-war accommodation plans.

The resulting scheme involved two developments – the first westwards from the existing Junior School in the MacRobert Block, and the other eastwards from the existing secondary building. The former envisaged a new wing of three storeys and included five classrooms, a second gym (over the existing gym) and a dining-room and servery, along with additional cloakrooms, toilets, staff space and storage and was estimated at £68,800. The latter entailed a four-storeyed building with five classrooms (three of these new), three benchwork rooms, three science labs, three art rooms, one technical drawing room, one lecture theatre, and a preparation room, at an estimated cost of £101,600.[49]

Although the exciting plans were adopted in principle by the Governors in April 1955 there was an appreciation that it would take some time for them to be completed. Nonetheless, the Chair of Governors, John F. Hall, along with the Convener of Finance and Buildings, Baillie James A. Mackie, and Headmaster Collier met with Sir William Murrie, Secretary of the SED, on 12 May that year, and it was agreed that the Governors should procure a loan of £75,000 and go ahead with the Junior School extension, deferring meantime the more ambitious project.[50] At least the first major accommodation development for the College at Schoolhill since the 1930s was underway.

Again the comparison with the Technical College was marked. Spurred on by pressure from its new Director, Dr West, the Governors added a third storey to its existing technical building, so adding a further 6,600 square feet of extra space. The extension was opened in November 1951 at a cost of £30,660.[51] Yet that still proved inadequate and a further 10,000 square feet were added by the creation of a building behind the MacRobert Hall in September 1960. Add to this the New School of Architecture at Garthdee from May 1957 and the new domestic science building at Kepplestone, opened in September 1963, and the charge, which had been made since 1909, that the College was very much 'a poor relation', continued to have substance.[52]

Staffing

The other major issue which Collier had to contend with was maintaining the quality and quantity of staff. The *Gordonian* lamented in December 1951 that the list of staff changes showed a 'melancholy lengthening'[53] with every passing year. The days were over when men (rather than women) entered in comparative youth and left only when 65 years of age compelled them. A number bemoaned the resulting loss of strength derived from teachers growing up in, and themselves becoming part of, the living tradition of an ancient foundation.

Although there was never an abundance of applicants for any particular teaching post, schools like Gordon's were seen as desirable and rewarding places to teach, particularly for the well-qualified academic. Like his predecessors, Collier continued the tradition of internal promotion for senior posts, which enabled him to employ young assistants, often straight from training college. This ensured a healthy age balance on the staff and created a cadre of enthusiastic young colleagues able and willing to support the extra-curricular life of the College. When William Copland, Deputy Headmaster and Principal Teacher of Classics, resigned in January 1948,[54] he was replaced by James Gordon, PT Science since 1930, as Deputy Headmaster,[55] and George Gibson was promoted to PT Classics. A similar process took place in October 1948 when George Bain, First Assistant in Modern Languages, retired after forty years in teaching[56] and in August 1949 when George Forbes, First Assistant in English, retired: after 41 years' service to his old school.[57] Loyalty to the College continued to be a hallmark of the Gordon's staff. In August 1958 another two stalwarts retired: John Mackintosh had joined the staff in 1920 and been PT History since 1933[58] and Jane C. Smith, who had arrived in 1922 and later become Special Assistant in French and Latin.

Collier's Legacy

If the quality of staff generally remained high, Collier's record in increasing its numbers was disappointing. In March 1946 some forty teachers were employed for 771 boys, a pupil-teacher ratio (PTR) of 19.3 – this at a time when education had reached its worst staffing run-down ever. When he retired in 1960 Collier left 864 boys and forty-four full-time staff and two part-timers – a PTR of 19.2. During Collier's tenure there had been no advance and indeed, as most of the pupil increase had been in the secondary department, the size of classes had grown.

Collier continued in post beyond his 60th birthday. He could be optimistic about accommodation, given that the Governors agreed to an Appeal for £100,000 for the second phase of the building development.[59] However, he must have been less sanguine over the new regulations brought in by the SED in 1959. The grant-in-aid which was so important for the College was to be taken over by central government and the £10,000 per annum contributed locally via the Town Council was to phased out completely by 1963 and would not be replaced. The level of fees needed revision upwards again – primary levels from January 1960 were £20 and secondary £32.

Collier was successful in maintaining the academic standards of the College. He was heartened that the College won the prestigious BBC 'Top of the Form' competition in 1951, although the team included one boy who had been written-off academically by Collier.[60] He was able annually to report to his Governors the successes of Gordon's in the University of Aberdeen Bursary Competition. Indeed, in his final session, 1959–60, seventeen boys gained bursaries, including two of the three most valuable in the Faculty of Arts, three of the seven open bursaries awarded in medicine, and four of fourteen open bursaries in science.[61] He also increased the number in the Sixth Form from twelve to 70 and the number of successes in the Leaving Certificate examinations also advanced to 180. Personally, he was probably most proud about his contribution to the Scout Movement and his personal invitation to join the elite body of British schoolmasters – the Headmasters' Conference (HMC) – in 1953. Gordon's was only the thirteenth Scottish school to join its ranks.[62] Although a personal accolade it also symbolised the high status and reputation of the College.

Despite these successes Collier was regarded as aloof and remote. More was increasingly being asked from headmasters than scholarship and strong discipline. There was little open criticism at the time, for Collier did not seem out of place in a period when authoritarian headmasters were still the norm. Unfortunately for the College he stood in marked contrast to his immediate predecessor. Collier remained respected but never loved for he lacked the common touch needed to gain popularity. Sadly he did not live long to enjoy his retirement for he died in hospital in Chichester on 1 November 1960.

There were 23 applications for Collier's post when he decided to retire, aged 62, in April 1960. A short-leet of four was interviewed on 18 December 1959, and after a second interview, John Marshall, Headmaster of North Berwick High School, was unanimously appointed.[63] He was officially introduced and welcomed to the College on Tuesday 19 April 1960 by John Milne, Convener of the Secondary School Committee, George M. Lawrence, President of the Gordonian Association, John B. Hugelshofer, Deputy Headmaster and Grant A. T. Allan, School Captain.[64]

Jack Marshall

John (Jack) Marshall was born in July 1915 and attended Airdrie Academy. He went on to study Classics at the University of Glasgow in 1935 and obtained a First Class Honours, gaining the Medley Memorial Prize in History and the John Clark Scholarship in Classics. After teaching for two years at Bluevale School, Dennistoun, he joined the staff of Coatbridge Secondary School, before being appointed in 1941 as Principal Teacher of Classics at North Berwick High School, where he was promoted to the post of Rector in 1950. After ten years running one school he applied and obtained the Headmastership at Gordon's College.

Marshall inherited an institution with a long list of requirements, of which the most pressing was an acute need for additional accommodation. Although the annual number of entrants to the College remained relatively steady, a considerable number of pupils were staying on longer at school.[65] This general trend was bolstered by the reorganisation of the Scottish Certificate of Education between 1960 and 1962. The introduction of the fourth year Ordinary Grade persuaded many pupils, who in an earlier time might have left school after three years of secondary education,[66] to carry on for an extra year and, with some success there, even further. Simultaneously, greater diversity and flexibility of subject choices were being developed,[67] and the sciences and geography were emphasising more practical work which entailed smaller class sizes. All such measures increased the demands on accommodation.

Fortunately, the extension to the Junior School had been completed.[68] Its nature illustrated the constraints of the built-up site, but clearly the architects had maximised the use of the limited space, and in doing so had created a new dining-room, doubled the gym area, and also come in under budget at £74,586.[69] Fortunately, too, Marshall inherited a Building Fund of £25,133,[70] the first but disappointing results of an ongoing Appeal launched the year before he arrived,[71] and plans for the next phase of building. However, these needed revisiting. Marshall did so and suggested significant changes.[72]

Marshall's Modernisation Programme

By May 1961 Marshall, following discussions with HMI, had convinced the Governors of the need for four additional classrooms beyond those provided for in the approved building plans.[73] However, in the course of producing new plans it became clear that the Crooked Lane site was becoming increasingly problematical for a major extension. Marshall suggested an alternative plan envisaging the provision of all the necessary accommodation in a block to the west of the main School building, adjacent to, and north of, the swimming pool. The block would have exits to the playground as well as connection at two levels with the west wing of the main building. By the use of 'stilts', playground space would be conserved (and indeed sheltered), the lighting for technical rooms would be improved, circulation of pupils would be eased and indeed congestion ameliorated, while the problem of how the College would function during building operations would also be solved. The more restricted Crooked Lane option – first agreed in 1955 and then deferred – was abandoned. The new scheme was four storeyed and would house Science, Technical and Art Departments, and would be detached from the Auld Hoose except for a flyover corridor connected to the existing first floor. The space released by these changes in the west wing made room for nine classrooms for the Geography, Languages and Music Departments. Altogether the plans were estimated at £171,000.[74] It was hoped that the publication of the College's ambitious proposals would help boost the languishing Appeal.

In the event the Appeal finally did pick up and reached its target: by June 1964 some 1,404 donors had committed £79,683 (which grossed up to £103,693),[75] allowing the Governors to meet more than half of the costs of their new building extension, with its sixteen labs, workshops and art rooms, which was opened by Dr John N. Milne, Convener of the Secondary School

Committee, on 26 April 1965. The result was a boost to science, engineering and art at the College.

Marshall was keen that the Governors continued their modernisation programme. He persuaded them[76] that the next priority was library provision,[77] for the handsomely furnished Library adjacent to the MacRobert Hall was only just coping with new standards of utilisation. Accommodation for pupils selecting books appeared adequate, but space for reference and private study purposes fell far short of requirements. In addition, Marshall argued that the Library's situation, remote from the heart of the College, was a handicap.[78] When the Library had been formed in the 1930s the College's Sixth Year numbered a mere twenty, but by the mid-sixties Marshall was proudly boasting that its numbers had gone over the hundred mark and the post-Higher Grade curriculum placed a premium on private study in suitable accommodation. In November 1965 Marshall visited Kirkcaldy High School to view the new Sixth Form study library there.

The initial plans for a Library were opposed by the Scottish Development Department on account of their effect on the existing building, which had been listed in the highest category of buildings of special architectural or historic interest by the Secretary of State.[79] By February 1967 new plans had been produced which had gained planning approval. The Library would be 3000 square feet in area and was estimated to cost £41,267.[80] It was erected in a central position adjacent to the 'bridge' between the new science block and the Auld Hoose; it had three zones of accommodation – for borrowing, for private study and for class teaching. It was officially opened by Dr Roy Strathdee in October 1968,[81] and held a Special Commemorative Exhibition to mark the Tercentenary of Robert Gordon's birth.[82]

Leadership

Marshall's style of leadership contrasted with that of his predecessor and the editor of the *Gordonian* magazine welcomed his new ideas which had brought 'an invigorating experience' to the College.[83] A number of his early decisions – his encouragement of school uniform, his emphasis on careers guidance and advice, the division of science into the separate disciplines of physics and chemistry[84] and the addition of another class in Primary 7 following the decision of the Town Council to close the Grammar School Primary[85] – were all welcomed.

However, Marshall very soon came to understand that there were serious economic and political issues facing the College which threatened the very future of Gordon's and, indeed, all grant-aided schools in Scotland. Within a year of becoming Headmaster he was warning of the need for the College to secure a sounder financial base if it was to survive and prosper. For Gordon's the threat seemed more acute as the SED insisted on the urgent need to upgrade the College while making no financial contribution to the process.[86]

The Governors discussed various options to improve finances. None of them were palatable. The Primary Department seemed more vulnerable and certain Governors contemplated its closure. Increasing the number of fee-paying pupils was another possibility but given the accommodation limitations this could only be done at the expense of bursars, who at this time numbered 257 out of a total roll of 850, and this would be alien to the traditions of the College.

Fortunately there was good news too. When the HMI inspected the College in June 1964 the resulting Report confirmed the good standards of achievement being attained throughout the College.[87] In the first and second years the streamed A, B and C classes took Latin, while the D and E classes took technical subjects. In third year forward there were two broad band ability groups who stayed on to fifth and sixth years (125 of 175), two-thirds of whom went on to higher education. The main issue of concern, other than accommodation, was the large class sizes, which were around 35 in younger years.

The Threat to the College

The arrival to power in 1964 of a Labour Government at Westminster, after a considerable period in opposition, led to the reorganisation of secondary education in Britain on comprehensive lines.[88] In local terms, the transfer exam at 11 plus which determined the secondary destination of children was deemed redundant and would no longer be available as the basis for bursaries and scholarships to Gordon's.[89] In national terms, the Public Schools (Donnison) Commission was set up in December 1965 to advise on the best way of integrating the public schools – which included Gordon's – within the state system of education.[90] A Sub-Committee of the Commission concentrated on Scotland with Sir Roger Young, Principal of Watson's College, as its Vice-Chairman. It took until 1970 to report.[91]

The principle behind Government grants had been accepted for almost a century. When the Government approved of schools run by other bodies – whether local boards or authorities, church authorities, or special governing bodies such as that set up by Robert Gordon in his Mortification – it shared with these bodies the expense of running the school. In Scotland, the norm was the management of a school by a local authority which made a financial contribution from the rates it levied, with the Government making usually a very substantial grant contribution. In the case of Gordon's its funding in the 1960s resulted from contributions from the AET and Town Council (sums set out by legislation), increasing amounts from fee-paying parents and the rest – in the region of 50–58% of the total – in the form of a grant from central government. In return for this support Gordon's saved the state money and accepted a growing number of rules and regulations.

As the twentieth century developed, central government became increasingly dominant in its relationship with local government, and Wilson's Governments (1964–70) determined to dictate to school-managing authorities a particular method of organising schools, viz. comprehensive education. With regard to grant-aided fee-paying schools, the Labour Government decided, as it awaited Donnison, to 'freeze' the annual grant payments which, during a period of inflation, whittled away the percentage of the grant. Fee levels, which had been kept as low as possible to enable those in comparatively humble circumstances to send their sons to the College, spiralled upwards.[92]

Temporary respite came with the advent of Heath's Conservative Government (1970–4) but the Governors appreciated that this was only a breathing space as the Labour opposition accepted Donnison's Report (1970) and was committed, when next in government, to giving grant-aided schools the choice of independence or integration into the state system. Professor George M. Burnett, Convener of the Secondary School Committee between 1968–74, guided a Policy Sub-Committee through a series of options which could confront the College and its viability at different sizes and different fee-levels.

Marshall and his Governors recognised that the most damaging effect of diminution and withdrawal of grant was to the College's most prized tradition: its record of educating able boys from all sections of the community almost regardless of the financial status of their parents.[93] They feared that the artisan class would be hard hit as the fees rose. They therefore determined that a second foundation of scholarships, alongside those administered by the AET, would be needed to retain the character of the College. This was the only way forward, for the alternative, of being absorbed by the local authority and becoming a neighbourhood comprehensive, was a fate which was already overtaking the Grammar School but was not one which appealed to the Gordon's community.

The return of Labour to power in 1974 brought the expected ultimatum to all grant-aided schools on their future. The SED gave a deadline[94] for the Governors to declare their intentions. They responded by determining to 'continue the College in its present form as the only guarantee of its high standards and distinctive character'. They were strengthened in their decision by the overwhelming support of the parents, despite substantial fee increases. The overdue Houghton Award had raised teachers' salaries by 30% in early 1975 and to cope with this the fee levels at Primary had to rise from £167 to £247, and Secondary from £172 to £252.[95] Then into the equation came the phasing out of the grant (frozen at 1972/3 levels over six years from the beginning of the 1976 session), which increased the fees for all fee-paying pupils by another £100. On 13 May 1975 a statement to the parents from the Governors set out the fee levels, the reasons for the considerable increase and a prognosis of the foreseeable future. With the grant in 1975/6 down to 28 per cent of approved expenditure, the Governors confidently expected to retain their numbers as they began the road to full independence. They were right, for the school roll went down by only twenty in the coming weeks.

There were talks between the Governors and a Working Party set up by Grampian Regional Council to discuss future arrangements for the College[96] but it was now clear that the Governors had reluctantly decided to move to independence and the discussions broke down. On 15 September 1975 the Governors informed the Council that the College would continue to operate in terms of the statutory instrument – the 1958 Educational Endowments Act – throughout the period of run-down of the Government grant and then in 1981 become wholly independent.

Simultaneously, in January 1976, the College Appeal, with an ambitious target of £250,000, was launched for the establishment of a new foundation of College Scholarships.[97] This time the target was handsomely surpassed,[98] and the new scholarships were first awarded in August 1977. Sixteen were introduced for First Year with a value of £200 per annum for six years: ten were given to boys from primaries other than Gordon's and six were available for the Junior School pupils of Gordon's. The total matched the number of awards from the AET, whose bursaries were primarily aimed at those who needed full fee assistance to attend the College.[99] The new RGC scholarships were meant to help those who could contribute to fees but needed some financial help to pay the full fee.

Under Marshall, relationships with the AET remained somewhat strained, especially when financial pressures led to the announcement reducing the number of annual bursaries to fifteen for session 1966/7.[100] The situation was aggravated in 1970 when the Trust gave over to the College only £19,350 as the residue of free income and not the expected £32,500.[101] A formal meeting was arranged to discuss matters[102] and the implications for future years. However, the Governors were not satisfied with the results and requested that the Secretary of State initiate a revision of the Educational Endowments Scheme (1958).[103] Fortunately, there was a realisation on both sides of the need to tackle the great disparity which had arisen between the amount paid by the Trust to the Governors in respect of free places and the possible total sum based on the current rate of fees.[104] This led to the decision that the provision for 'not less than thirty bursaries shall be offered each year to boys entering First Year' should be changed to 'not more than twenty foundations', and that the sum specified be deleted. Marshall also ensured that there was the beginning of regular meetings between the Governors and the AET to discuss the number and tenure of free places to be awarded for 1976/7 and thereafter.[105]

Staffing

During his tenure Marshall faced the usual staffing issues with the retiral of a number of long-serving teaching staff.[106] John B. Hugelshofer, Deputy Headmaster and Principal Teacher of Languages, retired in September 1963 and was replaced in the former post by Dr John Forrest, PT English,[107] and in the latter post by John Reid. Two years later John Foster retired[108] followed by Hector Donaldson, PT Chemistry, in October 1966 after 35 years' service.[109] Andrew Forbes, PT Art, retired in August of the following year, after 33 years, and Andy Robb, Swimming Instructor and Pond Superintendent from 1939, did likewise in June 1968. Davie Donald, PT Maths, was commended by the Governors for his loyalty after 40 years on the staff when he retired in June 1971, John Forrest had 28 years service when he followed suit in January 1973, and finally the remarkable George Barton, Head of the Junior School, relinquished his post in August 1974 after 41 years on the staff.[110]

The structure of promoted posts in Scottish secondary schools consisted at this time of a Head and a Deputy Head (very much a recent post to share in the increasing administration involved in running a school) and a line of usually well-qualified Principal Teachers of subject departments who were expected

The Auld Hoose in mid-Victorian times

James Robertson, Master of Gordon's Hospital 1829–32

Andrew Findlater, Headmaster of Gordon's Hospital 1842–49

Memorial to Robert Gordon in Drum's Aisle (1857)

William D. Strahan, Headmaster of Gordon's Hospital 1849–72

Peter Esslemont, Lord Provost of Aberdeen 1880–83, was the driving force behind Hospital reform

James Matthews, ex-Hospital boy who was Lord Provost of Aberdeen 1883-86

Hospital Staff in 1880 with Headmaster Alexander Ogilvie (pictured centre)

College Staff Outing to Muchalls in 1894 with future Headmaster Charles Stewart (in bowler hat)

Lord Provost Alexander Lyon's Dream. The proposed Technical College had become his 'special lobby' (December 1907)

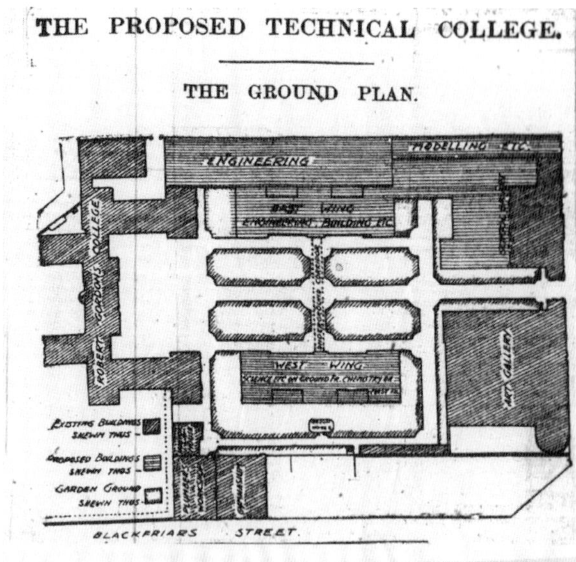

The proposed Technical College Plan of January 1908 of the Town Council on the ground allocated by the College Governors

The Fire of March 1911 caused extensive damage to the East Wing of the Auld Hoose

William Martin's Memorial in the ruined church at Auchendoir, Cabrach (1917)

Headmaster Charles Stewart (front row centre) with the College Staff in 1920

Opening of the Memorial Playing Field and Pavilion at Seafield by Sir Francis Ogilvie, with Headmaster George Morrison in the front row (March 1925)

In 1925 the Technical College began extensive building on the east side of the Quadrangle

On the west side of the Quadrangle the College built a new Hall, which was opened in March 1931. It was named after Lady MacRobert who generously donated towards the building costs

Headmaster Graham Andrew with School Captain Gilbert Gunn (on his immediate right) and the first College Prefects (1933)

The College Governors meet under Dr Walter A. Reid, Chairman 1924–42, in the Governors' Room (1937)

William Anderson, first Otaki scholar, unveils a plaque in the new Swimmimg Pool (1937)

College Headmaster, David E. Collier 1943–60

College Headmasters (left to right) George Allan (1978–96), the late Jack Marshall (1960–77) and Brian Lockhart (1996–2004)

HRH The Princess Royal opens the Library and Information Centre in the Anniversary Year (2000)

Presentation for Sir Graeme Catto (Chairman of Governors 1995–2005) from current Head of College, Hugh Ouston (left) and his successor as Chair, Colin Crosby (right) (2005)

to lead by example as well as supervise all that went on in the classes in their subject. In February 1971 the SED produced Circular 780, a Green Paper, which suggested a radical shift from the traditional structure. To help with administration the role of Assistant Head was to be created[111] and, as a move away from subject dominance, promoted posts in Guidance were introduced. Marshall persuaded the Governors that Gordon's should follow the guidelines and as a result they promoted John Gordon and Ken Anderson to the new posts of Assistant Head[112] and three Principal Teacher of Guidance positions were created, each in charge of advising two secondary year-groups. In doing so, Marshall laid the basis of a promotion structure which was built on by his successors.

Like some Heads in other schools around the same time Marshall found himself under pressure from his pupils, and a few parents, to relax a number of school rules. Unlike some Heads elsewhere, however, Marshall was not of a mind to give way. His staff supported his stance and he also received the backing of the Governors in his determination to implement existing Regulations on 'morals and manners' and on 'the dress appearance and bearing' of College pupils.[113] As a result Marshall was unpopular with the boys and that led to the claim that he never achieved a rapport with them.[114] Although there was substance in this it was not an age where this was expected. Indeed, in defence of Marshall the *Gordonian* suggested that no Head could have, or should have, such a relationship. Nonetheless, Marshall gave a hostage to fortune when he admitted that Headmasters had 'no opportunity of getting to terms with individual pupils' and holding that the pressure of administrative duties prevented him from getting to know all the boys.[115] On the other hand, Marshall had many friends and defenders on his teaching staff. For them, he had led them well during an unsettling period of change. He had exhibited imagination and drive in formulating plans while also being successful in persuading others of the correct course to be followed.

Marshall had been eligible to retire since his 60th birthday in July 1975 but felt it would be an inappropriate time given the political and economic situation facing grant-aided schools in general and the College in particular. The support of parents for the move to independence, the success of the College Appeal and the introduction of new scholarships changed matters dramatically. Marshall decided to retire in December 1977,[116] leaving a school in good heart with 1200 pupils (350 in primary and 850 in secondary).

Importance of Marshall

There were 22 applicants for the advertised post of Headmaster and a short-leet of four was selected for interview. Karl Hearne, the Headmaster of Kings Norton Grammar School for Boys in Birmingham, withdrew; the others were interviewed on 29 September 1977. George Allan, Deputy Headmaster at the College since early 1973, was chosen over Robert Campbell, Rector of Greenock Academy, later a successful President of the Headteachers' Association of Scotland (HAS) and Gordon Stewart, who was to continue as a very popular Deputy at the High School of Dundee until his retiral.[117] On 11 November John Gordon was promoted internally to be Deputy.[118] These promotions were not just a vote of confidence in the successful individuals themselves but also in Jack Marshall's leadership.

Robert Gordon's had benefited from Marshall's experience and expertise in the politics of education at a critical stage in the School's history.[119] The path to independence would inevitably change the College but Marshall and his Governors appreciated that it was the only way to preserve something of the uniqueness of the School and save the legacy of Robert Gordon for posterity. He also contributed substantially to education nationally, being a member of the Advisory Council for Education for Scotland (1955–7), President of HAS (1962–4) and a member of the new General Teaching Council of Scotland (1966–70).[120] In doing so he developed a resilience, toughness and resourcefulness, which were used to great effect when the challenge to the status of the College occurred. His classical training ensured a precision of thought and language, which was important in debate and the drafting of documentation, and his good communication skills made him a kindly interviewer, effective delegator and a regular contributor to Grampian Television. During his long and active retirement Marshall became Co-ordinator of the Scottish Scheme for Oxford Colleges' Admissions (1978–84), continued his work on the Gordon Cook Foundation and remained a JP of the City until 1995.[121] He died in January 2007.

12

TOWARDS THE MODERN SCHOOL, 1978–2007

George A. Allan

George A. Allan was born in February 1936 and educated at Daniel Stewart's College in Edinburgh, where he did well becoming School Captain, obtaining a Flying Scholarship and a University Bursary. He also achieved success at the University of Edinburgh, where, in 1957, he gained First Class Honours in Classics and became the Bruce of Grangehill Scholar. His first teaching appointment took him to Glasgow Academy (1958–60) before returning to Stewart's. After three years he was promoted to Head of Classics, a post he held for a decade. In 1973 he moved to Gordon's College to become Deputy Head and was chosen to succeed Marshall as Headmaster from January 1978.

Every comparatively new Headmaster has a 'shopping list' of priorities for his school and George Allan was no different. He had soon informed the Board of the capital development needed for both Schoolhill and Seafield[1] and been instructed to consult widely and bring forward precise requirements. When he did so his submission included a new biology laboratory, realignment of the Chemistry Department and the creation of two new laboratories, an-all weather hockey pitch suitable for conversion to eight tennis courts in the summer and a new cricket wicket.[2] The Governors were prepared for such expenditure and, having satisfied themselves that a similar pitch to that being proposed was a success at Stowe School and with assurances from Allan that he was not contemplating any other major capital development in the foreseeable future, they sanctioned the expenditure.

Following the Green Paper on Promoted Posts in 1971 the Governors had introduced special salary allowances to discourage College-promoted staff from making a 'sideways' move in status to a local authority school in order to attain a higher salary. That measure had proved effective. In 1979 in reviewing the position Allan persuaded the Governors to introduce a flat-rate special allowance of £100 per annum to all members of the teaching staff in addition to the enhanced responsibility elements. He argued persuasively that this would recognise the quality of the teaching staff and their contribution in and out of the classroom, while also helping to recruit and retain staff.

The Governors were also sensitive to the need to keep modernising the structure of posts in the College. The horizontal Guidance System was extended by Allan in March 1983 with the Assistant Head (Guidance) being supported by a third Principal Teacher and responsibility between the three PTs being divided into S1–2, S3–4 and S5–6.[3] The enhancement of different pathways in career development was thus appreciated and the Governors regularly revisited issues of salary levels, conditions of service,[4] staff professional development and career structure[5] to attract and maintain its traditional quality of staff. Such efforts helped enhance loyalty in times of uncertainty and the sensitivity of the Governors helped staff cope as workload intensified. Staff morale was a discussion topic for the Governors during the widespread disruption in schools following the introduction of the 14–16 Development Programme in December 1984. Allan was rightly proud to inform the Governors that no staff had resorted to strike action despite union pressure and in May 1985 the College allowance was increased to £600 for all teaching staff and the special responsibility elements revised and improved.[6]

One of the strands of Conservative Party thinking had been how a Government should support the grant-aided, soon to be fully independent, school sector. It returned to power in 1979 under Margaret Thatcher and produced the Assisted Places Scheme (APS) in 1981–2, offering bursaries to 'lower income families'. Although the educational intention was admirable – to ensure that the social mix of the schools was as wide as possible and that a lack of money should be no barrier for entry to them – it was politically contentious. Moreover, by now the Governors feared that any government support, however well meant, would bring political strings. There were also practical issues: the Scheme was only for secondary entrants and this might encourage parents to delay application so hitting primary enrolment. The other major drawback – that the election of a Government of a different political complexion would mean the withdrawal of the Scheme[7] – could be overcome by the setting up of a specific bursary fund to deal with this particular scenario.

Following discussions with other schools in the Scottish Council for Independent Schools (SCIS), Allan held the arguments for taking some financial aid were 'compelling' and the Governors decided on qualified support of, and involvement in, the APS.[8] When the Scottish Education Department (SED) inquired officially whether the College was participating, the Governors provisionally agreed.[9] Such a cautious approach led to ten boys being supported under the Scheme in its first year of operation – Albyn had four girls and St Margaret's two, but a number of other schools among the 39 Scottish schools participating committed heavily to remain in business.[10]

For Gordon's the emphasis was placed far more on the fee remissions made possible by the AET and RGC foundations, scholarships and bursaries. In that regard the Governors had been heartened by a letter from the former intimating its wish to award annually eight bursaries along with their sixteen foundations 'thereby re-establishing the 2:1 ratio' between them.[11] By 1984–5, the AET was providing eighteen presentation foundations, four open competition foundations and eight bursaries annually (with a total of 116 boys receiving such awards in the College) while the RGC scholarships were aiding some 86 boys. Even with its low take-up of Assisted Places Gordon's could continue to proclaim proudly that around a quarter of its secondary pupils were supported in their fees, a figure unsurpassed anywhere in the country.

Separation of College and Institute[12]

At various times in the post-war period there had been attempts to break the link between the College and Technical College (Institute) but these had been abortive. However, during session 1974–5 the first link between them was broken: when Charles Birnie retired from his post as Secretary of the Governors it was decided that RGIT appoint his successor while the College would appoint a Clerk and Treasurer to take over its administration.[13] The latter was to be housed in the ground floor of the old building with the School secretarial staff, and the Headmaster and his senior staff moved into offices on the first floor between the Governors' Room and Room 18. The Institute responded by pressing for the complete administrative separation of both bodies[14] and an ad hoc group under Convener Tom Phemister, with Headmaster Allan included, was set up.[15] It provided a framework for the proposed reconstitution of Governing Bodies in order to achieve separation, which was approved in principle by the Secretary of State on 12 October 1979. M. J. P. Cunliffe of the SED visited the Colleges a month later and this resulted in discussions on the division of the various properties and lands of the Colleges.

The resulting plan was approved by the ad hoc group of Governors on 19 December 1979. It seemed a fair distribution of the properties and was accepted as such by the Governing Body. Where the activities of the College and Institute impinged on each other, the former gained ownership of the workshops under the east wing of the old building, the boiler house and storage room and the house of the Head Janitor (all used by the Institute), while the MacRobert Hall, adjoining corridor, entrance hall, cloakrooms and basement store were to be jointly owned by the College and the Institute on the basis of five-sixth to the College and one-sixth to the Institute. (The basement workshops, despite being used by the Institute, were also to be owned on the same basis.) Although the College dining-room was to be retained by the College, the kitchen on the third floor was given over to the Institute despite the claim that it more properly adjoined the College section of the site. On the other hand, the College gained the Crooked Lane car park which had originally being bought for accommodation for the school although it had been used for car parking by Institute staff. The Main Gates were allocated to the Institute.

On the basis of usage, therefore, the College could be more than pleased with the arrangements agreed, but, given the history of the two institutions, there must have been some disquiet that the College had officially lost control over a large part of Schoolhill. At least the right had been reserved to restrict future developments on the site and each party agreed to give the other first option for purchase, should the first party wish to dispose of its interest in property at Schoolhill.[16]

The separation led to the formation of a new Board of Governors for the College.[17] Its first meeting after reconstitution took place on 4 February 1982. Calum A. MacLeod was elected Chairman two weeks later[18] and the previous Committee system – Policy, Playingfield and Scholarship – was enlarged to include two others on Finance and Property, and Staff Affairs. This suggested a Governing Body more focused on forward development and more sensitive to the needs of their stakeholders than ever before. Headmaster Allan was aware that schools similar to Gordon's were making provision for parental views to be included at Board level. On 15 November 1982 he formally proposed that College parents – an 'untapped reservoir' of support and expertise – be more involved, and, after some discussion, the Governors agreed on the setting up of a Parents' Association. Following a positive vote by the parents themselves in June 1983[19] the way was open for the new body, which met for the first time in March 1984. It was to fulfil completely its original aims of providing a focus for dialogue between the College and parents, creating fund-raising opportunities and making available the skills of parents, especially in the area of careers.

HMI visited the College in September/October 1983 and their Report was published in April of the following year.[20] The Governors could generally be pleased, but there were a number of areas requiring attention. The Junior School, in particular, was criticised for not meeting the needs of its pupils, and its Head had 'given no lead in the development of educational provision'.[21] As a result, the Chairman asked Allan to report to the Board on the last meeting of each term on the progress and activities of the College. A new age of accountability had arrived.

Slopefield

In January 1983 the College was approached with an offer which was to change the course of its history. Barratt Construction asked whether the Governors were interested in the possibility of developing 'Slopefield', a fifty-acre site mainly situated between Countesswells Road and Craigton Road but with a portion north of Countesswells Road. The first reaction was probably negative but, nonetheless, there was much to be said for having school, playing-fields and boarding house together in one location instead of three different places. Moreover, the Governors understood only too well that they faced ever-increasing development, maintenance and renewal costs in adapting Schoolhill to the needs of modern education and also the pressure on existing classrooms and accommodation in an already crowded site.

Throughout 1983 the Governors examined a number of sites and options for the College including Slopefield, which became the favoured proposal in their Development Plan of 30 April 1984 which still remained 'strictly confidential' (but not for much longer). Although the Governors knew that the District Council[22] had previously rejected applications to develop the site for housing and recreation, they still decided to apply for outline planning permission. Before the press release was issued on 14 May 1984 the staff were informed of the College plan to build a prestigious, high-quality modern establishment 'sympathetic to the rural nature of the site'.[23] The site owners appeared to be on board and, if approved, the project would take some three years to complete.

The immediate reaction of the local inhabitants to the proposal was hostile. At a public meeting held in Airyhall School in June 1984, concerns were raised about the erosion of the Green Belt with added traffic and parking problems, the adverse effect on the amenity of the neighbourhood and the pre-emption of the outcome of studies on a route for the proposed 'outer bypass' road. Opposition continued at a meeting of the Braeside and Mannofield Community Council.[24] Nonetheless, the Governors went ahead and produced their site plan and then a model, which was put on public display. On 28 January 1985 they submitted their plans to the District Council.

Surprisingly perhaps, there were only seven official objections.[25] Meantime, in the Conservative-controlled Grampian Regional Council there were discussions on the best way to preserve the Green Belt, with Regional Convener John Sorrie suggesting that the Gordon's Plan would conserve part of it and was a better alternative than the other eventual likelihood, which would be house-building.[26] However, the District Council was not persuaded and stood firm against changing the use of the land from agricultural to educational purposes, and its Planning Director, Bert Allan, deemed the application invalid because of lack of 'relevant information'. The Governors, when they did not receive a decision on their plans within the two month legal time-frame, appealed to Secretary of State Malcolm Rifkind, who ruled the application valid.

By this time the Governors had refined their plans: the eleven acres north of Countesswells Road would house the playing-fields and grandstand, while the main forty acres site would have three buildings in extensive grounds. The planned new school would be 25,000 square feet in size[27] and would include a Music School and a Games Hall; the boarding school would accommodate sixty pupils[28] and the total roll would be kept at the current 1170. However, despite these details being included in a second application it was turned down unanimously in August 1985 by the District planning committee.[29]

The College was not too dismayed at this decision and found support from a number of quarters – even the Department of Agriculture and Fisheries believed the arguments were finely balanced. The Under-Secretary of State for Education and Science, Allan Stewart, visited the College in September and, on 10 December 1985, Grampian Regional planning committee decided, by 9 votes to 6, to back the College move in principle.[30] Yet the Governors appreciated that they would need to go to a Public Enquiry and this would not happen immediately as the fate of their proposals depended on the Regional Structural Development Plan currently being reviewed and itself the subject of a public hearing.

Co-education

It was during this hiatus that Chairman MacLeod introduced the topic of co-education at the Governors' meeting on 21 April 1986. This was not a bombshell to those present, for almost a year earlier[31] he had gained the support of the Board to initiate meetings between Allan and himself and their counterparts in the girls' schools, Albyn and St Margaret's, 'to discuss matters of mutual educational interest'. It did not take much reading between the lines to appreciate the significance of these talks, especially as the like of them had never happened before. MacLeod spoke of national trends and the pressure, particularly from younger parents, for the College to consider the introduction of co-education. He asked Allan to produce a discussion paper on the topic and asked for maximum attendance at their next meeting for its debate.

When the Governors met next on 23 June 1986 most minds had already been made up and they decided in principle on a move to co-education, which was to be announced immediately to all the different sections of the Gordon's community. Why was there such overwhelming support for such a momentous decision? Fundamentally because the decision to abandon Schoolhill for Slopefield had been the dramatic break with the past and, with a new beginning on the cards for the College, it seemed sensible to modernise completely. Why then had Slopefield been accepted so readily? Perhaps because Schoolhill had lost some of its attraction now that half the site had been hived off to the Institute. In a real sense, Slopefield was seen as compensation for the loss of part of Robert Gordon's birthright.

As with all major decisions, one can find many contributing factors. The fear of being left behind as other schools moved forward. Change at Heriot's in Edinburgh had often in the past been a catalyst for change at Gordon's and since its introduction of co-education in 1979 Heriot's had made clear and significant progress. With fee levels spiralling upwards[32] as salary and curricular costs escalated[33] and the resulting concerns on the size of the roll[34] the Governors had to secure the future of the College, and to double the potential market was an important way to help do so. In retrospect, it is not difficult to understand why the Governors took their brave decision. It also led them – and others – naturally to be more focused on their discussions on the future organisation of independent schooling in Aberdeen.

Meantime, with the plans for co-education taking shape, the Governors instructed their lawyers to approach Barrett Aberdeen Ltd and, as a result, an offer from the College for Slopefield was accepted on 10 July 1986.[35]

Headmaster Allan explained in great detail that buildings would comprise only 20% of the total site.[36] Such arguments did not convince Nicol Stephen, a consistent opponent of the College's plans, who, as a result of the May 1986 elections, found himself the new planning convener of the Grampian Regional Council. On 2 September his Committee decided by 12 votes to 6 to withdraw support for the College, and the full Council instructed its officials to adopt a neutral stance. The loss of such support did not bode well for the Public Enquiry, which was now set for 2 March 1987.

Tripartite Talks

In the final months of 1986 the two separate, but related, issues, involving the Slopefield development, were the focus of attention of the Governors: the tripartite talks with Albyn and St Margaret's, and preparation of the College's case for the Public Enquiry. The former had quickly resulted in the setting up of a Working Party of representatives of the three schools chaired by David Adams.[37] However, when the schools issued a press release, the *Press and Journal* headline of 7 January 1987 expressed 'shock' and the talks captured the attention of press, radio and television. Despite this reaction, the Working Party made good progress at three meetings later that month. It discussed demographic trends, economic and political factors, and educational considerations[38] and then moved to discuss models based on a spectrum of options proposed by Headmaster Allan.[39] Further model refinements were reviewed along with pupil projections for independent schools to 1996.

By early 1987 news on the other front – preparing for the Enquiry – was disappointing. Despite ongoing discussions with both District and Regional Councils, no significant progress had been made on either the line of the proposed outer bypass road[40] or the roads/traffic issue.[41] At the Governors' meeting on 2 February Allan highlighted the escalating capital costs – on planning, solving the roads problem and dealing with the extensive electric cabling – and suggested that these 'probably put the development of an all-in-one campus at Slopefield beyond the College's means'. He also held that the tripartite talks on the rationalisation of resources indicated that Slopefield, in both area and configuration, might not be large enough to provide buildings, services, playing-fields and landscaping for a large co-eduactional school. His evaluation went further and envisaged Slopefield as a shared playing-field, which development would not infringe the Green Belt and indeed would enhance the amenity of the area providing a buffer zone for the local residents of Airyhall. In this scenario the roads/traffic problem would be reduced as the movement of pupils and traffic to and from the fields would be much less in total volume at any one time and would tend to occur at off-peak times. Allan had put together a 'strong case' for abandoning their plans and the Governors agreed with his arguments. Eight days later the College staff were informed that the College intended to lodge a planning application with the District Council for the development of Slopefield as playing-fields and associated facilities for pavilion and changing accommodation.[42]

By the end of March 1987 the Working Party decided to work up inventories of the existing staffing and accommodation in the three schools. However, there was a growing appreciation that a major issue would be the creation of a single governing body which increasingly was seen as central to any mergers. The Working Party set itself a deadline of six months to progress the issue. The problem here was the need to have the approval of the Court of Session for changes in Gordon's constitution, while Albyn and St Margaret's were both companies.

During May, Albyn sent home a questionnaire to all its parents and St Margaret's decided to follow suit in September.[43] By then the Working Party was concentrating its investigations on a medium-sized co-ed school (800 to 1500) and a smaller girls' school (below 800) as the most likely combination for the immediate future of independent education in Aberdeen. Further work was scheduled on precise sizes of the schools and the number of staff, classrooms and specialised areas. It was then planned to match the requirements to the sites available to decide which were the most suitable for the primary and secondary departments of the co-ed school and for the girls' school.

By September the difficult decision on which site would house the girls' school had to be taken. Unfortunately, it was not straightforward, as both schools were operating acceptably on their respective sites. Important criteria, however, were the relative proximity of the two sites to Schoolhill, the relative size of library and hall, the relative costs of upgrading expensive specialist rooms (especially science) and work already undertaken to develop improved facilities for the future.[44] As a result, the Education Working Party recommended that the girls' school should be housed in the Albyn school building, with the co-ed secondary at Schoolhill and the primary co-ed department in St Margaret's. It then turned its attention to staffing structures and educational adaptations to the building.

The Legal and Financial Working Party worked out the timetable for all matters of substance to be agreed by early 1988, for merger to be complete by autumn 1988 and for the new structures to be operating from autumn 1989. The communities of all three schools were advised by letter of the progress to date and a press release was issued and hit the headlines on 31 October 1987.[45] Parent meetings were organised for late November and were to be followed up by letters asking parents to commit themselves to one of the schools. However, as a result of meetings on 23 and 25 November a group of St Margaret's parents met to consider how the distinctive identity of the School might best be retained. The School Council[46] was requested to suspend merger talks meantime to allow further consultation to take place. Facing accusations of letting their parents down and failing to consult[47] the Council, stung by such criticism, decided not to proceed with the tripartite talks.

The reaction of the College Governors to this disappointing development was to continue talking with Albyn, while the latter had decided that it did not wish to become the primary department of the large co-ed school. Its representatives flirted with the idea of a small co-ed school catering for boys not taken by Gordon's, especially if it was strengthened by co-operation with the latter over playing-fields, Sixth Year subjects and boarding. However, there still remained the widespread view that Aberdeen would only support two independent schools and that without immediate action one of the schools would fail. Moreover, the record of girls' schools going co-ed successfully was not good and St Margaret's might be helped to survive if it was to be the only single-sex school operating. So Albyn decided to remain girls only and instead fell back on 'close collaboration' with RGC.[48]

For practical reasons it proved difficult to programme curriculum co-operation so fee concessions were the result of more discussions. From August 1989 both schools agreed to fee concessions – 5% for a second child in a family where the elder child was already a pupil at either school and 40% to third or subsequent children if the two elder children attended either school. This scheme[49] gave concessions to 274 families and initially was to cost Albyn £18,246 p.a. and Gordon's £29,198. As Gordon's had less need to attract pupils, the College Governors willingly accepted an expensive scheme in an effort to assist Albyn in its competition with St Margaret's.[50]

At the Board Meeting of 25 January 1988 the Governors, heartened by Allan's report that the overwhelming majority of parents would opt for their son to remain at College when co-education was introduced, agreed to proceed with their plans for admitting girls in Primary 1, 6 and 7 and Secondary 1 and

6 in August 1989. As this would need improvements and alterations at Schoolhill the Policy Committee was asked to take stock and examine all future options.

At Schoolhill this meant resuming informal talks with RGIT, which had shown a general interest in purchasing the College's buildings. The Principal, Dr Kennedy, knew that a minimum of £2 million[51] would be needed by the College to consider moving and building a new school. In the event it was believed that the SED would not approve an offer from RGIT beyond that of the District Valuer, which fell considerably short of the College's valuation, and so discussions did not get far. Schemes for moving the Junior School to another site were soon abandoned as costly and disruptive and the Property Committee was requested to examine the possibilities for expansion at Schoolhill. Permission for the development of playing-fields at Slopefield had been granted in September 1987 by the District Council subject to seventeen conditions which were still being negotiated, but the Governors expected an agreement to be reached. This meant that Seafield would be surplus to requirements and, although the Governors flirted with various thoughts,[52] it was decided that it needed to be sold for maximum profit, which meant persuading the planners to allow housing on the site.

Politically, since the advent of complete independence in 1985 the College had enjoyed the benefits which the extra freedom brought. Issues such as the use of corporal punishment were determined by the College itself.[53] The Governors were able to consolidate the Capital Fee with the Tuition Fee in March 1986 as they were no longer required to separate the two elements for the SED.[54] The lack of any disruption during national actions was another sign of the growing realisation that the College was increasingly independent. Economically, however, there was the downside that the College was now totally dependent on its own finances (and some help from the AET). Unfortunately, when the College needed the AET most it was in no position to help. Indeed, on 25 June 1987, it informed the Governors about the serious nature of the decline in productivity in the farming sector, from where the Trust derived most of its income. The financial crisis facing the AET meant that it could not sustain a system of pupil awards based on full funding, especially as the fees increased continuously. As a result the thirty awards of 1986/7 had to be reduced to twenty in 1987/8, to twelve in 1988/9, and then to eight in 1989/90.[55] Relationships between the College and Trust worsened. as the latter went to great lengths to ensure that applicants from within the College did not dominate the award lists.[56] Resentment grew on both sides and was only defused with the arrival of a new Trust Factor, William Russell, himself a Gordon's scholarship boy, who was able to improve co-operation significantly.[57]

By September 1988 the College overdraft had reached £900,000 and the Board was concerned at its level of borrowing at a time of high interest rates.[58] The Finance and Property Committee was strengthened by the addition of Alex Mair, Chairman of Grampian TV, who had been recruited for his financial expertise. This helped it decide that if the College was to remain competitive and fund its needs it would be necessary to increase fees to a level commensurate with comparable schools in the Central Belt. It argued that the fees had been kept artificially low[59] and now had to be raised significantly to reduce dependence on loans. A fee level of £2,500 per annum was recommended – up from £1915 – an increase of over 30%.[60] When this was announced to parents it provoked a storm of outrage.[61] Allan worked hard to calm matters[62] and the Parents' Asssociation played its part as a conduit.[63] Nonetheless, an Action Group was formed to resist the fee increases. The Governors, however, refused to back down, but at least appreciated the need to explain the background to its decision fully in writing to all parents.[64] An important lesson was also learned about the need to improve communication in the future and not take the fee-paying parents for granted.[65]

Blackfriars' and Countesswells

Despite such problems, the school roll held up well and, of the 1156 who attended the College in August 1989,[66] some 71 were girls. They were spread throughout the College with 26 in the Junior School, thirty in S1 and fifteen in S6.[67] A new Assistant Head, Rona Livingstone, was appointed to help settle them in[68] and generally this happened smoothly. There was a realistic appreciation that the ultimate aim of a College with 40% girls would take some years to achieve. Meantime Sillerton House had been redeveloped and modernised[69] and numbers were, at that time, holding up well,[70] while the news about Slopefield led to some optimism. However, Allan knew that the College's credibility with its parents, and the public at large, was under scrutiny. For five years possible developments had been mooted in public and he wanted decisions made to meet operational needs, to instil confidence within the school and wider community, and in so doing to boost the College's recruiting potential.[71] Specifically, he suggested a new building at the Blackfriars Street end of the back playground.

Thankfully, the Governors were immediately responsive to Allan's promptings and matters proceeded quickly. By June 1990 the initial talks with the

District Planning Department had made significant progress. Most importantly, given the height of surrounding buildings there was acceptance of a five-storey building.[72] Allan asked the College architect, Cos Pacitti, to meet specific priorities which included facilities for a Dining Hall, Art and Music Departments, general classrooms for both Junior and Senior School, Sixth Year facilities and conference and staff amenities. The building design details, which were in an architectural style which complemented Woolmanhill and the Cowdray Hall, were forwarded to the planners in late 1990. The estimated cost was in the region of £3.5 million.

On top of the estimates for the new Blackfriars' Building the Governors were determined that Slopefield would be converted into first-class sports' facilities,[73] for rugby, hockey with artificial astroturf pitch, athletics and cricket.[74] It was, therefore, crucial that the Governors sold Seafield at the most opportune time, and they decided to delay until after the Public Enquiry into the Aberdeen District Wide Local Plan, which opened the way to sell to a residential developer. These details were incorporated into the College's Ten-Year Business Plan of March 1991.[75] It made provision for an overdraft peak of £6.2m in September 1992 (before the Slopefield monies arrived); total borrowing of £7.2m and a Term Loan of £2.5m which would be repaid over fifteen years. It also envisaged an increase in College numbers from 1175 to 1375 (a hundred extra in Primary and another hundred in Secondary).[76]

The first half of 1992 was a momentous time for the College. In March, following the acceptance of the Design Brief for Seafield by the District Council Planning Committee, ten companies submitted offers. The College accepted that from Headland Properties – the sale price was £3.057m. The same month the official opening of Slopefield took place. For some time there had been disquiet over the name and the Governors decided to change it to Countesswells.[77] The weather was kind when HRH The Princess Anne unveiled the plaque. The total cost reached £3.065m. and the result was a playing-field three and a half times larger than Seafield. Meantime, in the same month, the main tender of contract for the Blackfriars Building was issued, Hall and Tawse's offer of £2.755m accepted and the first pile was driven into the west corner of the playground shortly afterwards.

It took only sixteen months for the completion of Blackfriars' Building, which opened for the beginning of session in late August 1993. The areas vacated were also refurbished and departments redistributed. The old dining-room was made into Nursery and Primary I accommodation – enabling the new Nursery unit to open at the same time;[78] the old art rooms were converted into biology and science labs, while a new computer suite was established in the modernised Technical Department. After four frenetic years Allan promised that it was time to draw breath and enter a period when the pace would be quieter. However, such days soon appeared few and far between.

The loss of Seafield was a psychological blow for some Gordonians, especially as it closely followed the introduction of co-education. To add insult to injury, the College then requested from the Association, what it termed 'a nominal rent' for 1992/2 of £2000 for the use of Countesswells and then a move to more 'realistic' charges for future years.[79] The Sports Sections requested a reduction and a moratorium during talks, but the Governors stood firm, claiming even at £4000 the Association would be paying only 7½% of expenditure while receiving 15% use of the facilities.[80] A meeting with the President of the Association, George Ross, failed to solve matters and Allan had to produce a detailed paper which he delivered to the Association Executive in November 1993. The resulting compromise of a reduction to £3000 for 1993/4 but future rentals to be based on percentage use did not please the Association and relationships between it and the College remained cool for a while.[81]

The changes at Schoolhill, especially the increasing school roll – which in session 1993/4 reached 1295 (365 in Primary and 930 in Secondary) – threw up new issues to tackle. Allan was concerned with the loss in corporate identity,[82] symbolised in the need to split morning assembly into S1–3 and S4–6 held on different days as the secondary could no longer meet altogether in the MacRobert Hall. The retiral of John Y. Duncan as Deputy[83] meant his replacement, Michael Duncan,[84] had to deal with the high use of accommodation, the crowding in corridors, damage to property (accidental as much as wilful), and demands on Guidance time and Library and study space. Parents were also disappointed that class sizes remained larger than those in the smaller independent schools locally.

Significance of Allan

Although Allan's focus was centred on strategic matters for much of his Headship he also had to contend with the day-to-day issues which affect a large school. He was also at the helm in a period of significant national curricular change, something which had not faced any of his predecessors, with perhaps the exception of Marshall. Following the Standard Grade and 5–14 Programme, the 1992 Howie Report[85] proposed reforms in teaching and learning in S4, 5 and

6 of the upper secondary. Allan convened a Working Party of senior staff and Governors and produced a powerfully argued riposte to the more radical of Howie's suggestions especially the principle of two pathways (academic and vocational), the group certificate, the points system of assessment and the moving of Standard Grade to Third Year.[86] Allan argued that the 'bold strategy' of Howie underestimated the 'psychological effect of such a sweeping reorganisation on a teaching profession wearied by the volume of change over two decades'. In the event, Allan and his senior colleagues, along with the Governors, were more in tune with the situation generally in the country than members of the Howie Committee, whose proposals shook the complacency of the educational establishment but were not 'evolutionary' enough to be adopted.

The partnership of Chairman and Headmaster had worked effectively for twelve years when Calum MacLeod decided to resign. He had made an immense contribution to the development of the College, in so doing strengthening and preparing it for the 21st century. His remarkable contribution of gifts – legal and financial expertise, shrewd management skills and a personable character – had made him an exceptional Chairman of Governors. There was no obvious long-term successor. James Cameron agreed to be an interim Chair for a year while an outsider was brought in and prepared for the task. George Allan took soundings and, with his Governor's hat, was instrumental in persuading Graeme Catto, Otaki Scholar and School Captain from 1963, to join the Board and take over the chairmanship in September 1995. His first crucial role was to organise the process for choosing a new Headmaster, as Allan himself had indicated his intention to retire in summer 1996. A new partnership was created between Chair and Head when Brian Lockhart was appointed.

Unfortunately Allan did not have a happy final year as Head, as the College found itself at the centre of much unwanted and unwarranted media interest. Its procedures and policies, particularly in the area of bullying, were put under severe scrutiny and critics were quick – too quick – to intervene. These happenings, however, should not detract from the significance of Allan's stewardship, when the College went through a period of immense change and improvement. The decisions to introduce co-education and develop Countesswells, in particular, strengthened the College and laid the basis for future success. Allan had been meticulous in all that he did and he displayed a mental toughness and gritty determination in seeing things through. He always put the interests of the College first and was not concerned if he courted unpopularity when doing so. He was sceptical of educational jargon and theories. He saw himself as a traditional schoolmaster and headmaster, rather than a manager, and the College benefited much from this perception of his role.

Brian R. W. Lockhart

There were thirty applications for the post of Headmaster following George Allan's decision to retire. On 10 November a long-list of eight was interviewed by a sub-committee of Governors under Professor Catto. The short-list of four candidates was interviewed again on 4 December and Brian Lockhart, Deputy Rector at the High School of Glasgow, was unanimously chosen to take up office on 1 August 1996.

Brian R. W. Lockhart was born in July 1944 and was educated at Leith Academy and George Heriot's School, where he won the Dux Medal in History in 1963. He went on to complete a Joint Honours Degree in History-Politics at the University of Aberdeen, before completing his post-graduate qualification at Moray House College and gaining a Diploma in Education from the University of Edinburgh. His former Headmaster at Heriot's, William McL. Dewar, was keen for him to return to his old school and he joined the Heriot's staff in June 1968. A combination of good fortune and innovative teaching strategies led to a rapid promotion, first to the post of Special Assistant and then to Principal Teacher of History and Economic History in 1972. His department grew significantly and was praised by the HMI who were impressed with the popularity of the subject, especially at Sixth Year level. In 1981 he moved to the new High School of Glasgow[87] which was being redeveloped at Old Anniesland and became an important part of the team responsible for its remarkable growth and success.[88]

Softening of the Culture

On arrival at Gordon's, Lockhart set out his 'vision' for the College: he stressed the importance of style, tone and ethos and saw the need to soften its culture.[89] In so doing he aimed at providing a high quality and enjoyable experience for all pupils and increasing the number and proportion of girls on the roll.[90] He also inherited an exciting agenda from his predecessor, George Allan, who had begun preparations for the forthcoming 250th Anniversary of the opening of the Hospital by planning an Appeal, which was launched officially on 14

September 1996.[91] It aimed at raising £1.55m. for accommodation and bursaries – the Governors again committing themselves to continuing the tradition of supporting children whose parents could not afford the fees. Although an added burden for a new Head,[92] it proved a useful focus for getting to know, and being known by, the Gordon's community. The contacts made then were soon to prove important in developing good relationships with parents and former pupils in particular.

In September 1996 the College overdraft was £3.2m and the Term Loan £1.9m,[93] while the pupil roll of 1350 was below the Business Plan budget. Despite these financial concerns, the Governors supported the new Head's early audit and the list of priorities he drew up. In staffing this involved offering early retiral to the few teachers who were not performing to the level expected, and the creation of new posts.[94] A School Nurse was appointed for the first time and, with the enthusiastic approval of Ian Black,[95] French was introduced into the Junior School. At the Policy Meeting of the Governors in January 1997 Lockhart pressed for the introduction of the recommendations of the Guidance Working Party,[96] a decision on which had been delayed until after his arrival. The Governors agreed to the significant reforms, which brought in a vertical system[97] and this, with later refinements,[98] proved central to strengthening the 'caring' side of the College.

Class organisation was re-arranged in order to create the best possible combinations of pupils for classes and to resist unhelpful labelling. Previously, pupils entering SI were allocated to a top, middle or lower class in which they were taught all their subjects, just as those designated less able had, in previous years, been allocated to the 'E' class. The new configuration of classes, however, proved much more flexible and provided ability sets in some subjects so that pupils could be taught at an appropriate pace when necessary.

Lockhart's passionate interest in the curriculum was evident in the many additions which were made during his time. One highly significant decision was to increase the S3/S4 provision from seven Standard Grades to eight, thus providing greater choice and challenge for pupils at this stage. At S3/S4 level, new subjects on offer included business management, drama, modern studies, religious studies and Spanish. In addition, the requirements of a new age were met by the inclusion of a general information and communications technology (ICT) course in S4 to complement the new SI and S2 ICT provision, while, in the Junior School, French was brought in for P3–P7 pupils and ICT featured as a subject in its own right in all years.

It was perhaps at S6 level, however, that the greatest number of changes occurred with new courses being offered at every level. Highers were made available for the first time in courses such as information systems, philosophy and psychology, while there was an ever-increasing provision at Advanced Higher level in order to ensure that pupils opting to take subjects at the S3/S4 stage could pursue them right through to the highest level available within the Scottish school system. The S6 Enhanced Curriculum courses proved very successful and their introduction was directly attributable to Lockhart's interest in this area. Gordon's became the first school in Britain to offer the European Computer Driving Licence (ECDL) to its pupils. Partnerships with the University of Aberdeen, Robert Gordon University and Aberdeen College were developed to offer subjects such as entrepreneurship, psychology and sociology, with the result that pupils were not only able to sample a discipline which they might want to study at university, but also learned to function in settings more akin to the lectures, seminars and tutorials in which they would find themselves once they left school. Pupils were also able to attend Scots Law and pre-medicine courses delivered by local practitioners, and the fact that cookery and Japanese were also on offer emphasised the stimulating breadth of choice which was available within the S6 curriculum.

Although Lockhart himself struggled somewhat to keep up with developing technology, he appreciated its increasing importance for improving communication and efficient administration, and, in time, learning and teaching. He was keen to ensure the College was at the forefront of new developments. The Governors, too, supported this aim and accepted the massive investment which such a commitment involved. Fortuitously, the College was the recipient of a significant legacy from the Will of Ronald Burnett[99] and with the Headmaster joining the Burnett Trustees it was agreed that £200,000 should be pledged immediately from that source to help the College ensure that every classroom had a networked computer and generous provision of computing suites, as well as to provide an extensive staff training programme to ensure that effective use was made of such resources.

Lockhart's view of his role as Headmaster was somewhat different from his predecessors'. He declined to serve as a Governor, preferring to attend Governor meetings as the representative of the staff and, in seeing their welfare as crucial in raising standards, he set about attempting to improve their salaries,[100] conditions of service, professional development[101] and career structure.[102] However, he was an 'interventionist': he introduced an annual Quality Assurance interview for each Head of Department and began to visit departments systematically. Then, causing a little concern, he visited classrooms to learn at first hand about his staff and the pupils' learning experience. Such monitoring was an attempt to break the culture of autonomy of the classroom teacher and result in the evolution of line-management and a Professional Review and Development Scheme. Paradoxically, despite these ventures Lockhart viewed himself more as a manager than a teacher[103] and he developed a strong management team, which was strengthened in numbers and given more time within the working day to contribute to management decisions.

Lockhart inherited outstanding senior staff[104] and was fortunate to gain Jennifer Montgomery as his Deputy in 1997. She proved an inspired choice and Lockhart was happy to delegate much of the day-to-day running of the College to her capable hands.[105] Some of his other senior appointments went to those already on the staff as he had much confidence in the quality and loyalty of the Gordon's staff and believed that it was good to reward them with internal promotion where possible.[106]

He placed much emphasis on having good relationships with all parts of the Gordon's community. His partnership with his Chairman was strong and they worked well together, involving Governors in workshops, especially on strategic matters.[107] He met regularly with parents' representatives and encouraged them to play an even more active role in College matters. He was keen for them to have an influence on school policies, believing that parents were an underused resource. He worked hard to keep the staff informed of ongoing developments, especially on in-service days, and his 'accessibility was well known to all'.[108] He wanted the pupils to be happy at school and he personally encouraged their involvement in extra-curricular activities at every opportunity. In particular, he promoted participation of senior pupils in decision making.[109] He widened the Playing Fields Committee to include former pupil representatives from rugby, hockey and cricket and supported the development of facilities at Countesswells for the sections. Such were examples of his inclusive style.

Good relationships were commented on by HMI after their inspection of the Secondary Department in May 1998.[110] Lockhart had made 'a considerable positive impact' and improved the climate and introduced a 'range of well-judged improvements'. The many traditional strengths were itemised, especially academic success, good behaviour, the good learning environment and the wide range of extra-curricular opportunities. The Junior School and Nursery had to wait until April 2002 for its full report but it too stressed the positive ethos, attainment and the 'highly motivated, happy and well-behaved pupils'.[111]

Accommodation and Financial Developments

Given the constraints of the College Business Plan, Lockhart was limited in what he could do to improve accommodation. The continuation of the phased rewiring programme, the refit of a biology laboratory and a refurbished main staff-room were all that could be afforded immediately. However, the feel of the Quadrangle was 'softened' by planting Gordon's roses, introducing more benches[112] and separating cars and pupils by creating a pedestrian walkway. Fortunately, the Appeal had reached £1m by May 1997[113] and Lockhart began to plan for the first-phase developments – a Grandstand complex at Countesswells[114] and the refurbishment of the Music Department on the upper floors of the Auld Hoose.[115] His attempt, however, to move the Nursery to the playing-fields was rejected by the Council planners as a breach of the Green Belt.[116] Nonetheless, the new Grandstand, opened on 2 September 2000 by Bert Bruce,[117]and the Music Department refurbishment projects were completed on target.

Lockhart also began discussions on the second phase – the Library extension and refurbishment and the Heritage Room. In the event the architects were able to produce exciting plans which envisaged a significantly enlarged and modernised Library and IT Centre,[118] and, in the space below, a Sixth Year Careers' Room and an Archive Room. The Governors' Room was to be modified to include display cabinets with inclusions to illustrate the heritage of Hospital and College. Again, on target, the Library was opened on 31 August 2000 by HRH The Princess Anne. It was an integral part of the 250th Anniversary Celebration of the Opening of the Hospital, which proved a great success that year.

Although these developments were significant in improving the quality of the Schoolhill site, the increasing school roll[119] put further pressure on accommodation. A five-year agreement with Robert Gordon University[120] (RGU) had been signed which leased some surplus Schoolhill space to the College but the Governors were forced to consider alternative sites to alleviate the situation.[121] With no obvious solution in sight the Governors opened a dialogue with Albyn School to see if some arrangement could be made for mutual benefit.[122]

Talks between the schools began well, if cautiously. The respective Chairmen of Governors, Graeme Catto and Andrew Lewis, met on 27 April 1999 and found the basis of an agenda for discussion. Eventually, more practical matters were discussed harmoniously between the Heads of the schools and there appeared a growing appreciation of the benefits of closer co-operation. However, despite Lockhart's 'Vision for the Future', which detailed the attractive 'entitlements' which were on offer to the pupils of both schools if they merged, the Albyn Governors on 27 November 2000 finally rejected further talks believing that a merger was 'irreconcible with the fundamental characteristics of Albyn'.[123]

The College Governors, pressed by Lockhart, focused again on Schoolhill. Their architects produced attractive plans to build on the Crooked Lane carpark; they envisaged four storeys and a teaching block of twenty classrooms and drama studio, which would be reached by a walkway, above the road, from the Auld Hoose. However, the Governors were unwilling to commit to such an expensive option which might need to be sold on and redeveloped if, as seemed possible, other space became available in the medium term at Schoolhill.

This was the central issue, for RGU had begun talks with Aberdeen University about a possible future collaboration in the autumn of 2001, with all options up to 'full merger' being explored. One of the major benefits for both universities of coming together would be a rationalisation of estates which would free up buildings. Under the separation agreement of 1981 between the College and RGU (RGIT), any building at Schoolhill which was up for sale had to be offered first to the other institution on the site at educational prices. If RGU determined to sell buildings, the College would want to be in a position to buy them. It seemed the wisest course for the College Governors to be patient and await the outcome of events. In the meantime, however, temporary measures were needed. RGU renewed its leasing agreement with the College but more significant was the buying of surplus modular units, sited at Kepplestone, from the University. During April 2003 these were positioned in the back-playground and customised for use in August of that year. They provided seven high-quality classrooms and a base area for technological studies.

The Governors appreciated that the measures were not ideal, especially the loss in playground space.[124] However, they determined to improve other areas of school provision. Proud of the claim that the rugby pitches at Countesswells were the best north of Edinburgh, they understood the importance of upgrading hockey facilities there. Indeed, like swimming, hockey at Gordon's had produced many internationalists and now a growing number of girls were playing the game as their major winter sport. The existing all-weather sand pitch had been laid in 1991 therefore needed refurbishment or replacement, and this was the priority for the College as the surface could be used for tennis in summer. However, for Gordonians, hockey at the top level was being played increasingly on water-based pitches and they put that at the top of their wish list. As early as May 2001 Lockhart had suggested that the record surpluses of the College[125] should be used to create two new pitches and Mrs Sheila Fyfe, Convener of the Playing Fields Committee, as always pressing for improvements, was also keen on this.

With Bursar, Bob Leggate, sympathetic, the Governors included the proposed expenditure in their new Business Plan. The contract was won by John H. Connon Ltd: the sand-based pitch was in operation by October 2003 and the new water-based pitch was proudly opened by Alan Innes, stalwart of Gordonian hockey, on 20 March 2004.[126]

Although merger talks between the universities broke down without agreement, RGU launched its own strategic review and increasingly appeared to be moving towards a further concentration of the university at Garthdee and a slimming-down of operations at Schoolhill. To speed matters on, the College Finance Convener, Colin Crosby, saw the need to take an initiative. As a result, a specific offer, above educational value,[127] was made to RGU for the building on the east side of the Quadrangle. In June 2003, the Principal of RGU, Bill Steveley, welcomed the offer and although he reiterated that any further discussions would have to await the completion of their estates review, it seemed highly likely that it would retain only a 'footprint' at Schoolhill. This was formally confirmed in May 2004 when RGU declared its intention to leave the site within ten years. At last, the way was open for the College to gain back the Schoolhill Quadrangle. It would happen in stages and would be a costly business for the College but the prospect of a vast improvement in accommodation and a far less congested environment would mean the beginning of a new era in the history of the school.

Lockhart was delighted at the turn of events, but he had already announced his impending retiral. He did so, knowing that the major problem facing the College was on the way to being solved. Although his successor might have to spend a great deal of time on accommodation issues at least the uncertainty over the College's site was now over.

Lockhart left the College in good shape. Indeed, during his term of office he had 'succeeded in changing and improving almost all aspects of the College'.[128] Moreover, the College was in great demand with its numbers at a record 1463,[129] partly because of its consistently excellent academic results, which were the result of a partnership between talented pupils and committed staff.[130] As its finances were also strong,[131] and the annual financial appeals were increasingly successful,[132] the Chairman of Governors, Sir Graeme Catto,[133] could still proudly boast that Robert Gordon's legacy continued as some 25% of the College's secondary pupils were being given financial help to attend – the highest figure in Scotland.

If Allan and his Governors had made the crucial decisions which safeguarded the College and laid the basis for future success, Lockhart and his Governors could claim to have taken it to new levels of success and achievement. By making the College the first choice for so many parents and by taking the gamble to increase the size of the College by around a hundred pupils they paid off the sizeable loans and debt incurred in the acquisitions of the early 1990s. They also created the surpluses which have enabled the College to be in a position to buy out RGU at Schoolhill. Hugh Ouston,[134] who had become the ninth Head of the College in August 2004, was the first to acknowledge what he owed to his predecessors.

The historic agreement with RGU was finally completed in October 2005 after lengthy and detailed negotiations on the part of the Governors, including Colin Crosby, who became the new Chairman of Governors replacing Sir Graeme Catto that same autumn. Almost a century after the fateful decision to give over land for the Technical College and share their site, the Governors of Robert Gordon's College have reached agreement to buy the buildings belonging to the Technical College's successor, RGU, and thereby are regaining control over the entire Schoolhill Quadrangle.

The University's Blackfriars' Building (at the back of the MacRobert Hall), to be handed over to the College on 15 June 2008, will be transformed into a modern and spacious Junior School. Two benefits of this are the long sought-for reduction in class sizes, achieved by increasing the number of classes in each year group, and the extension of the College's signature on the urban landscape of Aberdeen, in the creation of a new facade opposite the recently redeveloped Her Majesty's Theatre. Part of the engineering workshops on the east side will come into the College's ownership at the same point and, once vacated by RGU, will offer much needed space for performimg arts. Finally, the Technology Building (opposite the MacRobert Hall) will be taken over by the College at some point between 2012 and 2015. With the high quality of science laboratories thus made available and complete control over the central Quadrangle, opportunities for further developments on the west side will open up, especially in the area of physical education. The quality of life for the College will be dramatically improved and one can expect an exceptional campus to develop.

POSTSCRIPT – THE LEGACY

The contrast between the College of the early 21st century and the early Hospital is striking. In its earliest years the Hospital was a fragile experiment struggling to fulfil its Founder's intentions. Contrary to general expectation it began to produce a considerable number of boys who went on to contribute significantly to Aberdeen and further afield. However, the days of free charity schools were numbered.

The 1872 Education (Scotland) Act organised 'elementary education for the working classes' but failed to 'organise secondary education for the classes immediately above them'.[1] In these circumstances attention turned to using the funds locked up in charitable endowments to provide a network of secondary schools. The resulting change for Gordon's from Hospital to College in 1881 was, therefore, part of a national movement aimed at improving secondary education, and, as such, was supported by the mainstream of both major political parties. It led to Gordon's joining the front rank of Scottish schools, while inevitably changing its social make-up.

How, then, and how successfully, did the Hospital and College fulfil Robert Gordon's aim of helping to provide a solution to Scotland's needs by founding an institution to fit out and qualify boys for useful vocations and employments? Achieving this goal in the days of the Hospital involved apprenticeships to open the way to skilled occupations, while after 1881 the new College was expected to offer an education with a technical bias. However, quite rapidly, Gordon's began to succeed across the curriculum and its roll consequently increased as the school combined a growing reputation for high academic quality with moderate fees and social cachet.[2] Its great service was to make available good secondary education to the lower ranges of the middle class, in the process giving access to the universities and to the growing number of professions and careers which set examinations for entry.

As a reaction to the success of this dramatic change the movement for a Technical College, originally envisaged as a replacement for the College, had to be satisfied with a supplementary role. In this way the Governors, similar to the Governors of George Heriot's in Edinburgh, contributed not only to the development of secondary and, to a lesser extent, primary education, but from 1910 onwards to higher technical education in Scotland.

Today a prerequisite for skilled occupations would involve higher education and while the College regularly sends over 95% of its pupils on to university, the successor to the Technical College has become a higher education institution in its own right. Significantly, College pupils exhibit a distinct bias towards studying science and technical subjects, while Robert Gordon University (RGU) has built a reputation for vocational-type courses. The link, in both cases, with the Founder's vision is striking.

However, what about Robert Gordon's stress on his institution being free for 'indigent' boys? By the late 19th century this went against current orthodoxy, which supported fees because they brought in extra resources and encouraged regular attendance. In the very year they were introduced into Gordon's – 1881 – the Educational Institute of Scotland (EIS) was bitterly opposing free education, fearing the loss of fee income would lead to teacher salary cuts. It was only gradually after the extension of the franchise by the 1884 Reform Act that a demand for free education arose. Even then most of the endowed and 'higher class'[3] schools continued to charge fees – and did so until after the Second World War. Fees which were introduced remained low and only increased markedly in the remaining fee-paying sector after 1960. Until then Gordon's College, in particular, had an outstanding record of offering bursaries to guarantee free education to all who needed financial aid. Since then the College Governors have been remarkably successful in raising funds[4] to enable annually some 250 boys and girls to obtain financial aid, some 25% of the secondary roll. It is claimed that the total number of pupils and the sums of money involved are the largest in Scotland.[5]

Robert Gordon understood the need to countenance, even embrace, change in the Statutes of his Hospital. Nonetheless, what he wanted for his beneficiaries – a sound education, to be cared for, to be prepared for a career, and to be brought up on Christian principles – has remained consistently the basis of what the Hospital and the College offered and continues to offer.

As a result, because of its origins and these continuities, the College is proud of its history and traditions. It could justly claim to have played an important part in the system of secondary education as it developed and Robert Gordon as one of 'The Makers of Scottish Education'.[6] Even today, unlike those independent Scottish schools which look south of the border, Gordon's rightly regards itself as serving a local middle class, supplemented by a significant element of bursary pupils. It remains true to its Scottish heritage in terms of values, leadership, staffing, curriculum and examinations. In doing so, it is still the desired destination for many parents and children in north-east Scotland.

Thus the substantial results of Robert Gordon's Bequest have benefited thousands of children (and adults) in the last two and a half centuries. Robert Gordon cared sufficiently about education to spend his money, energy and time on its development. As a result, his College is a lasting testimony to his charity, which will bear his name and perpetuate his fame in the centuries ahead.

NOTES

Chapter 1

1 J. Malcolm Bulloch: 'The Grave Gordons' in *The Bicentenary Record of Robert Gordon's Hospital 1729–1929* (Aberdeen 1929).

2 R. B. Strathdee: *Robert Gordon* (printed privately, Aberdeen 1969) p. 2; John M. Taylor articles in *Gordonian,* December 1934, June and December 1935.

3 A small property north-west of Cruden Bay.

4 In the north-west of the parish of Rhynie.

5 North of Huntly, near Cairnie.

6 Around Gordon. Edward Gordon of Cairnfield: *History of the House of Gordon* (Aberdeen 1949) vol. I p. 131. Edward Gordon of Cairnfield: 'Ancestry of Robert Gordon', *Gordonian,* (June 1950) vol. I no. 2 p. 111.

7 Later called Huntly.

8 Rev. William Temple: *The Thanage of Fermartyn* (Aberdeen 1894) esp. pp. 302–317 and pp. 503–4 describes him as the most remarkable of men.

9 Three miles south of Keith in Banffshire.

10 North-west of Cairnie.

11 Near Auchleuchries.

12 Walter R. Humphries: 'Gordon of Pitlurg', *Gordonian* (December 1933) vol. V no. 2 p. 68.

13 His portrait hangs in Robert Gordon's College. It was painted in 1585 probably by John Anderson. John M. Taylor: 'House of Gordon', *Gordonian* (December 1934) vol. V no. 4 p. 143.

14 An effigy of Sir John is in the Boray Aisle, the remains of St Martin's Church, Cairnie.

15 These included 'Notes on Bede's History touching the Scottish Antiquities'; 'Origin of the Saxon Language among the Scots'; 'Origin of the Nation'; and 'Reasons for Scotland's sparse population'. No mean musician, he published 'An Playing Booke for the lute' (1627) containing 78 songs.

16 Kinmundy just south of Mintlaw as the Kinmundy in Newmachar was then in the hands of the Menzies family. Roy Bridges: *People and Places in Newmachar. Past and Present.* (Newmachar 2001) p. 18.

17 Founded in 1593, Marischal, compared with King's, placed more stress on

Protestant theology and on mathematics and more practical subjects. It has been suggested that commercial-minded burgesses of Aberdeen saw this curriculum as more useful to them. Bridges *ibid.*

18 *Thay Haif Said. The Story of Marischal College.* (Aberdeen 1982) p. 2; Bridges: (2001) *op. cit.* p. 18

19 Walter R. Humphries: 'Gordon of Straloch', *Gordonian,* (December 1932) vol. IV no. 6 pp. 262–265.

20 Ten miles north of Aberdeen.

21 Charter granted for Sir Thomas Gordon of Cluny, dated Straloch, 24 June 1606. The lands were sold by John Gordon Cumming of Pitlurg in 1760 to John Ramsay of Barra. (John Malcolm Bulloch: *The House of Gordon* (Aberdeen 1897) volume II p. 275.

22 East of Ellon.

23 Bridges (2001) *op. cit.* p. 19 suggests that Straloch's main efforts were 'devoted to saving his kinsmen [the Earls of Huntly] from the consequences of their maintaining Catholic sympathies and lacking astuteness in politics.'

24 1565–1614. Pont was minister of Dunnet in Caithness (1601–10) and was an accomplished mathematician. He personally surveyed and drew many parts of Scotland during the late 1580s and 1590s.

25 *Theatrum Scotiae* was completed in 1648 and first published in Amsterdam in 1654.

26 Some 65 manuscript maps by Straloch survive in the National Library.

27 Jeffrey C. Stone: *The Pont Manuscript Maps of Scotland. Sixteenth century origins of a Blaeu atlas.* (Tring, Hants 1989) esp. pp. 5–13 following his 1972 University of Aberdeen Ph.D. Thesis *Maps of Scotland By Timothy Pont, Robert and James Gordon and Joan Blaeu. A Study in Historical Cartography* esp. pp. 19 and 515 and 'Robert Gordon of Straloch: cartographer or chorographer?' *Northern Scotland* (1981) no. 4, pp. 7–22.

28 Stone (1989) *op. cit.* pp. 9–13 held that of the 47 regional maps in the Atlas, nine were drafted by Robert Gordon using Pont sources without significant alteration; three were drafted by Robert Gordon incorporating new material as well as information from Pont manuscripts and one map was drafted by James Gordon.

29 Inscribed 'Robertus Gordonius' it was handed over to the Royal Scottish Museum by the executors of Mrs Florence Cumming, 18 Ainslie Place, Edinburgh, in 1947. *Nature* 19 April 1947; *Gordonian* vol. IX no. 5 June 1947 p. 160; A. R. Hutchieson: Bequest to the Royal Scottish Museum – Astrolabe of Robert Gordon of Straloch, *Mariners' Mirror* 34, 1948, pp. 122–3.

30 *Dictionary of National Biography* (*DNB*) (Oxford 2004) vol. 22 pp. 954–955. Article by Shona M. Vance.

31 Where his son, George, was buried (and son, Patrick, was to be reburied).

32 *Scottish Notes and Queries* (October 1896) vol. X no. 5 p. 74.

33 John Marshall: 'Robert Gordon of Straloch – Scottish cartographer' *Leopard Magazine*

(September 1980) pp. 25–27 put the case for Straloch as a cartographer of significance.

34 James worked on the collection in 1683 and before his death in 1686 gave them to Sir Robert Sibbald, who also collected the Pont and Adair manuscript maps. After Sibbald's death in 1722 they were purchased and deposited in the Advocates' Library in Edinburgh, where they remain to this day.

35 Straloch had met, during his time in Paris, Robert Johnstone of Blackfriars, who had become one of executors of George Heriot's Will in 1624. When he came to make his own Will of 30 September 1639 Johnstone made numerous bequests including the mortification of £600 sterling to Aberdeen poor for setting them to work at lawful trades and manufactures. Brian R. W. Lockhart: *Jinglin' Geordie's Legacy. A History of George Heriot's Hospital and School* (East Linton 2003) p. 51.

36 In Robert Gordon's time the word "hospital" was used for a charitable institution for the education of the young, while "infirmary" referred to an institution for the care of those who were ill or injured.

37 See Appendix II for Genealogy.

38 By 1630 around 12,000 Scots were in Swedish service. Steve Murdoch: 'Scotland, Europe and the English "Missing Link"' in *History Compass* 5/3 (2007) p. 893.

39 There has been some debate on which member of the Gordon family won this medal. However, according to Mrs M. M. Gordon: *John Gordon of Pitlurg and Parkhill or Memoirs of a Standard-Bearer* (London 1885) it was preserved in the family as an heirloom originally awarded to Robert. This was confirmed by Alex M. Munro: 'Portraits in Possession of Robert Gordon's College' in *Scottish Notes and Queries* (January 1896) vol. IX no. 8 pp. 113–115 and Walter R. Humphries: 'An 18th Century Doctor', *Gordonian* (December 1935) vol. V no. 6 p. 241. It can be found today in the Governors' Room of Robert Gordon's College, having been given over as part of the Parkhill Bequest of March 1895.

40 David Stevenson: *King's College, Aberdeen, 1560–1641: From Protestant Reformation to Covenanting Revolution* (Aberdeen 1990) p. 91.

41 As a minister in his early years during the Covenanting Wars he was admonished more than once for failing to act against persons suspected of anti-Covenanting leanings, but he managed to hang on to his charge, perhaps because of his family connections. In May 1650 he was excused from attending Cummunion as he had to go south immediately as his brother-in-law, Gilbert Menzies, younger of Pitfodels, aged 22, had been killed at Crabstill defending the Royal Standard.

42 In the National Library of Scotland, Adv. MS.70.2.10, [Gordon] 52.

43 *Edinburgh Council Records* 2 April 1647.

44 *Aberdeen Council Register* 1661 vol. 54 p. 323.

45 Not written by Straloch as suggested by some.

46 The manuscript – a folio volume of 510 pages – remains in King's College Library.

47 Like his father, James endeavoured to steer a middle course between the opposing

sides which divided the nation. James Man (ed): *James Gordon's History of Scots Affairs 1637–1641* (Aberdeen 1841). vol. I (Spalding Club).

48 Sometimes Ludovick.

49 This suggests perhaps a close relationship with his deceased brother, Arthur, given that they were both younger sons, and that Lewis and Robert Gordon had kept in touch. Family was important to the Founder. *Services of Heirs in Scotland 1545–1799*, 8 December 1711 and 24 January 1712.

50 He entered in 1641 but classes were interrupted for long periods. *Peter John Anderson: Roll of Alumni at University and King's College, 1596–1860* (Aberdeen 1900) p. 486.

51 One of at least 138 advocates at that time. John Macpherson Pinkerton (ed): *The Minute Book of the Faculty of Advocates* vol. I 1661–1712 (Edinburgh 1976) p. v.

52 The Pitfodels branch of the Menzies family dominated Aberdeen local politics until 1635. In the previous 212 years it had occupied the civic chair (Lord Provostship) for 114 years. Alexander Keith: *Eminent Aberdonians* (Aberdeen 1984) pp. 12–15.

53 *Aberdeen Burgess Register* (October 1632–June 1694): 1661 p. 357.

54 Honorary burgesses were admitted by Aberdeen Town Council because of either the eminence of the individual being honoured or the good offices of friends. The composition fee, from 1629 on, had been 200 merks. Conversion rates at this time were: £1 sterling equalled eighteen merks equalled twelve pounds Scots.

55 Isobell was the only daughter of Lt. Colonel Thomas Menzies of Balgownie who, as an unrepentant Roman Catholic, fled the country for religious reasons. He took up arms under the Tsar of Russia, was badly wounded fighting the Poles at Slobodyshche (1660) and was buried in the Ukraine. Joseph Robertson (ed): *Passages from the Diary of Patrick Gordon of Auchleuchries in the years 1635–1699* (1859) pp. 31–32 ; Robert I. Frost: *The Northern Wars. War, State and Society in Northeastern Europe, 1558–1721* (Harlow, Essex, 2000) pp. 186–7.

56 Isobell assigned bonds valued at 14,400 merks to Arthur and some land in the barony of Slains, while Arthur added 10,000 merks of his own, the combined sum to be vested in land or annual-rent to provide for them jointly, the survivor for the terms of his or her life (Arthur did die first), then heritably to their children.

57 *Session Records of Old Machar* 3 May 1663. Alexander M. Munro: *Records of Old Aberdeen* (Aberdeen 1909) vol. II p. 59 and vol. III p. 228. There seem to have been a number of Roman Catholics in this parish and the Session was much exercised in their suppression.

58 His last Faculty attendance in Edinburgh was in November 1664 although he was still on the list of advocates there as late as November 1670. Pinkerton (1976) *op. cit.* pp. 9 and 21. However, he did not practise in Aberdeen, his name not appearing in the list of Aberdeen advocates of the time.

59 Became No. 12 Broad Street. The Row was demolished in 1867 to make way for the new Municipal Buildings and Advocates' Hall.

60 Alexander Walker: *Robert Gordon. His Hospital and his College* (Aberdeen 1886) p. 3.

61 'Maister Arthour Gordon and Isabel Menzies his spouse a son baptised by Mr John Menzies called Robert. Mr Robert Petrie, Provost, Robert Forbes late Baillie, Mr John Forbes and Andrew Thomson godfathers.' *Old Parish Register for Births/Christenings 1553–1854, 168/OA 004 Aberdeen.* Petrie of Portlethen was Lord Provost of Aberdeen 1664–5, 1667–70 and 1674–5, while Robert Forbes of Rubislaw became Provost 1671–3. Alexander M. Munro: *Memorials of the Aldermen, Provosts and Lord Provosts of Aberdeen, 1272–1893* (Aberdeen 1897) pp. 179 ff.

62 Anna and John died when young although John was still alive at the time of his father's death in March 1680. Mary married Sir James Abercrombie, 2nd of Birkenbog (near Cullen) (1668–1734) and had fifteen children. She died in 1742.

63 Bulloch (1929) *op. cit.* suggests that as he was called 'a pupil' when becoming a burgess. This was presumably at the Grammar School.

64 The 'heritable' estate of land and buildings came to the equivalent of £ 1,111. 2. 3d. sterling. £134,972 sterling in today's money. Laurence H. Officer: *Purchasing of British Pounds from 1264 to 2006* (Measuringworth.com 2007). His mother and two surviving siblings inherited the 'moveable' estate which amounted to £712 sterling. *Testament testamentar of Arthur Gordon.*

65 Francis Douglas: *A General Description of the East Coast of Scotland from Edinburgh to Cullen* (Paisley 1782) p. 123.

66 Until then he was under the guardianship of his mother and uncles, Alexander, seventh son of Straloch, a lawyer who became a Lord of Session in 1688 (Lord Auchintoul), and Lewis. This arrangement ensured that young Robert Gordon was not too influenced by the Catholicism of the Menzies family.

67 The charge that he dissipated his wealth on 'riotous living' was only suggested over a century after Robert Gordon's death by James Bruce: *Lives of Eminent Men of Aberdeen* (Aberdeen 1841) p. 289 and is not based on any contemporary evidence. It was partially based on the wrong assumption that Robert was born in 1665 and was three years older than he actually was.

68 When helping to plan the Grand Tour for his own son in 1696, John Clerk's father held Holland the 'epitome of the wholl world in which are to be found the greatest men of all professions, the best governed commonwealth and rarities of all kinds to satisfie a man'. Christopher A. Whately: *The Scots and the Union* (Edinburgh 2006) p. 72 and p. 83.

69 The custom arose in this period of admitting children as burgesses but it seems to have been a special privilege of those who held high office especially in the Town Council. Alexander Skene became a merchant burgess aged four in 1625; his wealthy father became Town Treasurer shortly afterwards. Baillie Gray's sons were admitted in infancy in 1658.

70 *Burgess Register Oct. 1632 – June 1694*; April 1684 pp. 726–7 quoted in full by Strathdee (1969) *op. cit.* p. 5.

71 In his time Aberdeen was a trading, rather than a craft, town. The stent roll of 1669 listed c.600 burgesses, around 350 of whom were merchants and 250 craftsmen (and only 75 of the merchants were involved in overseas trade, the rest operating mainly in the north-east of Scotland). Ian Blanchard, Elizabeth Gemmill, Nicholas Mayhew and Ian D. Whyte: 'The Economy: Town and Country in Aberdeen Before 1800' in *Aberdeen Before 1800. A New History.* (East Linton 2002) p. 152.

72 Peter John Anderson: (1900) *op. cit.* p. 503. Perhaps, however, the choice was determined by the fact that Marischal drew more heavily from students in Aberdeen. David Ditchburn: 'Educating the Elite. Aberdeen and its Universities' in *Aberdeen Before 1800* (2002) *op. cit.* p. 341.

73 Jennifer J. Carter and Colin A. McLaren: *Crown and Gown 1495–1995* (Aberdeen 1994) pp. 22–3.

74 Peter John Anderson (ed.): *Fasti Academiae Mariscballanae Aberdonensis* (Aberdeen 1898) vol. II Officers, Graduates and Alumni p. 255 and p. 259 shows one other example in the period – George Munro with his servant attending 1683–7.

75 *Ibid.* p. 260.

76 His grandfather, Robert of Straloch, however, was on record, in the 1650s, promoting trade as an occupation as an alternative to poverty and a military career for 'the better classes'. James Miller: *Swords for Hire. The Scottish Mercenary* (Edinburgh 2007) p. 219.

77 *Memorialls for the Government of the Royal Burghs of Scotland . . . as also, A Survey of the City of Aberdeen* (Aberdeen 1685). J. Robertson: 'Alexander Skene of Newtyle' in *Scottish Notes and Queries* 9 (March 1896) pp. 158-160. Gordon DesBrisay: Alexander Skene (1621-94) in *Oxford Dictionary of National Biography* 2004 edition.

78 This original copy now can be found in the Governors' Room of Robert Gordon's College. It was owned by Dr Alexander Walker in the 19th century but was returned to the College in the 1970s.

79 Plaiding, Fingrams, Stockings, Salmon and Herring, Stuffs, Serges, Sheep-skins and Lamb-skins.

80 Baillie Skene (1685) *op. cit.* p. 246.

81 *ibid.* p. 112.

82 *ibid.* p. 122.

83 *ibid.* p. 168.

84 *Diary of General Patrick Gordon* (1859) *op. cit.* p. 154 suggests that he wrote to Robert Gordon on 5 August 1686 in Danzig, but this seems a little early.

85 Known as Gdansk today.

86 Anna Bieganska: 'Scottish Merchants and Traders in 17th and 18th Century Warsaw', *Scottish Slavonic Review,* (Autumn 1985) no. 5, pp. 19–34. T. A. Fischer:

The Scots in Germany: being a Contribution towards the History of the Scot Abroad (Edinburgh 1902) pp. 3–65 and Robert I. Frost 'Scottish Soldiers, Poland-Lithuania and the Thirty Years' War' in Steve Murdoch (ed): *Scotland and the Thirty Years' War 1618–1648* (Leiden 2001) pp. 192–193.

87 Steve Murdoch (2007) *op. cit.* p. 895.

88 Waldemar Kowalski stresses these as the 'push' factor from Scotland. 'The Placement of Urbanised Scots in the Polish Crown during the 16th and 17th centuries' in Alexia Grosjean and Steve Murdoch: *Scottish Communities Abroad in the Early Modern Period* (Leiden 2005) p. 65.

89 The Polish-Lithuanian reputation for religious toleration gave it added appeal to Scots of both Protestant and Roman Catholic persuasion. Anna Bieganska: 'Scottish Immigrants in Poland', *Scottish Slavonic Review* (Autumn 1991) no. 19. Anna Bieganska: 'In Search of Tolerance. Scottish Catholics and Presbyterians in Poland', *Scottish Slavonic Review,* (Autumn 1991) no. 17. pp. 37–59.

90 James Miller: (2007) *op. cit.* pp. 68-69. The Scots were primarily foot soldiers while the Polish army was mainly cavalry. The resulting success led to thirteen Scottish soldiers being granted the right to join the Polish nobility in the 17th century.

91 T. A. Fischer: *The Scots in Eastern and Western Prussia* (Edinburgh 1903) pp. 3–119. According to Laurence Fountaine: *History of Pedlars in Europe* (Durham, NC 1996) p. 10 the Scots who settled in Poland came from 140 locations in the north and north-east of Scotland and can be identified in more than 420 locations in their new homeland.

92 The Lanark traveller, William Lithgow, visited Poland in 1616 and found Scots everywhere. He estimated 30,000 Scots families. He saw Poland as the 'mother and nurse of the youth and youthlings of Scotland . . . in cloathing, feeding and inriching them'. [*The Totall Discoveries of the Rare Adventures and Painefull Perigrinations.'* (1632 repr. Glasgow 1906 pp. 367–8.)]. The Scots influx was so great that James VI and I's representative in Poland between 1606 and 1622, Patrick Gordon, reported a number destitute and the King attempted to limit their emigration to those with friends or with the resources to subsist for a year. Anna Bieganska: 'The Learned Scots in Poland from mid 16th century to close of 18th century', *Canadian Slavonic Papers,* 43/1, March 2001. The Englishman John Chamberlain wrote in March 1621 to Dudley Carleton estimating the same figure (M. A. Everett (ed.): *Calendar of State Papers. Domestic Series of Reign of James I 1619–23* [London 1858] p. 33 and 237). This was corroborated by Sir James Cochrane, English Ambassador to Poland, who claimed many thousands of Scots in Poland in 1652 (A. Francis Steuart (ed): *Papers Relating to the Scots in Poland 1576–1793* [Edinburgh 1915]). Lawrence Fountaine (1996) *op. cit.* (p. 10) mentions 30,000 while Robert I. Frost (2001) *op. cit.* p. 192 suggests the number may be as large as the 40,000 mentioned in an aside by Flamineo, a character in John Webster's tragic play, 'The

White Devil' (first acted in 1608). Steve Murdoch (2007) *op. cit.* p. 895 reports an estimate of 50,000 in mid-17th century, although suggests such figures should be viewed with 'scepticism'.

93 = Stary Szkoty (Old Scotland).

94 The Hussites were a reforming religious movement following Jan Hus. They raided German towns and provinces committed to defeating their objectives. They burned Alt Schottland again in 1520.

95 Steve Murdoch: *Network North: Scottish Kin, Commercial and Covert Associations in Northern Europe 1603–1746* (Leiden 2006) p. 135

96 James Lithgow being especially successful in the latter in Danzig.

97 Postmaster Robert Low at Danzig was a benefactor of the 1700 Marischal Appeal and the Principal responded by commissioning Charles Whyt to paint his portrait, which hangs on the wall in Elphinstone Hall. (ABDUA 30100). Alasdair M. Stewart: 'Aberdeen and Gdansk', *Aberdeen University Review* (Spring 1977) no. 157 pp. 45–51. Peter John Anderson (ed): *Fasti Academiae Mariscballanae Aberdonensis* (Aberdeen 1889) vol. I pp. 357–360. Probably the most outstanding success story was that of Alexander Chalmers (Czamer), who four times was elected Mayor of Warsaw and died in 1703. S. Seliga in *Scotland and Poland; A Chapter of Forgotten History* eds. S. Seliga and L. Koczy (Dundee 1969) chapter I.

98 Billy Kay: *The Scottish World. A Journey into the Scottish Diaspora* (Edinburgh 2006) pp. 41–56.

99 Poland-Lithuania took no official part in the War.

100 The Sejm's property tax of 10% on Scots/English settlers raised £10,000 sterling: of the nearly five hundred who paid they were overwhelmingly Scots, judging by their names, and included eleven with the surname Gordon. Andrew B. Pernal and Rosanne P. Gasse: 'The 1651 Polish subsidy to the exiled Charles II' in *Oxford Slavonic Papers* (Oxford 1999) No. 32 pp. 1–50. Frost (2001) *op. cit.* p.195.

101 Dauvit Horsbroch: 'Wish You Were Here? Scottish Reactions to 'Postcards' Home from the 'Germane Warres'' in Steve Murdoch (2001) *op. cit.* pp. 245–267.

102 A considerable number of Scottish immigrants were affluent people hoping to increase their wealth.

103 The most significant included 1622 Jacob Balfour; 1658 Jacob Anderson; 1670 William Robertson; and 1688 John Turner. Maria Bogucka: 'Scots in Gdansk (Danzig) in the Seventeenth Century' in A. I. Macinnes, T. Riis and F. G. Pedersen (eds.): *Ships, Guns and Bibles in the North Sea and the Baltic States c.1350–c.1700* (East Linton 2000) pp. 39–46

104 The first preacher to the Scots congregation in 1692 in the Church of St Peter and St Paul, Alexander Burnet, took services in his own home in Frauengasse.

105 Norman Davies: *God's Playground. Vol. 1. The Origins to 1795. A History of Poland* (Oxford rev. ed. 2005) pp. 199–200.

106 Ibid. p. 198. Mostly rye, but also significant quantities of wheat and barley. The

decline was a result mainly of an increase in domestic grain production in Western and Southern Europe and the cessation of population growth in the same areas.

107 Milja van Tielhof: *The 'Mother of All Trades': The Baltic Grain Trade in Amsterdam from the Late Sixteenth to the Early Nineteenth Century* (Leiden 2002) sees the period of contraction as 1650–1760 before revival, and that Amsterdam and Gdansk were closely integrated as markets for two centuries.

108 J. A. Faber: 'Structural changes in the European economy during the eighteenth century as reflected in the Baltic trade' in W. G. Heeres et al. (eds): *From Dunkirk to Danzig. Shipping and Trade in the North Sea and Baltic, 1350–1850* (Hilversum 1988) p. 90. These trends continued and intensified in the later 18th century.

109 *Ibid.* pp. 84–85.

110 The main colonial products were coffee, tea, indigo, rice, sugar and pepper.

111 Norman Davies (2005) *op. cit.* p. 210.

112 Eric J. Graham: *A Maritime History of Scotland, 1650–1790* (East Linton 2002) p. 161.

113 *Ibid.* pp. 212–3.

114 Andrew Davidson had completed six years as an apprentice and three as a journeyman but he was younger with less financial backing and had arrived in Poland much earlier in the century. Anna Bieganska: 'Andrew Davidson (1591–1660) and his Descendants in Poland', *Scottish Slavonic Review,* (Spring 1988) No. 10, pp. 7–18.

115 Attempts to restrict the trade of the immigrant Scots had been a feature of the reaction of vested interests in Poland and elsewhere in the 16th and early 17th centuries. Lawrence Fountaine (1996) *op. cit.* esp. ch. 1.

116 Legal documents exist from 1699 onwards describing him as a 'merchant in Aberdeen'. Strathdee (1969) *op. cit.* p. 14; Alexander Du Toit 'Robert Gordon' in *Oxford DNB* (Oxford 2004) vol. 22 pp. 955–6.

117 Including the Pilica, Western Bug, San, Wieprz and Niemen.

118 Danzig stood at the mouth of the Motlawa (Mottlau) and was connected to the Leninka, a branch of the delta of the Vistula.

119 Called Folwarks.

120 Other exports may have included rye, wheat, linseed and potash to Amsterdam, Bordeaux, La Rochelle and Lisbon.

121 Including wine, cloth, spices and paper.

122 Lubomirski was the King's most important adviser and highest official in the Treasury.

123 'wegen unterschiedenen bei des reichs Zollen verubte Excessen'. *Acta Vice Prasidialia* 1696–7, Danzig City Archives (22 November 1696) 300. 5/129a pp. 769–770, 784–5, 790, 835–41 and 859–860. Danzig City Archives (6 September 1697) 300. 5/130 pp. 727–731.

124 In later 17th century zloty coins struck by mint master, Andrzej Tymff, were quickly christened 'Tymfy'.

125 Karin Friedrich: *The Other Prussia, Royal Prussia, Poland and Liberty, 1569–1772* (Cambridge 2000) pp. 66–7.

126 Born in 1647, the son of Andrew Davidson and his second wife, Anna Iwaszkiewicz, he became a Danzig burgess (citizen) in 1681. Anna Bieganska: *op. cit.*

127 From Aberdeen he became a burgess in 1685.

128 A Scottish burgess from Dundee who had arrived in Danzig in 1668 and by Robert Gordon's time had become British Resident in the town.

129 Or Gellatly. Anna Bieganska (1988) *op. cit.*; Danzig City Archives 300. 60/5, pp. 216, 251, 300; 300. 1/84 p. 457; 300. 1/ 88 pp. 82, 213; 300. 1/ 90 pp. 332, 351, 374.

130 Caution = financial guarantee.

131 His total fine was 4710 florins, half of which went in compensation to Susanna Gordonowa, who may have been the Miss Gordon living in Konska Street in Kedainiai in Lithuania. Rimantas Zirgulis: 'The Scottish Community in Kedainiai c1630 – c1750' in Grosjean and Murdoch (2005) *op. cit.* p. 237.

132 To avoid such instances a number of Scots attempted to gain citizenship usually after a ten-year residence. Robert Gordon appears not to have been keen to do this, even though with his background and networking he was rich enough to enter the local upper class and so obtain citizenship.

133 Douglas Catterall: 'At Home Abroad: Ethnicity and Enclave in the World of Scots Traders in Northern Europe c.1600–1800,' *Journal of Early Modern History* (2004) vol. 8 nos. 3–4 pp. 319–357.

134 The Polish translation of 'Englishe Haus' was 'cathedral angieleki'. The Poles omitted the 'g' and the resulting 'cathedral anieleki' became 'angel house'. Soon after Robert Gordon's departure in 1720 it became a hotel and in time the best-known hotel in the city. It was badly damaged in 1945 and reconstructed in the 1970s.

135 T. C. Smout: *Scottish Trade on the Eve of Union 1660-1707* (Edinburgh 1963) p. 165.

136 Steve Murdoch: 'The French Connection: Bordeaux's 'Scottish' Networks in Context, c1670–1720' in Gilles Leydier: *Scotland and Europe, Scotland in Europe* (Newcastle 2007) p. 38.

137 Bill Purdie: 'Ralph Carr: a Newcastle merchant and the Baltic trade in the mid-18th century' in Patrick Salmon and Tony Barrow: *Britain and the Baltic. Studies in Commercial, Political and Cultural Relations 1500-2000* (Sunderland 2003) pp. 157–168.

138 *Council Register* vol. 57 (August 1682–December 1704) pp. 423–4.

139 *Burgh Sasine Register* vols. 52 pp. 3, 15–17, 51–52, and vol. 55 pp. 307–8.

140 *List of Pollable Persons in Aberdeenshire for 1696* (Aberdeen 1844) vol. II pp. 622–623. He was assessed for three pounds, six shillings Scots. His uncle, Lewis, a doctor, with no wife, nor child nor servant was assessed at twelve pounds, six shillings Scots.

141 Copies extant in College Archive include an account for 1701–2 (dated 27 January 1703) for 41 barrels of salmon, sold by Gordon and Rickart and shipped on 'John of Aberdeen' to Le Havre, and a letter from Jacques Quesnel of 3 February 1703 (in French) regarding a bill for salmon. Rickart's Accounts also refer to salmon trading with Gordon on 10 December 1700 and 9 July 1703 in *Scottish Notes and Queries*, VI, (1913) p. 104 and p. 203. Rickart's papers (including Accounts) are held in the University of Aberdeen Special Libraries (GB 231).

142 Rickart's Accounts 7 July 1701 in *Scottish Notes and Queries*, (1913) vol. VI, p. 112.

143 *Ibid.* p. 262.

144 *Treasurer's Accounts of Aberdeen* (1700–25) vol. 3 and (1725–50) vol. 4. Gordon was one of twelve heritors with half-nets annually till his death, when Rickart regained the salmon rights. *Scottish Notes and Queries* (1915) vol. VIII p. 53.

145 Christopher A. Whatley: (2006) *op. cit.* p. 117.

146 T. M. Devine: *The Scottish Nation 1700–2000* (London 1999) p. 6. Douglas Watt: *The Price of Scotland. Darien, Union and the Wealth of Nations* (King's Lynn 2007). Although there was interest in the Company of Scotland in Danzig (p. 99) English opposition scared off foreign investors (p. 103).

147 Founded in 1695.

148 *Council Register* (June 1705–September 1721) vol. 58 p. 133.

149 F. Douglas (1782) *op. cit.* p. 125.

150 Unfortunately Anna Bieganska: 'Subscribers from Poland to the Restoration of Marischal College in the Late Seventeenth Century' in Paul Dukes (ed): *The Universities of Aberdeen and Europe. The First Three Centuries* (Aberdeen 1995) pp. 152–3 wrongly adds 'of Tillielt' to the name of the Founder. Tillielt married in 1687 Elizabeth, daughter of James Hearn but the marriage was childless. His wife died in 1702 and following his death his sister, Jean, made a claim for his estate on 17 June 1712, *Book of Propinquity*, Volume II (1706–1732), while his nephew, Alexander Charles (son of another sister, Isobell) was granted a passport to Poland on 5 August 1712 to look after his uncle's effects. Margaret R. Mackenzie: *Calendar of Town Council in-letters* (Aberdeen 1918) vol. 8 no. 183.

151 Peter J. Anderson (ed): (1889) *op. cit.* pp. 358–9.

152 The letter which betrays a growing Germanisation in style and spelling is extant in the University of Aberdeen Special Libraries Collection M387/14/3/4/1.

153 Sometimes termed the 'English' Church.

154 T. A. Fischer (1902) *op. cit.* ch. 7; R. B. Strathdee (1969) *op. cit.* pp. 16–17. Although this Church was destroyed in 1945 during the Second World War, according to Frank S. N. Dunsby, its minister earlier that century, it had carved on its communion table the figure of a pelican feeding its young from its own breast. This has led some to surmise that Robert Gordon, having received sacrament from this table, perhaps obtained the idea of a pelican as an appropriate symbol for his foundation. A. Stewart (1977) *op. cit.* p. 50.

155 Eric J. Graham (2002) *op. cit.* p. 168.
156 In 1694 some 68 appeals from Gdansk widows were heard against the 'jus caducorum'. State Archives in Gdansk: *Acta Praesidialia* 1693–4 pp. 480–2.
157 The estate of George Allan of Konigsberg took four years to clear up between 1725 and 1729 as a result of these complications.
158 Smout chose as an example of significant economic success Andrew Russell, a merchant-trader and banker, centred on Rotterdam between 1669 and 1697, who left 90,000 pounds Scots on his death. T. C. Smout (1963) *op. cit.* p. 115. Robert Gordon brought home the same amount from Danzig a few years later.
159 Walker (1886) *op. cit.* p. 8.
160 A charity school.
161 F. Douglas (1782) *op. cit.* stressed Robert Gordon's lack of interest in 'private connexions' (p. 124). He suggested that Lord Provost Cruickshank pleaded the case for Robert's sister, Mary, to benefit from his wealth. Robert Gordon's response was curt – what could be expected if the head of the Town pleaded against a settlement from which its citizens would benefit?
162 Robert Gordon Hospital (RGH) *Minutes* vol. 2 – February 1738–November 1742 (20 November 1738) p. 13.
163 Today, suitably inscribed, the books can be found in the rare books section of King's College Library. *Liber Academiae Mariscellanae Abredonensis: Ex Dono Moderatorum Paedotrophii Gordonii A.D. 1738.*
164 *AU MS 139 Bible.*
165 RGH *Minutes op. cit.* pp. 13–4. Boethius was the last of the great pagan writers of Rome, who produced his 'Consolatione' at the beginning of the sixth century A.D. His insistent message stressed the vanity of misdirected human wishes. It was work which men of culture in the Middle Ages knew well. Cato's work of wise, homely maxims appealed to Gordon. 'From Robert Gordon's Library', *Gordonian,* (June 1938) vol. VI no. 5 p. 215.
166 *AU MS 148 Cato and Boethius.*
167 Hector Boece was the first Principal of King's College (1505–35) and produced his history in Latin in 1527.
168 D. H. Willson: *King James VI and I* (London 1958) p. 133.
169 5th edition – Oxford 1638.
170 Details and signature found on flyleaf.
171 James Bruce: (1841) *op. cit.* p. 295.
172 1568–1658.
173 James Man (1841) *op. cit.* p. 35 R. B. Strathdee: *Sit Bona Librorum Copia* (privately published 1968).
174 RGH *Annual Accounts* 1738–9.
175 Bookseller 1736–49 who left 1126 books which sold for £220.
176 This last paragraph is based on Alastair J. Mann: *The Scottish Book Trade 1500–1720.*

Print Commerce and Print Control In Early Modern Scotland (East Linton 2000) p. 205.

177 William R. MacDonald: 'Book Auctions and Book Values in the Aberdeen Area 1749–1800', *Aberdeen University Review,* (1967) no. XLII, pp. 114-132.

178 1637–1714.

179 1640–1703.

180 See Book 10 of Gordon's engravings for examples from both.

181 Straloch's links with Holland were long-term and included outstanding figures in engraving and painting.

182 In particular his 1622 '*Balli di Sfessania*' in Books 3 and 4.

183 Book 1.

184 John Marshall 'Robert Gordon, Merchant in Danzig' (October 1980) *Leopard* Part II p. 29.

185 Melvin.

186 *Catalogue of the Coins and Medals belonging to Robert Gordon's College in Aberdeen* (Aberdeen 1893) p. vi. Organised by Michie of the University of Aberdeen and A. M. Munro, City Chamberlain's office.

187 The only earlier Scottish collection of coins appears to be that of James Sutherland (d. 1719) who sold his cabinet in 1705 to the Faculty of Advocates.

188 These paragraphs rely heavily on Donal Bateson, University of Glasgow, who viewed the catalogue in November 2006.

189 According to the explanation in 'Bon Accord' on 26 May 1904 it may have been part of the original Blackfriars property Gordon purchased in Schoolhill. A less likely suggestion is that it refers to Sillerton between Fyvie and Turriff.

190 R. B. Strathdee (1969) *op. cit.* p. 18 mentions six different examples from this time including a number of bonds for Sir Alexander Cunmming.

191 'Sealbhar' = a Celtic word meaning rich in cattle. As the b and h were both silent they were omitted. The resulting 'sealar' became 'siller', the Scottish word for wealth. Sillerton was therefore a local name for the Hospital, as it was built on the farm and, as it was near a loch, it produced much grass. The name was transferred to a farm in Turiff on an estate purchased by the Governors. This was the theory of John Milne: *Celtic Place Names in Aberdeenshire* (Aberdeen 1912) pp. 289–290. Other contributions to the debate can be found in 'The meaning of 'Sillerton'' *Gordonian,* (June 1937) vol. VI no. 3 p. 96. 'Where is Silverton?' *Gordonian,* (June 1939) vol. VII no. 1 pp. 7–8.

192 R. B. Strathdee: *A Gordonian Looks at The School Hill* (privately published 1973) p. 17.

193 Robert Gordon Hospital (RGH) *Accounts,* City Archives, DD/61/A/1/1, 24 April–8 November 1731 p. 10 (Whitsun 1730–1) and 8 November 1731–13 November 1732 p. 14 (Whitsun 1731–2).

194 An Aberdeen baker and poet.

195 Francis Douglas (1782) *op. cit.* p. 123. The tradition probably owed something to those disappointed when Gordon bequethed his entire fortune to found a Hospital.

196 *Ibid.* viz. To found a Hospital for poor boys.

197 Walter Thom: *The History of Aberdeen, containing an account of the Rise, Progress and Extension of the City.* (Aberdeen 1811) p. 77.

198 William Kennedy: *Annals of Aberdeen from the Reign of King William the Lion to the End of the Year 1818, with an account of the City, Cathedral and University of Old Aberdeen.* 2 vols. (Aberdeen 1818) vol. II p. 140.

199 *Selected Writings of John Ramsay with Memoir and Notes by Alexander Walker (his literary executor)* (Aberdeen 1871) pp. 182 ff. ('The Letter of Masque' was written in 1834.)

200 Editorial writer for *Aberdeen Journal.*

201 1841 pp. 289–302. Principal John Murray in his Oration spoke of Bruce publishing 'a century's sweepings of scurrilous gossip' with an 'admixture of the author's own historical venom'.

202 *Ibid.* Preface xi. This statement and his stated intention not to deal with 'undeserved eulogiums' (*ibid*) made his pen-portrait less than objective.

203 The charge of misogyny was based on a misunderstanding of Robert Gordon's beliefs. Gordon's provision in the Statutes of his Hospital that females had no place there was founded on the premise that a small number of women would be problematic in a monastery of boys and men.

204 Robert Chalmers (ed): *A Biographical Dictionary of Eminent Scotsmen* (Glasgow 1855) 4 vols. new edition vol. II pp. 475–479 repeated the criticisms of Gordon's character but in less colourful terms.

205 Alexander Walker: *Robert Gordon 1665–1731 and His Hospital 1750–1876* (Aberdeen 1876).

206 Alexander Walker: (1886). *op. cit.* p. 9.

207 Alex. M. Munro: *Scottish Notes and Queries* (Feb. 1888) vol. I pp. 133–4 had already suggested 'that he was no miser goes without saying' and Anderson developed this theme in a talk at the Auld Lads' Reunion in the Imperial Hotel in Aberdeen on 19 December 1890 *Scottish Notes and Queries* (February 1891) vol. IV pp. 169–170. William Robbie: *Aberdeen. Its Traditions and History* (Aberdeen 1893) p. 281 also gave a balanced approach.

208 Robert Anderson: *The History of Robert Gordon's Hospital, Aberdeen 1729–1881* (Aberdeen 1896) p. 7.

209 *Ibid.* p. 8. Unfortunately, even though they agree that the stories about Gordon's meanness are much exaggerated, more recent works still detail some of these stories. John S. Smith: 'Robert Gordon the 'Merchant Miser' Founder of Gordon's College' *Deeside Field* (1987) no. 19 pp. 10–12; Henry Ellington: *The Robert Gordon University. A History* (Aberdeen 2002).

210 Shona M. Vance: 'Poverty and Pursuit of Learning' in *History of Universities* [2003], XVIII (2) pp. 90–146.

211 Shona Vance: *Mortifications (Bursaries and Endowments) for Education in Aberdeen, 1593–1660 and their Implementation in 17th Century.* Ph.D. Thesis, University of Aberdeen 2000.

212 Provision had been made for the maintenance and education of ten orphans, a number of daughters of decayed burgesses of guild, eleven bursaries at the Grammar School, six divinity bursaries, chairs in mathematics and divinity, as well as subsidised salaries for the Principal and four teaching regents, a librarianship, four teachers at the Grammar School, two schoolmistresses and several personal libraries and a collection of mathematical instruments. Shona Vance (2003) *op. cit.* p. 94.

213 *Ibid.* p. 97ff.

214 *Ibid.* p. 43.

215 Rebuilt in 1631 as a home for 'decayed' brethren of guild including merchants who had fallen on difficult times and could not support themselves in old age.

216 *Mortifications under the charge of the Provost, Magistrates and Town Council of Aberdeen.* (Aberdeen 1849) pp. 149–155.

217 *Ibid.* pp. 117–8 footnote.

218 K. J. Peters: *Burgess of Guild* (Aberdeen 1982) p. 13.

219 Eventually established in the Gallowgate in 1664. *Ibid.*

220 Heriot's Hospital in Edinburgh had been followed at the end of the 17th century by the foundation of a number of other Hospitals, while the Hutcheson brothers had founded a Hospital in Glasgow.

221 Jean Guild's mortification of 1649 to maintain and educate ten orphans had followed this pattern, as had the benefaction of Catharine Rolland in 1659. *Mortifications* (1849) *op. cit.* pp. 128–130 and pp. 135–140.

222 The burgess class was the 30% or so of urban families that belonged to an incorporated guild or trade.

223 In fact in 1696 Aberdeen there were 50 professionals: 16 law; 15 education; 7 surgeons; 7 church; 4 medicine and 1 other – a 'significant number'. Michael Lynch and Helen M. Dingwall: 'Elite Society in Town and Country ' in *Aberdeen Before 1800* (2002) p. 193.

224 Gordon DesBrisay and Elizabeth Ewen, with H. Lesley Diack: 'Life in the Two Towns' in *Aberdeen Before 1800* (2002) p. 67.

225 The corporate poor referred to the distressed members of the burgess class, the 30% or so of urban families that belonged to an incorporated guild or trade. *Ibid.* p. 58 ff.

226 Dr James C. P. Logan: *Founder's Day Oration* 13 May 1977.

227 R. A. Houston: *Scottish Literacy and Scottish Identity* (Cambridge 1985).

228 He himself gifted over £11,000 sterling.

229 Brian R. W. Lockhart (2003) *op. cit.*

230 Shona Vance (2000) *op. cit.* pp. 153–4 and p. 156.

231 To manage the unprecedented outpouring of bequests the Town appointed a Master of Mortifications (or charitable legacies) in 1632. However, the Wars of the Covenant seriously interrupted this flow and Aberdeen borrowed some £77,000 from the mortifications alone to pay its debts. As a result, there were fewer new charitable mortifications in the second half of the 17th century than in the decade of the 1630s. *Mortifications* (1849). By 1695, despite significant attempts to service the debt, the Town still owed £92,392 to its charitable trusts. Gordon DesBrisay: 'The civill warrs did overrun all. Aberdeen, 1630–90' in *Aberdeen Before 1800* (2002) *op. cit.* esp. pp. 264–5.

232 William Cruickshank, Lord Provost of Aberdeen; William Smith, late Baillie of Aberdeen; John Rickart of Achnacant, merchant in Aberdeen; Alexander Thomson, advocate in Aberdeen, while James Moir, writer, produced the document which was signed on every page by Robert Thomson, Town Clerk. It was recorded on 24 May 1731.

233 Presented and accepted by the Heriot Governors on 4 July 1627 and having taken Balcanquall over three years to complete. Brian R. W. Lockhart (2003) *op. cit.* pp. 20–5.

234 The result of work by Charles Binning, John Osburn, John Inglis and three ministers and dating from 1 May 1724.

235 Helen M. Dingwall: *Late 17th Century Edinburgh: a demographic study*. (Aldershot 1994) pp. 266–7.

236 Note the order, which suggests that the prime purpose was to create a home rather than a school, with the emphasis on a Christian upbringing.

237 This stress on Menzies, as well as Gordon, suggests a respect for his mother's family, but note that priority was given to any boy relation.

238 F. Douglas (1782) *op. cit.* p. 122 saw this as 'very sensible' but Ramsay (1871) *op. cit.* was more critical, suggesting such a cautious approach meant an unnecessary delay in opening.

239 Or widower in the same situation.

240 Robert Gordon remained a committed Protestant, although his Catholic relatives and his time in Poland ensured a toleration of other religions. On his death his estate included a portrait of Pope Clement XI (1700-21), whom Gordon probably admired for his charitable work and his attempts to bring harmony to Poland. Eamon Duffy: *Saints and Sinners. A History of the Popes* (3rd ed. Yale 2006) pp. 237-240.

241 Celibacy was the norm in all hospitals and was accepted without comment. Bruce (1841) *op. cit.* p. 299 held that it was not in line with Protestant principles and was an unnatural and miserable state. The celibacy model at Gordon's was probably based mainly on cost. However, both Luther and Calvin pressed only for the ending of mandatory celibacy, and Wesley commended celibacy for those who could accept it.

242 Explaining the fact that most of the Masters and Schoolmasters were ministers of religion or had a religious background.
243 Later lowered to 14.
244 Made £5 sterling for all on 21 August 1842.
245 Made £5 sterling for both on 3 April 1755.
246 Professor Robert D. Lockhart *1943 Oration*. The boys would be watched over until they were 22.
247 Heriot's Statute XIII and Watson's Statute XIV.
248 Defined as 2000 merks (Scots) of free stock paying back one half of the costs of their education; 4000 merks (Scots) of free stock paying back all that was bestowed on them.
249 Article XV.
250 Seeking legal opinion in August 1840.
251 However, this clause proved controversial in the instance of the first case, and then impractical as a number of other significant endowments were left to the Governors.
252 Baillie John Munro: *1st Founder's Day Oration*. 27 April 1934.
253 Article XX.
254 Walter Humphries: *Founder's Day Oration* 1941.
255 King's and Marischal.
256 The link with Heriot's suggested this. It was based on Christ's Hospital, then in London.
257 Lord Provost 1728–30 and 1732–4.
258 On 24 May 1731.
259 Witnessed by Cruickshank; William Smith and William Chambers, ex-Baillies of Aberdeen; James Thomson of Portlethen, advocate in Aberdeen; Alexander Thomson, advocate in Aberdeen, and written by James Moir. It was recorded on 24 May 1731.
260 £2000 sterling.
261 The Appendix also included his instructions that his coins and medals should be preserved in a box in the Hospital, while his pictures and prints were also not to be sold but be subject to inventory and kept in the Hospital.
262 Under Scots Law a feu was a perpetual lease of land at a fixed rent.
263 Following a gift of land by Alexander II in 1240 a monastery of Blackfriars (Dominicans) had grown up. It suffered greatly during the Reformation and most of its property passed to the Crown, being acquired by Earl Marischal in 1587 for the endowment of Marischal College. G. M. Fraser: *Historical Aberdeen* (Aberdeen 1905).
264 *Council Register* (September 1728–September 1741) vol. LX. (1730) pp. 171–177. The Council held the land as Trustees for Jean Guild's Mortification, which owned it, hence the £10 was accepted. Otherwise it may have been free.

265 RGH *Accounts* (April–November 1731) Drs John and James Gordon for medicines to Robert Gordon on his deathbed and for a care-cloath and incense at the interment 86 pounds Scots. To Drs Gordon and Donaldson and William Abercrombie, surgeon, 'for their pains at attendance upon Robert Gordon at this time' 667 pounds Scots.

266 His death after an evening out Douglas (1782) *op. cit.* p. 125 was put down to 'overeating' by Ramsay (1834) *op. cit.* p. 185 and turned into a 'debauch' where he gorged himself by Bruce (1841) *op. cit* p. 297.

267 F. Douglas (1782) *op. cit.* p. 125.

268 At a cost of 20 pounds Scots. *Kirk and Bridge Work Accounts 1725–50.* Bell-ringing at funerals occurred at a frequency of less than once a year in this period. Although ended by the Reformation the practice had crept back in during the famine of the 1690s. Anne Gordon: 'Death and Associated Customs' in John Beech, Owen Hand, Mark A. Mulhearn and Jeremy Weston (eds): *The Individual and Community Life* (Edinburgh 2005) pp. 104-5.

269 Mortcloaths were funeral shrouds, which in the case of the poor were rented, while those of the rich were lined with velvet and bordered with lace fringing. Anne Gordon (2005) *ibid.* p. 107.

270 Between September 1730 and August 1731 113 burials were recorded and Gordon's was the only one to use two mortcloaths. Even Lady Finzach's funeral on 23 April 1731 only used one. City of Aberdeen *Treasurer's Accounts* 1725–1750.

271 *Kirk and Bridge Work Accounts* (1725–50) vol. 4. Drum's Aisle was the traditional burial place of the Irvine of Drum family. Despite Reformation strictures, burials of the upper class or wealthy continued in church probably until the mid-18th century, as recent archaeological work at St Nicholas has shown.

272 RGH *Annual Accounts* November 1731–November 1732 p. 8.

273 25 pounds Scots. The total figure excluded the generous honorarium given later by the Governors to the physicians who attended Robert Gordon in his final days.

274 Douglas (1782) *op. cit.* p. 298.

275 The purse and shoe exhibited in the Governors' Room in the College are reputed to have belonged to the Founder.

276 RGH *Quarterly Accounts* 1 May–1 August 1734; at a cost of 76 pounds Scots.

Chapter 2

1 Lord Provost 1730–2.

2 Udny had borrowed 500 merks from Robert Gordon, expecting a legacy on his death but despite the claim that he had worked 20 years without payment no bequest was forthcoming, The Governors came to an accommodation with Udny

on 17 November 1735. RGH *Minutes* vol. I (May 1731–November 1737) p. 129.

3 The Governors determined on an Inventory of Robert Gordon's 'medals, prints and picturs' and considered an inventory of his library (7 February 1732): *Minutes* I, p. 35.

4 Cruden remained Treasurer until 18 July 1737 when the Accounts were cleared 'upon a suspition [sic] of the Treasurer's affairs being in disorder'. *Annual Accounts* November 1736–July 1737. A bond was immediately produced for the outstanding sum of 1168 pounds Scots which ensured the books balanced. Cruden was replaced by John Midleton, who remained in office until November 1747 when his son, William, took over until 13 November 1749 when he was replaced by William Gordon, merchant. *Minutes* vol. III (Nov. 1742– Nov. 1758) p. 70.

5 £10,333 sterling – £1,493,790 in today's money. L. Officer (2007) *op. cit.*

6 RGH *Minutes* vol. I p. 3.

7 John Gifford: *William Adam 1689–1748. A Life and Times of Scotland's Universal Architect* (Edinburgh 1989) pp. 163 ff.

8 John Fleming: *Robert Adam and his Circle in Edinburgh and Rome* (London 1962 repr. 1978) p. 51

9 In the event some of his designs were deemed too elaborate. Howard Colvin: *A Biographical Dictionary of British Architects* (London 1978) p. 57; R. Anderson (1896) *op. cit.* p. 28; RCAHMS: *Tolbooth and Town Houses. Civic Architecture in Scotland to 1833* (London 1996).

10 Lord Provost 1728–30 and 1732–4.

11 RGH *Minutes* vol. I p. 4.

12 Their Account when rendered totalled 1734 pounds Scots. (RGH *Accounts* 24 April – 8 November 1731) p. 9.

13 James Macaulay: 'The Growth of a New Town' in *Aberdeen Before 1800. A New History* (2002) *op. cit.* p. 408. It was published later in William Adam: *Vitruvius Scoticus: being a collection of plans, elevations and sections of public buildings, noblemen's and gentlemen's houses in Scotland* (Edinburgh 1812) plate 108.

14 RGH *Minutes* vol. I p. 4.

15 Adam's stonemason at Haddo House in 1731.

16 RGH *Minutes* vol. I p. 14.

17 *Ibid.* vol. I p. 32.

18 Peter John Anderson: Marischal College v. Gordon's College, *Scottish Notes and Queries,* (April 1892) V, p. 164.

19 The Charter from Marischal College was signed on 17 March 1732 and a Charter was given over by the Master of Mortifications on 13 September 1732. *Burgh Sasine Register* vol. 58 pp. 48–9. The College handed over the lands for twenty bolls of bear 'good and sufficient merchant stuff' annually. *Council Register* vol. LX p. 264 and 'Gordon's Hospital Site', *Scottish Notes and Queries*

(December 1909) vol. II pp. 377–8. The feu duty of twenty bolls was later converted into cash.

20 RGH *Minutes*. vol. I. p. 42.

21 G. M. Fraser (1905) *op. cit*; Tom Donnelly: *The Aberdeen Granite Industry* (Aberdeen 1994) p. 2; J. S. Smith: 'The Rise and Fall of Aberdeen's Granite Industry', *Aberdeen University Review*, (Spring 1982) no. 167, pp. 163–7.

22 RGH *Accounts* 24 April – 8 November 1731 p. 9.

23 Between 2 Dec. 1731 and 28 April 1732 they were paid 1015 pounds Scots; between 28 April and 1 August 1732 some 2481 pounds Scots and between 1 August and 1 November 1732 some 1919 pounds Scots. RGH *Annual Accounts* Nov. 1731–Nov. 1732. Between 3 and 21 Nov. 1732 they were paid some 105 pounds Scots, excluding work on the garden. RGH *Annual Accounts*: Nov. 1732- Nov. 1733.

24 The use of surface stones was the cause of the 'beautifully weathered surface which the granite has now taken on, a surface quite different from that assumed by quarried stone'. W. Douglas Simpson: 'Gordon's College and its Architect', *Gordonian*, (June 1928) vol. III no. 3, p. 139.

25 Who hailed from Elphinstone.

26 RGH *Minutes* vol. I. (29 March 1732) p. 45.

27 *Ibid.* p. 55.

28 *Ibid.* p. 65.

29 *Ibid.* p. 74. The appointment of a gardener, Alexander Drysdale of Old Raine for four years, suggests good progress.

30 *Ibid.* p. 78.

31 *Ibid.* pp. 82 and 101.

32 181 pounds Scots.

33 *Ibid.* pp. 116–7.

34 *Ibid.* p. 146, p. 150 and p. 160. The stone came from John Davie in 'Stonehyve'. RGH *Quarterly Accounts* July–Nov. 1737.

35 RGH *Minutes* vol. I p. 137.

36 *Annual Accounts* November 1737–8: accounts paid in February, May and November.

37 RGH *Minutes* vol. II p. 41.

38 *Ibid.* p. 46.

39 RGH *Accounts*: and on three of those occasions Adam spent time in Mrs Cooper's coffee house with the Governors, the cost of which totalled 171 pounds Scots. Payments to Adam for his designs were 448 pounds Scots. He 'communed' with the Governors again in Mrs Leslie's coffee house in late 1736 at cost of 7 pounds Scots. RGH *Quarterly Accounts* August–Nov. 1736.

40 Kennedy: *(1818)* vol. II *op. cit.* p. 141.

41 Robert Wilson: *An Historical Account and Delineation of Aberdeen* (Aberdeen 1822) p. 57.

42 James H. Wilson: *The Bon Accord Repository of Local Institutions* (Aberdeen 1842) p. 95.

43 James R. Rettie: *Aberdeen Fifty Years Ago* (Aberdeen 1868) p. 102.

44 David Murray: 'Robert Gordon's Hospital and its relationship to the other Public Buildings of William Adam'. *Scott Sutherland School of Architecture Dissertation* 1975 p. 9.

45 RGH *Minutes* vol. II p. 116

46 J. F. Wyness: 'Robert Gordon's Hospital. A Sketch of its History and Architecture', *Gordonian*, (December 1930) vol. IV no. 2 pp. 62–65.

47 Others no longer surviving include Dundee Town House, Glasgow University Library, Edinburgh Orphan's Hospital, Edinburgh Royal Infirmary and Watson's Hospital.

48 David Murray: (1975) *op. cit.* p. 29.

49 William Adam: (1812) *op. cit.* plate 108.

50 James Macaulay: (2002) *op. cit.* p. 408.

51 In 1751 from John Thom, blacksmith and Governor. RGH *Minutes* vol. III p. 108 and p. 135. The iron door was to ensure that the Founder's coins, medals and prints, and the Hospital papers, were kept secure and fireproof. It cost 112 pounds Scots. *Quarterly Accounts*, 1 May – 1 August 1752.

52 *Annual Accounts* 1749–50: February bill for 498 pounds Scots.

53 With shaped back, pierced vase splat and carved mask cresting, serpentine drop-in seat, with shell carved apron, cabriole legs and claw feet. Provided by Provost Alexander Robertson in May 1750 for 25 pounds Scots. *Annual Accounts* 1749–50.

54 With shaped backs, solid vase splats and drop-in seats, on cabriole legs with pad feet, united by turned side and central stretchers. The set numbers 23.

55 With rectangular tops over club legs and claw and ball feet.

56 With fringe drawer on square tapered legs.

57 With rounded corners, fringe drawer and turned legs with claw feet.

58 Francis Douglas: (1782) *op. cit.* p. 119.

59 James H. Wilson: (1842) *op. cit.* p. 95.

60 Kennedy (1818) II *op. cit.* p. 144.

61 W. Douglas Simpson: (1928) *op. cit.* p. 141.

62 J. F. Wyness: (1930) *op. cit.* p. 64.

63 Auditors spoke to Barnes about his debt and executed a summons against Glenbucket. (RGH *Minutes* vol. I p. 4). Both discharged their debt in October 1732 (*ibid.* p. 63).

64 By John Arbuthnot of Fordoun and Colonel Partick Ogilvie of Insch on 12 June 1732; by William Burnet of Craigie and Alexander Frasier (elder and younger) on 19 July 1732; Sir James Dunbar of Durno on 14 August 1732; William Duff of Braco, George Keith (advocate) and James Cattanach (advocate) on 1 November 1732; and William Baird of Auchmedden and James Eithern of Pitroddie on 19 February 1733.

65 The Governors had received a Memorial from Seton as early as 20 August 1731 and inspected his lands at Whitehill (RGH *Minutes* vol. I, p. 11). A further Memorial from Seton resulted in him being lent 44,000 merks (*ibid.* p. 28). In 1750–1 the Hospital rents from Orchardtown raised 1665 pounds Scots.

66 *Annual Accounts* November 1733–November 1734.

67 RGH *Minutes* vol. I p. 111.

68 *Ibid.* p. 112.

69 The Hospital rents from Dumbreck in 1750–1 raised 1210 pounds Scots.

70 RGH *Minutes* vol. I pp. 120–2.

71 RGH *Annual Accounts* November 1734 – November 1735.

72 Sasine was the registration of a deed transferring ownership of property.

73 RGH *Minutes* vol. I p. 142. *Annual Accounts* November 1736 – July 1737. Lying in the parish of Banchory–Devenick in the county of Kincardineshire.

74 RGH *Minutes* vol. I p. 139. Crookstown rents raised 1835 pounds Scots for the Hospital in 1750–1.

75 RGH *Minutes* vol. III p. 22.

76 *Ibid.* p. 28.

77 RGH *Minutes* vol. VI (June 1792–December 1816) pp. 168–9.

78 RGH *Minutes* vol. III p. 58: 2 August 1747.

79 *Ibid.* p. 77. In the parish of Kincardine–O'Neal, Kincardineshire, just south of Torphins.

80 Birkenbog House lay two miles south-east of Cullen. It incorporated an older round tower.

81 RGH *Minutes* vol. I p. 19. Walker (1896) *op. cit.* pp. 6–7.

82 RGH *Minutes* vol. I p. 23.

83 *Ibid.* p. 21.

84 From Duncan Forbes advocate, Robert Dundas, late Lord Advocate, and local advocate, Alexander Gordon of Troup. *Inventory of Title Deeds and Other Documents* (17 November 1823) p. 2; Margaret R. Mackenzie: *Calendar of Letters of Burgh of Aberdeen* (Aberdeen 1918) Supplementary volume I no. 40 (6 December 1731).

85 RGH *Minutes* vol. I p. 40. The Deed of consent was signed by the principal citizens of the Town in March 1732.

86 Totalling 571 pounds Scots. RGH *Annual Accounts* Nov. 1731 – Nov. 1732.

87 *Inventory* (1823) p. 2. Following 'retour' confirmation that Mary was heir to Robert Gordon. *Services to Heir* 2 May and 11 May 1732.

88 The Governors' description of the 1746 Jacobite Rebellion, which was the last attempt to return the Stuart dynasty to the throne of Scotland. RGH *Minutes* vol. III p. 33.

89 R. B. Strathdee: 'Fort Cumberland' in *Aberdeen University Review* (Autumn 1952) vol. XXXIV, no. 107 p. 356.

90 Son of George II.
91 Kennedy (1818) I *op. cit.* p. 303.
92 Strathdee (1952) *op. cit.* p. 357. Cumberland occupied the house created by Sir George Skene, Provost of Aberdeen 1676–84 and owned by Alexander Thomson, advocate: the second house requisitioned belonged to the widow of Gordon of Hallhead. William Robbie: (1893) *op. cit.* pp. 308–311. The leading citizens, pleased at the restoration of their position, granted Cumberland the freedom of the Burgh on 6 March.
93 Kennedy (1818) *op. cit.* vol. I p. 303.
94 Part of the War Office '*Surveys of Military Works in Scotland*' in the National Library of Scotland.
95 Christopher Duffy: *The '45* (London 2003) p. 478.
96 1744–6 (and again in 1752–4).
97 Alexander Keith: *A Thousand Years of Aberdeen* (Aberdeen 1972) p. 278.
98 Which included ex-Provosts Robertson and Chalmers; John Osburn and Robert Pollock, both ministers.
99 RGH *Minutes* vol. III p. 35.
100 *Ibid.* p. 40.
101 *Ibid.* p. 43.
102 Aberdeen City Archives L / N / 1(17 February 1746–10 October 1747). *Papers relating to the attempted recovery of the costs of repair of Robert Gordon's Hospital.*
103 Aberdeen City Archives L / N / 6. *Detailed estimate of repair work of Hospital gardens.*
104 *Ibid.* L / N / 4. *Detailed estimate of repair costs to mason work.*
105 *Ibid.* L / N / 8. *Detailed estimate of wright work, glass windows, locks and other iron work.*
106 *Ibid.* L / N / 11. *Total costings of repair.*
107 *Ibid.* L / N / 12. *Draft Petition to Magistrates in Edinburgh.* RGH *Minutes* vol. III p. 44.
108 Anderson (1896) *op. cit.*
109 RGH *Minutes* vol. III p. 47.
110 Lt. Col. David Watson to Rt. Hon. Lt. Gen....of H.M. Ordnance, Fort Augustus, 21 August 1747. James Allardyce: *Historical Papers relating to the Jacobite period 1699–1750* vol. I (Aberdeen 1895) pp. 304–5. RGH *Quarterly Accounts* 1 May – 1 August 1747.
111 Lord Provost 1746–8.
112 RGH *Minutes* vol. III p. 51.
113 *Annual Accounts* November 1747–8.
114 RGH *Minutes* vol. III pp. 54–55.
115 *Annual Accounts* 1747–8, 1748–9, 1749–50.
116 RGH *Minutes* vol. III (15 August 1748). Confirmed also by the purchase of Mid Beltie.
117 *Ibid.* p. 65.

118 An Officer, Roderick McCulloch, had been appointed from 1 November 1746.

119 RGH *Minutes* vol. III p. 69. (20 August 1749).

120 Taylor's map of 1773 showed the bowling green in the area later occupied by the Art Gallery. It was used until the 1830s building developments but by then was being neglected. Alexander Clark: 'The Bowling Green at Gordon's Hospital' *Gordonian*, (May 1929) vol. III no. 5 p. 248.

121 RGH *Minutes* vol. III p. 70 (13 November 1749).

122 *Ibid.* p. 80.

123 Tuesday 6 March 1750, Number 114 and Tuesday 13 March 1750, Number 115.

124 One Governor voted for the other candidate, James Taylor, merchant.

125 James Bissett dissented and protested in writing. RGH *Minutes* vol. III p. 84.

126 *Ibid.* p. 84.

127 *Ibid.* p. 81.

128 On 21 May 1751 he was given an annual salary of 12 guineas, besides payment for his 'drogs', which in his first year of service totalled £1/19/7 Sterling. *Ibid.* p. 107.

129 *Ibid.* p. 82. As a printer he was also given the contract to supply paper, pens and ink. He had begun publication in 1748 of *The Aberdeen Journal*, the oldest newspaper in Scotland. He was also Master of the Sang School and Precentor of the West Kirk of St Nicholas.

130 *Aberdeen Journal* Tuesday 17 July 1750 Number 133 reported that the 'boys were received, genteelly clothed'.

131 RGH Minutes vol. III p. 91.

132 *Ibid.* p. 90.

133 The numbers in square brackets refer to the number given to the boy in the original Registers of the Hospital. RGH *Register of Admissions and Departures* vol. I (1750–1854).

134 His burial crepe and funeral expenses of 26 pounds Scots were paid by the Hospital. *Quarterly Accounts* 1 May – 1 August 1751.

135 Perhaps he was annoyed as one of only a few ex-Hospital pupils who was reminded by letters in February 1788 about the expectations of the Governors that he should pay the cost of his education. RGH *Minutes* vol. V (November 1779–May 1792) p. 279. He did not reply (V, p. 289.), and probably heard that the Governors considered going to court to force him to pay but decided that it would be 'inexpedient' to do so. (V, p. 341).

136 With his departure the Governors began to keep a book detailing charges, so that it would be available when a boy was able to pay back the cost of his education. RGH *Minutes* vol. III. p. 135. Formalised on 17 November 1761 but discontinued on 1 July 1767 when it was thought that such obligations from minors could not be binding.

Chapter 3

1 RGH *Minutes* vol. III p. 100.
2 Son of Rev. Robert Abercrombie of Leslie.
3 Later extended to boys serving their apprenticeshaip.
4 Exceptions were George Smith, who was specially admitted on 17 August 1752 because he was the son of a widow with eleven children; John Tough was admitted in April 1784 because of the poverty of his parents and the size of his family – RGH *Minutes* vol. V p. 108; and twins were taken in April 1824 as they had no father and their mother, through incapacity, was unable to maintain them. RGH *Minutes* vol. VII (February 1817–April 1831) p. 229.
5 RGH *Minutes* vol. III p. 176.
6 The decades broke down as follows: 1750s 41 burgess of guild, 41 burgess of trade = 82 admissions; 1760s 17 b. of gild, 46 b. of trade, 8 relations of Founder (and 2 unknown) = 73; 1770s 25 b. of guild, 93 b. of trade, 7 relations (and 1 unknown) = 126; 1780s 43 b. of guild, 92 b. of trade, 3 relations (and 1 unknown) = 139.
7 Parental occupations were wrights (65), weavers (43), shoemakers (31), hammermen (31), tailors (18) and fleshers (18). Apprenticeship destinations were wright (73), hammerman (39), shoemaker (37), tailor (19) and weaver (13).
8 Those apprenticed to clerk/writers (11) and medical related occupations (12).
9 Anderson (1896) *op. cit.* p. 39. RGH *Minutes* vol. V p. 153. Both Master and father seem to have compromised: Marr was apprenticed to a writer (clerk) and later went abroad to seek his fortune in the West Indies.
10 See Appendix II for his relation to the Founder.
11 Anderson (1896) *op. cit.* pp. 12–3.
12 RGH *Minutes* vol. V p. 167. *Annual Accounts* 1784–5.
13 RGH *Minutes* vol. V p. 342.
14 *Annual Accounts* 1795–6 and 1796–7.
15 RGH *Minutes* vol. III p. 107. Curiously these were: that the Hospital was for the relief, maintenance and education of boys of names Gordon and Menzies in preference to others; that the Hospital was always to be called Robert Gordon's Hospital; that the administration of the Hospital was to remain with the Governors as stipulated by Robert Gordon; and that no part of the stock or profits of the Hospital was to be applied to other than the use and benefit of the Hospital.
16 John Mackintosh: 'A School of the North East', *Scottish Field,* April 1962. p. 73. *Annual Accounts* 1749–50 paid in November.
17 Sometimes termed Mistress or Matron. RGH *Minutes* vol III p. 116. *Quarterly Accounts* 1 August – 1 November 1752.
18 RGH *Minutes* vol. III p. 119.
19 *Ibid.* p. 138.

20 Walker (1886) *op. cit.* p. 20.
21 R. B. Strathdee: *A Pride of Masters* (privately published 1972) pp. 7–8. Anderson (1896) *op. cit.* p. 39.
22 RGH *Minutes* vol. III p. 145.
23 *Ibid.* p. 101 (12 March 1751).
24 *Ibid.* p. 109 (21 May 1751).
25 *Ibid.* p. 130.
26 *Ibid.* p. 129.
27 *Ibid.* p. 149.
28 *Ibid.* p. 132. Lord Provost 1744–6 and 1752–4.
29 *Quarterly Accounts* 1 November 1751 – 1 February 1752.
30 RGH *Minutes* vol. III p. 149.
31 Until November 1765.
32 By 1760 the Governors were paying two pounds Scots a quarter for the boys to be seated regularly in the loft in the West Kirk. *Quarterly Accounts* 1 August – 1 November 1760. As numbers increased they took up the gallery and the middle area from summer 1807 and the servants began to attend the East Kirk. *Quarterly Accounts* 1 May – 1 August 1807. When in 1840 the Governors agreed to allow, as an experiment, forty boys and a master to attend public worship in the North Church the Session of the West Kirk made a strong protest.
33 RGH *Minutes* vol. III p. 120.
34 Lord Provost 1748–50.
35 RGH *Minutes* vol. III p. 125.
36 From 1737. The yard, which could be seen by travellers entering London by stagecoach from the West, was illustrated in Hogarth's 'Analysis of Beauty' (1753). Hogarth's depiction of the yard seems, from surviving contemporary written descriptions, to be accurate and shows at least some of the wide range of stock.
37 In order to have some idea of what a full life-size statue would look like, they commissioned Cheere to produce a terracotta statuette model of Robert Gordon two feet high. They liked what they saw and approved.
38 French-born sculptor, active in England for virtually his entire career. He had made his reputation with a full-length seated statue of the composer, Handel (Victoria and Albert Musuem, London 1738). He was the greatest sculptor ever to work in England and the greatest sculptor of his time.
39 *Evening Gazette* 11 July and 3 August 1888.
40 Mrs Arundell Esdaile: 'The Statue of Robert Gordon and its Sculptor', *Gordonian*, (December 1930), vol. IV no. 2 pp. 66–67.
41 It was shipped on the Aberdeen Packet *Captain Gordon*. James Rettie: *Memorandum 18* (1753 ff) p. 7.
42 *Quarterly Accounts* 1 August – 1 November 1753.
43 *Aberdeen Journal* Tuesday 14 August 1753, Number 292 related that the previous

Saturday 'a magnificent statue of Robert Gordon . . . was erected in a niche over the Great Entry'.

44 *Quarterly Accounts* 1 August – 1 November 1801.
45 RGH *Minutes* vol. III p. 150.
46 *Ibid.* p. 127.
47 *Ibid.* p. 141.
48 *Ibid.* p. 195.
49 *Ibid.* p. 158.
50 Rev. George Abercrombie became a Governor when he took up the ministry of St Nicholas in 1772. He remained a Governor until his death in 1790.
51 One compensation for the heavy workload was an increased salary to £25 sterling per annum.
52 Littlejohn was paid £60 sterling and Wallace £76 sterling. The first Hospital Accounts to use sterling. *Quarterly Accounts* 1 November 1760–1 February 1761.
53 Agreement reached 30 June 1761 RGH *Minutes* vol. IV (November 1758–October 1779).
54 Mosman had studied with Aikman in London, then in Rome under Francesco Imperiali. He worked in Edinburgh until 1745, settling in Aberdeen in the 1750s.
55 In Scotland in 1763 Wesley's congregations were large and composed of all classes of the community. Following his visit a Methodist chapel was founded in Aberdeen in 1764. David Wilson: *Methodism in Scotland* (Aberdeen 1850) p. 6.
56 Hucheon was minister at Fetteresso until his death on 27 February 1800.
57 Appointed October 1755.
58 RGH *Minutes* vol. V p. 20.
59 Lord Provost 1768–70,1772–4, 1776–8, 1780–2, and 1786–7.
60 RGH *Minutes* vol. V p. 23.
61 *Ibid.* p. 27.
62 James was the third son of the Robertsons to be educated in the Hospital.
63 *Ibid.* p. 28.
64 *Ibid.* p. 32.
65 *Ibid.* p. 38.
66 *Ibid.* p. 54.
67 *Ibid.* p. 45.
68 Statute XV.
69 Woven locally.
70 The fashion of the day.
71 RGH *Minutes* vol. V p. 83. The leather caps were to be found 'expensive and inconvenient' and were replaced by blue woollen bonnets. *Ibid.* p. 195 (15 August 1757). In late 1793 corduroy breeches were adopted 'as a cheaper and more frugal ware' instead of knee breeches. By the 1820s a cocked bonnet had been introduced.

72 Instead of a tie.
73 RGH *Minutes* vol. V p. 97.
74 *Ibid.* p. 101.
75 Lord Provost 1778–80 and 1782–4.
76 RGH *Minutes* vol. V p. 105.
77 Two and a half hours of lessons in the morning were followed by an hour of music (Monday, Tuesday and Wednesday) or an hour of drawing (Thursday, Friday, Saturday) and the afternoons saw three hours of lessons. Private prayers were said by the boys first thing in the morning and formal worship took place both morning and evening. Play was restricted to less than an hour after breakfast.
78 The Hospital paid a fee for this from 1760 onwards.
79 Following Gillet in November 1765 James Pringle took over as Music Master until November 1773. James Chalmers returned from May 1774 till February 1797.
80 Drawing was introduced in 1773 under Hugh Morison.
81 RGH *Minutes* vol. V pp. 111–134.
82 *Foundation Statutes and Rules of Robert Gordon's Hospital in Aberdeen* (Aberdeen 1784). Six were bound in calf and the others stitched.
83 *Ibid.* (1784) pp. 3–57.
84 *Ibid.* pp. 59–61 The most important being those of 19 August 1751 and 3 April 1755, the others being minor procedural matters.
85 *Ibid.* pp. 62–66.
86 *Ibid.* pp. 67–74.
87 *Ibid.* pp. 75–76.
88 *Ibid.* pp. 80–102. These also include an updated description of the duties of Mistress and Maid-servants.
89 *Ibid.* pp. 103–116. As a result the Governors clarified their right to acquire lands, and raise and defend legal actions.
90 RGH *Annual Accounts* Nov. 1783–Nov. 1784. The Clerk received eleven guineas, the Treasurer ten guineas and the Officer one guinea.
91 RGH *Minutes* vol. V p. 153.
92 *Ibid.* p. 174.
93 *Ibid.* p. 179.
94 Lord Provost 1784–6 and 1789–91.
95 RGH *Minutes* vol. V p. 197.
96 *Ibid.* p. 225.
97 *Ibid.* p. 254.
98 *Ibid.* p. 261.
99 *Ibid.* p. 262.
100 *Ibid.* p. 265.

101 *Ibid.* p. 278.
102 *Ibid.* p. 290. In May 1790 after Mrs Mark's resignation after 38 years' service she was awarded an annuity of £20 stg. *Ibid.* p. 343. She was replaced by Miss Jean More, who remained Housekeeper until 1816.
103 *Ibid.* p. 180.
104 *Ibid.* p. 181.
105 *Ibid.* p. 189.
106 *Ibid.* p. 334.
107 Jenkins was fifteen years old while Wilson was ten and Martin nine years old.
108 *Ibid.* p. 337 (3 April 1790).
109 *Ibid.* p. 339.
110 James Donald had been appointed in February 1789.
111 *Ibid.* p. 342.
112 On his death in November 1822 his remains were brought to the Hall of the Hospital and from there the funeral cortege left for the interment, which was attended by the Hospital boys. RGH *Minutes* vol. VII pp. 158–9.
113 RGH *Minutes* vol. V p. 345.
114 *Ibid.* pp. 28–9 and 35.
115 *Ibid.* p. 81.
116 These included James Crookshank [186] in October 1783, Archibald Robertson [221] in October 1785, Patrick Copland [306] in October 1788 and James Robertson [251] in April 1789. *Ibid.* pp. 95–96, 186, 201–2 and 314–5.
117 RGH *Annual Accounts* 1784–5.
118 RGH *Minutes* vol. V p. 185.
119 Kennedy (1818) *op. cit.* vol. I p. 322 footnote.
120 *Ibid.*
121 James H. Wilson (1842) *op. cit.* p. 12.
122 By February 1817 the Town's debt had risen to £225,741 sterling and its insolvency was only combated by special measures *ibid.* pp. 12 ff. On 21 May 1817 a legal decree was obtained by the Hospital treasurer, William Shepherd, against Hugh Gordon, Town Treasurer, for outstanding monies.
123 RGH *Minutes* vol. V p. 239. The expenditure on each boy per annum in the 1780s was just over £17 sterling. RGH *Abstract of Accounts* 1781–90.
124 RGH *Minutes* vol. V pp. 186, 189 and 275.
125 *Ibid.* p. 231.
126 *Ibid.*
127 *Ibid.* p. 289 and 293.
128 *Annual Accounts* 1787–8. The Opinion cost £9 sterling.
129 RGH *Minutes* vol. V p. 328. Against John Sligo [10] who had succeeded in a spirit distillation business in Leith, and James [33] and John Malcom [57], deceased merchants.

130 *Ibid.* p. 338.
131 *Ibid.* p. 341.
132 *Ibid.* p. 40.
133 *Ibid.* p. 228.
134 *Ibid.* p. 237.
135 *Ibid.* pp. 169–170.
136 *Ibid.* p. 247.
137 *Ibid.* p. 343.
138 *Ibid.* p. 348. Built by Patrick Scott, mason, at a cost of £37 sterling. *Quarterly Accounts* 1 February – 1 May 1793.
139 The iron gate for the front of the Hospital had been supplied by James Thain for £36 sterling. *Quarterly Accounts* 1 May – 1 August 1772.
140 Seen in the sketches by George Taylor of the garden surveyed in 1773.
141 Feuars named their own streets without reference to the Town Council until 1795 when the Police Commissioners took this over.
142 David Kidd [113] and James Shand [120] in April 1768.
143 Clearly a family problem as his younger brother, Robert, was later dismissed for the same offence.
144 RGH *Annual Accounts* 1801–2.
145 Some 4%.
146 Some 3%.
147 RGH *Register op. cit.* vol. 1
148 Baillie 1821–3, 1824–6, 1827–9 and 1830–2. Died 1849.

Chapter 4

1 This decision was to become very significant in 1841.
2 Robert Cruickshank: 'Reminiscences; or Strong Recollections of Gordon's Hospital Forty Years Ago'. *Paper read to the Social Meeting in Robert Gordon's Hospital on 23 January 1866* (Aberdeen 1866) p. 3. Cruickshank was a pupil in the Hospital between 1822 and 1827, was apprenticed to a grocer and ultimately set up his own business. He repaid 100 guineas for his education when he was a Governor in 1861.
3 RGH *Minutes* vol. V p. 349 and p. 352.
4 *Ibid.* p. 354.
5 *Ibid.* pp. 365–370.
6 *Ibid.* p. 380.
7 *Ibid.* p. 394.
8 RGH *Minutes* vol. VI p. 150.
9 *Ibid.* p. 173 and pp. 235–6.
10 *Ibid.* pp. 239–240. He remained until 1811.

11 *Ibid.* p. 212. Anderson (1896) *op. cit.* p. 152.
12 RGH *Minutes* vol. VI pp. 280–1.
13 *Ibid.* p. 386. Later, in 1828, ex-pupil William Simpson [692], who attended between 1809–14, was appointed Music Master.
14 RGH *Minutes* vol. V p. 348.
15 RGH *Minutes* vol. VI p. 23.
16 *Ibid.* p. 163.
17 *Ibid.* p. 335; RGH *Committee Book* (1796–1831) p. 54. In retrospect there may have been substance to the complaint.
18 RGH *Minutes* vol. VI pp. 344–5.
19 *Ibid.* p. 346.
20 RGH *Committee Book* (1796–1831) p. 1.
21 It was built by John Snetzler (1710–c1800), the celebrated Swiss organ-builder who settled in London in 1740 and who, in terms of quantity and to some extent quality, dominated the scene of chamber organs. David Welsh: 'Organs prior to 1820 in North-East Scotland', *British Institute of Organ Studies Reporter* (July 2004) vol. XXVIII no. 3. pp. 14–19. It was erected by Messrs. Guild and Massie. *Quarterly Accounts* 1 May – 1 November 1806.
22 And his successor, William Kedward, who taught in the Hospital between 1824 and 1828.
23 James Bruce, organ builder, was called in to report on its state in May 1830. Although he concluded that it was worth repairing at a cost of £26 sterling (RGH *Minutes* vol. VII p. 415.) the Governors decided not to do so. Another organ was fitted up in the Public School in April 1856. Anderson (1896) *op. cit.* p. 183.
24 George III.
25 Cruickshank (1866) *op. cit.* p. 8.
26 *Gordonian*, April 1910, vol. 11 no. 3 p. 312.
27 Employed from 1798 to 1821.
28 RGH *Minutes* vol. VI p. 12. (19 November 1792).
29 *Ibid.* p. 115.
30 *Ibid.* p. 121. RGH *Committee Book* (1796–1831) pp. 32–4. Later the jurisdiction of the Censors was extended to the Dining Room and Bedroom. In 1840 the Governors recognised the office and defined the duties. In 1855 Headmaster Strahan awarded a book prize to the best bedroom Censor. Censors continued to operate until 1881; Prefects were not introduced until the 1930s. R. B. Strathdee: 'Prefects or Censors?' *The Gordonian*, (December 1948) vol. X no. 2 pp. 51–52. At the Annual Dinner of the Gordonian Association before members and guests partake of the meal, the old Sillerton grace is sung, the President introducing the ceremony, as of old, with the words: 'Censor, Grace.' R. B. Strathdee: (1968) *op. cit.* p. 7.

31 RGH *Minutes* vol. V p. 373.

32 RGH *Minutes* vol. VI p. 72.

33 Walker (1876) *op. cit.* p. 12.

34 She was also remembered for her carelessly cooked 'Thursday's Dinner' as the caterpillars were frequently left in the cabbage. Many boys went hungry then and on other occasions.

35 RGH *Minutes* vol. VII p. 20. According to one source she was the natural daughter of Marshall Keith, who participated in the 1715 Jacobite rising. She dressed and acted like a lady and was always treated with marked respect. Alexander Walker (1886) *op. cit.* pp. 25–7.

36 RGH *Minutes* vol. VII pp. 274–5.

37 Walker (1876) *op. cit.* p. 14.

38 RGH *Minutes* vol. V pp. 386–7.

39 *Ibid.* p. 389.

40 Anderson (1896) *op. cit.* p. 193.

41 Indeed the only change in 1755 had been downwards, while the Wars of the late 18th century resulted in increasing prices.

42 RGH *Minutes* vol. V pp, 402–7.

43 Or Kingsford. In the parish of Auchterless in Aberdeenshire.

44 RGH *Minutes* vol. VI p. 2. The sasine in favour of the Governors was dated 26 August 1794. Walker (1876) p. 21 stressed the 'essential service' of the clerical Governors to the Hospital. An example of this included the important role of Rev. Hugh Hay of the East Kirk in the decision to buy the Towie estate.

45 RGH *Minutes* vol. VI p. 103.

46 RGH *Committee Book* (1796–1831) p. 30.

47 RGH *Minutes* vol. VI pp. 110–1.

48 *Ibid.* p. 238. *Annual Accounts* 1803–4.

49 *Annual Accounts* 1804–5.

50 RGH Minutes vol. VI pp. 281–2.

51 *Ibid.* p. 307. *Annual Accounts* 1808–9.The ground in front of the Hospital, to within 50 feet, was enclosed by a three-foot wall and iron railing, and the space tastefully laid out in flowers. The area beyond this, and running to Schoolhill, was occupied by a market-gardener, Saunders Sherriffs. His property on both sides of the entry walk was unprotected, yet rarely did boys take apples, berries, carrots or turnips. Cruickshank (1866) *op. cit.* p. 3.

52 RGH *Minutes* Vol. VI pp. 327–8.

53 RGH *Committee Book* (1796–1831) p. 54. Property facing Schoolhill was bought from Alexander Sherriffs in February 1823, while tenements in Woolmanhill were bought for £400 from George Duncan's Trustees in 1833. *Quarterly Accounts* 1 November 1833–1 February 1834.

54 RGH *Minutes* vol. VI p. 336. Thom's salary had already been increased to 30

guineas in August 1791 RGH *Minutes* vol. V p. 387 then to £42 in May 1799. RGH *Minutes* vol. VI p. 163.

55 RGH *Minutes* vol. VI p. 354; RGH *Committee* Book (1796–1831) pp. 58–62.

56 RGH *Minutes* vol. VI pp. 354–9.

57 *Ibid.* pp. 412–3.

58 *Ibid.* p. 424; RGH *Committee Book* (1796–1831) p. 88.

59 The Hospital was the largest creditor in February 1817 when the Town was insolvent. RGH *Minutes* vol. VII pp. 2–3. The use of Hospital funds by the Town raised questions over the ability of the latter to deal with the interests of the Hospital without sacrificing them to the Town. The situation was compounded when Lord Provost Alexander Fraser was appointed the Hospital representative on the Board of Trustees in charge of the Town repayments to its creditors. *Ibid.* p. 7.

60 *Ibid.* p. 80.

61 *Ibid.* pp. 84–5.

62 *Ibid.* p. 92. *Annual Accounts* 1820–1.

63 The book and account-keeping had been changed in May 1811 after criticism of the then system by George Hogarth, Dean of Guild. RGH *Minutes* vol. VI p. 329, pp. 333–4 and p. 336.

64 The Cautioners pledged to guarantee financially any deficiencies of the Treasurer.

65 RGH *Minutes* vol. VII p. 96.

66 *Ibid.* pp. 103–112.

67 *Ibid.* p. 117.

68 *Ibid.* pp. 125–6.

69 The arbitrators were John Davidson and David Hutchison.

70 *Ibid.* p. 142.

71 By 1852 they had become a 'dressing room' and the Steward's room – these were still the purposes in 1883. Today they are the janitors' room and an interview/administration office.

72 By 1852 it had been converted into 'bath and washrooms' and now further subdivided into rooms for various functions and a corridor continues through the original gable into the west wing of 1831–2.

73 By 1852 a corridor had been inserted and the kitchen had become pantries, the other rooms being for the use of Matron. Now the rooms are reception, administration and classrooms.

74 Use not stipulated in 1852 but now Guidance room to front and toilet to rear.

75 Which has remained unaltered.

76 By 1883 a vestibule, now a senior management room.

77 By 1852 this had been split by a corridor and steps up to the new east wing. In 1883 the front room was a tutor's room and the rear a sewing room. Now they house the Head at the front and Depute Head at the back.

78 It remained so in 1883.

79 By 1883 the sleeping room remained but the counting room had become a classroom.
80 By 1883 there were bedrooms front and back.
81 A bedroom by 1883.
82 A clothes closet in 1883.
83 By 1883 a single large bedroom.
84 By 1883 the front part was a cloakroom.
85 Simpson was born in October 1791. Collyhill was a small parish in Bourtie, just south of Oldmeldrum.
86 *Aberdeen Journal* Wednesday 21 August 1816. Simpson was inexperienced at grouse shooting and accidentally discharged his gun. The resulting wound on the left side of his head killed him instantly.
87 RGH *Minutes* vol. VII pp. 115–6; *Minutes* of the first meeting of the Collyhill Trust 29 June 1821.
88 *Additional Endowment to Robert Gordon's Hospital in Aberdeen* (Aberdeen 1836).
89 RGH *Minutes* vol. VII pp. 154–5 and 160–5.
90 Alexander Simpson's financial contribution to the Hospital was vital to its development. However, probably because the Collyhill Trustees were independent of the Governors for the next half-century Simpson does not appear to have gained the credit he deserves and it took till April 1942 for the granite memorial to him to be erected on the east wall of the College buildings. *Press and Journal* 6 December 1941.
91 RGH *Minutes* vol. VII p. 247. (15 November 1824). RGH *Committee* Book (1796–1831) p. 180.
92 Bought from William Spark for £52/10/-. RGH *Quarterly Accounts* 1 February–1 May 1825.
93 Lord Provost 1820–2, 1824–6, 1828–30 and 1832–3.
94 He embarked on a 'distinguished ministry' for fourteen years. R. B. Strathdee: (1972) *op. cit.* p. 14. He died on 11 July 1843.
95 The Governors bought in four dozen bottles of wine from Robert Duthie costing £5/17/-. *Quarterly Accounts* 1 November–1 February 1828.
96 RGH *Minutes* vol. VII p. 295. Provided by William Jamieson for £100. RGH *Quarterly Accounts* 1 February–1 May 1827.
97 Walker (1876) *op. cit.* p. 11.
98 Cruickshank (1866) *op. cit.* p. 4.
99 Parental occupations were dominated by weavers (57), shoemakers (38), wrights (35), fleshers (30), hammermen (30), bakers (22) and tailors (20).
100 Apprentice destinations were wright (102), hammerman (81), clerk (53), shoemaker (39), grocer (39), tailor (29), printer (28), sailor/seaman (25), medical (21), haberdasher (19), merchant (17) and weaver (16); there were even a few apprenticed to writers (3), architects (3) and a solitary surgeon.

101 Eight went 'abroad', destination imprecise, while 13 went to London, with others going to the West Indies (5), Africa (5), Canada (3), East Indies (3), Gibraltar (2) and Australia (1).
102 Cruickshank (1866) *op. cit.* p. 4.
103 RGH *Minutes* vol. VI p. 143.
104 *Ibid.* p. 167.
105 *Ibid.* p. 186.
106 *Ibid.* p. 212.
107 RGH *Minutes* vol. VII pp. 15–6.
108 *Register of Boys attending RGH* vol. I p. 41.
109 *Ibid.* p. 52.
110 His 'Whalers in Peterhead Bay' (c.1813) is in the Arbuthnot Museum.
111 *The Gordonian,* June 1919 no. 9.
112 R. Anderson (1896) *op. cit.* pp. 177–180.
113 RGH *Minutes* vol. VII pp. 299–300 [3 October 1826].
114 John Smith (1781–1852) had been made responsible for public works in Aberdeen in 1807 and had reshaped much of the Town. The Governors saw him as the in-house architect for the Hospital.
115 RGH *Committee Book* (1796–1831) p. 202.
116 Archibald Simpson (1790–1847) was committed to the neo-classical style and was responsible for the museum part of Marischal College and the Music Hall.
117 RGH *Minutes* vol. VII pp. 302–303. [20 November 1826]. Smith and Simpson had a mutual respect for each other, very often competing for the same commission and both were frequently consulted over the same project. David F. Miller: Archibald Simpson. *Architect. His Life and Times 1790–1847* (Kinloss 2006) p. 9.
118 Lord Provost 1822–4, 1826–8.
119 RGH *Minutes* vol. VII p. 308. RGH *Committee Book* (1796–1831) p. 229.
120 James Skene (1775–1864) of Rubislaw was an artist and legal friend of Walter Scott, who was instrumental in the founding and building of the Edinburgh Academy in 1824, designed by William Burn.
121 William Burn (1789–1870) was a distinguished architect who had already completed work on Blairquhan Castle in Ayrshire, Lauriston Castle outside Edinburgh and the school buildings for Edinburgh Academy and John Watson's Hospital.
122 RGH *Committee Book* (1796–1831) p. 241.
123 Clearly Burn was keen to meet this major criticism of his design.
124 RGH *Minutes* vol. VII p. 319.
125 *Ibid.* p. 328.
126 *Ibid.* p. 328 and p. 337. *Quarterly Accounts* 1 November 1827–1 February 1828. Burn was paid 30 guineas on 24 November 1827. *Annual Accounts* 1827–8.
127 RGH *Committee Book* (1796–1831) p. 250 [7 January 1828]. He gave 'information to builders' *Annual Accounts* 3 November 1828 and was paid £18/15/10.

128 RGH *Minutes* vol. VII p. 346. RGH *Committee Book* (1796–1831) p. 266 [3 April 1828].

129 RGH *Committee Book* (1796–1831) p. 269.

130 Along St Andrews Street and Blackfriars Street, given the decay of existing walls and problems daily from 'troublesome and idle people' who caused nuisance and disturbance. *Ibid.* p. 266.

131 RGH *Minutes* vol. VII p. 350. [19 May 1828].

132 He received £270/10/6. *Ibid.* p. 351 [18 August 1828]. *Annual Accounts* 8 September 1828.

133 RGH *Minutes* vol. VII pp. 359–360.

134 *Ibid.* p. 379.

135 *Ibid.* p. 380.

136 *Ibid.* p. 384. RGH *Committee* Book (1796–1831) p. 287. Simpson was appointed joint Professor of Hebrew and Oriental Languages at Marischal College in 1831. He took over Kintore Church on 18 September 1833, and after the Disruption in 1843 he joined the Free Church of Kintore and continued in that charge until his death on 29 June 1870.

137 Probably introduced as a result of the erection of a 25 foot reflecting telescope in the Hospital gardens by John Ramage, who was an optical instrument maker of some renown. It was sold after Ramage's death but in 1866 the Governors bought a telescope for the use of the boys.

138 RGH *Minutes* vol. VII p. 388.

139 Rev. A. H. Charteris: *Life of the Rev. James Robertson D.D.* (Edinburgh 1863) p. 23.

140 *Ibid.* p. 24.

141 What is perhaps most surprising is that no previous Master, even one as lauded as Thom, had openly commented on these underlying tensions. That they existed is clear but, unlike Heriot's Hospital, where a major drive was undertaken to defeat these evils from the mid-18th century, they had been ignored at Gordon's.

142 This was achieved despite his dwarf-like appearance and shrill voice. Jack Webster: *The Auld Hoose. The Story of Robert Gordon's College* (Edinburgh 2005) p. 42.

143 RGH *Minutes* vol. VII p. 393.

144 *Ibid.* p. 400.

145 Brian R. W. Lockhart (2003) *op. cit.* p. 139.

146 Rev. A. H. Charteris (1863) *op. cit.* p. 26.

147 The work on the enclosing walls had been completed already at a cost of £287. *Quarterly Accounts* 1 November 1828 – 1 February 1829.

148 The new total was £9293. RGH *Minutes* vol. VII p. 405. RGH *Committee Book* (1796–1831) p. 300

149 RGH *Minutes* vol. VII p. 407. [14 December 1829].

150 RGH *Committee Book* (1796–1831) pp. 301–2.

151 *Ibid.* pp. 303–4.

152 RGH *Minutes* vol. VII p. 421.
153 RGH *Committee Book* (1796–1831) p. 315.
154 RGH *Minutes* vol. VII p. 426.
155 George Hogg (1749-1826), an Aberdeen merchant who owned an estate in Maryculter parish.
156 *Ibid.* pp. 369–370.
157 £1750 was paid on 20 December 1827 and the rest the following year. *Annual Accounts* 1827–8.
158 RGH *Minutes* vol. VII p. 243.
159 £8400 principal with £336 interest per annum (4%). *Ibid.* p. 394 and p. 408.
160 The Statutes of Heriot's were compiled by a divine – Rev. Walter Balcanquall.
161 RGH *Minutes* vol. VIII (May 1831 – September 1845) pp. 9–10.
162 'Shirley' (Sir John Skelton): Review of Dr Charteris's 'Life of Robertson', *Fraser's Magazine,* August 1863.
163 Rev. A. H. Charteris (1863) *op. cit.* p. 35.
164 *Ibid.* and RGH *Minutes* vol. VIII p. 32. Robertson had a glittering career in the Church. Successful at Ellon he went on to become Professor of Divinity and Ecclesiastical History at the University of Edinburgh in 1843 and Moderator of the General Assembly of the Church of Scotland (1857–60) before his death in 1860. Robert Anderson: 'Dr. James Robertson', *Gordonian* (December 1912) vol. IV, no 2, pp. 27–30.
165 RGH *Minutes* vol. VIII p. 37.
166 RGH *Minutes* vol. VI p. 132. The Governors did so again in 1803. R. B. Strathdee: *In A Monastery Garden* (private publication 1970) p. 8.
167 RGH *Minutes* vol. VI p. 237.
168 *Ibid.* p. 193.
169 Clive Lee: 'Social Welfare. Poverty and Health' in *Aberdeen 1800–2000* (2000) *op. cit.* p. 268.
170 RGH *Minutes* vol. VII p. 407.
171 The wine bill was £30 and other expenses were £7. *Quarterly Accounts* 1 November 1829 – 1 February 1830.
172 The evening in December 1834 was in the Lemon Tree Hotel and an annual supper was still being held in 1849. R. Anderson (1896) *op. cit.* p. 180.

Chapter 5

1 His elder brother, James, was to become a famous Rector of the Grammar School.
2 Making it £63 per annum. RGH *Minutes* vol. VIII p. 40.
3 Estimated cost was £89. *Ibid.* p. 6
4 *Ibid.* p. 19. By March 1836 the Governors were complaining of its expense and

appealed to the Gas Company for 'an abatement to a charitable institution'. RGH *Letter Book* [20 November 1834 – 22 January 1846] no. 1 pp. 53–54.

5 RGH *Committee Book (CB)* vol. 1. (January 1832–September 1845) pp. 18–19. RGH *Minutes* vol. VIII p. 37. The Governors had, in October 1831, decided that with increasing numbers of boys a Porter was needed. *Ibid.* p. 17.

6 Accepted by the Building Committee on 26 November 1832. *CB* vol. I pp. 23–4.

7 *Ibid.* pp. 22–3. RGH *Minutes* vol. VIII p. 50.

8 *CB* vol. I p. 27. Completed by George Milne for £60. *Ibid.* p. 32. In the 18th century the Hospital grounds had been laid out in four large rectangular sections, with dividing paths – the south-west section being used at one time as a bowling green. Smith altered levels of gardens and walks and made considerable changes. *Aberdeen Observer* 1 February 1833; G. M. Fraser: 'Archibald Simpson, Architect and his Times. A Study in the Making of Aberdeen' in *Aberdeen Weekly Journal,* 14 June 1918.

9 RGH *Minutes* vol. VIII p. 55.

10 *Ibid.*

11 *CB* vol. I p. 32.

12 Smith's final work was to design two cast-iron lamp-posts to be placed on the pillars of the Hospital gate. RGH *Minutes* vol. VIII p. 91 [5 June 1833].

13 His general station between 9.30am and 9pm.

14 RGH *Minutes* vol. VIII p. 88.

15 Minuted 18 November 1833 *Ibid.* p. 98.

16 £150 in February–May 1831 and £200 in August–November 1833. RGH *Quarterly Accounts.* He also received some incidental expenses.

17 And in so doing appeared to lose much of its Renaissance feeling. Wyness (1930) *op. cit.* p. 64.

18 David Murray (1975) *op. cit.* p. 65.

19 *Quarterly Accounts* 1 May – 1 August 1833 and 1 August – 1 November 1833.

20 It was removed in the 1880s to the gate of St Nicholas Kirk in Schoolhill.

21 RGH *Minutes* vol. VIII p. 15.

22 *Ibid.* p. 27.

23 *Ibid.* pp. 42–3.

24 *Ibid.* p. 63.

25 *Ibid.* p. 92.

26 *Ibid.* p. 178.

27 By August 1875 when the last three Collyhill boys were elected some 241 had benefited.

28 Walker (1886) *op. cit.* p. 27.

29 RGH *Minutes* vol. VIII p. 55.

30 Dated 4 April 1831 but not minuted by the Governors until 4 April 1833. *Ibid.* pp. 71–76.

31 *Ibid.* p. 55.
32 *CB* vol. I pp. 30–1. [29 January 1833].
33 RGH *Minutes* vol. VIII p. 60.
34 *CB* vol. I pp. 33–4.
35 *Ibid.* pp. 36–8.
36 RGH *Minutes* vol. VIII p. 65.
37 *Ibid.* p. 66.
38 W. Hamish Fraser: 'Politics before 1918' in *Aberdeen 1800–2000* (2000) *op. cit.* pp. 178–180.
39 Clive H. Lee: Local Government in *Ibid.* p. 243.
40 RGH *Visiting Book 1832–50* p. 11.
41 Letter from 'An Old Hospital Boy' to *Aberdeen Shaver* 14 November 1833.
42 Lord Provost 1833–36.
43 RGH *Minutes* vol. VIII pp. 95–6.
44 *Ibid.* p. 109.
45 There was evidence that two boys had gone to see Muil on their return on 12 November, because it was thought he would be pleased to hear of the indiscipline. It was reported that he was!
46 *Ibid.* p. 112.
47 They had taken the back-gate keys and seized and beat the Hospital Drum.
48 *Ibid.* p. 114.
49 *Ibid.* p. 115.
50 After applying for his job back and for an annuity in separate letters to the Governors he was given £25, which was to be paid annually but only at the Governors' pleasure.
51 John Murray [1030]; James Donald [1033]; Duguid Laurence [1040]; Alexander Joss [1042]; Daniel Finlayson [1044]; Robert Strachan [1045]; Duncan Robertson [1056]; James Fyfe [1078]; and John Johnstone [1088].
52 RGH *Minutes* vol. VIII pp. 120–122. The compiler of the RGH *Register* vol. I p. 88 placed the comment 'last of the Tyrants' next to the name of James Donald [1033].
53 In May 1834 the new schoolmaster, Alexander Gerard, began to teach French an hour every alternate day to the Fourth Division. (*CB* vol. I p. 53). Given more responsibility his salary was increased to £52 p.a. – the same as the other schoolmasters. On the death of Arthur Simpson, arithmetic, Gerard moved from English to arithmetic, and from the six applicants William Thomson was chosen. (*CB* vol. I p. 127 and p. 129).
54 This seems not to have been carried through. In May 1839 the Education Committee was pressing for Latin to be taught. *CB* vol. I p. 163 and p. 181.
55 RGH *Minutes* vol. VIII p. 123.
56 R. Anderson (1896) *op. cit.* pp. 163–4. Although not mentioned, music continued

to be taught by Alexander Colston (appointed 1832). He developed instrumental instruction which not only kept the boys occupied purposefully but was also seen as a necessary adjunct to drill on its introduction. R. B. Strathdee: *Oh, The Brave Music of a Distant Drum* (privately published 1970) p. 5.

57 RGH *Minutes* vol. VIII p. 129.

58 *Ibid.* pp. 133–5.

59 *Ibid.* p. 139.

60 *Ibid.* p. 142. *CB* vol. I p. 53. Alexander Jamieson.

61 First expenditure of £5 appeared in *Quarterly Accounts* November 1839–February 1840.

62 RGH *Minutes* vol. VIII p. 174 The Visiting Committee of Governors had recommended prizes in August 1833. *Quarterly Accounts* 1 February–1 May 1840 included a small sum for 'prizes'.

63 *Ibid. Quarterly Accounts* 1 August–1 November 1840 include a small sum for 'good conduct'. This was not totally novel as Thom had given books for good behaviour in 1807. *Annual Accounts* 1807–8.

64 R. Anderson (1896) *op. cit.* pp. 59–60. The Out-going Prize was replaced by a Silver Medal in November 1854.

65 *CB* vol. I p. 187.

66 *Ibid.* p. 26.

67 Up till 1821 the Treasurer and Factor roles were combined. The Factor role was moved to the Clerk (£50 and £40 for Factor duties), leaving the Treasurer at £40. The Governors wanted to avoid duplication. Two options were examined: dispense with the rule that the Treasurer must be a merchant combining all three roles and paying salary of £100 or retaining Treasurer at £40 and reducing salary of Clerk/Factor to £70. RGH *Minutes* vol. VIII p. 158. The Governors chose the latter course, reasoning that the Treasurer post could not be dispensed with.

68 *CB* vol. I pp. 85–7. In December 1838 the Governors cut the Treasurer's attendance in the Hospital to three times a week between 10am and noon.

69 RGH *Minutes* vol. VIII p. 212. On the death of Charles Walker in November 1835.

70 *Ibid.* p. 173.

71 *CB* vol. I p. 66. Dyce became Lecturer in Midwifery at Marischal College in 1841 (and a professor after the 1860 union). He was Physician to the Infirmary as well as the Hospital.

72 *Ibid.* p. 69. In January 1837 the Governors gave an allowance to two housemaids for 'great exertion' during an outbreak of sickness in the Hospital: as a result Miss Rose was able to dispense with the assistance of a regular sick nurse. RGH *Minutes* vol. VIII p. 223.

73 Situated near the main walk (right hand side) in St Nicholas Kirkyard. She died 1 April 1835 aged 61.

74 Which was not in the Regulations.
75 RGH *Minutes* vol. VIII p. 176. Although the Hospital lost a number of their officials through death in the mid-1830s the most shocking was that of Lord Provost James Blaikie. He died immediately after chairing a Governors' meeting on 3 October 1836. As his son said 'within its [i.e. the Hospital's] walls was closed the last scene of his earthly labours'. *Ibid.* p. 221.
76 *CB* vol. I p. 143.
77 *Ibid.* pp. 90–1. RGH *Minutes* vol. VIII pp. 214–5.
78 Ground and enclosing walls, £3500; old building, £1300; new buildings, £13,000; furniture, books, instruments, plate, £860 = £18,660.
79 *CB* vol. I p. 131.
80 Walker (1886) *op. cit.* p. 27.
81 R. B. Strathdee (1972) *op. cit.* p. 22. These included the 'skulls of several notorious criminals' – perhaps from the skeletons excavated from the Old Blackfriars' Graves.
82 RGH *Minutes* vol. VIII p. 231.
83 Walker (1876) *op. cit.* p. 22.
84 RGH *Minutes* vol. VIII p. 142.
85 RGH *Visitors' Minute Book* (1832–50) p. 21.
86 RGH *Minutes* vol. VIII p. 252.
87 The *Aberdeen Shaver* of 1835–7 and the *New Shaver* (1838–9) made much of 'military drilling' and although taken up by Baillie Forbes there was no evidence that this was the cause of the problems faced. Anderson (1896) *op. cit* pp. 60–1.
88 RGH *Minutes* vol. VIII. p. 226.
89 *Ibid.* pp. 268–9. *Quarterly Accounts* 1 May–1 August 1839.
90 RGH *Minutes* vol. VIII pp. 272–3.
91 *Ibid.* p. 278.
92 *Ibid.* p. 279.
93 *CB* vol. I p. 179.
94 RGH *Minutes* vol. VIII p. 282.
95 Later ruled out on grounds of expense.
96 *Ibid.* p. 283.
97 *Ibid.* and *CB* vol. I p. 179.
98 RGH *Minutes* vol. VIII p. 283.
99 It began visiting the Hospital in November 1832.
100 *Ibid.* p. 306.
101 Lord Provost 1839–47 and 1853–6 (younger brother of James Blaikie).
102 *CB* vol. I p. 213.
103 *Ibid.*
104 RGH *Minutes* vol. VIII p. 309.
105 *Ibid.* p. 310. Since 1790 contracts of employment were for one year only and renewed every November.

106 Alexander Gerard had resigned in April 1841 just before the incident. He took up an appointment as Naval Instructor and Schoolmaster of HMS *Indus*. *CB* vol. I p. 210.

107 Anderson (1896) *op. cit.* p. 61.

108 RGH *Minutes* vol. VIII p. 316.

109 At Watson's too there had been problems between staff and the need to change was acknowledged, but the Governors there were not yet supportive of non-residence.

110 *Ibid.* p. 317.

111 RGH *Letter Book* no. I pp. 244–5 and pp. 248–9.

112 RGH *Minutes* vol. VIII p. 319. *CB* vol. I p. 215.

113 RGH *Minutes* vol. VIII p. 319.

114 *Ibid.* p. 322. Miss Rose did not go to law and was given a testimonial by the Governors which stated that her services had been dispensed with 'as a result of new arrangements introduced by the Governors for the better regulation of the Hospital'. RGH *Letter Book* no. I pp. 285–6.

115 Legal costs alone cost £150. *Quarterly Accounts* 1 February – 1 May 1842.

116 After a delay of eighteen months Melvin was appointed Headmaster of Tarves Public School, where he proved a success. For many years after leaving Gordon's a few of his former Hospital boys, who much admired and respected him, paid Melvin an annual visit of honour. He also held the office of Inspector of the Poor but regularly was out of pocket on account of his generosity. He died on 15 May 1864. Shortly before his death he married his old housekeeper so she might benefit from an annuity from the widows' fund into which he was forced to pay. The rest of his estate was left to benefit Tarves, and the result was a splendid public hall and an excellent public library.

117 From his headstone in Tarves Churchyard.

118 On 17 January 1842.

119 *Scottish Notes and Queries* (December 1895) vol. IX no. 7 p. 105.

120 The issue of the irregular cleaning of shoes had been raised by the Visiting Committee in November 1832.

121 *CB* vol. I p. 235.

122 James Hughes, Porter since May 1833, had his salary increased from March 1842 (£10 a quarter to 15 guineas).

123 RGH *Minutes* vol. VIII p. 344.

124 RGH *Minutes* vol. VIII p. 275.

125 In October 1843 the Governors determined that the April 1833 change was null and void as it had not been approved by three-quarters of all the Governors on two occasions. *CB* vol. I pp. 286–7.

126 Anderson (1896) *op. cit.* pp. 164–5.

127 RGH *Minutes* vol. VIII p. 345.

128 *CB* vol. I p. 256.

129 These were produced and issued. RGH *Minutes* vol. VIII pp. 348–350. Useful information was gathered from them. Between 1843–6 the apprentices worked on average a nine-hour working day; two-thirds went to Church regularly and one-third read regularly, especially Scriptures. 90% of masters were satisfied with their apprentices. RGH *Answers to Queries* (1843–6) vol. I.

130 Introduced in November 1842 mainly for financial reasons. About 36 boys were now leaving annually. *CB* vol. I p. 233.

131 Dyce had been put under some pressure by the Governors earlier in 1842 on the issue of scrofulous habits. He had been instructed to be very particular when examining candidates for admission to ensure they were free from them. *CB* vol. I p. 236. Also he had been quizzed on Hospital routines to combat Itch, when eight cases were reported. *Ibid.* pp. 237–8.

132 The afternoon meal was done away with and the evening meal served an hour earlier at 7pm. On his own initiative Findlater suggested a cup of tea or coffee on Sunday afternoons. Anderson (1896) *op. cit.* p. 65.

133 RGH *Minutes* vol. VIII pp. 357–8.

134 *CB* vol. I p. 229.

135 From his Evidence to the Colebrooke Commission on Hospitals in 1873.

136 *Colebrooke Commission*: Report of Oral Evidence 30 April 1873 p. 322 Qns. 3710–3711.

137 *CB* vol. I p. 283. He had six fixed wooden seats placed in the playgound in May 1843. RGH *Minutes* vol. VIII p. 372.

138 It included 'The Proof Catechism, with Paraphrases, Notes and Analysis', 'Select Psalms and Paraphrases', 'Select Hymns and other Pieces', 'Forms of Prayer', 'Outlines of Geography', and 'Chronological Tables and tables of weights and measures'. The original edition extended to 192 pages and Strahan introduced new editions in 1857 and 1869. The final edition in 1874 still operated when the Hospital ended in 1881. By then it was bound in canvas covers. Anderson (1896) *op. cit* pp. 174–6.

139 The boys produced 'Ovid in the Aberdeenshire Dialect', printed at the Gordon's Hospital Press in Aberdeen in 1848. R. B. Strathdee (1972) *op. cit.* p. 53. A copy was presented to the Aberdeen Public Library in 1912. R. B. Strathdee (1968) *op. cit.* p. 7.

140 *CB* vol. 2 (September 1845–July 1859) p. 3.

141 The Sillerton band marched regularly through the town and once a week played in the grounds, the public being admitted. The boys and their band played an increasing part of the life of Aberdeen and they participated in public ceremonies. They led the ceremonial procession for the founding of the second Marischal College on 18 October 1837. Walker (1876) *op. cit.* p. 23. They were present at the foundation of the New Market on 8 October 1840 and played

during its opening ceremony on 29 April 1842. Again the band led the boys to the foundation ceremony of the Mechanics' Institute in Market Street on 13 August 1845. G. M. Fraser: *Aberdeen Mechanics' Institute. A Record of Civic and Educational Progress* (Aberdeen 1912) p. 32. The boys sang at the founding of the Victoria Dock on 9 June 1846. Walker (1876) *op. cit.* p. 23.

142 Ben Pitman was greatly pleased with the aptitude of the boys, who made much progress in the study of shorthand. William Skea: *Gordonian*, (March 1914) vol. V, no. 3, p. 73.

143 *Quarterly Accounts* 1 May – 1 August 1845.

144 The main parental occupations were merchant (43), shoemaker (42), wright (41), tailor (27), hammerman (25), baker (22), weaver (19) and flesher (10).

145 Apprenticeships were to hammerman (62), clerk (62), mariner (58), wright (43), grocer (28), tailor (20), printer (15), shoemaker (14), merchant (9) and medical (8).

146 Clerks, medical, architect (2), solicitor (2) and teacher (1) becoming more prominent.

147 He was also a member of Gordon's Governing Body between 1863–71 and chaired it as Lord Provost 1883–5.

148 To become Minister of the Free Greyfriars' Church in Edinburgh.

149 RGH *Minutes* vol. VIII p. 378. He was replaced by Alexander Gerard, late teacher in the Hospital, who returned in January 1844. *Ibid.* pp. 382–3.

150 *Ibid.* p. 391. The House Steward was paid £30 with board and lodging, the Gatekeeper £10 with accommodation. Gray remained until 1879. He displayed 'good tact in managing boys' C. M. Lawrence: 'Sillerton from Inside', *Gordonian* (June 1910) vol. II no. 4 p. 356.

151 RGH *Minutes* vol. VIII p. 412.

152 *CB* vol. I p. 334.

153 RGH *Minutes* vol. VIII p. 413.

154 This has resulted in the extravagant claim that he 'may be regarded as the founder of the Technical College'. Alexander Keith (1972) *op. cit.* p. 342.

155 RGH *Minutes* vol. IX (November 1845 – November 1875) p. 17.

156 *Ibid.* p. 53.

157 Lord Provost 1847–50.

158 *Ibid.* p. 54.

159 *Gordonian*, (December 1911) vol. III no. 2, p. 45.

160 Alexander Bain: *Autobiography* (1904 rev. ed. 2004 Kila, Montana) p. 116 and p. 156.

161 RGH *Minutes* vol. IX p. 55.

162 After his departure from the Hospital Findlater supervised the production of the *Chambers' Information for the People* and took on the monumental task of editing the first edition of *Chambers' Encyclopedia*, to which he contributed numerous articles. He went on to edit *Chambers' Etymological Dictionary*, a pioneer in its time. He gained an honorary LL.D. from Aberdeen University in 1864. 'A scholar of wide

and varied learning, equally at home in the physical sciences, in the history of ancient religions and in modern comparative philology.' *Chambers' Encyclopedia.* He died on 1 January 1885.

163 *Report of May 1849* p. 2.
164 RGH *Minutes* vol. IX pp. 58–9.
165 *Report of 1849* pp. 2–3.
166 RGH *Minutes* vol. IX p. 57.
167 *Ibid.* pp. 58–9.
168 Brian R. W. Lockhart (2003) *op. cit.* pp. 136–7. Nonetheless, there were 21 applicants for the post including Alexander Gerard, who was on the leet of five but was eliminated after the first ballot having obtained five votes. William D. Strahan was elected 12–7 on the second ballot as the new Head.

Chapter 6

1 Baillie George Bothwell's proposed reduction was based on the practice in parochial schools where 50 to 80 children appeared to be instructed successfully in one class. He believed the object of Robert Gordon's Hospital was 'principally to give a plain useful education to its inmates'. His motion was defeated 10–4 on 25 June 1849. RGH *Minutes* vol. IX pp. 58–9.
2 Bridewell = prison. There he comforted two murderers before their separate executions in 1849.
3 Anderson worked in the Sheriff Clerk's office before becoming Chief Sub-Editor of the Aberdeen *Free Press* (1873–1903) and then Editor of the Aberdeen *Daily Journal* (1903–10).
4 Robert Anderson: *Some Reminiscences of Gordon's Hospital* (privately published 1894). Robert Anderson: 'Rev. W.D. Strahan. Headmaster of Robert Gordon's Hospital 1849–72', *Gordonian,* (December 1913) vol. V no. 2 pp. 34–35.
5 One of the teachers, Dr Ogilvie, had stated that he found the boys on Sunday evenings 'in general, more inclined to misbehave, to be inattentive, restless and troublesome than on any other occasion on weekdays'. He put this down to the length of time devoted to religious observance. Gerard concurred and both schoolmasters related how they often had to stop in the middle of prayers to punish the more disorderly.
6 *CB* vol. 2 pp. 114–5.
7 RGH *Minutes* vol. IX p. 71.
8 It had failed to persuade the Governors to make changes to the Hospital uniform in 1842–3.
9 *CB* vol. 2 p. 126; RGH *Minutes* vol. IX, p. 79 and 93. The lighter clothing was judged 'a great improvement' by chairman Baillie Watson in November 1851,

when it was agreed that the boys be allowed to wear a small cloak to put over their shoulders in wet or cold weather. RGH *Minutes* vol. IX, p. 113.

10 Brian R. W. Lockhart (2003) *op. cit.* p. 159.

11 RGH *Minutes* vol. IX p. 122. He had been drawing master since August 1842. Interestingly, when first suggested by the Education Committee, Strahan believed it inopportune, preferring to emphasise accuracy in English. However, within the year he held the time right for its introduction. *CB* vol. 2, pp. 153–4 and p. 169.

12 RGH *Minutes* vol. IX p. 85.

13 This was to counter the occasional attacks on the Governors for not taking the most needy at various times. *Aberdeen Shaver* March 1836. Robert Anderson (1896) *op. cit.* p. 61.

14 *CB* vol. 2. p. 143. It went to Stonehaven. Occasionally outings had occurred before this. A casual trip to Inverurie was undertaken in Melvin's time. Alexander Walker (1876) *op. cit.* p. 25.

15 Called the 'Jaunt' by the boys.

16 RGH *Minutes* vol. IX p. 119.

17 An annual trip continued until the 1870s.

18 *Ibid.* pp. 97–8.

19 *CB* vol. 2, p. 106.

20 The House Steward lived in instead.

21 Unlike Heriot's where there had been an annual ceremony since its opening in 1659.

22 RGH *Minutes* vol. IX p. 84.

23 *CB* vol. 2 p. 128.

24 RGH *Minutes* vol. IX p. 120. *CB* vol. 2 pp. 172–6. Although in 1876 Walker was complaining that the 'mean heraldic effort in marble' was little better than the original wooden eschutcheon which had lasted such a short time. *Op. cit.* p. 28.

25 The assessment of Lord Provost Thompson in November 1850. RGH *Minutes* vol. IX p. 94.

26 *Ibid.* p. 110.

27 *Ibid.* p. 114.

28 *Ibid.* p. 141.

29 *Ibid.* p. 203.

30 In May 1852 Strahan had felt it necessary to bring to the Governors the issue of the teacher of the Mathematical School wanting to alter the seats in his classroom!

31 RGH *Minutes* vol. IX p. 157; *CB* vol. 2 p. 211.

32 First Silver Medal was won by William Gellan [1721] who left the Hospital in November 1855 to be apprenticed to a clerk; he was followed by Alexander Orr [1727] who left in August 1856 to study at Marischal College.

33 RGH *Minutes* vol. IX p. 283.

34 *Ibid.* p. 215.
35 *CB* (August 1859 – October 1870) vol. 3 p. 56.
36 Former Rector of Jedburgh School.
37 RGH *Minutes* vol. IX p. 201; *CB* vol. 2 pp. 240–1.
38 RGH *Minutes* vol. IX p. 234.
39 *Ibid.* p. 318.
40 *Ibid.* p. 269.
41 *CB* vol. 3 pp. 31, 39 and 50–4.
42 John Ogilvie (1797–1867) had a leg amputated as a young man; graduated AM with distinction at Marischal in 1828 with highest honours in mathematics; was appointed to the staff of the Hospital in May 1831. He established a national reputation as a lexicographer, editing the first edition of the *Imperial Dictionary* (1850–1) and gained the honorary degree of LL.D. from Marischal in 1848. He was described by Dr Forsyth as 'A tall gaunt man in spectacles, John Ogilvie, stern and dignified yet kind and with a happy sense of humour, had eminent abilities as a teacher. His name shed no small lustre on the institution.' He was buried in Nellfield Cemetery and was uncle to four brothers who all were awarded an honorary LL.D. from Aberdeen University, one of whom, Alexander, was to become Headmaster of Gordon's.
43 RGH *Minutes* vol. IX p. 262; *CB* vol. 2 pp. 330 and 332–5. Joseph Ogilvie: *John Ogilvie. Lexicographer LL.D.* (Aberdeen 1902) p. 124.
44 RGH *Minutes* vol. IX pp. 119–120.
45 *Ibid.* p. 169.
46 *Ibid.* p. 215; *CB* vol. 2 pp. 300–1.
47 RGH *Minutes* vol. IX p. 232.
48 Jennifer J. Carter and Colin A. McLaren: (1994) *op. cit.* p. 73; Colin A. McLaren: *Aberdeen Students 1600–1860* (Aberdeen 2005) p. 134.
49 RGH *Minutes* vol. IX p. 284.
50 *CB* vol. 3 pp. 112–3; RGH *Minutes* vol. IX pp. 322–3. In 1862 the cost was £20/16/- for the four scholars.
51 Robert Anderson: *Auld Days in 'The Auld Hoose': Discipline in Robert Gordon's Hospital* (Aberdeen 1896) privately published p. 7 held that the two most common offences were – 'not rising when called' and 'not attending to the second bell'. His view was that 'really serious offences were few'. *Ibid.* p. 10.
52 *Black Book for Weekly Reports* (March 1851–September 1853): Saturday 7 June 1851.
53 *Ibid.* Saturday 12 March 1853.
54 Jadzowski was a Polish refugee who arrived penniless in London in 1832. He was appointed Hospital drawing master in 1842. Tall and erect with dark eyes and dark hair, he was a striking personality. He had a fiery temper and the boys continually tried to provoke him. However, 'he was much respected in the City'. *Scottish Notes and Queries* (July 1915) no. 8 p. 153.

55 *Black Book for Weekly Reports* (January 1856–February 1858): thirteen on detention on 24 December 1856 and seventeen on 22 April 1857. J. R. E. [Elder]: 'The Black Books of Robert Gordon's Hospital', *Gordonian* (March 1909) vol. I no. 7 pp. 148–150.

56 *Black Book for Weekly Reports*: 16 May 1857.

57 *Ibid.* 20 February 1856.

58 RGH *Minutes* vol. IX pp. 245–7; *CB* vol. 2 p. 299.

59 RGH *Physician's Visiting Book* (1832–50).

60 *Ibid.*

61 RGH *Physician's Visiting Book* (1851–81). J. R. E. [Elder]: 'The Visiting Books of Gordon's Hospital', *Gordonian,* April, May, June and December 1909 pp. 173–5, 198–9, 224–5 and 277–8.

62 RGH *Minutes* vol. IX p. 203.

63 RGH *Physician's Visiting Book 1851–81.*

64 RGH *Minutes* vol. IX p. 185.

65 *Ibid.* p. 187.

66 *Ibid.* p. 209.

67 *Ibid.* pp. 192–3.

68 *Ibid.* p. 194.

69 *Ibid.* p. 200.

70 Ringworm (or Tinea) is a contagious itching skin disease occurring in small patches, caused by fungi and affecting chiefly the scalp or the feet.

71 RGH *Physician's Visiting Book* (1851–81).

72 Who was married to a Russian princess.

73 RGH *Minutes* vol. IX p. 235.

74 *CB* vol. 2 pp. 326–7.

75 *Herald* 12 October 1864.

76 *Journal* 15 July 1866.

77 *Gordonian,* (June 1944), vol. VIII no. 5.

78 RGH *Minutes* vol. IX p. 423.

79 Increasingly being used as the term for ex-pupils.

80 1796–1859. An American historian who made a study of Spanish history and wrote *The Conquest of Mexico* and *The Conquest of Peru.*

81 1792–1848. In particular *Mr Midshipman Easy, Masterman Ready* and *Peter Simple.*

82 1818–83. An Irishman who lived in America and wrote *The Scalp Hunter* and *The Headless Horseman.*

83 It was first discussed in 1786–9.

84 In 1839–40 when the Governors had taken legal advice, which had held that there was no legal obligation for ex-pupils to pay the Hospital back. RGH *Minutes* vol. VIII p. 295 *CB* vol. I pp. 183–4.

85 *CB* vol. 3 pp. 57–60.

86 *Ibid.* p. 62.
87 RGH *Minutes* vol. IX p. 359.
88 *Ibid.* p. 408.
89 *Ibid.* p. 303.
90 The Grammar School had vacated its Schoolhill site and moved to its present position in 1863.
91 *Ibid.* pp. 345–6.
92 *CB* vol. 3 p. 158.
93 RGH *Minutes* vol. IX p. 350.
94 *CB* (November 1870 – September 1880) vol. 4 p. 12.
95 *Ibid.* pp. 19–22.
96 There was also a chronic state of 'war' between the Hospital boys and those of the Industrial School (the 'Fudgies'), then in Skene Square, as well as those from the Boys' Hospital in King Street. The latter believed that Gordon boys were of superior birth and upbringing, while the Gordon boys looked on the others as rough and scum. On occasion Strahan had threatened to call in the police to end the fighting.
97 Rev. John Ewen: 'Gordon's Hospital Forty-Five Years Ago', *Gordonian,* (March 1913) vol. IV no. 3 p. 62.
98 Pope from the Grammar School was invited to join the Hospital staff with drawing co-joined with writing.
99 Jadzowski resigned in February 1872 and was given £50 for his long service. He was replaced by M. des Clayes.
100 *CB* vol. 4 pp. 33–41 and 44–5.
101 Lord Provost 1869–74.
102 He died in 1875.
103 Of total 29.
104 To be nicknamed Rufus because of his red hair.
105 RGH *Minutes* vol. IX p. 478. *Scotsman* 21 October 1872.
106 From 1817 to 1860. He became a mentor to Ogilvie.
107 *CB* vol. 4 pp. 90–1.
108 *Ibid.* p. 82.
109 And later Head of the Normal Training College in the North of Scotland.
110 In 1868. He later became HMCI for Scotland. *Scottish Notes and Queries* (September 1893) vol. VII no. 4 .
111 The history of a remarkable family was documented in the privately published article 'The Ogilvies in Ternemny, Rothiemay. A Famous Scholastic Family' (1938).
112 RGH *Minutes* vol. IX p. 485.
113 *CB* vol. 4 p. 99
114 *Ibid.*
115 *Ibid.* p. 127; RGH *Minutes* vol. IX pp. 504–5.

116 Lord Provost 1874–80.
117 RGH *Minutes* (November 1875 – December 1885) vol. X pp. 8–11.
118 Anderson: *The History* (1896) *op. cit.* p. 89. Scott had joined the staff in 1845, while Gerard has arrived in 1834 (with a gap between 1841–3 when he missed the clear-out of staff).
119 Gerard had a great weakness for sarcasm and was nicknamed 'Bottler', while Scott was a quiet, kind, generous man, nicknamed 'Tripe'. C. M. Lawrence: (1910) *op. cit.* pp. 355–360.
120 Both were bachelors, dressed invariably in broadcloth. Scott was more pompous but fair and just with the boys, while Gerard was a genial, conscientious character.
121 RGH *Minutes* vol. IX p. 513.
122 The portrait, by Sir George Reid, was given to Aberdeen Art Gallery in 1903. Gerard died on 23 March 1880 in his 69th year.
123 A. C. 1872–81 [probably Alexander Clerk]: 'Dr Alexander Gerard', *Gordonian* (December 1925) vol. II no.4 pp. 126–7.
124 A new assistant teacher, John Wattie, was appointed to replace Lobban when he left to become Rector of Nairn Academy in 1881(a post Lobban retained until 1920).
125 RGH *Minutes* vol. X p. 39.
126 Dale had been a teacher at Leadhills in Lanarkshire and had a marked accent. He was deemed 'a born teacher'. He retired in 1896. Rev. J. Ewen (1913) *op. cit.* p. 62.
127 'The Doctor', *Gordonian* (January 1916) no. 2, pp. 4–5.
128 RGH *Minutes* vol. IX p. 493.
129 *CB* vol. 4 p. 110.
130 RGH *Minutes* vol. IX pp. 495–7.
131 *CB* vol. 4 p. 114.
132 Annually at the end of session there were 51 out-resident boys in 1877–8, then 63, then 77, then 114 at the end of session 1880–1.
133 'Musings of an Old Boy', 1872–81, *Gordonian* (June 1921) vol. I no. I p. 5.
134 Lord Provost 1880–3.
135 RGH *Minutes* vol. X p. 114.
136 Alexander Walker (1876) *op. cit.* p. 35.

Chapter 7

1 Brian R. W. Lockhart (2003) *op. cit.* pp. 152–3.
2 Evidence (following queries issued by a Committee of Boys' and Girls' Hospitals, Aberdeen) on *Hospital system and the Industrial Training of Youth*, Aberdeen 1854. p. 5 Answer 9.

3 Including Dr John Forbes of Donaldsons' Hospital; Rev. J. P. Bell, Minister of the United Presbyterian Church, Midmar; and Rev. David Biggar, Headmaster of Cauvin's Hospital, Duddingston.
4 The average annual cost of a child in an industrial school was £5, while the cost at Gordon's was £20. *Evidence 1854* para. 51 p. 26.
5 Between August 1849 and May 1854.
6 *Ibid.* p. 57 para. 402.
7 In confidence he related that when he had arrived at Gordon's he had found vices but he struck at the root of the problem by ending communication between the boys and the female domestic staff. His predecessor had tackled the problem of the tyranny of the older boys and he thought that this was decreasing. *Ibid.* para. 412 p. 57.
8 Those supporting day schools were Cochran, Henderson, Urquhart, Reid, Bothwell, Berry and Oswald, with Edmond supporting hospitals.
9 RGH *Minutes* vol. IX pp. 161–2.
10 *Ibid.* pp. 166–7.
11 *Ibid.* pp. 170–4.
12 *Ibid.* p. 173.
13 *Ibid.* pp. 176–181.
14 Supported by Baillies Watson, Henderson and McHardy; Councillors (Hugh) Ross, Webster, Oswald and Williams; Dean of Guild Rose; and Master of Mortifications Bothwell.
15 Knighted early in 1856.
16 *CB* vol. 2, pp. 220 and 228–9.
17 *Ibid.* pp. 248–9. A great divergence of opinion was exhibited. Alexander Walker (1876) *op. cit.* p. 29. John Webster was Lord Provost from 1856–59.
18 RGH *Minutes* vol. IX p. 225.
19 *Ibid.* p. 230.
20 Adopted in 1850.
21 *Ibid.* pp. 228–9 and 253.
22 The roll of 142 was eight short of capacity.
23 *Ibid.* p. 277. *CB* vol. 3 pp. 28–9. This, however, only lasted until 15 May 1865 when, with more applications again, the ten-year burgess qualification was re-instated. RGH *Minutes* vol. IX p. 361. Nonetheless in May 1865 the Collyhill Trustees added sixteen more boys to the Collyhill roll in the Hospital and the Governors responded by pledging to reach their full complement of 140 boys (i.e. 180 boys in total) as soon as practicable. RGH *Minutes* vol. IX p. 356.
24 In the case of Watson's Hospital, which had introduced day boys (to join their boarders) by Act of Parliament as early as 1852, Laurie recommended the relaxation of the severity of the regime, a shortening of the long day, the abandonment of uniform and the encouragement for boys to be sent home to their

families at weekends. Simon Laurie: *Report on the Hospitals under the administration of the Merchant Company, Edinburgh, and general remarks on Hospital Training* (Edinburgh 1868). Les Howie: *George Watson's College. An Illustrated History* (Edinburgh 2006) pp. 38-9.

25 Lord Provost 1865–9.

26 RGH *Minutes* vol. IX p. 404.

27 *Ibid.* p. 408.

28 *Ibid.* pp. 410–1.

29 *Ibid.* p. 414.

30 William Henry Sykes, Liberal MP for Aberdeen, 1857–72.

31 RGH *Minutes* vol. IX p. 414.

32 *Ibid.* p. 417.

33 Watson's for boys, with a new girls' equivalent; Stewart's for boys and a Young Ladies' Institution (formerly the Merchant Maiden) – all four to be middle-class schools taking pupils at eight years of age and providing a full liberal education. The fifth – Gillespie's – was aimed at the upper working class and took some time to become a Higher-Grade school, being handed over to the School Board of Edinburgh in 1908. R. D. Anderson: *Education and Opportunity in Victorian Scotland. Schools and Universities* (Oxford 1983) p. 179. Les Howie (2006) *op. cit.* pp. 40-41.

34 Brian R. W. Lockhart (2003) *op. cit.* pp. 198 ff.

35 RGH *Minutes* vol. IX pp. 428 and 431.

36 Lord Provost 1869–74.

37 *CB* vol. 4 pp. 7–9 and pp. 13–15.

38 Completed by July 1871 it broadly followed the Merchant Company example, reducing the number of foundationers and establishing day and evening classes.

39 RGH *Minutes* vol. IX pp. 438–9.

40 *Ibid.* p. 441.

41 Hutcheson's Hospital in Glasgow was experiencing the same problems.

42 *Ibid.* pp. 445–448.

43 *Reply to Memorial and Queries for the Governors of Robert Gordon's Hospital,* 20 September 1871.

44 RGH *Minutes* vol. IX pp. 462–3. Esslemont (1834–94) was on the Governing Body 1869–75 and 1877–82. He was Lord Provost 1880–2. He was Liberal MP for East Aberdeenshire between 1885–92.

45 Preference would still be given to boys with surname Gordon and Menzies, then sons and grandsons of decayed burgesses of guild, then sons and grandsons of burgesses of trade and then the children of those residing in Aberdeen (within the parliamentary boundary). The preferences would only operate when all else was equal. This wider admission reflected the increase in Aberdeen's population by two and a half times since 1818 and the decline of the guildry numbers to about one-third of the total of 1818.

46 RGH *Minutes* vol. IX p. 467.
47 Apprentice fees and allowances at the end of apprenticeships.
48 *Ibid.* p. 468. *Scotsman* 20 August 1872. By 1879 some seven boys had received the £5 allowance because they were needy, in place of the £8/6/8 which previously had been given to all apprentices at the end of their apprenticeship. *CB* vol. 4 p. 226. It was held, however, on 18 June 1879 that it needed a three-quarters of Governors' majority (of twenty-nine) to be carried and so the 1842 enactment was still binding.
49 Chaired by Sir Thomas (Edward) Colebrooke, Liberal MP for Lanarkshire North. It included two representatives of the north-east – M. E. Grant Duff, Liberal MP for Elgin Burghs and James W. Barclay, Liberal MP for Forfarshire.
50 The net revenue for the year to 31 October 1872 was calculated at £5611 and expenditure at £4858. The property evaluation was £170,167 with borrowing of £164,417.
51 Estimated at between 500 and 600 cubic feet.
52 Compared with Heriot's 407 cubic ft; Watson's 560; John Watson's 670; Stewart's 600. Brian R.W. Lockhart (2003) *op. cit.* p. 188.
53 Of the 400 boys admitted between 1862–72 some five had died in the Hospital.
54 *Colebrooke Commission* 1873 vol. XXVII pp. 513 ff. Also included in *Appendix to 3rd Report* 1875 pp. 344–348. RGH *Minutes* vol. IX pp. 483–4.
55 Rev. Dr Findlater was to give evidence on his experience of the Hospital System. Qn. 3694 ff.
56 Qn. 3727.
57 Qn. 3733.
58 Qn. 4879–4998. Locally elected School Boards were set up under the 1872 Education Act to run education.
59 Qn. 5061–5067.
60 This had been Esslemont's original intention but he probably modified it to ensure no opposition.
61 *Colebrooke Commission 3rd Report* (1875) vol. XXIX pp. 33–4.
62 *Ibid.* p. 82. Following the 1864 Report conclusion.
63 *Ibid.* p. 39.
64 *Ibid.* p. 71.
65 Alexander Walker (1825–1903) was to be Dean of Guild until 1880 and was an influential member of the Governors. He was much involved in educational and charity work. He wrote, in 1886, *Robert Gordon. His Hospital and His College* although he was a Grammar School boy himself. For a time he was President of the Conservative Association.
66 Dining in the Hospital was an issue in October 1877 when some of the Collyhill Trustees stressed the importance of ensuring that the boys had one substantial meal a day. Collyhill Trustees: *Sederunt Book* (1871–85) no. 2 p. 28.

67 Robert Anderson: *The History* (1896) *op. cit.* p. 92.
68 Lord Provost 1874–80.
69 RGH *Minutes* vol. IX pp. 516–7.
70 *CB* vol. 4 p. 159.
71 The figure of £7/10/- was agreed.
72 *Ibid.* and RGH *Minutes* vol. X pp. 8–9.
73 *CB* vol. 4 pp. 162–3.
74 RGH *Minutes* vol. X pp. 10–11. *CB* vol. 4 pp. 160–1.
75 *Ibid.* p. 163 and p. 167. This large proportion was not maintained. In February 1877, the next exit date, only two were retained for exhibiting 'superior attainments'.
76 *Ibid.* p. 188.
77 RGH *Minutes* vol. X p. 33.
78 *CB* vol. 4 p. 189.
79 *Ibid.* pp. 191–2.
80 RGH *Minutes* vol. X p. 39. An ex-Grammar School pupil he became Rector of Elgin Academy in 1883, before being appointed first Headmaster of Madras College in 1889. He retired in 1915.
81 First Reading: *Hansard* (3rd series) vol. 239 col. 192–200.
82 RGH *Minutes* vol. X pp. 41–2.
83 Chaired by Lord Moncrieff.
84 RGH *Minutes* vol. X p. 45.
85 *Ibid.* p. 51.
86 *Ibid.* p. 57.
87 Moved by Baillie Donald and seconded by Baillie Esslemont. Agreed 10–2. Ibid. pp. 58–9. *Scotsman,* 13 August 1879.
88 The first mention of this title.
89 Baillie Duffus dissented and Rev. Mitford Mitchell reserved his position. *CB* vol. 4 p. 259.
90 Even then Duffus dissented, joined by Councillor Tennant. RGH *Minutes* vol. X p. 73. However, the reaction of the Collyhill Trustees was even more dramatic. They threatened to oppose the Provisional Order and go 'independent'.
91 *Ibid.* pp. 75–6.
92 Dr Beveridge, Baillies Smith and Duffus.
93 RGH *Letter Book* 10 (despatched) [5 December 1879–22 December 1881] p. 76. Meantime, the Collyhill Trustees prepared to submit their own evidence opposing the amalgamation of funds and the composition of the new Governing Body which minimised the influence of the Trustees. Simpson of Collyhill Trust *Sederunt Book* 2 pp. 54–6.
94 *CB* vol. 4 p. 269. *Moncrieff Commission Evidence* (1880) pp. 112ff. (Qn. 609–691) and pp. 137ff (Qn 729ff).

95 *Moncrieff Commission Evidence* (1880) pp. 125ff. (Qn. 692–708).
96 Professor of Church History at the University of Aberdeen.
97 *Moncrieff Commission Evidence* (1880) pp. 130ff. (Qn. 709–728).
98 *CB* vol. 4 pp. 274–5.
99 This was, however, contentious for a number of Governors as only the Lord Provost's casting vote (13–12) defeated Duffus and his allies who argued that no scheme for union would be satisfactory unless there was complete amalgamation of both funds.
100 Ten from the Town Council, three from the Collyhill Trustees, and ex-officio Lord Provost, Dean of Guild, Principal of University and a clerical Governor.
101 Included in the fundamental principles were to be (i) number and constitution of Governing Body, (ii) maintenance of religious instruction as in Robert Gordon's Deed, and (iii) provision for elementary and secondary education respectfully.
102 Alexander Duffus was on the Governing Body between 1878–83 and, although a Liberal, was an outspoken critic of Esslemont.
103 Signed by Messrs Duffus, Smith, Tennant, Hunter, Ogilvie, Donald, Paterson, Gray, Gordon, Croll, Beveridge, Henderson, Kilgour, Gill and Findlay. This was a majority of the twenty-nine Governors.
104 *Moncrieff Commission Evidence* (1880) pp. 154ff. (Qn. 854–896) and pp. 167–8. (Qn. 954–6).
105 *Ibid.* pp. 162ff. (Qn. 910–953).
106 *Ibid.* pp. 160ff. (Qn. 897–909).
107 *Ibid.* pp. 168ff. (Qn. 957–969).
108 RGH *Minutes* vol. X p. 97.
109 1881 *Sessional Papers*, vol. 26, clxx, p. 423.
110 Nine to be elected by the Town Council, two elected by the Principal and professors of the University, two clerical Governors elected by the six City ministers, and including the Lord Provost, Dean of Guild, University Principal and Chair of School Board (there to prevent undue competition between schools).
111 RGH *Letter Book* 10. Letter from Clerk to solicitors, 12 October 1880, p. 337.
112 Ibid. p. 417.
113 RGH *Committee Book* vol. 5 [4 October 1880 – 8 August 1881].
114 The Governors wished to restrict foundationers to boys belonging to the City of Aberdeen; they believed that the needy would send boys to work so the level for entry should be lowered to 2nd Standard; they wished those gaining bursaries to attend the College schools; they wished the power to establish day and evening classes for boys, girls and adults. RGH *Minutes* vol. X p. 107.
115 Messrs. Duffus, Smith, Hunter, Beveridge, Gordon, Kilgour and Gray.
116 Simpson of Collyhill Trustees *Sederunt Book* no. 2 p. 69.
117 *Third Report* (1881) C. 3076 p. 1061.

118 RGH *Letter Book* vol. 10 p. 644.
119 *Ibid.* p. 719.
120 The year of the Scottish Education Act.
121 Robert Anderson (attended 1857–62) writing in 1894: 'Some Reminiscences of Robert Gordon's Hospital' quoted in his 1896 *op. cit.* p. 97.
122 The claim of James Bruce: *Lives of Eminent Men of Aberdeen* (Aberdeen 1841) p. 300 that the Hospital produced no man of genius other than Frederick Cruickshank, the miniature painter, can be dismissed.
123 *Second Report of Endowed Institutions (Moncrieff) Commission* (1881). Including rents from Dumbreck and Orchardtown (£70,288); rents from Towie (£97,895); rents and feu-duties from Findon (£4296); rents and feu-duties from the Heritage in Aberdeen (£3433) and value of Hospital building and furniture (£18,660). Deductions included sums borrowed (£9850).
124 Had the Governors dragged their feet on reform in 1881 then the Hospital would have been dealt with under the Educational Endowments (Scotland) Act of 1882, which set up the Balfour Commission with compulsory powers to reform endowments.

Chapter 8

1 The use of the term 'College' was a deliberate ploy to attract the 'better class' who needed encouragement to attend a former Hospital. This attitude also affected the level of fees, which if set too low would put off the higher classes.
2 Clause 2.
3 Foundationers were the children or grandchildren of burgesses of guild or of trade of the City of Aberdeen who were orphans, or whose parents were in receipt of weekly wages or belong to the labouring classes.
4 Thirty.
5 Clauses 5 and 6.
6 Clause 7.
7 Clause 8.
8 Clause 10.
9 Clause 11. The Education Committee decided on 24 August 1881 on twenty bursaries, each one year in length for day pupils.
10 Clause 13.
11 Clause 17. Aimed specifically at bringing the Mechanics' Institute under the wing of the Governors.
12 In Edinburgh, the Watt Institution had been taken over by the Governors of Heriot's Hospital and the resulting Heriot-Watt College was to become a university in modern times. In Glasgow, the Allan Glen's Institution came under the

Governors of the new Allan Glen's School, and a number of other colleges combined to form the Glasgow and West of Scotland Technical College (later Strathclyde University).

13 Clause 15.

14 He had already been developing some evening classes under the syllabus of Art and Science Department in London (created in 1853). These continued and in December 1881 Ogilvie reported on numbers: chemistry 100 (62 external and 38 pupils and ex-pupils); theoretical mechanics 23 (3 and 20); agriculture 27 (3 and 24); botany 67 (10 and 57); magnetism and electricity 77 (8 and 69) and physiography 60 (37 and 23).

15 John Strong: *A History of Secondary Education in Scotland. An Account of Scottish Secondary Education from Early Times to the Education Act of 1918.* (Oxford 1909) p. 208 ff. The teacher received one-third of the fees with only external students paying 5/- fee per subject per session.

16 RGH *Minutes* vol. X p. 143.

17 Ogilvie's Curriculum for the College can be found in Appendix III. Despite the wide curriculum there was no room for music. According to James Thomson: 'Music in Robert Gordon's College', *Gordonian* (May 1929) vol. III no. 5 p. 256 it seemed that 'games and merry-making must be put away with all childish things'.

18 The Audit Committee remained at four in number.

19 The foundationers were boarded out in stages, the last twenty going in May 1882. This involved an extensive series of home visits by the Governors of the House Committee to ensure that they were suitable for the boys. Rules were finalised for parents/guardians in charge of foundationers, which included the provision that boys had to attend church at least once every Sunday. The maintenance and clothing allowance was £15 p.a.

20 RGH *Minutes* vol. X p. 161.

21 RG College *Minutes* 1882 p. 114. This increase owed something to Ogilvie personally for it included a number of country boys who arrived as a result of Ogilvie's reputation as an excellent schoolmaster at Monymusk. It was probably also encouraged by Ogilvie's appointment of assistants from the country which widened the appeal of the College and made it better known.

22 The west wing rooms (Rooms 1–5) had a total capacity of 58,240 cubic feet and could accommodate 387, while the capacity of the east wing rooms (Rooms 6–9) was 49,530 cubic feet and took 305.

23 The west wing rooms (10–14) had capacity of 52,011 cubic feet and took 305, while the east wing rooms (15–18) measured 48,741 cubic ft and accommodated 256.

24 RGC *Minutes* 1882 p. 151. It had a capacity of 8610 cubic feet and held about thirty boys.

25 RGH *Minutes* vol. X pp. 138–9.

26 In heraldic terms, the first and fourth quarters were azure, three boars' heads erased with a bordure or; the second quarter argent, on a chief indented vert, three crescents of the field; and the third quarter, gules, a tower triple-towered argent, masoned sable.

27 To supersede the Hospital motto of 'Imperat hoc natura potens'.

28 Few seem to have accepted his translation. 'Omni nunc arte magistra', *Gordonian,* (March 1914) vol. V no. 3 pp. 79–80. A more straightforward translation would be 'Now you should use all your masterly skill'. R. B. Strathdee: 'The Seals of the Hospital and College', *Gordonian,* (June 1950) vol. I no. 2 pp. 84–7, and (December 1950) vol. I no. 3 pp. 180–4.

29 *Inventory* 1883.

30 RGH *Minutes* vol. X p. 125.

31 *Ibid.* p. 126.

32 *Ibid.* p. 127.

33 On 19 June 1888 the *Free Press* editorial stressed the unfair competition from Gordon's and the need to raise its fees as the College was 'underselling the Grammar School in the educational market'.

34 RGH *Minutes* vol. X p. 145.

35 Alexander Walker (1886) *op. cit.* pp. 49–51 counters this: in the early years of Hospital there were 26 foundationers, while in the early years of the College there were 120 foundationers of the same class.

36 Indeed, that was one of the main reasons why the name had been changed to a 'College'.

37 RGH *Minutes* vol. X p. 182.

38 *Ibid.* p. 183. Competitive exams were believed to favour 'middle-class' children.

39 Indeed enabling the Governors to admit boys of a 'better class' so raising the tone was a distinct aim of the 1881 Order.

40 With instruction given in English, arithmetic, French, German, theory of music, phonography and political economy.

41 With classes for practical plane and solid geometry, machine and building construction and drawing, applied mechanics and steam, metal-working tools, carpentry and joinery, magnetism and electricity, electrical engineering, inorganic chemistry and botany.

42 He remained on the College staff until 1886 when he left to become Principal of the Heriot-Watt College in Edinburgh.

43 'The College and Science', *Gordonian,* (December 1923) vol. I no. 6 p. 168.

44 *Scottish Notes and Queries,* (May 1898) vol. XI, no. 11 p. 165.

45 Taking 8th, 22nd, 30th, 34th and 35th places.

46 The changes in 1881 had thus met a strong demand.

47 Vice-President of the Committee of Council in Education, between 1880-5, A. J. Mundella.

48 'A Practical Science and Art School: Gordon's College, Aberdeen': *Chambers's Journal*, 22 March 1884 p. 185.
49 RGH *Minutes* vol. X pp. 144–5.
50 *Ibid.* pp. 154–5.
51 Architect Smith valued the houses belonging to the Governors (including the Entrance Lodge) with areas attached at £1251, and a block of ground, eighty foot deep, behind the boundary wall of the house property, at £284. Including the property recently bought by the Governors at 66 Schoolhill for £1875, Smith estimated the value of the whole area at £3410 with the Lodge another £200.
52 RGH *Minutes* vol. X . p. 159. With Baillies MacDonald and Duffus dissenting.
53 *Scottish Notes and Queries* , (October 1895) vol. IX no. 5 p. 69.
54 RGC *Minutes* 1883 p. 55.
55 John Gray (1811–91) came from Cuminestown in Aberdeenshire where his father was a millwright and carpenter. He moved to Aberdeen when a young man and prospered in his chosen profession.
56 As a result of a competition, the plans of Matthews and Mackenzie, architects in Aberdeen, were chosen, and the Italian Renaissance style building of Art Gallery and Museum, with a frontage of 130 feet on Schoolhill, was opened in December 1884. *Scotsman* 6 December 1884 gave a full description.
57 On digging the foundations of the Gallery, bones of those interred in the original Blackfriars' burial ground were disturbed. They were reburied in a specially constructed brick vault. R. B. Strathdee: *In A Monastery Garden* (private, 1970) pp. 7–8.
58 RGH *Minutes* vol. X pp. 172–3. The only loser was the College which lost a ready-made Library of 16,000 volumes with all its furniture and fittings, which were transferred to the Town Council.
59 G. M. Fraser (1912) *op. cit.* pp. 58–67.
60 Lord Provost 1883–6.
61 This resulted in the Porter's Lodge being dismantled stone by stone and re-erected at the Schoolhill entrance to the West Kirk of St Nicholas. The new College entrance archway involved a janitor's house on its west side. It was occupied until December 1957. Governors' *Minutes* 27 December 1957 p. 49.
62 'After exposure to the climatic conditions of Aberdeen for nearly a quarter of a century the floral decorations of the gate became much eroded and part of these decorations was removed' in 1909. *Jubilee of Gray's School of Art, Aberdeen 1885–1935* p. 9. More recently the bronze shields were also removed.
63 *Ibid.* p. 7. In 1896 two further classrooms were added by extending eastwards of the original building at a cost of £600.
64 R. B. Strathdee: *Scientia et Opera* (private, Aberdeen 1971) p. 17. This involved 60 and 189 students respectively. Among the subjects taught were freehand drawing, shading, painting from life, landscape and still life in oil and water

colour, modelling, sketching, perspective and geometrical drawing, artistic anatomy, etching and design.

65 The Art School was reconstructed between 1928 and 1931 and occupied its extended buildings until it moved to a completely new building at Garthdee in 1967. Henry Ellington: *The Robert Gordon University. A History.* (Aberdeen 2002) pp. 99–101.

66 The British general, Charles Gordon, had become a national hero following his ill-fated defence of Khartoum against Sudanese rebels in 1885.

67 *Scotsman,* 12 April and 16 May 1888.

68 RGC *Minutes* June 1888 p. 108.

69 Or free scholars.

70 *Balfour Commission,* 3rd Report, 31 December 1885: Question 4124 p. 507.

71 *Ibid.* Qn. 4240–2.

72 *Ibid.* Qn. 4172.

73 *Ibid.* Qn. 4159.

74 *Ibid.* Qn. 4397.

75 *Ibid.* Qn. 4401–2.

76 *Ibid.* Qn. 4218ff.

77 This remained until October 1891 when the figure was raised to 80. *RGC* Minutes 1891 p. 5.

78 The argument against fee differentials held that universities were subsidised by private benefaction but the rich were not charged higher fees. Moreover, libraries, parks and galleries were similar. Even in schooling many high school scholars (as in Edinburgh) had endowments and lower fees as a result. According to this argument the reason schools like Gordon's were popular was not because they were cheap but because of their reputation. *Scotsman* 2 August 1888.

79 The lowest group included city parents earning under £75 p.a. and between £75 and £100 p.a. and county parents earning under £80 p.a. The middle group included city parents earning between £100–£150 and £150–£250 and county parents earning £80–£150. The highest group included city parents earning between £250–£350 and over £350 and county parents earning over £150.

80 Lowest city 122; lowest county 56: middle city 139; middle county 129: highest city 111; highest county 55.

81 By 1909–10 (with the same fee structure) the College had seen a significant increase in city families with lowest and middle wages and a small increase in families with high wages. Out of Aberdeen there had been an increase in lowest wage families but the number of highest and middle wage families had dropped very significantly. Overall the College seemed to be appealing to all sections of the working class. There were ten boys who joined from the Grammar School in 1909–10 and of these eight of the families were to pay the highest fees.

82 Liberal MP for Perth. He was the son of a Liverpool merchant and a Fellow of University College, Oxford.
83 Parker Committee *3rd Report* (1888). C.5425
84 *Ibid.* Qns. 2485, 2491, 2806 and 2812.
85 Regius Professor of Anatomy at Aberdeen University since 1863.
86 Parker (1888) *op. cit.* Qn 2808.
87 *Ibid.* Qn. 2256 and 3145.
88 By Frederick Fuller, recently retired Professor of Mathematics at Aberdeen University, and James Donaldson, Rector of the High School in Edinburgh.
89 The School Board lost patience with Moir in November 1892. He escaped dismissal but had to accept the indignity of being reduced to the position of co-Rector and Senior Classics Master with control of the Grammar being given to his co-Rector, Morland Simpson. (Thanks to Arthur McCombie for sharing his unpublished material on the Grammar School with me.)
90 Parker (1888) *op. cit.* Qn. 2932–3003.
91 *Ibid.* Qn. 2933.
92 Instead of the one-quarter previously.
93 Those earning over £200 p.a.
94 Parker (1888) *op. cit.* Qn. 2946.
95 *Ibid.* Qn 2355.
96 The unreformed hospitals were Shaw's Hospital (founded 1807); the Aberdeen Female Orphans' Asylum (founded in 1840 by Mrs Mary Emslie it operated in Albyn Place. It closed in July 1891 and the building was sold to Aberdeen School Board for £45000 and became the High School for Girls.); the Orphans and Destitute Children's Hospital (founded 1849); and the Boys' and Girls' Hospital (founded 1852, its building in King Street proved 'magnificent premises' [W. Robbie (1893) *op. cit.* p. 459] for the headquarters of the Aberdeen Educational Trust).
97 *The Scheme of Administration* (Aberdeen 1889) of the Aberdeen Educational Trust was approved by the Queen in Council on 17 November 1888.
98 Aberdeen Educational Trust was reponsible for the reconstruction of the Boys' and Girls' Hospital School (200 educated and maintained five days a week, with clothing allowance) and the development of a School of Cookery, which took place in October 1891. It was limited to 60 foundationers, half residing in and half boarded out, whose curriculum was cooking, dressmaking and laundry. It was converted into the School of Domestic School (under the Technical College) in October 1912 with 713 students. Alexander Walker: *Mrs Emslie and her Orphan Hospital* (Aberdeen 1898).
99 *Aberdeen Free Press* 24 March 1888.
100 Lord Provost 1886–9.
101 RGC *Minutes* 1888 p. 85.

102 *Ibid.* p. 88.

103 *Aberdeen Free Press* 3 August 1888. Parnell was the leader of the Irish Nationalist Party at Westminster which was renowned for its obstructionist tactics in the House of Commons in the 1880s.

104 *Aberdeen Journal* 7 August 1888

105 *Scotsman* 15 December 1888.

106 *Aberdeen Free Press* 12 March 1889.

107 RGC *Minutes* 1889 pp. 47–8.

108 The SED (Scotch Education Department, changed to Scottish in 1918) had been set up by the Education Act of 1872 as a committee of the Privy Council in London to oversee a new national system of education. The schools' inspectorate, founded in 1840, continued to be based in Scotland. In 1885 the SED came under the auspices of a Secretary of State for Scotland, and from then until 1904 the Permanent Secretary of the SED, Henry Craik, was influential in policy making. Lindsay Paterson: *Scottish Education in the Twentieth century* (Edinburgh 2003) pp. 37ff.; James Scotland: *The History of Scottish Education* (London 1969) vol. 2 pp. 25–27.

109 RGC *Minutes* 1886 p. 48.

110 McLellan (called 'Mac' by the boys) was one of the first staff to call the boys by their first name. He remained Senior Mathematical Master until 1912. On his retiral he was held to be 'one of the finest Mathematical Teachers the country has ever seen'. He was also admired and respected by the staff and pupils as a 'very perfect gentleman'. *Gordonian,* (October 1912) vol. IV no. 1 pp. 1–2.

111 Buchanan came with a great reputation, having been a Whitworth Scholar and with a BSc. from London University. He was to prove 'a teacher of rare merit' and retired from the College in 1919. 'The College and Science', *Gordonian,* (December 1923) vol. I no. 6. p. 168.

112 Lowrie was appointed Principal of Roseworthy College, Adelaide, Australia in November 1887.

113 Bruce was appointed Rector of Inverness Academy in February 1888.

114 Riddoch was Classical Master from1888–93 and then became Rector of Mackie Academy, Stonehaven. He had 'volcanic energy'. *Gordonian,* (December 1928) vol. 3 no. 4 p. 180. On his death in March 1942 some of his former College students from half a century earlier thought it appropriate to commemorate his 'brilliant' work by introducing a Memorial Prize. *RGC Minutes* , 26 November 1943 p. 29.

115 RGC *Minutes* 1886 p. 67. On the death of Treasurer John Morison in February 1886, the posts of Treasurer and Clerk were merged and from the 27 candidates the Governors selected Thomas Fotheringham.

116 Gordon's was the only Aberdeen school to put forward candidates in 1888.

117 RGC *Minutes* 1888 pp. 183–4.

118 RGC *Minutes* 1891 p. 4.

119 The first Gordonian First Bursar was Robert H. Strachan, who became a professor in Westminster College, Cambridge. He was followed in 1890 by Thomas Bruce, who worked for the Clarendon Press, Oxford, in 1891 by William Low who became Rector of Cambridge Secondary School and in 1892 by Alex Taylor, who joined the India Office. Further First Bursars were produced in 1895 (Alex Hutchison, who became a G.P.), 1896 (John Murray, mentioned later), 1898 (James Dawson, who joined the Indian Civil Service), 1899 (John Gray, who did the same) and 1900 (John Michie, who became Professor of Classsics at Brisbane University).

120 *Scotsman* 27 October 1890.

121 Given that classics totalled 750 of 1000 marks in the Competition at this time the contribution of Riddoch to these results was outstanding.

122 RGC *Minutes* 1892 p. 132. This became two gold medals in 1898, showing the acceptance by then of the classical side being the equal of the modern side of the College curriculum.

123 Riddoch was appointed Rector of Mackie Academy, Stonehaven, in August 1893 and was replaced by James Clark, who was appointed Headmaster of Dumfries Academy in June 1895. George Morrison was promoted to First Classical Master then.

124 RGC *Minutes* 1895 p. 74.

125 *Ibid.* pp. 169–170.

126 The small numbers reflected the lack of bursaries for science.

127 The *Gordonian* of 1922 held him to be the greatest man the College had given to the world.

128 The growth of a 'feel-good' factor about the College led to a successful first Reunion of boys, who attended between 1881–88, at Mollinson's Restaurant on 29 December 1896.

129 In 1918 the Pharmacy School moved into accommodation in the temporary wooden buildings, which had been erected in the front quadrangle after the 1911 fire (see next chapter) pending the construction of a permanent Technical College building. A second fire in 1926, which resulted in the destruction of the hutted chemistry and pharmacy laboratories, entailed a further temporary change of accommodation until, in October 1928, the Pharmacy School moved into the new Technical Building built on the Harriet Street side of the campus.

130 Stewart was Ogilvie's chief assistant and had been groomed for succession. Indeed, according to the reminiscences of one College boy, Ogilvie had been putting more responsibility onto Stewart as early as the later 1880s. 'Reminiscences of John R. Reid (1886–9)', *Gordonian*, (December 1946) vol. IX no. 4.

131 RGC *Minutes* 1901 p. 71.

132 His nickname came from either the shape of his hat or his large girth.

133 *Ibid.* p. 72.

134 Three, in fact, but one withdrew.

135 *Ibid.* p. 120.

136 John Murray: 'Gordon's in the Nineties', *Gordonian,* (April 1923) vol. I no. 5 p. 136. He even had a small hole bored in some classroom doors so he could 'spy' what was going on.

137 Probably the most unusual praise came from Pytor Kropotkin, one of Russia's leading anarchists, who was enthusiastic about the substantial science and technical education at the College. During a visit Kropotkin was particularly struck by the experimentation and survey work undertaken. *Fields, Factories and Workshops, or Industry Combined with Agriculture and Brain Work with Manual Work* (London 1898).

138 RGC *Minutes 1901* p. 149. Ogilvie retired to 'Braidwood', Corrennie Gardens, Edinburgh, on the edge of the Hermitage. He died suddenly on 2 August 1904 and was survived by his wife and family of five sons and two daughters (one daughter dying in infancy). He was buried in the family lair in Allenvale Cemetry, Aberdeen. (Grave Number D145A).

139 R. D. Anderson (1983) *op. cit.* p. 200.

140 R. D. Anderson: *Education and the Scottish People 1750–1918* (Oxford 1995) p. 270.

141 *Ibid.* p. 266.

Chapter 9

1 Stewart's relationship with former pupils was also close. He and a number of other Old Boys had wished to foster a spirit of camaraderie and develop the corporate life of the College and so he called a meeting on 21 April 1900. They decided to form a Former Pupils' Association, which was set up on 19 May. Under its first president, Dr John R. Levack, it had 81 members but a membership crisis in 1905 was averted by Stewart becoming President. George A. Burnett: 'The Former Pupils' Association. Its Genesis and Growth', *Gordonian,* (April 1923) vol. I no. 5 pp. 156–159.

2 He gave up teaching completely in June 1905. *Free Press* and *Scotsman* 30 May 1905.

3 *Scotsman* 17 February 1899. New Higher Grade schools were formed after 1899 for those who were pupils undertaking certificate work. James Scotland: (1969) *op. cit.* p. 70.

4 *Aberdeen Journal,* 30 October 1901.

5 When the Central School had opened in 1894 in Little Belmont Street, accommodating 489 children, it had adversely affected the College roll. RGC *Minutes* 27 February 1899 p. 66.

6 Of 393 boys between twelve and fifteen years of age, Gordon's retaining 97 foundationers and bursars, 128 from country and 50 paying highest level of fees.
7 RGC *Minutes* 1898–9 p. 72.
8 Letter to Governors, dated 21 July 1899 in RGC *Minutes* 1898–9 p. 116.
9 Anderson (1995) *op. cit.* p. 249.
10 RGC *Minutes* 1900–1 p. 76.
11 Fees had been abolished in elementary schools in 1890 but controversially had been retained in Higher Grade secondary schools. Anderson (1995) *op. cit.* p. 190.
12 RGC *Minutes* 1900–1 p. 79.
13 'Robert Gordon's College as a Secondary School. Memorandum by the Head Master.' November 1901.
14 *Free Press*, 29 November 1901 and 17 January 1902.
15 *Aberdeen Journal*, editorial, 14 September 1905.
16 Anderson (1995) *op. cit.* p. 286.
17 Originally £221,000 but eventually £100,000.
18 He had recently replaced the retired Craik as Permanent Secretary of the SED.
19 Lord Provost 1905–8.
20 Representatives attended from the Town Council (9), University (4), Incorporated Trades (3), Chamber of Commerce (3), United Trades Council (2) and, showing the significance for the College, some 19 Governors as well as 50 others.
21 *Free Press* 18 October 1906.
22 In 1903 the School Board took over elementary and intermediate continuation school work, leaving the Governors in charge of advanced work.
23 RGC *Minutes* 1906–7 pp. 2–4.
24 January 1907 Report, RGC *Minutes* pp. 80–1.
25 RGC *Minutes* 1906–7, pp. 82–85.
26 He had just been knighted, during the Royal Visit to Aberdeen in September 1906.
27 RGC *Minutes* 1906–7 p. 42.
28 *Ibid.*
29 *Bon Accord*, 3 October 1907.
30 It came up with £15,000 on 13 June 1907. Treasurer Meff believed that this and the RGC site with Gray's School of Art represented £50,000 and he expected the SED to match this figure. *Scotsman*, 18 June 1907.
31 RGC *Minutes* 1906–7 p. 93. Their legal opinion held that these resolutions could only be carried through following a Provisional Order. Lyon was supported by the Governors when he moved that they should obtain the necessary powers. *Scotsman*, 28 May 1907.
32 Parliamentary approval first and plans to be accepted by the Governors. *Scotsman* 26 November 1907.
33 RGC *Minutes* 1907–8 p. 4. Lyon valued the gift of the site from the Governors at £25,000. *Scotsman* 30 November 1907.

34 Town Council decision by 24–2 on 21 January 1908. To a considerable extent the result of SED pressure for the Town Council to play a more official role.

35 Town Council, College Governors, School Board and the Aberdeen Educational Trust.

36 RGC *Minutes* 1908–9 p. 165.

37 *Aberdeen Journal,* 24 October 1908.

38 Including a raising of the school leaving age, the end of fees in elementary schools, supplementary courses and competition from Higher Grade schools.

39 RGC *Minutes* 1908–9 p. 169.

40 Stewart was also in favour of ending open competiton and leaving the Governors to select from a clearly defined class of the community, which would receive maintenance and education.

41 The introduction of smaller class sizes at Watson's meant numbers being cut by 100, ten additional staff being employed and an increase in fees for the first time in a number of years. *Scotsman,* 19 November 1908.

42 This was felt particularly strongly felt by the ministers, led by Rev. Dr C. C. Macdonald, as they would be excluded from its management.

43 Councillor Kemp, Rev. Dr C. C. Macdonald, William Watson, Professor Harrower and Baillie Coutts at this stage opposed the end of the College.

44 *Evening Express,* 2 December 1908.

45 Dr (later Dame) Maria M. Ogilvie Gordon (1864–1939) was a brilliant academic and geologist, publishing more than thirty scientific papers and books. In later life she was active in politics and the international women's movement. She married John Gordon, an Aberdeen physician, and they sent their son to Gordon's. *Scotsman* 11 August 2005: *Great Scottish Scientists.*

46 Full details of her talk, 'Some Educational Problems in Aberdeen', were published in the *Aberdeen Journal,* 21 December 1908 and a précis in the *Scotsman* of the same date.

47 A deficit of £289 on expenditure on educational purposes of £12,204.

48 Stewart claimed this had been a failure. The Classical Department of the College had 72 pupils spread over three years and the Grammar School had 57; the Modern Department of the College had 80 while the Grammar had 37, again over three years. He held this to be bad finance and also bad school management, and that there was no room in Aberdeen for two classical and two modern schools.

49 Combating the argument that the Technical College could use College buildings, which she believed would need complete gutting and refurbishment, costing as much as a new building.

50 Lord Provost 1908–11.

51 Compared with the efficiency of the College where Stewart had much greater power in these areas.

52 *Free Press* and *Scotsman,* 9 April 1909.
53 RGC *Minutes* 1908–9 p. 57.
54 *Ibid.* p. 26.
55 *Ibid.* pp. 55–6.
56 One to run the College and the other to run its property. The concept of two bodies had probably come from the SED and was seen as preparing the way for the demise of the College.
57 *Inquiry,* August 1909, Question 74 p. 31.
58 *Ibid.* Qn 120 p. 36.
59 He was exasperated that the Governors had been discussing the issue for almost four years.
60 *Ibid.* Qns. 131–132 pp. 37–8.
61 *Ibid.* Qns. 134–135 p. 38.
62 RGC *Minutes* 1908–9 pp. 71–74.
63 *Ibid.* p. 75.
64 *Inquiry* Qns 239–244 pp. 49–51.
65 *Ibid.* Qn. 515 p. 75.
66 *Ibid.* Qn. 516 p. 75.
67 An accountant who had been a member of the Governing Body since 1892.
68 *Inquiry* Qn 650 p. 87.
69 Minister of St Clement's Church, a Governor since 1883–4 and Convener of the Education Committee.
70 *Inquiry* Qn 771 p. 99.
71 *Ibid.* Qn 805 p. 103.
72 Little mention was made of the financial situation at the time but given this excess of expenditure and an accumulated liability of £14,684 (to 31 July 1908), it was presumably believed that the new arrangements would help rectify this embarrassment.
73 *Ibid.* Qn. 833 p. 106.
74 Darroch was also Professor of Education at the University of Edinburgh.
75 *Inquiry* Qn. 1330 p. 158.
76 Significantly the jobs had been amalgamated then because of the belief that they would be more efficiently done by one man.
77 *Inquiry* Qn 1113 p. 137.
78 *Ibid.* Qn. 1207–1210 p. 146.
79 *Ibid.* Qn. 1216 p. 147
80 *Ibid.* Qn. 1228 p. 148.
81 *Ibid.* Qn. 1257 p. 151.
82 *Ibid.* Qn 1259 p. 151.
83 *Ibid.* Qn. 1262 p. 152.
84 The first bursar of 1896.

85 *Ibid.* p. 169.
86 Clause 64.
87 The autocracy of Struthers, since he took over the SED from Craik in 1905, was a matter of contention. According to one complaint: 'the veiled prophet of Dover House was pre-eminent among the oligarchy of eminent public servants which dominated Scottish affairs'. R. Munro-Ferguson in the House of Commons: *Hansard* 4th series, 196. 10 November 1908, 130. Quoted by Anderson (1995) *op. cit.* p. 289.
88 Lord Belhaven and Stanton; Earl of Dunmore; Sir John A. Dewar (Liberal MP for Inverness-shire) and Sir John Jardine (Liberal MP for Roxburgh) with P. F. Wood as Clerk.
89 *Inquiry* p. 183.
90 Clause 37.
91 Clause 64.
92 *Inquiry* p. 185.
93 Clause 65.
94 The Bill had its second and third readings in the House of Commons on 28 October and 3 November. It received royal assent on 25 November 1909.
95 Lord Provost; 9 appointed by Town Council; 3 by School Board; 2 by Senatus; 2 by County Council; 1 by Harbour Commissioners; 1 by Presbytery; 1 by Incorporated Trades; 1 by Endowments Trust; and 9 by the Governors.
96 9 appointed by Town Council; 3 by School Board; 2 by Parish Council; 1 by Senatus; 1 by Presbytery; 1 by Incorporated Trades; 1 by Society of Advocates; 1 by Governors; 1 by Six Presbyterian ministers of Aberdeen; and 1 non-Church of Scotland minister by Town Council.
97 All figures in this paragraph refer to per annum.
98 These remained the same as before, viz. 90 boys – previously elected by the Governors now to be elected by the Trustees – between eight and eleven years of age who had passed an entrance examination and were children or grandchildren of burgesses of Guild or Trade of Aberdeen, or boys of the city who were orphans, or whose parents were in receipt of weekly wages or belong to the labouring class; and thirty boys aged between eleven and fifteen by open competitive examination who were suitable in respect of health and character.
99 Thirty presentation bursaries (age 8–12), 10 restricted competition (12–13) and 30 open competition (15 and over) in value between £3 and £7 p.a. for families on weekly wages or the labouring classes or orphans in needy circumstances
100 *Minutes of Governors* 1909 pp. 157–160. Other scholarships inherited from the Educational Trust included £1075 for the maintenance and education of 60 girls – 'educational foundationers'; Davidson's free scholars for seafaring persons residing in Footdee; Grammar School (2) and McRa Bursaries (2); 'Public School'

bursaries for help with elementary education and AET bursaries for evening classes and the Technical College. *Scotsman,* 12 January 1911 p. 8

101 Details were published in the local press.

Robert Gordon's College	*Gross acreage*	*Capital value*
Estate of Towie and Barclay	3,542	£73,036
Estate of Dumbreck and Orchardtown	2,000	£50,476
Lands of Haremoss	82	£2,702
Estates of Barrack and Crichie	1,926	£38,802
		add feu-duties etc.
	=	*£171,011*
Aberdeen Educational Trust		
Estate of Muchalls	2,234	£70,751
Easter Muchalls Estate	250	£7,147
Estates of Elrick and Annochie	2,100	£45,000
		add feu-duties etc.
	=	*£142,234*

Free Press, 15 February 1910.

102 Including Herbert F. Stockdale, Secretary and Director of the West of Scotland Technical College since 1899. *Inquiry* Qn 433 p. 67.

103 RGC *Minutes* 1910 p. 10.

104 The Governors agreed plans for a large extension to the Domestic Science School, costing £11,000, in February 1911. It was opened by Lord Provost Maitland on 24 October 1912. *Free Press* 25 February 1911.

105 The first two classes learned the subjects of elementary school, including, from 1907, vocal music with Alexander Hendry, who also supervised an orchestra outside of school hours with Morrison as leader, McLellan as principal viola and Elder as the only cellist. This ended in 1913. James Thomson (1929) *op. cit.* p. 256. The two highest classes worked at the 'Qualifying' stage with, in addition, Latin and geometry.

106 First Year with six classes (admission at 12–13 years of age) and a curriculum of English, mathematics, Latin, science, drawing and handicraft; 2nd Year with four classes (13–14) adding French; 3rd Year with four classes (14–15) adding Greek with one class; and 4th Year with one class (15–16) with boys choosing between Latin and German.

107 With a two-year Modern side for two classes (15–16) with English, mathematics, Latin or German or technical work, French, physics and chemistry, or a three year classical side for three classes (15–16) with English, mathematics, Latin, Greek, French or dynamics.

108 And as a consequence deducted 10% from the school grant for session 1908–9, threatening even more dire penalties if numbers were not reduced.

109 Outwith Aberdeen fees ranged from £3 for £80 p.a. and under to £7 for £150 p.a. and over.

110 RGC *Minutes* 1910 p. 40.

111 *Ibid.* p. 43.

112 By 1914–5 the roll was 693 (primary 48; intermediate 488; and post-intermediate 157) RGC *Minutes* 1914–5 p. 122, although it is likely that the drop owed much to the War. Senior boys were enlisting and a number left as a result of the increased demand for boy labour.

113 Early estimates of the damage were put at £12–15,000, which was covered by insurance.

114 *Gordonian,* (March 1911) vol. II no. 7 pp. 469–471.

115 Evening classes were cancelled for a week.

116 'The New Chemistry Rooms', *The Gordonian,* December 1913 vol. V no. 2 p. 41. The Chemistry Master, Herbert Williams, visited a number of schools north and south of the border, and prepared plans which made the new laboratory 'the best of its kind in Britain at that time'. 'Retiral of Mr. Herbert Williams BSc.', *Gordonian,* (December 1929) vol. III no. 6 p. 305.

117 *Free Press* 27 September 1913.

118 The school had already lost the semi-detached block off Crooked Lane to the Technical College.

119 The plans were costed at £9250. RGC *Minutes* 1914 pp. 63–6.

120 *Ibid.* p. 106. Plans for the School of Engineering were well advanced and the Aberdeen Harbour Commissioners had offered a site near the harbour for the new School of Navigation and Fisheries.

121 RGC *Minutes* 1914–5 p. 18.

122 Firstly as a result of the fire and then through the expansion of the Technical College, both of which necessitated the occupation of the gym as classrooms.

123 *Free Press* 30 October 1914. The Germans had dismissed all British nationals teaching in German schools within a week of the outbreak of the War.

124 Numbers had increased from 766 (1917–8) to 853 (1918–9).

125 Lord Provost 1914–9.

126 RGC *Minutes* 1918–9 pp. 61–2.

127 Rejecting the appointment of a new Headmaster for the school. *Ibid.* pp. 175–6.

128 *Ibid.* p. 176.

129 *Free Press* 26 April 1919.

130 Under the 1918 Act evening classes were taken over by the local authorities and became continuation classes taught during the day.

131 Duncan later disputed this as the EA had no authority to buy schools. He assumed that if pupils transferred then the buildings would also be transferred. *Free Press* 13 December 1919.

132 RGC *Minutes* 1918–9 p. 242.

133 RGC *Minutes* 1919–20 p. 24.

134 *Free Press* 29 November 1919.

135 Printed on 24 and 25 December 1919 and 6 January 1920. The *Gordonian* of December 1919 (no. 10) strongly defended the College and its traditions. 'There is no other school which has given quite the same opportunities and creates the same atmosphere of strenuous work, and to hamper these facilities or to take away the individuality of the School is to shatter a force which has proved itself of the greatest value to Aberdeen and the district' (p. 14).

136

	To secondary school	*To Technical College*
1914	£100	£1240
1915	£100	£1408
1916	£ 76	£1231
1917	£234	£ 876
1918	£ 76	£1437
1919	£ 76	£ 923

Aberdeen Daily Journal; The Future of Robert Gordon's College (December 1919/January 1920).

137 Adding to the three already on the Committee.

138 Leaving unsolved the issue of Technical College funding and its growing deficit. George Duncan claimed that there was little to show for the large sums contributed to it and this resulted in more criticism of Stewart's leadership. *Free Press* 1 May 1920. It was suggested that the management should be pruned and each department have its own head responsible directly to the Governors, particularly in finance. A Special Committee was set up to review the whole situation. Unfortunately for Stewart, discord at the Domestic Science School led to two inquiries, the second of which, in June 1920, suggested that Stewart had aggravated matters by failing to clarify precise job specifications. This led to further demands for management reorganisation.

139 *Minutes of Governors* 1919–20 p. 225.

140 *Daily Journal* 24 August 1920.

141 RGC *Minutes* 1919–20 pp. 364–6.

142 Lord Provost 1919–25.

143 RGC *Minutes ibid.* 23 September p. 369.

144 Although details were leaked in the *Free Press* on 20 November.

145 RGC *Minutes* 1920–1 pp. 81–90.

146 *Ibid.* pp. 91–109.

147 *Free Press* 29 January 1921. Stewart wished to call the police! Immediately after the meeting Croll sent a written apology which the Provost had published in the press.

148 RGC *Minutes* 1920–1 p. 170; *Daily Journal* and *Free Press* 26 February 1921.

149 RGC *Minutes* 1920–1 pp. 396–7.

150 And indeed during his Headmastership continued to produce a large number of pupils who were successful in later life, including continuing the tradition of producing First Bursars: 1904 Harold G. Gruer; 1905 William D. Barron; 1909 J. Ernest Gillies; 1910 Alan J. Low; and 1912 Kenneth Bruce. A number of Stewart's former pupils also went on to gain knighthoods including a newspaperman (Francis Low); civil servant (William Scott Brown); two engineers (Duncan Anderson and Robert McLennan); administrator (Keith Cantlie); two medics (Alexander Anderson and George McRobert); a schoolmaster (William Forbes); and an admiral (Colin Cantlie).

151 R. B. Strathdee: *A Pride of Masters* (private, 1972) p. 40.

152 *Ibid.*

153 He inherited a permanent staff of 12 and an enrolment of 200 in day classes; he left a permanent staff of 40 (and a part-time staff of 80) and day classes of 1441.

154 RGC Minutes 26 June 1974 pp. 126–7.

155 Articles in *Gordonian* (June 1917) no. 5 pp. 5–6; December 1938, vol. VI no. 6 pp. 253–256; and June 1945 vol. IX no. 1 pp. 35–36.

Chapter 10

1 The loss of county pupils (from Aberdeenshire and Kincardineshire) was accelerated by the 1918 Education Act and the Governors tried to counteract the trend by abolishing the extra fee, introduced by the Act, on pupils attending the College from outwith the city boundaries.

2 RGC *Minutes* 1923–4 p. 18

3 She remained in charge of the Kindergarten until her retiral in 1947.

4 RGC *Minutes* 1921–2 pp. 79–80. This was encouraged by Morrison who, at his first Annual Aberdeen Dinner as Headmaster on 3 December 1920, suggested searching for a playing-field, which would be an excellent war memorial.

5 Rugby had been introduced in 1895 by Peter Smith, using the University grounds on a Saturday afternoon. In 1904 the Governors officially recognised the sport and began paying £30 a year for the use of the University grounds three evenings a week as well as Saturday mornings. Peter Smith: 'Sport in the College up to 1923', *Gordonian*, May 1929, vol. III, no. 5 pp. 262–3. *Press and Journal* 19 May 1925.

6 Hockey had begun in 1908–9.

7 Of four shillings per boy per annum. The Grammar School had a Games Fee of ten shillings.

8 The bazaar raised £1500.

9 It bore the Memorial tablet 'Ad Maiorem Dei Gloriam'.

10 'Opening of the Memorial Playing Field and Pavilion', *Gordonian,* June 1925, vol. II no. 3. pp. 78–80.
11 Despite this, throughout the history of Seafield (1925–92) Gordonians used its facilities regularly, paying only for the overtime of the groundsmen. Otherwise the College bore all capital, maintenance and repair costs. In return, the Former Pupils gave significant gifts to Seafield, in particular the Stand, opened in September 1925.
12 *Press and Journal* 26 February 1927.
13 *RGC Minutes* 1920–1 p. 9.
14 Repeated the following year.
15 Sir Arthur Somervell declared the College could only be matched musically by one or two of the great English public schools. James Thomson (1929) *op. cit.* p. 257.
16 Whose nickname became 'Holy Joe'.
17 To 31 July 1920 the deficit of the secondary school was £4731 and that of the Central Institution £4607, making £9338 in total.
18 RGC *Minutes* 1921–2 p. 410.
19 The EA was being asked in effect to maintain the School but could not send any boy without paying full fees.
20 Munro believed that some estates should have been sold and the monies reinvested.
21 *Free Press* 4 November and 27 November 1922.
22 The implication was that the Governors would always favour boys already at the College over those from other schools sitting the exams.
23 *Press and Journal* 9 December 1922.
24 *Press and Journal* 7 February 1923. AET gained three seats (from one) on the Governing Body, while the latter gained two representatives on the AET (up from one).
25 However, the AET argued that if the Trusts were united, the monies would need to be transferred to a number of bodies as well as the College. This threat, if carried through and legally proper, would cost the College dear. This argument still stands today especially as by the later 1990s College pupils benefited from AET endowments at least twenty times more than all other beneficiaries.
26 The Local Government (Scotland) Act of 1929 resulted in the functions and duties of the EAs being taken over by Town Councils after May 1930. In Aberdeen the Town Council representation on the Governing Body rose from six to fifteen (including the Lord Provost who was ex-officio). RGC *Minutes* 10 January 1930 pp. 9–10.
27 Reid had attended the Hospital between 1870–5 being Dux before attending Marischal College and becoming a chartered accountant in 1884. He had been chair of the Former Pupil Association and so was sympathetic to the College's plight.
28 RGC *Minutes* 1924 p. 6.
29 He remained its Convener until 1942 when he took over as Chairman of the Governors for a decade.

30 A further attempt by the Former Pupils in January 1928 also failed. *Ibid.* 30 March 1928 p. 57.

31 *Press and Journal* 7 February 1925.

32 *Ibid.* 26 September 1925.

33 *Ibid.* 15 October 1925.

34 *Free Press* 4 December 1920.

35 *Press and Journal* 28 February 1925.

36 *Press and Journal* 31 March 1928.

37 RGC *Minutes* 1928 p. 132. *Press and Journal* 11 August 1928.

38 *Press and Journal* September 1928.

39 Under it was placed a sealed lead casket containing a copy of a brochure prepared by the Governors and a copy of the prospectuses for 1929–30, together with newspapers giving an account of proceedings. A few coins, past and current, were included.

40 The trowel he used was later gifted to the College by his daughter and was placed in the Governors' Room.

41 The administrative offices and two classrooms were to be situated on the lower floor and two other classrooms on the first floor.

42 *RGC Headmaster's Log* Book. (1930). Rooms 35 and 36 were taken over a month before Rooms 37 and 38.

43 *Press and Journal* 30 May 1931.

44 The total costs of the accommodation improvements were apportioned £10,000 (five-sixths) to the school and £2,000 (one-sixth) to the Technical College. RGC *Minutes* 1930 p. 107.

45 They had almost 200 years' service between them, James Rennie 'with perfect attendance'. *Gordonian,* (December 1921) vol. I no. 2 p. 47.

46 James Gordon had won the Town Council medal as the Dux of the College in 1903 and was 5th bursar at Aberdeen University that year. *Press and Journal* 26 April 1903.

47 RGC *Minutes* 1929 p. 178.

48 *Press and Journal* 3 March 1930. The school had a holiday on 2 March 1930 to celebrate the honour.

49 RGC *Minutes* 1930 p. 60.

50 The presentation foundationers were not so distinguished for their diligence and achievement.

51 He went on to mention twenty university professors, sixteen Indian civil servants, school inspectors, men of science and medicine, and those who had done well in industry, commerce and finance. 'Some Reflections on the Half-Century', *Gordonian,* (December 1932) vol. IV no. 6 pp. 260–2.

52 For over twenty years he was a member of the Provincial Committee for the Training of Teachers and from 1919–30 he served on the EIS Council before becoming its President.

53 *Press and Journal* 25 June 1932.
54 *Press and Journal* 29 September 1929. The idea had been first suggested by Robert Anderson in 1880 at a meeting of the 'Auld Lads'. *Gordonian,* (December 1930) vol. IV no. 2 p. 70.
55 *Ibid.*
56 *Ibid.* 15 November 1929.
57 RGC *Minutes* 28 October 1932 p. 170.
58 *Ibid.* 25 November 1932 p. 174.
59 He gained 18,070 votes, defeating his Labour advocate opponent, Robert Gibson, who received 4,750 votes. *Scotsman* 15 March 1934.
60 Graham Andrew (aged 39), Rector of Elgin Academy; Alexander Dingwall, Rector of Jedburgh Grammar School; Andrew Miller, Rector of Preston Lodge School, Prestonpans; George Milne, Rector of Keith Grammar School; and John Robertson, Headmaster of the Central School, Aberdeen.
61 RGC *Minutes* 1933 pp. 16–17.
62 I. G. Andrew: *Unpublished Autobiography* p. 53.
63 Later Rector of the Royal High School, Edinburgh.
64 He won the coveted John Clark Scholarship.
65 Later Rector of Aberdeen Grammar School.
66 This led on 9 February 1922 to a letter signed by all members of the Elgin staff protesting against Andrew's appointment on the grounds of his youth, lack of experience, limited scholarship and service: *Unpublished Autobiography* pp. 148–9.
67 Rugby in winter and soccer in spring.
68 Numbering 48.
69 Copland refused to countenance extra payment for the work.
70 RGC *Minutes* 1933 p. 74.
71 *Ibid.* p. 96.
72 RGC *Headmaster's Log* 14 November 1933.
73 RGC *Minutes* 1933 p. 95.
74 *Headmaster's Log-Book*; *RGC Minutes* 1934 pp. 46–47. The Boards are now to be found on the ground floor of the east wing of the Auld Hoose.
75 *Ibid.* p. 121.
76 McKenzie saw his role primarily as Secretary of the Technical College. However, having had poor relationships with the School and Morrison, in particular, McKenzie was probably keen to improve matters with Andrew, particularly as there was some thought of making Andrew the Principal of the Technical College, as Stewart had been before him. Fortunately, Andrew had done his homework and, knowing the problems of the past, was anxious not to repeat them. He dismissed the idea. *Unpublished Autobiography* p. 198.
77 School Captain Gilbert Gunn laid a wreath of daffodils, with the College badge, a pelican, worked out in violets, while Joseph Bissett laid a laurel wreath.

78 RGC *Minutes* 1933 p. 187.

79 Later extended by Headmaster Lockhart to include all staff (teaching and non-teaching).

80 The role of the janitor was played by the Head Janitor, William Murray, who was to retire from the post in April 1936 after 38 years' service to the College. *Press and Journal* 1 May 1936.

81 The Governors also did not demur at the expense of fitting out excellent metal and woodwork rooms.

82 Dux of Banff Academy, Savage had entered Aberdeen University as 10th bursar. He contributed to the College on both the classical and modern sides. *Gordonian,* (June 1936) vol. VI no. 1 pp. 4–5.

83 RGC *Minutes* 1936 p. 206: *Daily Mail* 20 August 1936. Barclay returned when Savage was called up and he taught commercial subjects until his death in December 1943. RGC *Minutes* 31 December 1943 pp. 37–8.

84 *Ibid.* 1935 pp. 77–80.

85 *Ibid.* 1935 pp. 122–4. At a cost of £11,300. The College had developed a fine swimming tradition since the time of Robert Semple, a chemistry teacher, who founded the first College swimming club in the 1880s. 'Thirty Years On' *Gordonian* (June 1917) no. 5 p. 17.

86 *Educational Endowments in Scotland* (Edinburgh 1927) Nos. 30–74.

87 *Press and Journal* 11 January 1930.

88 *Scotsman* 25 June 1930.

89 *Memorandum for the Town Council* 16 January 1933 p. 4; *Press and Journal* 16 January 1933.

90 Councillor George Duncan, Convener of the Town Council Education Committee as quoted in *Press and Journal* 10 March 1934.

91 A much more contentious issue was the Commissioners' attempt to pool the monies of various bequests (including the significant Milne Bequest) previously controlled by the University of Aberdeen and give them over to the Education Committee of the County Council as a general fund to be used for school bursaries and the provision of playing-fields for children. [*Scotsman* 28 June 1934]. This, and the general belief that the Commissioners were ignoring the intentions of founders in their various Schemes, led to a bitter reaction. [*Scotsman* 23 November 1934] Dr George Morrison, former Headmaster, played a significant role in debates in the House of Commons and its Standing Committee, promoting the 'spirit of the intentions of the founders' especially in locality, economy and the provision of competitive bursaries. The result was a restriction in powers for the Commissioners created in the Act which gained royal assent on 15 February 1935.

92 Of £6 p.a.

93 Continuity was also the order of the day with the AET, as eleven of the new body of sixteen were already Trustees. The AET held its last meeting in the

Trust Offices in the Domestic Science Building at 352 King Street at the end of 1937, moving to leased premises at 16 Bridge Street. The vacant rooms at King Street were converted into classrooms.

94 Seven from the Town Council (down from 14); 3 from Senatus (3 before); 1 from County Council (2); 1 from Harbour Commissioners (1); 2 from Presbytery (2); 1 from Incorporated Trades (1); 1 from AET (3); 1 from College FP Association (none); and 4 co-opted (6). George Hall was the first FP representative on the Board. The Association had 2500 members. Heriot's had included FP representation on their Board in 1928 following the Fettes example.

95 RGC *Minutes* 14 October 1935 pp. 7–8.

96 *Ibid.* 28 October 1935 pp. 6–7.

97 *Press and Journal* 23 November 1935.

98 G. E. C. Barton: *Sillerton 1937–87* (Aberdeen 1987) p. 1.

99 *Press and Journal* 23 April 1937.

100 As a memento Peck was presented by School Captain, Douglas Fox, with a writing cabinet, made in the College's own workshop.

101 The appointment of Andy Robb as Pool Superintendent from a field of 59 applicants in February 1937 was to result in astonishing success for the School in swimming.

102 Owned by the New Zealand Shipping Company.

103 'Pro Patria', *Gordonian,* (June 1920) no. 11 pp. 17–18.

104 Remarkably one of few other casualties that day was another Gordonian, fourteen-year-old Midshipman William E. Martin. He had left the College from class IVD early in 1917. Presumably he was on board the *Otaki* as a result of the Gordonian connection. His last letter to his girlfriend can be seen in the College. His memorial plaque can be seen on the north wall of the ruined church at Auchendoir, Cabrach, Aberdeenshire. John Marshall: 'The Otaki Story', *The Pelican* no. 2 (Autumn 2005) pp. 7–9; and *Gordonian* (December 1917) no. 6 p. 9.

105 RGC *Minutes* 25 June 1937 p. 211

106 Otaki Day (10 March) is commemorated annually in the College and a Reunion of Otaki Scholars took place in 2003. Bob Duncan, Development Director of the College under Headmaster Lockhart, compiled a commemorative booklet *Otaki Reunion 15 August 2003*, which included detailed profiles of all the Otaki Scholars. Another, more modern, generous benefactor, Robert G. Crawford, (attended College 1936–9), has ensured that the girls of the College have an equivalent to the Otaki: the Crawford Travel Scholarship has enabled the girl School Captain also to experience the trip of a lifetime.

107 Attended College 1895–8.

108 It is not surprising that Andrew saw 1936 as the 'annus mirabilus'.

109 He had attended the College between 1893–6.

110 At its peak Sillerton accommodated over sixty boys, and 14 Albyn Place was

purchased to provide the necessary room. Only when boarding became less fashionable did numbers drop and Sillerton was closed in 1995.

111 The Hospital Library had disappeared with the Hospital in 1881 and the concept was revived after 1909 when the Committee of the *Gordonian* Magazine, then run by staff and boys, offered the Governors £10 from their funds for any object of advantage to the College. In 1912 Principal Stewart decided to use the money to lay the foundation of a reference library. In the 1920s the Governors supported the idea.

112 From the 129 applications received, John W. Barclay was appointed with effect from 1 April 1938. RGC *Minutes* 28 January 1938 pp. 85–6.

113 It was unveiled by School Captain Fox. RGC *Minutes* 31 December 1937 p. 68.

114 *Ibid.* 25 June 1937 p. 211.

115 *Press and Journal* 2 July 1938.

116 His replacement, George Logan, did not arrive until January 1940.

117 Kindergarten returned during October.

118 A winter timetable was introduced on 20 November: morning 8.45am–12.25pm; afternoon 12.40pm–4.20pm.

119 Pupil 1889–96 and member of staff from 1901. He contributed to swimming, athletics, scouts, school camps and summer excursions. His retiral was followed in December 1942 by that of George Sheach, also an ex-pupil, who had returned to the staff in 1904. He was a violinist in the School Orchestra, 'father' of the forestry camps and 'one of the last of the old giants'. *Gordonian,* (December 1942), vol. VIII no. 2, p. 47.

120 RGC *Minutes* 27 September 1940 p. 176.

121 *Ibid.* p. 207.

122 *Ibid.*

123 With the exception of 14 May 1941 when the alarm lasted over four hours.

124 RGC *Minutes* 30 May 1941 p. 116. A College Army Cadet Corps was formed in April 1942 and reached a strength of 160. RGC *Minutes* 25 September 1942 p. 154.

125 RGC *Minutes* 28 November 1941 pp. 34–5.

126 RGC *Minutes* 30 October 1942 p. 2.

127 At his funeral on 17 January 1944 the College was represented by senior staff, the School Captain and prefects.

128 *Unpublished Autobiography* p. 235.

129 RGC *Minutes* 29 January 1943 p. 44.

130 It was £950 p.a.

131 Clapton proved a loss. He was a successful head at Warrington until 1950 and then at King Edward VII Grammar School from 1950–65. Humphries was very disappointed at not becoming Head of his 'own' school. On 4 February 1945 he left the College to become an HMI.

132 Hector Waugh: *George Watson's College. History and Record 1724–1970* (Edinburgh 1970) p. 149. What Andrew saw as his greatest successes at Watson's – Founder's Day and the development of the Blair Library – were the result of his tried and tested formula. For the boys of Watson's, however, 'his greatest achievement was getting rid of the ridiculous short trousers in which his predecessor had imprisoned all from S1 to S6 and bringing back "longs" for seniors.' Les Howie: (2006) *op. cit.* p. 131.
133 *The Watsonian,* May 1953, vol. XLVIII no. 1, pp. 1–2.
134 *Unpublished Autobiography* p. 249.
135 He had been plagued with ill-health earlier in his career. According to his unpublished autobiography he was close to a nervous breakdown in 1920 (p. 135) and declined the post of Rector at Dumfries Academy in 1931 on medical grounds (p. 185).

Chapter 11

1 A successful school in Islington. It had recently sent Selig Brodetsky, later famous for his work on aerodynamics and fluid mechanics, and Jacob Bronowski, the great scientist, to Cambridge University on scholarships.
2 A school with 600 boys which still exists as Portsmouth College.
3 On the casting vote of the Convener of Dundee Education Committee. The decision was 12–11. Andrew Millar, Rector of Preston Lodge School, Prestonpans, was the defeated candidate. The salary was £850 (rising to £1000 in increments).
4 R. B. Strathdee (1972) *op. cit.* p. 50.
5 Carnon had already been on the staff of Heriot's for some 36 years.
6 The salary on offer – £950 (rising in increments of £25 to £1150) – was on the low side. The Governors decided to increase it to £1150 before offering it to Collier.
7 In a letter dated 3 June 1943 Andrew endowed a silver medal for the Dux of the Junior School as a token of his appreciation of the loyal and generous support which he had received from the Governors and staff while he was at the College. RGC *Minutes* 25 June 1943 p. 116.
8 Sir Thomas Mitchell, Lord Provost 1936–47.
9 *Ibid.* 29 October 1943 p. 2.
10 Murray died on 29 September 1943, aged 62, having no time to enjoy his retirement. He was a Former Pupil of the College, and had, from 1905–22, taught English, geography, history, French and German, before becoming Head of French in 1922, a post he held until 1943. He had co-written a popular French textbook and produced *The Gordonian.*
11 Principal Teacher of Modern Languages at Perth Academy.
12 Cullen had been a pupil of the College between 1890–6. From 1907 he taught

English and French but latterly only German. He was a great supporter of foreign travel to improve languages and had organised the very successful visit to Austria in 1937.

13 Lentz had come to the College at the end of the First World War when wounded. After the Second World War he returned to the College but left finally in early 1946 to take up a post with the French consulate in Southampton. *Press and Journal,* 1 February 1946.

14 Being paid £20 p.a. for the extra duties he undertook. RGC *Minutes* 29 October 1943 p. 3.

15 McKenzie had been Bookkeeper (from 1896), Cashier (from 1899), and Secretary (from 1909) and his total service amounted to 47 years 8 months. He took over six funds in 1896 with £2586 and by his retiral there were 33 funds worth £62,215. A native of Durris, he died in May 1946.

16 R. B. Strathdee: (1971) *op. cit.* p. 34.

17 He had been educated at Montrose Academy, apprenticed to an engineer before graduating BSc. from St. Andrews in 1929 and then gaining a PhD from King's College, London.

18 Charles Birnie, a pupil from 1922–26, becoming Cashier and principal assistant.

19 RGC *Minutes* 31 December 1943 p. 40.

20 The boys were to be charged fourpence (old) for 'dinner'.

21 The figures soon rose to 200 regularly. Staff did lunch duty voluntarily.

22 RGC *Minutes* 30 May 1947 p. 107.

23 A pipe band was formed from its ranks. *RGC Minutes* 28 May 1948 p. 104.

24 Which Collier himself took a personal interest in.

25 RGC *Minutes* 25 February 1955 p. 72. Despite this, music as a subject did make significant advances as a result of the efforts of Douglas Tees, Principal Teacher of Music between 1956 and 1983. A man of boundless energy and enthusiasm he motivated countless boys and made music enjoyable for them. *Gordonian* (June 1995) vol. IX no. 2 p. 11.

26 RGC *Minutes* 31 October 1958 p. 2.

27 Black travelled to Rome without his coach, Andy Robb, who was needed at College for his coaching duties. Given his preparation problems he, unsurprisingly, came fourth in his event and retired from swimming soon afterwards.

28 RGC *Minutes* 25 January 1946 pp. 63–4. The Sillerton Boarding House pupils still attended the West Kirk, continuing the tradition of the Hospital and the Minister of the West Kirk became the College Chaplain. *Gordonian* (June 1947) vol. IX no. 5 p. 160.

29 He attended the College 1895–1901 and became a prominent accountant.

30 By 1953 some £21,644 had been received. RGC *Minutes* 29 November 1946 p. 18 and 27 February 1953 p. 62.

31 William Mackenzie, the Science Dux in 1898, had been successful in the minefields

of South Africa. More recently the terms of this award have been modified.
32 RGC *Minutes* 28 January 1949 pp. 50–1.
33 Costing £2000.
34 RGC *Minutes* 30 June 1950 p. 136; 29 June 1951 p. 130; 28 September 1951 p. 153; and 26 October 1951 p. 3.
35 *Ibid.* 28 November 1952 p. 14.
36 Unfortunately for the School this was the priority of the Governors despite the College's accommodation problems. RGC *Minutes* 31 July 1953 p. 136.
37 *Ibid.* 29 January 1954 p. 41 and p. 46.
38 *Gordonian* Editorial (June 1947) vol. IX no. 5 attacked irreverence for the past.
39 *Aberdeen Grammar School Magazine* LII no. 2 July 1949. Rector J. J. Robertson held that the abolition of fees 'has not materially altered the make-up of the School'. p. 106.
40 Even as early as 1946 FPs of the Grammar School feared these consequences, which they thought would result from the ending of fee-paying, and which would destroy the special character and traditions of the School. *Aberdeen Grammar School Magazine* L no. 1 December 1946 p. 2.
41 RGC *Minutes* 25 January 1952 and 27 June 1958 pp. 163–4.
42 RGC *Minutes* 31 October 1952 p. 2.
43 The AET retaining control of who would gain their awards. RGC *Minutes* 24 November 1952 p. 11.
44 Himself a Gordonian.
45 Bursaries had ended at the Grammar School with the discontinuance of fees in 1947.
46 This would have been a usurption of the original College funds.
47 The Educational Endowments Scheme, when it finally did arrive in 1958, tinkered with representation again: the number of College Governors on the AET being increased to two (from one).
48 RGC *Minutes* 29 October 1954 p. 8.
49 *Ibid.* 29 April 1955 pp. 108–111.
50 *Ibid.* 28 October 1955 pp. 2–3.
51 *Ibid.* 28 April 1950 p. 90. Later it was suggested (certainly by the College) that a better alternative at this time would have been for the Technical College to have moved elsewhere and the buildings given over to the College at a cheap price.
52 Although this was partly explainable by the fact that the funding for the central institution came from public funds.
53 *Gordonian* (December 1951) vol. I no. 4 p. 221.
54 Copland was a Former Pupil of the College and had been on the staff since 1908, becoming Principal Teacher of Classics in November 1924. On three occasions in twenty years he had taken charge of the College in the absence of the

Head and in November 1943 had been recognised officially as Deputy Headmaster. RGC *Minutes* 26 December 1947 p. 32

55 Gordon himself retired in August 1949 and was replaced as Deputy by George Logan, PT Maths. Hector Donaldson became Head of Science.

56 27 at Gordon's. John Reid (later President of FP Association) joined the Department. RGC *Minutes* 25 March 1948 p. 78

57 Forbes had joined the staff in 1908 and taught English, Latin, history and geography.

58 RGC *Minutes* 28 February 1958 p. 70.

59 *Ibid.* 26 March 1959 p. 93.

60 Jack Webster: (2005) *op. cit.* p. 233.

61 RGC *Minutes* 1 July 1960 p. 159.

62 Twenty Scottish school Headmasters are members today including the present Head, Hugh Ouston.

63 RGC *Minutes* 24 December 1959 p. 51.

64 *Ibid.* 27 May 1960 p. 132.

65 50% more than in 1955.

66 Marshall thought that the practice of forcing some boys to leave 'at pistol point' at the end of the Third Year unacceptable.

67 Marshall introduced certificate music in September 1960. RGC *Minutes* 30 September 1960 p. 190.

68 Of the five new classrooms, three housed Primary 5, 6 and 7 (transferred from the main building), one was used for art and the other by the Secondary Department. Four rooms in the old building were released for secondary work.

69 RGC *Minutes* 29 September 1961 p. 206.

70 When grossed over seven years – the length of the covenants – this reached £52,400. *Ibid.* 30 September 1960 pp. 217–8.

71 In the first year of the Appeal some 15% of Gordonians had responded and two years after its launch the response was deemed 'greatly disappointing'. *Gordonian* Editorial, (December 1961) vol. III no. 2, p. 83.

72 *Governors Minutes* 25 November 1960 p. 19. *Notes on the Discussion at the Secondary School Meeting* 16 December 1960.

73 RGC *Minutes* 26 May 1961 p. 136.

74 *Ibid.* 29 December 1961 pp. 46–7. *Evening Express* 17 January 1962. *Press and Journal* 18 January 1962.

75 RGC *Minutes* 26 June 1964 pp. 136–7.

76 With support from HMI.

77 RGC *Minutes* 29 January 1965 p. 42; 15 December 1965 p. 20; 18 May 1966 p. 133.

78 John Marshall: *Robert Gordon's College 1950–1980, Part V. Leopard,* February 1981 p. 27.

79 RGC *Minutes* 18 May 1966 pp. 133–4.
80 *Ibid.* 28 June 1967 pp. 235–6.
81 *Gordonian* (June 1969) vol. IV no. 3. The area near the MacRobert Hall which had housed the old library became part of a further development when the Governors' administrative offices (which then still served the College and RGIT) were transferred to the former Gray's School of Art building (which had decamped to Garthdee). Two areas, on ground and first floors, were converted into Junior School classrooms, including particularly spacious infant rooms. RGC *Minutes* 6 December 1972 pp. 33–4.
82 RGC *Minutes* 23 October 1968 pp. 6–7. Meantime the Aberdeen College of Education building in St Andrew Street was bought by the Governors in 1968 and modernised for Technical College use. A second breakthrough occurred in the following year when Mitchell and Muil's premises in Schoolhill and Harriet Street were bought.
83 *Gordonian* (December 1960) vol. III no. 1 p. 41.
84 Hector Donaldson, PT Science, became PT Chemistry with salary conserved, and Donald Cameron, first assistant in science, became PT Physics. Marshall also introduced biology courses in the mid-1960s. RGC *Minutes* 30 December 1960 pp. 34–5.
85 Leaving Gordon's the only all-through boys' school in Aberdeen.
86 *Gordonian* (December 1961) vol. III no. 2.
87 HMI have a habit of choosing the most inconvenient times for their inspections. This was certainly the case for the College, as the session had been totally disrupted by the typhoid epidemic in Aberdeen which had closed the school for the first time in living memory.
88 Circular No. 600 dated 27 October 1965.
89 RGC *Minutes* 30 June 1966 p. 152. This led in 1969 to the addition of a third Primary 6 class, which cut down entry to S1. Total annual entry was one class in P1, two in P6 and two in S1.
90 The local authority began such talks with the College in April 1966.
91 *Second Report vol. III Scotland* (HMSO 1970).
92 RGC *Minutes* 19 March 1969 p. 112.
93 The College's extensive free places meant it gathered 'from a wider sweep of the social structure' than other grant-aided or independent schools. John Highet: *A School of One's Choice. A Sociological Study of the Fee-Paying Schools of Scotland* (London 1969) p. 168.
94 30 September 1975.
95 RGC *Minutes* 26 March 1975 p. 42.
96 *Ibid.* 22 October 1975 p. 7.
97 The College employed Craigmyle and Co. (Scotland) Ltd. as their fund-raising consultants. *Ibid.* 22 October 1975 p. 7.

98 When it was wound up in April 1977 the gross contributions amounted to £267,533 representing 884 donations. *Ibid.* 22 June 1977 p. 74.

99 And also included seven Open Foundations which were awarded on merit with no regard to need. *Ibid.* 15 December 1976. p. 31.

100 *Ibid.* 15 December 1965 p. 21.

101 *Ibid.* 17 March 1971 p. 110. Marshall objected to the significant AET expenditure on buildings coming from the annual income of farm rents rather than being treated as capital expenditure.

102 Especially given that the free income in the previous year (1969) had been £36,937.

103 RGC *Minutes* 22 March 1972 p. 93.

104 The College had to meet the shortfall.

105 RGC *Minutes* 22 October 1975 pp. 2–3 and p. 6. The curiosity of the AET nominating who would attend the College was resolved by the introduction of a common entrance examination.

106 Including Miss Herbert in December 1961 after 45 years' service.

107 RGC *Minutes* 31 May 1963 p. 100.

108 *Ibid.* 29 January 1965 p. 2

109 *Ibid.* 26 October 1966 p. 6. He died soon after on 16 April 1967.

110 *Ibid.* 26 June 1974 p. 101.

111 Marshall claimed that his time was 'almost wholly taken up nowadays with the direction of the school's policy as laid down by the Board of Governors and in dealing with the machinations of the politicians'. *Gordonian* (June 1972) vol. IV, no. 6 p. 440.

112 Although the majority of their time was still taken up by teaching.

113 RGC *Minutes* 21 October 1970 p. 8.

114 *Gordonian,* (June 1978), vol. V, no. 6, p. 459.

115 *Ibid.* (June 1972) vol. IV no. 6 p. 451.

116 RGC *Minutes* 22 June 1977 p. 80

117 *Ibid.* 29 September 1977 p. 3.

118 The unsuccessful short-list candidates included Urwin Woodman and Brian Lockhart.

119 George Barton speaking at Marshall's retiral dinner on 21 December 1977. *Gordonian,* (June 1978), vol. V, no. 6 p. 488.

120 He was also a member of the University and College Admissions' Service (UCAS) and, with travel dear to his heart, a Trustee of the Scottish Schools' Travel Trust (1960–78). He was the latter's Chairman (1971–78) and Secretary (1978–80).

121 He also continued his foreign travel and wrote *Off the Beaten Track in Switzerland* (1989), *Visitors' Guide to Switzerland* (1990, rev. 1995) and *Visitors' Guide to the Rhine and Mosel* (1992).

Chapter 12

1 RGC *Minutes* 22 October 1980 p. 3.
2 *Ibid.* 25 March 1981.
3 Although he rejected the idea of the House System incorporating Guidance. Instead the latter developed into two Assistant Heads in charge of S1–3 and S4–6 with a PT and APT for each age group.
4 Where Howard Smith, PT Geography, became the guardian of staff interests. Despite great financial pressure, Allan was able to persuade the Governors to reverse their decision to cut fee remission for staff children, which remained at a generous 80% remission. *Finance Committee Minutes* 25 June 1990.
5 In 1989 when the maintained system introduced the post of Senior Teacher, Allan decided not to follow suit but instead added Assistant Principal Teachers to both Guidance teams. He also created the post of APT of Outdoor Education to take charge of field trips and educational excursions. Headmaster's Paper on 'Additional Promoted Posts' 14 June 1989.
6 In April 1992 Allan was successful in having the flat-rate increased to £800 p.a., which went some way to stifling the criticism, which was mounting, that the College annual salary reviews had failed to produce any increase in the figure for over six years. Headmaster Memo to Finance Committee 30 April 1992.
7 This was eventually to happen to the Scheme in the 1990s, but the worst effects of withdrawal were mitigated by its being phased out over a number of years.
8 RGC *Minutes* 26 March 1980 p. 45.
9 *Ibid.* 22 October 1980 p. 3.
10 This remained the College approach throughout the life of the APS. When the Scheme was ended by Labour in 1997 Gordon's had a low dependency on it (some 70 pupils – 7% – of secondary were included). *Governors' Minutes* 29 January 1996.
11 *Governors' Minutes* 27 June 1979 p. 73.
12 The Technical College changed its name in 1965 to Robert Gordon's Institute of Technology (RGIT) to reflect more accurately the nature and standard of the work that was then being carried out. 'It was felt that this would provide a clear signal to the outside world that the institution had ceased to be a part of the Further Education (FE) sector, and was now firmly established as a major player in the Scottish Higher Education (HE) sector'. Henry Ellington (2002) *op. cit.* p. 106.
13 Noel Gwynne became Clerk and Treasurer to the Governors while Chris Anderson was the RGIT appointment. *Ibid.* p. 114.
14 *RGC Meeting* 28 June 1978 p. 88.
15 *Ibid.* p. 95.
16 These clauses proved their worth as early as January 1983 when the Secretary of RGIT wrote to the College suggesting the conversion of part of the lawn in

the Quadrangle in order to provide further car-parking spaces. The idea was rejected by the College Governors!

17 It was composed of Convener of Grampian Regional Council (ex officio); 3 from Grampian Regional Council; 2 from the AET; 2 from the University Senate; 2 from the Church of Scotland Presbytery; 2 from the Gordonian Association; 1 from Incorporated Trades; 1 from Chamber of Commerce; 1 from Trade Unions and between 4–6 co-opted members. The Educational Endowments Act of 1985 confirmed two Governors on the AET Board.

18 Calum MacLeod had been a partner in the legal firm of Paull & Williamsons between 1964–80. He held a number of chairmanships and served on a number of public bodies. W. Hamish Fraser and Clive H. Lee (2000) *op. cit.* pp. 151–2.

19 Parents voted for a PA by 763 votes to 116 against.

20 The first all-school inspection since 1972.

21 Which led to significant comment in the local press.

22 In the two-layer local government arrangements, while the Regional Authority (Grampian) laid down general planning principles it was the District Council (Aberdeen) which determined individual applications.

23 *Press and Journal* 15 May 1984.

24 *Ibid.* 24 January 1985.

25 One from the Community Council and six from local residents.

26 The *Evening Express* of 28 February 1985 agreed.

27 Two and a half times the size of the existing College.

28 Sillerton House accommodated a maximum of 54 boys.

29 *Evening Express* 20 August 1985.

30 *Evening Express* 10 December 1985 and *Press and Journal* 11 December 1985.

31 On 27 May 1985.

32 Annual fee increases averaged over 10% in the mid-1980s. The government grants were down to 5% of costs and ended completely in 1985.

33 The Main Report meant significant salary increases for teachers and the introduction of Standard Grade courses was proving extremely expensive.

34 Numbers held up reasonably well, although Allan was worried when 6th Year numbers fell significantly in the period before 1985.

35 The College was to pay £8000 an acre for the ground as it stood with no planning permission or £20,000 an acre if the College appeal to the Secretary of State, for change of use of the land, was upheld.

36 *Evening Express* 10 July 1986.

37 Each school was represented by its Head and two Governors under the Chairmanship of Adams, who was Principal of the College of Education and a Governor of both St Margaret's and RGC.

38 Pros and cons of co-education, size of school, parental choice and possible market research.

39 Models examined included (i) large co-educational school of 1200 in secondary and 700 in primary on one site; (ii) small girls' school of 500+ and large separate co-ed school with 1050 boys and 250 girls; and (iii) large co-ed and small co-ed schools on separate sites.

40 The Region was keeping its options open. Option A (the eastern line) ran along the eastern boundary of Slopefield and this meant leaving a fifty-metre strip of land there for possible future road development.

41 In particular the junction of Countesswells Road and Seafield Road with Springfield Road.

42 When the application was lodged the Gordonian Association representatives on the Board raised the matter of the War Memorial, in the form of the Seafield Pavilion. RGC *Minutes* 11 May 1987.

43 Both surveys had a consensus against a very large co-ed school (over 1500) and for the retention of a small girls' school.

44 Albyn had already obtained planning permission for additional science facilities.

45 The specifics of which sections would use which buildings was not released.

46 = Board.

47 *Evening Express* 26 November 1987.

48 Press release of 29 January 1988.

49 One of four examined.

50 The bipartite talks made little progress on other issues. In July 1989 the College rejected Albyn's request to buy or lease six acres of Slopefield (because the whole area was needed by RGC) and the discussions on boarding were ended when Albyn could not afford to contribute to the refurbishment of Sillerton House. The fee concessions were ended by Headmaster Lockhart a decade later.

51 The value of the buildings and site according to Kenneth Ryden.

52 Including moving the College there.

53 The College prohibited its use in May 1985.

54 Capital expenditure was now more sensibly judged as for the benefit of all pupils.

55 RGC *Minutes* 24 November 1986; *Policy Committee Minutes* 9 March 1988 and *Finance and Property Minutes* 15 February 1989.

56 Traditionally the AET made decisions on its awards without any reference to the entrance exams. Only in 1987 did it begin to use them, having been dissuaded from introducing its own entrance exams (to be held two weeks before Gordon's own entrance exams). RGC *Minutes* 27 January 1986. In 1993, the AET insisted on selecting its own mathematics paper for the entrance exams *Policy Committee Minutes* 10 November 1992, while the College determined to avoid such "interference" in the future.

57 RGC *Minutes* 28 November 1994.

58 *Ibid.* 19 September 1988.

59 The projected fee increase for 1987/8 was 12.4% but the actual increase was restricted to 10.5%. *Ibid.* 11 May 1987.

60 *Finance and Property Minutes* 26 October 1988. The College fee figure of £1950pa compared with £2229 for High School of Dundee; £2355 for George Heriot's; £2400 for High School of Glasgow; and £2526 for George Watson's.

61 *Press and Journal* and *Evening Express* 6 April 1989; *Press and Journal* 18 May 1989.

62 He found that pupil/teacher ratio was highest at RGC at 13.9 compared with Dundee HS at 10.5; Glasgow HS 11.5; Heriot's at 13.1; and Watson's at 12.0, showing staff costs were less than elsewhere.

63 RGC *Minutes* 8 May 1989.

64 The Governors also sold £350,000 of shares to cut the College overdraft. *Ibid.*

65 A direct debit scheme for paying fees was introduced. Following meetings with the parents the fee increase was set at 9.6%, and in 1991/2 at 11.3% (inflation plus 2%). By then the secondary fee was over £3000 p.a.

66 835 in secondary and 321 in primary.

67 A further six joined the Junior School in January 1990.

68 RGC *Minutes* 23 January 1989.

69 In 15 and 16 Albyn Terrace only at a cost of £33,000 which was paid for by the sale of 14 Albyn Terrace for £192,000. Its capacity was restricted to 35. *Ibid.* 19 June 1989.

70 This did not last. Boarding went increasingly out of fashion and Sillerton closed. Its buildings were sold for £454,000 in December 1995. *RGC Minutes* 2 October 1995.

71 Allan's Memo 'Development of Schoolhill' 8 May 1990.

72 It had been hoped for four storeys in the first instance.

73 As they were geared to include Gordonian use, the hockey pitch was of national standard and the cricket square was relaid from Seafield, also symbolising continuity with the ground's War Memorial tradition.

74 There was an interesting discussion on introducing football as a curricular game with the Chairman supporting and Allan (firmly backed by the Head of PE, Andy Dougal) opposing. The Playing Field Committee, under Dr. Gordon Smylie, had an 'open mind'. Allan won the argument, at least for the meantime. RGC *Minutes* 19 June 1989.

75 Drawn up by the College auditors, Coopers and Lybrand Deloitte, who also were instrumental in advising the new College Bursar, Bob Leggate, appointed in August 1991, on restricting VAT liabilities. *Ibid.* 30 September 1991. The plan adopted of lease and lease-back ensured a significant cash flow advantage resulting from the deferment of VAT. Despite challenge, the College won its case in a landmark House of Lords decision on 16 November 1995. RGC *Minutes* 29 January 1996.

76 This entailed a two-classroom portacabin in the playground until the Blackfriars' Building was complete.

77 General dislike of the name had first surfaced at the Playing Field Committee meeting on 8 February 1989 and discussed by the Governors in September 1991.
78 *Policy Committee Minutes* 10 November 1992.
79 Beginning at £4000 for 1993/4. *Playing Fields Committee Minutes* 2 March 1993.
80 As the Gordonian Sports Sections had recently decided on open membership (i.e. up to 80% of members had no connection to the College) the Governors argued that it was unreasonable to continue to allow access to high-quality facilities at an uneconomic cost to persons who had no connections with the College and whose parents had made no financial contribution to its development.
81 *Playing Field Committee Meetings* 20 April and 25 June 1993; *Governors' Minutes* 20 September and 6 December 1993. Fences were mended by the introduction of a scheme by which a small proportion of fees of senior pupils was transferred to the FP Association and in return all College leavers automatically became members of the Association.
82 Something he had warned the Governors about.
83 He had been a pupil at the College 1944–50, had returned to the staff in 1957 and served 37 years.
84 An internal promotion. He had been PT English from 1978 and Assistant Head from 1985.
85 Professor John Howie was a distinguished Former Pupil of the College and was Professor of Mathematics at the University of St Andrews.
86 *Policy Committee Minutes* 10 November 1992.
87 Originally a state school, it was closed by Strathclyde Regional Council in 1976 and reopened as an independent school on land belonging to its Former Pupils in 1977.
88 He had also begun to play a national role, which he continued when at Gordon's. He was Assistant Secretary and Executive member of the HAS (1988–94) and also a Council member (1988–2004); represented the independent sector on the Higher Still Implementation Group (1998–2001); Convener of the UCAS Scottish Standing Committee (2001–3); and Secretary, then Chairman of HMC Scottish Division (2002–4).
89 (Sir) Graeme Catto: 'The Lockhart Years', *Gordonian* (2004) vol. XI no. 6 p. 10.
90 He revived the target of a school with 40% girls, believing that the optimum proportion for a co-ed school.
91 The Appeal team of Alan Amoore (Appeal Chairman), Bob Duncan (Appeal Director) and Headmaster, were supported by professional advisers, Craigmyle & Co. Ltd with Miles Paterson of the P. A. much involved.
92 Lockhart had to speak at some fifteen Appeal meetings in his first term.
93 Part of the price paid for Countesswells and building the Blackfriars' Building.
94 In time further new posts were created – Junior School ICT Co-ordinator, Network Manager, Administration Systems Supervisor, Art Technician, Web Master

and Junior School Assistants, as well as subject specialists in areas such as Spanish, Junior School French and PE/Games. Lockhart saw back-up staff as crucial in allowing teaching staff to work most effectively. His view was coloured by his own secretary, Ann Gannon, who was outstanding in her support role.

95 The world-famous swimmer who had returned to Gordon's in 1993 and become the charismatic Head of the Junior School.

96 Chaired by Mrs Rona Livingstone, Assistant Head.

97 With Principal Teacher and Assistant Principal Teachers of Guidance, all with more guidance time, for each of the four School Houses, with an enhanced role for House staff.

98 All eight guidance staff were given the status of Principal Teacher and the Form Classes were created from the four Houses throughout the secondary school. This reinvigorated the House System with the result that pupils from all years participated regularly and enthusiastically in the large number of House events ranging from Swimming Gala and Sports Day to House Drama, Karaoke and Mind Games!

99 In total this reached £1.6m. Burnett had been the Modern Dux of 1935.

100 In 1997 the Gordon's Allowance increased for all members of the teaching staff from £800 p.a. to £880. This was restructured in 2002 and all teaching staff were paid 6% over the national scales – a significant and increasing differential was thus created.

101 He was particularly keen to develop the Principal Teacher role as 'academic' experts and make them more accountable for departmental results and their staff.

102 He used the McCrone Settlement in 2001 as a basis for developing a career structure in the secondary unique to Gordon's in the hope of attracting and retaining quality staff. In the Junior School he introduced a non-teaching management team to share the burden previously the responsibility of the Head and a teaching Deputy.

103 He willingly covered classes when staff were absent, but believed nobody could do the job of teaching properly unless they did it day in, day out.

104 Urwin Woodman and Rona Livingstone proved exceptionally able Assistant Heads until their retirements. Woodman had spent most of his teaching career at Gordon's and was much respected as an exceptional schoolmaster, while Livingstone had done much to ensure the smooth introduction of the girls. Fortunately, Michael Elder was to remain at Gordon's throughout this period and made a vital contribution in a number of different areas. He can be particularly proud of his crucial part in the College's development of information technology

105 Michael Duncan, Deputy Head at Gordon's, had been appointed as Rector of the High School of Dundee.

106 Philip Skingley and Anne Everest were examples of such promotions and both were great successes.

107 The 'Communications Strategy' (March 1999) and the '2020 Vision' (December 2000) resulted. Lockhart was helped in this by Clif Collier of Fifth Ring.
108 G. Catto (2004) *op. cit.* p. 10
109 The School Captains were joined by eight House Captains in a committee meeting weekly with the Headmaster. All Fifth Year voted for the Prefect Body (which was made up entirely of Sixth Formers). A School Council was introduced as a sounding-board for pupil opinion.
110 *Extended Inspection Report* 5 May 1998. p. 15.
111 *Inspection of Standards and Quality* 30 April 2002 p. 11. The Nursery Department gained particular credit.
112 A number donated by the Parents' Association.
113 Supported by the Burnett Trust. The Appeal reached £1.35m. by May 1998.
114 A long-term commitment to the Former Pupils.
115 Costing £300,000.
116 Unfortunately the Reporter rejected the College appeal, against the planning decision, on 11 September 2002.
117 Ex-President of the Gordonian Association and a Scottish rugby internationalist.
118 Costing £354,000.
119 By 1999 it had reached 1423, with 516 girls (36%).
120 RGIT had gained university status in 1992.
121 At this time Walker Dam School, property in Albyn Place and Woolmanhill were investigated, while later in 2002–3 Hilton, Kepplestone and Countesswells, where the College owned eleven acres across the road from its playing-fields, were looked at. All proved unsuitable as solutions to the College's accommodation needs.
122 With numbers going down Albyn had surplus space.
123 Referring to size and gender.
124 The parents, too, were unhappy with this development.
125 Reaching £600,000 given the failure to embark on a major building programme.
126 The total cost was £938,000.
127 In the belief that this would counter any tendency to sell property at other sites, where they would get the market (rather than educational) value.
128 Graeme Catto (2004) *op. cit.* p. 11.
129 In 2003–4 with 575 girls (39 per cent).
130 Particularly in terms of Higher Grade results, which led to over 95% of leavers going annually to university.
131 The good stewardship of Bursar, Bob Leggate, was an important factor in this.
132 Bob Duncan, Development Director, raised £152,000 in 2002–3.
133 He remained until 2005 as Chairman before giving way to Colin Crosby. He had proved an outstanding Chairman. *Gordonian* 2006.
134 Previously Vice-Principal of Watson's College, Edinburgh.

Postscript

1 Alexander Martin, Rector of Aberdeen Grammar School, quoted in *Educational News*, 30 December 1876 p. 666.
2 R. D. Anderson: (1983) *op. cit.* p. 200.
3 A group of originally eleven schools given special status under the 1872 Education Act to rely solely on fees and catering for mainly professional and commercial classes. They included Aberdeen Grammar School.
4 Robert Gordon had enjoined those who had benefited from financial assistance to give generously so that others might do so too. A number of generous donations have been given. Most recently in 2007 was that in memory of Lt. William Duguid, who had gone to Gordon's from Dunecht on a bursary and went on to excel in classics at Aberdeen University before being tragically killed in 1945.
5 And should be compared with the maintenance of a maximum of 180 pupils in the Hospital.
6 Alexander Morgan: *The Makers of Scottish Education* (London 1929).

APPENDIX I

Excerpt from Robert Gordon's Will

Source: – Aberdeen Commissionary Court, 12 January 1731 and Hospital Accounts, 24 April 1731–8 November 1731.

OWED TO ROBERT GORDON ON HIS DEATH:

Date of Loan	*Sum*	*By*	*Total (pounds Scots)*
27 June 1707	2500 merks	Patrick Ogilvie of Inchmartin	1750
1 June 1708	350 m	Lewis Gordon of Kinmundy	251
29 June 1708	1000 m	Lewis Gordon of Kinmundy	717
17 Dec. 1708	1000 pounds	Patrick Strachan of Glenkindy	1075
1 Feb. 1710	2000 m	Alexander Irvine of Drum & James Gordon of Barnes	
23 Dec. 1718	2500 m	Alexander Irvine of Drum & James Gordon of Barnes	
25 Sept. 1724	1000 p	Alexander Irvine of Drum & James Gordon of Barnes	3548
19 June 1711	300 m	Major-Gen. Thomas Buchanan	411
8 Dec. 1711	3000 p	James Udny	
17 Dec.1711	500 m	James Udny	3475
12 Dec 1711	1000 m	James Gordon of Tilliefour	717
20 Nov.1712	500 m	William Erskine of Pittrodie	367
24 Aug. 1713	1000 m	William Forbes (merchant) of Echt	950
11 June 1718	2000 m	John Gordon of Wardhouse	1467
14 June 1718	3000 m	John Forbes of Kincardin	2300
14 June 1718	2000 m	Charles Collinson of Auchleunies	1433
1 July 1718	1000 m	James Gordon of Auchlyne	717
22 Dec. 1718	1000 m	Andrew Burnet of Elrick	700
31 Dec. 1718	1100 m	Sir James Gordon of Lesmoir	862

15 June 1719	4000	p	Viscount John Arbuthnot	4400
3 Sept. 1720	2700	m	Alexander Irvine of Saphock	2260
22 June 1721	3000	m	Thomas Forbes of Echt	2150
27 June 1721	1000	m	Sir Archibald Grant of Monymusk	800
23 Dec. 1721	1000	p	Thomas Erskine of Pittrodie	1075
27 Feb. 1722	1000	m	Alexander Davidson of Gight	700
10 July 1722	630	p	Col. Patrick Ogilvie of Inchmartin	662
21 Nov. 1722	6000	m	Sir James Dunbar of Durno	4300
30 May 1723	3500	m	Sir Alexander Reid of Barradale	2567
26 June 1723	1000	p	Sir James Gordon of Lesmoir	1175
4 Nov. 1723	500	m	William Burnet of Craigie	342
7 Dec. 1723	2000	m	John Arbuthnot of Fordoun	1433
6 Jan. 1724	4000	m	Sir James Dunbar of Durno	2867
29 May 1724	2500	m	Alexander Frasier of King's Coll.	1750
2 June 1724	10000	m	Henry Fletcher of Saltoun	7000
23 June 1724	6000	m	John Urquhart of Meldrum	4200
26 Nov. 1724	1000	m	Sir Patrick Strachan of Glenkindy	717
21 Dec. 1724	7000	m	William Menzies of Pitfodels	4783
23 Dec. 1724	1000	m	James Gordon of Techmurie	700
1 July 1725	308	p	Lewis Gordon of Kinmundy	331
3 July 1725	2000	m	Alexander Davidson of Gight	1400
23 Sept. 1725	2000	m	Alexander Irvine of Saphock	1700
11 Nov. 1725	825	p	Robert Gordon of Cluny (advocate)	3825
16 June 1726	1000	m	Alexander Irvine of Saphock	833
12 July 1726	19	p	William Ross, factor of Udny	23
9 Aug. 1726	2000	m	Alexander William Reid of Glassell	1467
24 Oct. 1726	200	m	Robert Paterson, Commissary of Aberdeen	163
24 Dec. 1726	500	p	John Fullerton of Dudwick	7167
17 Jan. 1727	750	p	ex-Baillie William Gellie of Aberdeen	919
26 April 1727	100	p	Alexander Irvine of Saphock	120
31 May 1727	3000	m	William Baird of Auchmedden	2400
19 Dec. 1727	6000	m	George Skene	4700
14 Dec. 1728	6000	m	John, Lord Gray	4200
21 Dec. 1728	1000	p	Alexander & George Gordon of King's	1125
21 Dec. 1728	1200	m	Thomas Forbes of Watertown	900
11 Jan. 1729	4000	m	Sir Alexander & Thomas Burnet (of Leys)	2733

17 May 1729	500 m	Alexander Gordon of Logie	367
31 May 1729	1000 m	William Dingwall of Bracklaw	733
31 May 1729	5000 m	George Skene	3667
1 June 1729	3083 p	Earl of Erroll	3160
19 June 1729	4000 m	Sir Alexander & Thomas Burnet (of Leys)	2933
21 June 1729	2000 m	Alexander Reid & William Baird of Glassell	1467
28 June 1729	3000 m	Alexander Davidson of Newtown	2200
11 Nov. 1729	1000 m	Alexander Bannerman of Elrick	683
6 Dec. 1729	5000 m	Countess and Earl of Erroll	3583
9 Dec. 1729	400 m	John Arbuthnot of Fordoun	287
26 Jan. 1730	6000 m	Alexander Thomson of Fechfield	4100
22 June 1730	2000 m	John Elphinstone of Glack et. al.	1400
23 Oct. 1730	791 p	George Keith (advocate)	
11 Nov. 1730	325 p	George Keith (advocate)	
22 Mar. 1731	200 p	George Keith (advocate)	948
18 Dec. 1730	2000 m	Thomas Forbes of Watertown	1367
21 Dec. 1730	4000 m	John, Earl of Kintore	2733
2 Jan. 1731	1000 m	Sir Alexander Bannerman of Elrick	683
3 Jan. 1731	2000 m	John, Lord Gray	1367

*Adjudication of 20 December 1727 which had accumulated to 2858 Scots pounds by the time of his death.

	Scots pounds
Total sum owed to Robert Gordon at his death	133,163
Money lying at time of his death	791
	Sterling
Total	£11,163
Equivalent in purchasing power today	£1,613,780

(Lawrence Officer: *Measuring Worth* 2007).

APPENDIX II

Genealogy of Gordon and Abercrombie Families.

JOHN GORDON of Pitlurg, Botarie & Kinmundy 1547–1600
m. (1567)
Isobel Forbes 1548–?1622.

- John of Pitlurg 1573–1619 *m.* Nicolas Kinnaird
- Barbara *b.* 1577 *m.1.* Gilbert Keith of Troup *m.2.* John Elphinstone of Bannockburn
- ROBERT OF STRALOCH 1580–1661 *m. (1608)* Katherine Irvine 1585–1662
  - Robert of Pitlurg 1609–81 *m. (1638)* Katherine Burnett 1610–98
    - Robert of Pitlurg 1641–82 *m.* Jean Maitland
      - Alexander of Pitlurg d. 1747 *m. (1717)* Mary Gordon
        - Alexander d. 1743
        - Jane d. 1743
      - Mary d. 1710 *m. (1698)* William Baird 1676–1720
        - William of Auchmedden 1701–75 *m.* Anne Duff
        - Mary
        - Jean 1705–22
    - Charles of Woodgrove 1642–98 (to New Jersey 1684)
    - John MD 1643–1718 of Collieston *m. (1675)* Katherine Fullerton
      - John MD of Collieston & Hilton d.1735 *m.* Margaret Dowell
        - 3 sons and 2 dau. inc. James MD of Straloch d. 1755
    - Katherine 1644–92 *m. (1667)* Robert Arthbuthnot (Vt) d. 1682
      - Elizabeth b. 1669 *m. (1686)* Andrew Wood
      - Anne 1672–1742 *m. (1693)* John Hay of Westhill
      - John of Fordoun 1673–1737 *m.* Margaret Falconer
      - Alexander b. 1674 *m.* Jean Maitland
      - Catherine 1675–1746 *m. (1687)* Robert Gordon of Cluny
      - Helen 1675–1741 *m.2* (1720) John Spottiswood
      - Jean b. 1679
      - Thomas 1679–1745 *m.* Elizabeth Falconer
    - Thomas 1652–1722 (Chief Justice in New Jersey)
      - 6 children
    - George

(continued line)
- Alexander 1692–1716
- James 1693–?1713
- Robert 1695–?1705
- Elizabeth b. 1696
- Lewis 1697–?1716

The Menzies of Balgownie Family.

Lt. Col. Thomas Menzies *m.1.* Margaret Gordon *m.2.* 1651 (Riga) Lady Marie Farserson

- John Ludovick (Lewis) 1620–60
- Alexander, Lord of Balgownie 1621–63
- Francis 1622–63 *m. (1655)* Margaret Oliphant
  - William, Lord of Balgownie 1664–5
- William b. 1627
- Gilbert b. 1628
- Michael b. 1631
- John b. 1645
- ISOBELL *m. (1663)* *ARTHUR GORDON

*ARTHUR GORDON was assigned the lands of Balgownie from William as security for a loan of 9,940 merks in 1665.

- John of Fechil 1611–98
  - John of Fechil
- William 1613–49
- Alexander 1614–5
- Isabel 1615–67 *m. (1640)* Alexander Urquhart of Craighouse 1615–48
- Mary b. 1616 *m.* Sir Richard Maitland
  - Jean 1645–1711 *m.1* Robert Gordon of Pitlurg *m.2* John Gordon of Fechil
- JAMES OF ROTHIEMAY 1617–86 *m.1* Margaret Menzies of Pitfodels *m.2* Katherine Gordon
  - James of Zeochrie *m. 1686* Jane Fraser
    - Alexander d. 1722
    - James d. 1760
    - Margaret
  - Alexander of Kinmundy d. 1722
  - Lewis of Kinmoir d. 1734.
- George 1618–36
- ALEXANDER 1620–1705, Lord Auchintoul
- Jean b. 1621 *m.* Middleton of Johnston
- Barbara b. 1622 *m.* Alexander Menzies of Kinmundy
- Hugh b. 1624
- ARTHUR 1625–80 *m. (1663)* ISOBELL MENZIES of Balgownie
  - Robert (Founder) 1668–1731
  - Anna b. 1669
  - MARY 1671–1742 *m. (1690)* SIR JAMES ABERCROMBIE OF BIRKENBOG 1668–1734
    - Mary b. 1698
    - Anne b. 1700 *m.* George Stewart of Tanachie
    - Jean b. 1701
    - Isabell b. 1703 *m.* James Dunbar of Kincorth
    - (Sir) Robert, 3rd Bt. of Birkenbog 1705–87 *m.* Helen Abercrombie of Tullibody 1713–91.
      - 3 sons & 4 dau. inc (Sir) George 4th Bt. 1750–1831.
    - George 1706–76 *m. (1746)* Ingleby d. 1754
    - Arthur 1707–71 East India Co.
    - William 1710–39
    - John b. 1711
    - James b. 1713
  - John b. 1673
- Anne 1626–1714 *m. (1650)* Alexander Bisset of Lessendrum
- Patrick 1628–49
- Margaret b. 1629 d. infancy
- LEWIS 1631–1704 MD

APPENDIX III

1881 Curriculum of Ogilvie for the College

Junior Department

1st Year (under 10 years, level of Standard III) – English, Geography, History, Scripture, Writing, Arithmetic, Singing (fee 7/6 per quarter).

2nd Year – adding Physiography, Elementary Botany (fee 10/-)

3rd Year – adding Mathematics with Book-keeping, French or Latin, Freehand Drawing and Practical Geometry, Elementary Mechanics, Elementary Physics and Phonography (fee 12/6).

Senior Department

Commercial – emphasis on Modern languages but one hour daily of science with practical emphasis.

4th Year – English, Geography, History, French and German, Mathematics, Book-keeping, Ornamental Writing, Drawing, Phonography, Physics and Chemistry with laboratory practice. (15/-)

5th Year – English Literature, French, German, Mathematics, Book-keeping, Drawing, Phonography, advanced work in some science subjects.

Trade and Engineering – still English and a Modern Language, but emphasis mostly on Mathematics, Experimental Science and Drawing.

4th Year – English, Mathematics, Mechanics, Physics and Chemistry with laboratory practice, French or German, Practical Plane and Solid Geometry, Drawing in Perspective and from models. (15/-)

5th Year – English Literature, Mathematics, Applied Mechanics, Machine Construction and Drawing, French or German, and for engineering – steam and steam engine; for building trades – building construction and drawing. (15/-)

Classical – for entry to the university Arts' Course but still including Experimental science and Drawing for three hours a week – a decided advantage for the College boys when at University. Classes max. 40.

4th Year – English, Ancient History and Geography, Latin, Greek, Mathematics, Physics and Drawing. (15/-)

5th Year – English, Ancient History and Geography, Latin, Greek, Mathematics, Chemistry and Drawing. (15/-)

6th Year – English, Latin, Greek and Mathematics. (15/-)

Preparation for Preliminary Examinations for University Entry for Medicine and General Knowledge Examinations for Law Students

4th Year – English, Mathematics, Geography, History, Latin, French or German, Physics and Chemistry with laboratory practice, Phonography and Drawing. (15/-)

5th Year – English Literature, Mathematics, Latin, French or German, Animal Physiology, Drawing after models and casts. (15/-)

SELECTED BIBLIOGRAPHY

The Robert Gordon's College Archives were set up in 2000 and under the Librarian/Archivist, Mrs Penny Hartley, an impressive collection of documents and materials has already been acquired and catalogued. An asterisk in the bibliography denotes the source as the College Archive.

Aberdeen City inherited a number of documents in the 1990s, especially from the Robert Gordon University, and these are stored either at the Town House or the Old Town House in Old Aberdeen, signified as TH and OTH respectively.

A. PRIMARY SOURCES

Robert Gordon's Hospital (RGH) Sederunt Books of Minutes.*

Volume I. May 1731–November 1737.

This volume was lost for many years, then, in the early 20th century, was found in an advocate's office in Aberdeen.

Volume II. February 1738–November 1742.

Volume III. November 1742–November 1758.

Volume IV. November 1758–October 1779.

Unfortunately this volume was lost early on in the Hospital's history and has not been recovered. All that remains is a table of contents.

Volume V. November 1779–May 1792.

Volume VI. June 1792–December 1816.

Volume VII. February 1817–April 1831.

Volume VIII. May 1831–September 1845.

Volume IX. November 1845–November 1875.

Volume X. November 1875–December 1885.

Robert Gordon's College (RGC) Governors' Minutes* have been produced annually since the change from a Hospital to a College in 1881–2.

The RGC Magazine was produced regularly following its first edition in 1908 and is a valuable source of information. Although originally a pupil then a Former Pupil magazine it took early on as its title the *Gordonian* (and I have used that title for all the issues).

The 'Deed of Mortification and Disposition by Robert Gordon, merchant in Aberdeen, 1731'* had all 43 of its pages signed by Robert Thomson, the Town Clerk of Aberdeen, and was duly witnessed on 13 December 1729. The Deed included the Statutes and Rules, which Robert Gordon produced for his Hospital. The 'Appendix to the foregoing Deed of Mortification and Disposition'* was added on 19 September 1730. Both documents were included in every publication of 'Foundations, Statutes and Rules' – in 1784,* in 1823* and in 1850*, and these also included the Hospital Charter of 1772*, which 'erected the President and Governors into one body politic'.

The Hospital worked through a series of Committees and fortunately the books detailing their work from 1796–1880 have survived. RGH Committee Book (CB)* (unnumbered) for 1796–1831, then CB vol. 1* (January 1832 – September 1845); CB vol. 2* (September 1845 – July 1859); CB vol. 3* (August 1859–October 1870); CB vol. 4* (November 1870 – September 1880) and CB vol. 5* (October 1880 – August 1881). Of particular interest are the reports of the Governors' Visiting Committees and its Visiting Committee Minute Books of 1832–50 and 1851–81 (TH: DD61/M/1/4 and DD61/M/1/5). The RGH Journals of 1810–20 and 1864–85 (TH: DD61/A/9/1) and the Physician's Visiting Book of 1857–87 (TH: DD61/M/1/6) are also important sources.

Usually the Hospital Treasurers kept meticulous Account Books both quarterly and annually. The Town House has the bulk of these.

a. RGH ANNUAL ACCOUNTS.

Volume 1. (1731–51). (TH – DD61/A/1/1).
These include 24 April–8 November 1731 then continue annually from November to November. There is a short break in the Accounts caused by the Jacobites (1745–6).

Volume 2. (1760–80). (TH – DD61/A/1/2).
The Accounts between 1751–62 are missing.

Volume 3. (1780–90). (TH – DD61/A/1/3).

Volume 4. (1790–1800). (TH – DD61/A/1/4).
Volume 5. (1800–12). (TH – DD61/A/1/5).
Volume 6. (1819–31). (TH – DD61/A/1/6).
The Accounts from 1812–9 are missing. [Volume 7 is a duplicate of this]
Volume 8. (1831–60). (TH – DD61/A/1/8). [Volume 9 is a duplicate of this]
Volume 10 (1840–50)* and Volume 11 (1851–60)* are both in the College Archives.
Volume 12 (1861–70). (TH – DD61/A/1/12). [Volume 13 is a duplicate of this]
Volume 14 (1871–72)* is in the College Archives.
Volume 15 (1872–1881)* is also in the College.
The Annual Accounts of RGC* from 1881 on are all available.

b. RGH QUARTERLY ACCOUNTS.
The Town House has 21 volumes of these from DD61/A/2/1 to DD61/A/2/21.
Volume 1. November 1731–November 1734.
Volume 2. November 1734–July 1737.
Volume 3. July 1737–November 1743.
Volume 4. November 1743–May 1747.
Volume 5. May 1747–February 1748.
Volume 6. February 1748–November 1748.
Volume 7. November 1748–November 1749.
Volume 8. November 1749–November 1751.
Volume 9. November 1751–August 1754.
(Missing 1754-9.)
Volume 10. August 1760–August 1765.
Volume 11. November 1765–November 1775.
Volume 12. November 1775–November 1792.
(Missing 1780–90.)
Volume 13. November 1792–November 1810.
Volume 14. November 1810–November 1827.
(Missing 1812–9.)
Volume 15. November 1827–November 1834.
Volume 16. November 1834–November 1840.

Volume 17. November 1840–November 1844.
Volume 18. November 1844–November 1851.
Volume 19. November 1851–November 1859.
(Missing 1860–6.)
Volume 20. November 1867–November 1878.
Volume 21. November 1878–November 1881.

The Town House also has RGC College Accounts between 1880–86 in the series DD61/A/3/1 to DD61/A/3/6.

Other Accounting records held by the Town House of interest include –
RGH Cash Book 1810–20.
RGH Abstract of Income and Expenditure 1813–51. (DD61/A/6/)
RGC Abstract of Accounts 1885–1900. (14 volumes).
Book of Payments to Out-resident Boys 1876–86. (DD61/A/3/6)

Periodic inventories of Title Deeds and other significant documentation were taken. The most important for RGH was in 1823* and for RGC in 1883*. A 'Catalogue of the Coins and Medals belonging to Robert Gordon's College in Aberdeen'* was compiled in 1893 (Aberdeen).

The very important RGH Register of Admissions and Departures vol. 1 (1750–1854)* and vol. 2 (1854–84)* is the starting point for all research into the pupils attending the Hospital, and their backgrounds, although information about their subsequent careers is unfortunately very sketchy.

In terms of Correspondence, the ten volumes of RGH Despatched Letter Books (OTH: DD61/L/2) are helpful. They cover the following periods: vol. 1 November 1834–January 1846; vol. 2 January 1846–March 1850; vol. 3 March 1850–March 1857; vol. 4 March 1857–July 1861; vol. 5 July 1861–December 1864; vol. 6 December 1864–November 1868; vol. 7 November 1868–September 1872; vol. 8 October 1872–July 1876; vol. 9 July 1876–November 1879; vol. 10 December 1879–December 1881.

For RGH Correspondence Received, vol. 11 (November 1879–July 1881: OTH – DD61/L/1) is most interesting.

For RGC Correspondence the Clerk's Despatched Letters (vol. 2 1887–8; vol. 3 1888–9 and vol. 4 1889–90, are worth consulting (OTH: DD61/L/7), as are the Scotch [sic] Education Department Correspondence from 1890–1893 inclusive (OTH: DD61/L/10). The volumes of the RGC Principal's Letters concentrate on the Technical College but vol. 17 (April–August 1919) throws some light on the Stewart/Morrison issue. (OTH: DD61/L/12)

Apprentices and apprenticeships can be followed in RGH Register of Indentures 1833–76 (TH: DD61/M/1/1), RGH Answers to Queries vol. 1 1843–6 (OTH: DD61/L/3) and RGH Enactment Book 1863–79 (OTH: DD61/M/1/3)

Discipline issues are illuminated in the fascinating 'Black Books for Weekly Reports'* for March 1851–September 1853 and January 1856–February 1858.

The Collyhill debates can be better understood (at least from the Collyhill side) by reference to RGH Sederunt Book no. 2 of Simpson of Collyhill 1871–85. (TH)

Government Commissions are a useful source of information on the hospitals in general and RGH in particular. The Argyll Commission (Scotland) Third Report (1868) and the Colebrooke Commission into Endowed Schools and Hospitals (Scotland) its First Report (1873), Second Report (1874), Third Report (1875) and Appendix to the Third Report, 2 vols. (1875), have a wealth of material, while also important are the Moncrieff Commission on Endowed Institutions in Scotland, its First Report (1880), Second Report (1881), Third Report (1881), Special Report (1881) and the Balfour Commission especially its Third Report (1885). See also the Third Report of the Parker Committee 'appointed to inquire into certain queries relating to Education in Scotland'. (1888)

Local inquiries also provide background material. Most important in that regard was that on the 'Hospital system and the Industrial Training of Youth' following evidence given after queries issued by a Committee of the Boys' and Girls' Hospital', Aberdeen. (Aberdeen 1854)

Comparisons can be drawn between the unsuccessful Provisional Order of 1878 (TH: PLP/L2B/3) and the successful Provisional Order of 1881 (TH: PLP/L2B/4).

Some material bears specific scrutiny including –

August 1840 – Memorial for Resident Teachers.*

1841 – Melvin v. Rose Affair.*

September 1871 – Reply to Memorial and Queries for the Governors.*

In the modern period the Headmaster's Log* completed daily without interruption between 1920 and 1969 is extremely important.

RGH appeared periodically in local newspapers – the *Aberdeen Journal* from 1748 onwards, the *Aberdeen Chronicle* between 1806–32, the *Aberdeen Herald* between 1832 and 1876, and the *Aberdeen Free Press* from 1869 forward. Fortunately RGC collected newscuttings, which were made into chronological volumes. Strangely, those before 1928 can be found in OTH (DD61/N/1). Vol. 1 (1881–6); vol. 2 (1886–1901); vol. 3 (1901–06); vol. 4 (1906–1910); vol. 5 (1910–3); vol. 6 (1913–21) and vol. 7 (1921–8). Two unnumbered volumes deal with the Technical College (1906–08 and 1912–20). (OTH: DD61/N/2). The material since 1928 can be found in the College Archives, beginning chronologically but becoming more thematic in recent years.

Aberdeen has a wealth of primary sources in the Town House covering Robert Gordon's period, viz. the late 17th and early 18th centuries. Of particular use were:

Council Registers especially vol. 57 (August 1682–December 1704); vol. 58 (January 1705–September 1721); vol. 59 (September 1721–September 1728) and vol. 60 (September 1728–September 1741).

Treasurers' Accounts vol. 2 (1659–1700); vol. 3 (1700–25) and vol. 4 (1725–50).

Burgh Court Registers of Deeds vol. 13 (1689–1703), vol. 14 (1704–10), vol. 15 (1711–15), vol. 16 (1715–20), vol. 17 (1721–24), vol. 18 (1725–29) and vol. 19 (1730–35).

Shore Work Accounts volumes for 1656–1700 and 1700–1770.

Burgess Admissions Register of October 1632–June 1694.

Books of Propinquity vol. I (1637–1705) with Index, vol. II (1706–32) and vol. III (1733–65).

Kirk and Bridgework Accounts vol. 4 (1725–50).

Burgh Register of Sasines volumes 52, 53, 54, 55, 57 and 58, with Index books 1573–1694 and 1694–1791.

Margaret R. Mackenzie: Calendar of Letters of the Burgh of Aberdeen vols. 1–4 and vols. 7–14 (Aberdeen 1918).

List of Pollable Persons in Aberdeenshire for 1696 (Aberdeen 1844).

Valuation of the Burgh of Aberdeen 1712.

St Nicholas Kirk Session Minutes especially vol. 3, vols. 19–25 and 29–30.

Parcel L/N/1–L/N/15 (17 February–10 October 1747) which includes papers relating to the attempted recovery of the costs of repair of RGH after the events of 1745–6.

Other primary sources used were:

Services of Heirs in Scotland 1545–1799.

Old Parish Register for Aberdeen for Births/Christenings 1553–1854 (168/OA).

Marriage Contract between Arthur Gordon and Isobell Menzies (1663).*

Testament Testamentar of Arthur Gordon (1680).*

Acta Vice Prasidialia especially 300.5/129a; 300.5/130; 300.60/5; 300.1/84; 300.1/88; 300.1/90 in the Gdansk (Danzig) State Archives.

Manuscripts AU MS Bible, and Cato and Boethius (part of Robert Gordon's Library) in the Aberdeen University Special Libraries' Collection. (M387/14/3/4/1).

Committee of the Council of the City of Aberdeen on the Town's Public Schools: Interim Report. (Aberdeen 1834).

Report on the Grammar School and other educational institutions under the patronage of the Town Council of Aberdeen. (Aberdeen 1854).

Aberdeen Educational Trust Scheme of Administration 17 November 1888*. (Aberdeen 1889).

Robert Gordon's Technical College and Aberdeen Endowments Trust Order Confirmation Act 1909* (Aberdeen 1910).

B. EARLY PRINTED SOURCES (LISTED BY CHRONOLOGY)

Lithgow, William: *The Totall Discoveries of the Rare Adventures and Painefull Perigrinations* (original 1632; Glasgow 1906).

Skene, Alexander (under the pseudonym Philopoliteius): *Memorialls for the Government of the Royal Burghs in Scotland . . . as also, A Survey of the City of Aberdeen* (Aberdeen 1685).

Orem, William: *Old Aberdeen* (London 1782).

Douglas, Francis: *A General Description of the East Coast of Scotland from Edinburgh to Cullen.* Letter XV pp. 119–126. (Paisley 1782).

Thom, Walter: *The History of Aberdeen (containing an account of the Rise, Progress and Extension of the City).* 2 vols. (Aberdeen 1811).

Adam, William: *Virtuvius Scoticus: being a collection of plans, elevations and sections of public buildings, noblemen's and gentlemen's houses in Scotland.* (Edinburgh 1812).

Kennedy, William: *Annals of Aberdeen from the Reign of King William the Lion to the end of the year 1818, with an account of the City, Cathedral and University of Old Aberdeen.* 2 vols. (London 1818).

Wilson, Robert: *An Historical Account and Delineation of Aberdeen.* (Aberdeen 1822).

Orem, William: *A Description of the Chanonry, Cathedral and King's College of Old Aberdeen in the years 1724–5.* (Aberdeen 1830).

Simpson, Alexander (of Collyhill): *Additional Endowment to Robert Gordon's Hospital in Aberdeen.* (Aberdeen 1836).

Smith, Lewis (ed.): *Smith's Pocket Guide to the City of Aberdeen and its Environs.* (Aberdeen 1836).

Robertson, Joseph: *The Book of Bon-Accord: or a Guide to the City of Aberdeen.* (Aberdeen 1839).

Bruce, James: *Lives of Eminent Men of Aberdeen.* (pp. 289–302 on 'Robert Gordon') (Aberdeen 1841).

Man, James (ed.).: *James Gordon's History of Scots Affairs 1637–41.* vol. I (Aberdeen 1841).

Wilson, James H.: *The Bon-Accord Repository of Local Institutions.* (Aberdeen 1842).

Mortifications under the charge of the Provost, Magistrates and Town Council of Aberdeen. (Aberdeen 1849).

Wilson, David: *Methodism in Scotland.* (Aberdeen 1850).

Chalmers, Robert (ed.): *A Biographical Dictionary of Eminent Scotsmen* vol. II pp. 475–9 on 'Robert Gordon'. (Glasgow 1855).

Everett, M. A. (ed.): *Calendar of State Papers. Domestic Series of Reign of James I 1619–23.* (London 1858).

Robertson, Joseph (ed.): *Passages from the Diary of Patrick Gordon of Auchleuchries in the years 1635–1699.* (orig. 1859, New York 1968).

Charteris, (Rev.) A. H.: *Life of the Rev. James Robertson D.D.* (Edinburgh 1863).

Cruickshank, Robert: *Reminiscences ; or Strong Recollections of Gordon's Hospital Forty Years Ago.* [Paper read to the Social Meeting in Robert Gordon's Hospital on 23 January 1866]. (Aberdeen 1866).

Rettie, James R.: *Aberdeen Fifty Years Ago.* (Aberdeen 1868).

Laurie, Simon S.: *Report on the Hospitals under the administration of the Merchant Company, Edinburgh, and general remarks on Hospital Training.* (Edinburgh 1868).

Walker, Alexander (ed.): *Selected Writings of John Ramsay* [with pp. 182–201 on 'Gordon's Hospital']. (Aberdeen 1871).

Walker, Alexander: *Robert Gordon 1665–1731 and his Hospital 1750–1876.* (printed privately, Aberdeen 1876).

Smith, Alexander: *The History and Antiquities of New and Old Aberdeen.* (Aberdeen 1882).

Gordon, M. M.: *John Gordon of Pitlurg and Parkhill or Memories of a Standard-Bearer.* (London 1885).

Walker, Alexander: *Robert Gordon, His Hospital and His College.* (Aberdeen 1886).

Anderson, Peter John (ed.): *Fasti Academiae Mariscallanae Aberdonensis.* Vol. I Endowments. (Aberdeen 1889).

Robbie, William: *Aberdeen. Its Traditions and History.* (Aberdeen 1893).

Temple, Rev. William: *The Thanage of Fermartyn* (Aberdeen 1894).

Anderson, Robert: *Some Reminiscences of Robert Gordon's Hospital.* (privately published, Aberdeen 1894).

Allardyce, James (ed.): *Historical Papers relating to the Jacobite period, 1699–1750.* vol. I (Aberdeen 1895).

Anderson, Robert: *Auld Days in 'The Auld Hoose'. Discipline in Robert Gordon's Hospital.* (privately published, Aberdeen 1896).

Anderson, Robert: *The History of Robert Gordon's Hospital, Aberdeen 1729–1881.* (Aberdeen 1896).

Munro, Alexander M.: *Memorials of the Aldermen, Provosts and Lord Provosts of Aberdeen, 1272–1893.* (Aberdeen 1897).

Bulloch, John Malcolm: *The House of Gordon.* vol. II (Aberdeen 1897).

Anderson, Peter John (ed.): *Fasti Academiae Mariscallanae Aberdonensis.* vol. II Officers, Graduates and Alumni. (Aberdeen 1898).

Walker, Alexander: *Mrs Emslie and her Orphan Hospital.* (Aberdeen 1898).

Macleod, John: *Commissariat Record of Aberdeen Register of Testaments 1715–1800.* (Edinburgh 1899).

Anderson, Peter John: *Roll of Alumni at University and King's College 1596–1860.* (Aberdeen 1900).

Ogilvie, Joseph: *John Ogilvie. Lexicographer. LL.D.* (Aberdeen 1902).

Terry, Charles S. (ed.): *The Albemarle Papers vol. 1 and 2 being the correspondence of William Anne, 2nd Earl of Albemarle, Commander-in-Chief in Scotland 1746–7.* (Aberdeen 1902 ed.)

Fischer, T. A.: *The Scots in Germany. Being a Contribution towards the History of the Scot Abroad.* (Edinburgh 1902).

Fischer, T. A.: *The Scots in Eastern and Western Prussia.* (Edinburgh 1903).

Bain, Alexander: *Autobiography* (1904; rev. ed. Kila, Montana 2004).

Fraser, G. M.: *Historical Aberdeen.* (Aberdeen 1905).

Fischer, T. A.: *The Scots in Sweden* (Edinburgh 1907).

Munro, Alexander M.: *Records of Old Aberdeen* vol. II and III (Aberdeen 1909).

Strong, John: *A History of Secondary Education in Scotland. An Account of Scottish Secondary Education from Early Times to the Education Act of 1908.* (Oxford 1909).

Milne, John: *Topographical, Antiquarian and Historical Papers on the City of Aberdeen.* (Aberdeen 1911).

Milne, John: *Celtic Place Names in Aberdeenshire.* (Aberdeen 1912).

Fraser, G. M.: *Aberdeen Mechanics' Institute. A Record of Civic and Educational Progress.* (Aberdeen 1912).

Steuart, A. Francis (ed.): *Papers Relating to the Scots in Poland 1576–1793.* (Edinburgh 1915).

C. SECONDARY WORKS (LISTED ALPHABETICALLY)

Anderson, R. D.: *Education and Opportunity in Victorian Scoyland, Schools and Universities* (Oxford 1983).

Anderson, R. D.: *Education and the Scottish People 1750–1918.* (Oxford 1995).

Andrew, I. Graham: *Unpublished Autobiography.* (n.d.)

Barton, George E. C.: *Sillerton 1937–1987.* (Aberdeen 1987).

Bicentenary Record of Robert Gordon's Hospital in Aberdeen 1729–1929. (Aberdeen 1929).

Bridges, Roy: *People and Places in Newmachar. Past and Present.* (Newmachar 2001).

Carter, Jennifer J. and McLaren, Colin A.: *Crown and Gown 1495–1995.* (Aberdeen 1994).

Cieslak, Edmund and Biernat, Czeslaw: *History of Gdansk* (Gdansk 1995).

Clark, Victoria E.: *The Port of Aberdeen. A History of its Trade and Shipping from 12th Century to Present Day.* (Aberdeen 1921).

Clarke, Peter: *RGIT past, present and future 1903–1978. 75th Anniversary Souvenir Brochure.* (Aberdeen 1978).

Colvin, Howard: *A Biographical Dictionary of British Architects.* (London 1978 ed.).

Davies, Norman: *God's Playground vol. 1. The Origins to 1795. A History of Poland.* (Oxford 2005 rev. ed.).

Dennison, E. Patricia, Ditchburn, David and Lynch, Michael: *Aberdeen Before 1800. A New History.* (East Linton 2002).

Devine, T. M.: *The Scottish Nation 1700–2000.* (London 1999).

Dingwall, Helen M.: *Late Seventeenth Century Edinburgh: a demographic study.* (Aldershot 1994).

Dobson, David: *Scots in Poland, Russia and the Baltic States 1550–1850.* (Baltimore 2000).

Donnelly, Tom: *The Aberdeen Granite Industry.* (Aberdeen 1994).

Duffy, Christopher: *The 'Forty Five.* (London 2003).

Duffy, Eamon: *Saints and Sinners. A History of the Popes* (3rd ed. Yale 2006).

Ellington, Henry: *The Robert Gordon University. A History.* (Aberdeen 2002).

Fleming, John: *Robert Adam and his Circle in Edinburgh and Rome.* (London 1978 repr. ed.).

Fountaine, Laurence: *History of Pedlars in Europe.* (Durham, N.C. 1996).

Friedrich, Karin: *The Other Prussia. Royal Prussia, Poland and Liberty 1569–1772* (Cambridge 2000).

Frost, Robert I.: *The Northern Wars. War, State and Society in Northeastern Europe 1558–1721.* (Harlow, Essex 2000).

Fry, Michael: *The Union. England, Scotland and the Treaty of Union.* (Edinburgh 2006).

Gifford, John: *William Adam 1689–1748. A Life and Times of Scotland's Universal Architect.* (Edinburgh 1989).

Gordon, Edward (of Cairnfield): *History of the House of Gordon.* (Aberdeen 1949).

Gordon, G. and Dick, B. (ed.): *Scottish Urban History.* (Aberdeen 1983).

Graham, Eric J.: *A Maritime History of Scotland 1650–1790.* (East Linton 2002).

Grosjean, Alexia: *An Unofficial Alliance: Scotland and Sweden 1569-1654* (Leiden 2003)

Grosjean, Alexia and Murdoch, Steve (eds.): *Scottish Communities Abroad in the Early Modern Period.* (Leiden 2005).

Grosjean, Alexia and Murdoch, Steve: *Scotland, Scandinavia and Northern Europe Biographical Database* (SSNE) at www.st-andrews.ac.uk/history/ssne

Highet, John: *A School of One's Choice. A Sociological Study of the Fee-Paying Schools of Scotland* (London 1969).

Houston, R. A.: *Scottish Literacy and Scottish Identity.* (Cambridge 1985).

Howie, Les: *George Watson's College. An Illustrated History* (Edinburgh 2006).

Kay, Billy: *The Scottish World. A Journey into the Scottish Diaspora.* (Edinburgh 2006).

Keith, Alexander: *A Thousand Years of Aberdeen.* (Aberdeen 1972).

Keith, Alexander: *Eminent Victorians* (Aberdeen 1984).

Kropotkin, Pytor: *Fields, Factories and Workshops, or Industry Combined with Agriculture and Brain Work with Manual Work.* (London 1898).

Lockhart, Brian R. W.: *Jinglin' Geordie's Legacy. A History of George Heriot's Hospital and School.* (East Linton 2003).

Lynch, Michael: *The Early Modern Town in Scotland.* (London 1987).

Macaulay, James: *The Gothic Revival 1745–1845.* (Glasgow 1975).

Mackenzie, Hugh (ed.): *The Third Statistical Account of Scotland.* (Aberdeen 1953).

McLaren, Colin A.: *Aberdeen Students 1600–1860.* (Aberdeen 2005).

Mann, Alastair J.: *The Scottish Book Trade 1500–1720. Print Commerce and Print Control in Early Modern Scotland.* (East Linton 2000).

Marren, Peter: *Grampian Battlefields. The Historic Battles of North East Scotland from 84–1745.* (Edinburgh 1990).

Meldrum, Edward: *Aberdeen of Old.* (Aberdeen 1986).

Miller, David: *Archibald Simpson. Architect. His Life and Times 1790-1847* (Kinloss 2007).

Miller, James: *Swords for Hire. The Scottish Mercenary* (Edinburgh 2007).

Milne, J. C.: *Chronicle of the Aberdeen Demonstration School.* (Aberdeen 1946).

Morgan, Diane: *Lost Aberdeen. Aberdeen's Lost Architectural Heritage* (Edinburgh 2004).

Murdoch, Steve (ed.): *Scotland and the Thirty Years' War 1618–1648.* (Leiden 2001).

Murdoch, Steve: *Network North: Scottish Kin, Commercial and Covert Associations in Northern Europe 1603–1746.* (Leiden 2006).

Officer, Lawrence H.: *Purchasing Power of British Pounds from 1264 to 2006* (MeasuringWorth.com 2007).

Peters, K. J. : *Burgess of Guild* (Aberdeen 1982).

Pinkerton, John Macpherson (ed.): *The Minute Book of the Faculty of Advocates vol. 1 1661–1712.* (Edinburgh 1976 ed.).

Potter, Harry: *Bloodfeud. The Stewarts and Gordons at War in the age of Mary Queen of Scots.* (Stroud, Gloucs. 2002).

RCAHMS: *Tolbooths and Town Houses. Civic Architecture in Scotland to 1833* (London 1996).

Rettie, James: *Aberdeen One Hundred and Fifty Years Ago.* (Wakefield 1972). [originally published in Aberdeen in 1868 as '*Aberdeen Fifty Years Ago*'.]

Roberts, John L.: *Lost Kingdoms. Celtic Scotland and the Middle Ages.* (Edinburgh 1997).

Scott, Patrick W.: *The History of Strathbogie.* (Aberdeen 1997).

Seliga, S. and Koczy, L.: *Scotland and Poland. A Chapter of Forgotten History* (Dundee 1969).

Shewan, Alexander: *The Record of the Gym (Chanonry House School) Old Aberdeen.* (Aberdeen 1923).

Simpson, Dr H. F. Morland: *Bon Record. Records and Reminiscences of Aberdeen Grammar School from the Earliest Times by Many Writers.* (Aberdeen 1906).

Smout, T. C.: *Scottish Trade on the Eve of the Union.* (Edinburgh 1963).

Smout, T. C. (ed.): *Scotland and Europe 1200-1850* (Edinburgh 1986)

Stevenson, David: *King's College, Aberdeen 1560–1641. From Protestant Reformation to Covenanting Revolution.* (Aberdeen 1990).

Stone, Jeffrey C.: *The Pont Manuscript Maps of Scotland. Sixteenth century origins of a Blaeu Atlas.* (Tring, Hants 1989).

Strathdee, R. B.: *Sit Bona Librorum Copia.* (privately published, Aberdeen 1968).

Strathdee, R. B.: *Robert Gordon.* (privately published, Aberdeen 1969).

Strathdee, R. B.: *In A Monastery Garden.* (privately published, Aberdeen 1970).

Strathdee, R. B.: *Oh, The Brave Music of a Distant Drum.* (privately published, Aberdeen 1970).

Strathdee, R. B.: *Scientia et Opera.* (privately published, Aberdeen 1971).

Strathdee, R. B.: *A Pride of Masters.* (privately published, Aberdeen 1972).

Strathdee, R. B.: *A Gordonian Looks at The School Hill.* (privately published, Aberdeen 1973).

Tielhof, Maria van: *The 'Mother of All Trades': The Baltic Grain Trade in Amsterdam from the Late Sixteenth to the Early Nineteenth Century.* (Leiden 2002).

Trail, Katherine E.: *Story of Old Aberdeen.* (Aberdeen 1929).

Turner, John R.: *Scotland's North Sea Gateway. Aberdeen Harbour 1136–1986.* (Aberdeen 1986).

Watt, Douglas: *The Price of Scotland. Darien, Union and the Wealth of Nations* (King's Lynn 2007).

Waugh, Hector (ed.): *George Watson's College: History and Record 1724–1970.* (Edinburgh 1970).

W.B. (Borowny): *Scots in Old Poland* (Edinburgh 1941).

Webster, Jack: *The Auld Hoose. The Story of Robert Gordon's College.* (Edinburgh 2005).

Whatley, Christopher A.: *The Scots and the Union.* (Edinburgh 2006).

Wills, R.: *The Jacobites and Russia 1715–1750* (East Linton 2002).

Willson, D. H.: *King James VI and I.* (London 1958).

Wyness, Fenton: *City by the gray North Sea. Aberdeen.* (Aberdeen 1965).

D. ARTICLES

Allan, George: 'Century of fundamental and cataclysmic change' in *Leopard Magazine* (August 2000) no. 266 p. 34.

Anderson, Peter John: 'Marischal College v. Gordon's College' in *Scottish Notes and Queries* (April 1892) vol. V.

Anderson, Robert: 'Dr. James Robertson. Headmaster of Robert Gordon's Hospital 1829–32' in *Gordonian* (December 1912) vol. IV no. 2 pp. 27–30.

Anderson, Robert: 'Rev. W.D. Strahan. Headmaster of Robert Gordon's Hospital 1849–72' in *Gordonian* (December 1913) vol. V no. 2 pp. 34–35.

Anderson, Robert: 'Discipline in Gordon's Hospital' in *Gordonian* (August 1916) no. 3 Part I pp. 5–7 and December 1916 (December 1916) no, 4 Part II pp. 5–8.

Anderson, Robert: 'Robert Gordon and his Hospital' in *Gordonian* (April 1923) vol. I no. 5 pp. 128–131.

Bieganska, Anna: 'Scottish Merchants and Traders in Seventeenth and Eighteenth Century Warsaw' in *Scottish Slavonic Review* (Autumn 1985) no. 5 pp. 19–34.

Bieganska, Anna: 'Andrew Davidson (1591–1660) and his Descendants in Poland' in *Scottish Slavonic Review* (Spring 1988) no. 10 pp. 7–18.

Bieganska, Anna: 'In Search of Tolerance. Scottish Catholics and Presbyterians in Poland' in *Scottish Slavonic Review* (Autumn 1991) no. 17 pp. 37–59.

Bieganska, Anna: 'Scottish Immigrants in Poland' in *Scottish Slavonic Review* (Autumn 1991) no. 19.

Bieganska, Anna: 'The Learned Scots in Poland from mid-sixteenth century to close of 18th century' in *Canadian Slavonic Papers,* No. 43, March 2001.

Bieganska, Anna: 'Subscribers from Poland to the Restoration of Marischal College in the Late Seventeenth Century' in Dukes, Paul (ed.): *The Universities of Aberdeen and Europe. The First Three Centuries.* (Aberdeen 1995) pp. 143–165.

Bisset, John C. S.: 'Twenty One years of FP Cricket' in *Gordonian* (June 1946) vol. IX no. 3 pp. 99–100.

Blanchard, Ian, Gemmill, Elizabeth, Mayhew, Nicholas and Whyte, Ian D.: 'The Economy: Town and Country in Aberdeen before 1800' in Dennison, E. Patricia et al.: (2002) *op. cit.*

Bogucka, Maria: 'Scots in Gdansk (Danzig) in the Seventeenth Century' in Macinnes, A.I, Riis, T. and Pedersen, F.G.: *Ships, Guns and Bibles in the North Sea and the Baltic States c.1350–c.1700* (East Linton 2000) pp. 39–46.

Brown, James J.: 'Merchant Princes and Mercantile Interests in Early Seventeenth Century Scotland' in Lynch (1987) *op. cit.* pp. 125–146.

Bulloch, John Malcolm: 'The Gordons in Poland' in *Scottish Notes and Queries* (August 1898) vol. XII pp. 23–25.

Bulloch, John Malcolm: 'How the Scots Traded in the Baltic' in *Aberdeen Free Press* 2 June 1899.

Bulloch, John Malcolm: 'The Grave Gordons' in *The Bicentenary Record of Robert Gordon's Hospital 1729–1929.* (Aberdeen 1929).

Burnett, George A.: 'The Former Pupils' Association. Its Genesis and Growth' in *Gordonian* (April 1923) vol. I no. 5 pp. 156–159.

Catterall, Douglas: 'At Home Abroad: Ethnicity and Enclave in the World of Scots Traders in Northern Europe c. 1600–c. 1800' in *Journal of Early Modern History* (2004) vol. 8 nos 3 and 4 pp. 319–357.

Catto, (Sir) Graeme: 'The Lockhart Years' in *Gordonian* (2004) vol. XI no. 6 pp. 9–11.

Clark, Alexander: 'The Bowling Green at Gordon's Hospital' in *Gordonian* (May 1929) vol. III no. 5 p. 248.

C[lerk], A[lexander] (1872–1881): 'Dr. Alexander Gerard' in *Gordonian* (December 1925) vol. II no. 4 pp. 126–127.

Collier, D. E.: 'Fortune Made in Danzig Founded a Great School' in *Press and Journal* 28 June 1950.

Des Brisay, Gordon: 'The civill wars did overrun all. Aberdeen 1630–90' in Dennison, E. Patricia et al. (2002) *op. cit.*

Des Brisay, Gordon and Ewen, Elizabeth with Diack, H. Lesley: 'Life in the Two Towns' in *ibid.*

Devine, T. M.: 'The merchant class of the larger Scottish towns in the Seventeenth and early Eighteenth Centuries' in Gordon and Dick (ed.): (1983) *op. cit.*

Dictionary of National Biography. (Oxford 2004 ed.) especially:
vol. I pp. 213–214 James Macaulay on William Adam;
vol. 8 pp. 880–883 David M. Walker on William Burn ;
vol. 11 pp. 284–285 Matthew Craske and Malcolm Baker on John Cheere;
vol. 22 Jeffrey C. Stone on Parson James Gordon of Rothiemay pp. 915–917, Shona Macleod Vance on Robert Gordon of Straloch pp. 954–955 and Alexander Du Toit on Robert Gordon (Founder) pp. 955–956.
vol. 31 Howard Ellis on Sir Arthur Keith pp. 57–59.
vol. 39 B. W. Clapp on John Murray pp. 961–962;
vol. 47 p. 238 Lionel Alexander Ritchie on James Robertson and pp. 930–933 Malcolm Baker on Louis Francois Roubiliac.

Ditchburn, David: 'Educating the Elite. Aberdeen and Its Universities' in Dennison, E. Patricia et al. (2002) *op. cit.*

E[lder], J. R.: 'Robert Gordon: Our Founder' in *Gordonian* (October 1908) vol. I no. 2 pp. 25–26.

E[lder], J. E.: 'Robert Gordon's Hospital' in *Gordonian* (November 1908) vol.I no. 3 pp. 46–47; *Gordonian* (December 1908) vol. I no. 4 pp. 71–73; *Gordonian* (February 1909) vol. I no. 6 pp. 125–126.

E[lder], J. R.: 'The Black Books of Robert Gordon's Hospital' in *Gordonian* (March 1909) vol. I no. 7 pp. 148–150.

E[lder], J. R.: 'The Visiting Books of Gordon's Hospital' in *Gordonian* (April 1909) vol. I no. 8 pp. 173–175; *Gordonian* (May 1909) vol. I no. 9 pp. 198–199; *Gordonian* (June 1909) vol. I no. 10 pp. 224–225; *Gordonian* (December 1909) vol. II no. 2 pp. 277–278.

E[lder], J. R.: 'The Sederunt Book of Robert Gordon's Hospital, No. I' in *Gordonian* (June 1910) vol. II no. 4 pp. 350–351.

Esdaile, Arundell: 'The Statue of Robert Gordon and its Sculptor' in *Gordonian* (December 1930) vol. IV no. 2 pp. 66–67.

Esslemont, Alex. L.: 'Swimming in Aberdeen' in *Gordonian* (May 1929) vol. III no. 5 pp. 253–255.

Ewen, Rev. John: 'Gordon's Hospital Forty-Five Years Ago' in *Gordonian* (March 1913) vol. IV no. 3 pp. 59–62.

Faber, J. A.: 'Structural changes in the European economy during the eighteenth century as reflected in the Baltic trade' in Heeres, W. G. et al.: *From Dunkirk to Danzig. Shipping and Trade in the North Sea and Baltic, 1350–1850* (Hilversum 1988).

Fairley, T. S.: 'Sport and Athletics in Robert Gordon's College' in *Gordonian* (May 1929) vol. III no. 5 pp. 271–272.

Fraser, Alex: 'The Portraits in the College Hall' in *Gordonian* (December 1930) vol. IV no. 2 pp. 68–69.

Fraser, G. M.: 'Archibald Simpson, Architect and his Times. A Study in the Making of Aberdeen' in *Aberdeen Weekly Journal,* 14 June 1918.

Fraser, G. M.: 'The Site of Robert Gordon's College' in *Gordonian* (April 1923) vol. I no. 5 pp. 121–127.

Fraser, W. Hamish: 'Politics before 1918' in Dennison, E. Patricia et al. (2000) *op. cit.*

Frost, Robert I.: 'Scottish Soldiers, Poland-Lithuania and the Thirty Years' War' in Murdoch, Steve (ed.) (2001) *op. cit.* pp. 191–213.

Glennie, Charles E.: 'Rambling Recollections' in *Gordonian* (December 1927) vol. III no. 2 pp. 68–71.

Gordon, Anne: 'Death and Associated Customs' in John Beech, Owen Hand, Mark Mulhearn and Jeremy Weston (eds.): *The Individual and Community Life* (Edinburgh 2005) pp. 104 ff.

Gordon, Edward (of Cairnfield): 'Ancestry of Robert Gordon' in *Gordonian* (June 1950) vol. I no. 2 pp. 101–104.

Gordon, Maria M. Ogilvie: 'Some Educational Problems in Aberdeen' in *Aberdeen Journal,* 21 December 1908.

Grant, Ruth: 'The Brig o' Dee Affair, the Sixth Earl of Huntly and the Politics of the Counter-Reformation' in Goodare, Julian and Lynch, Michael (ed.): *The Reign of James VI* (East Linton 2000) pp. 93–109.

Harvey, George R.: '1900–1905' in *Gordonian* (April 1923) vol. I no. 5 pp. 141–143.

Horsbroch, Dauvit: 'Wish You were here? Scottish Reactions to 'Postcards' Home from the 'German Warres' in Murdoch, Steve (ed.): (2001) *op. cit.* pp. 245–267.

Humphries, Walter R.: 'Gordon of Straloch' I in *Gordonian* (December 1932) vol. IV no. 6 pp. 262–265; II in *Gordonian* (June 1933) vol. V no. I pp. 10–13.

Humphries, Walter R.: 'Gordon of Pitlurg' in *Gordonian* (December 1933) vol. V no. 2 pp. 67–69.

Humphries, Walter R.: 'An Eighteenth Century Doctor' in *Gordonian* (December 1935) vol. V no. 6 p. 241.

Hutchieson, A. R.: 'Bequest to the Royal Scottish Musuem – Astrolabe of Robert Gordon of Straloch' in *Mariners' Mirror* (1948) no. 34. pp. 122–3.

Keith, Alexander: 'Eminent Aberdonians No. 13. Robert Gordon, Merchant in Danzig and Founder of Gordon's College' in *Aberdeen Chamber of Commerce Journal* (Winter 1959–60) vol. 41 no. 2 pp. 80–85.

Kowalski, Waldemar: 'The Placement of Urbanised Scots in the Polish Crown during the 16th and 17th centuries' in Grosjean, Alexia and Murdoch, Steve (2005) *op. cit.*

Lawrence, C. M.: '"Sillerton" and Its Surroundings' in *Gordonian* (April 1910) vol. II no. 3 pp. 311–316.

Lawrence, C. M.: 'Sillerton from Inside' in *Gordonian* (June 1910) vol. II no. 4 pp. 355–360.

Lee, Clive H.: 'Social Welfare. Poverty and Health' in Dennison, E. Patricia et al. (2000) *op. cit.*

Lee, Clive H.: 'Local Government' in Denison, E. Patricia et al. (2000) *op. cit.*

Levack, J. R.: 'Reminiscences of Gordon's College in the Eighties' in *Gordonian* (June 1926) vol. II no. 5 pp. 175–176.

Lockhart, Brian R. W.: 'Vision for the Future' in *Leopard Magazine* (December 2000) no. 270 p. 20.

Lyell, John L. (1842–6) in *Gordonian* (December 1911) vol. III no. 2 p. 45.

Lynch, Michael and Dingwall, Helen M.: 'Elite Society in Town and Country' in Dennison, E. Patricia et al.:(2002) *op. cit.*

Macaulay, James: 'The Growth of a New Town' in *ibid.*

MacDonald, William R.: 'Book Auctions and Book Values in the Aberdeen Area 1749–1800' in *Aberdeen University Review* (1967) no. XLII pp. 114-132.

Mackintosh, John: 'Swimming in Gordon's' in *Gordonian* (May 1929) vol. III no. 5 p.257.

Mackintosh, John: 'Fort Cumberland' in *Gordonian* (December 1945) vol. IX no. 2 pp. 59–60.

Mackintosh, John: 'A School of the North East' in *Scottish Field* (April 1962) pp. 70–75.

Marshall, John: 'Robert Gordon and his College' in *The Scots Magazine* (August 1968) vol. 89 no. 5 pp. 423–432.

Marshall, John: 'The Robert Gordon Story' in *Press and Journal*, 28 September 1968.

Marshall, John: 'Robert Gordon of Straloch – Scottish cartographer' (Robert Gordon Story part I) in *Leopard Magazine* (September 1980) pp. 25–27.

Marshall, John: 'Robert Gordon, Merchant in Danzig' (Robert Gordon Story part II) in *Leopard Magazine* (October 1980) pp. 28–30.

Marshall, John: 'Robert Gordon's Hospital 1750–1881' (Robert Gordon Story part III) in *Leopard Magazine* (November 1980) pp. 28–29.

Marshall, John: 'Robert Gordon's College and Robert Gordon's Technical College 1881–1950' (Robert Gordon Story part IV) in *Leopard Magazine* (December 1980/January 1981) pp. 19–21.

Marshall, John: 'Robert Gordon's College 1950–80' (Robert Gordon Story part V) in *Leopard Magazine* (February 1981) pp. 27–29.

Marshall, John: 'A look back at 250 years of Robert Gordon's College' in *Leopard Magazine* (May 2000) No. 262 pp. 36–37.

Marshall, John: 'The Otaki Story' in *The Pelican* (Autumn 2005) pp. 7–9.

Morrison, G. A.: 'Some Reflections on the Half-Century' in *Gordonian* (December 1932) vol. IV no. 6 pp. 260–262.

M[orrison], G. A.: 'The Principal' in *Gordonian* (June 1917) no. 5 pp. 5–6.

M[orrison], G. A. et al.: 'Principal Charles Stewart MA' in *Gordonian* (December 1938) vol. VI no. 6 pp. 253–256.

Munro, Alex M.: 'Portraits in Possession of Robert Gordon's College' in *Scottish Notes and Queries* (January 1896) vol. IX no. 8 pp. 113–115.

Murdoch, Steve: 'The French connection: Bordeaux's "Scottish" Networks in Context c.1670-1720' in Gilles Leydier: *Scotland and Europe, Scotland in Europe* (Newcastle 2007).

Murdoch, Steve: 'Scotland, Europe and the English "Missing Link"' in *History Compass* (2007) no. 5/3 pp. 890-913.

Murray, Arthur F.: 'Soccer at Gordon's College in the 'Nineties' in *Gordonian* (May 1929) vol. III no. 5 pp. 261–262.

Murray, John: 'Gordon's in the Nineties' in *Gordonian* (April 1923) vol. I no. 5 pp. 136–138.

Nicol, R. Gordon: 'Robert Gordon and Danzig' in *Gordonian* (December 1931) vol. IV no. 4 pp. 174–175.

Ogilvie, Joseph: 'Early Life of Alexander Ogilvie, Late Headmaster of Gordon's College' in *Gordonian* (March 1911) vol. II no. 7 pp. 440–443.

Pernal, Andrew B.: 'London Gazette as a primary source for the biography of General Patrick Gordon' in *Canadian Journal of History* (April 2003).

Pernal, Andrew B. and Gasse, Rosanne P.: 'The 1651 Polish subsidy to the exiled Charles II' in *Oxford Slavonic Papers* (1999) no. 32 pp. 1–50.

Purdie, Bill: 'Ralph Carr: a Newcastle merchant and the Baltic trade in the mid-18th century' in Patrick Salmon and Tony Barrow: *Britain and the Baltic. Studies in Commercial. Political and Cultural Relations 1500-2000* (Sunderland 2003) pp. 157–168.

Reid, John R.: 'Reminiscences of John R. Reid (1886–9) in *Gordonian* (December 1946) vol. IX no. 4.

Reid, Walter A.: 'Life at Gordon's Hospital' in *Gordonian* (April 1923) vol. I no. 5. pp. 132–135.

Robertson, J.: 'Alexander Skene of Newtyle' in *Scottish Notes and Queries*, 9, March 1896 pp. 158-160.

Ross, William: 'The Vocabulary of the 'Auld Hoose'' in *Gordonian* (June 1939) vol. VII no. 1 pp. 13–14.

Shirreffs, John G.: 'Men's Hockey in Aberdeen' in *Gordonian* (May 1929) vol. III no. 5. pp. 249–252.

Simpson, W. Douglas: 'Gordon's College and its Architect' in *Gordonian* (June 1928) vol. III no. 3 pp. 139–141.

Skea, William: 'Two Milestones in the History of Old Gordon's. A Rebellion and a Revolution' in *Gordonian* (December 1913) vol. V no. 2 and in *Gordonian* (March 1914) vol. V no. 3 p. 73.

Skelton, Sir John ('Shirley'): 'Review of Dr. Charteris's 'Life of Robertson'' in *Fraser's Magazine* (August 1863).

Smith, J. S.: 'The Rise and Fall of Aberdeen's Granite Industry' in *Aberdeen University Review* (Spring 1982) no. 167 pp. 163–167.

Smith, John S.: 'Robert Gordon the 'Merchant Miser' Founder of Gordon's College' in *Deeside Field* (1987) no. 19 pp. 10–12.

Smith, Peter: 'The History of Sport in Robert Gordon's College' in *Gordonian* (April 1923) vol. I no. 5 pp. 154–155.

Smith, Peter: 'Sport in the College up to 1923' in *Gordonian* (May 1929) vol. III no. 5 pp. 262–263.

Stewart, Alasdair M.: 'Aberdeen and Gdansk' in *Aberdeen University Review* (Spring 1977) no. 157 pp. 45–51.

Stewart, Charles: 'Robert Gordon's College as a Secondary School'. *Memorandum by the Headmaster* (Aberdeen 1901).

Stewart, R. R.: 'Hockey in Gordon's' in *Gordonian* (May 1929) vol. III no. 5 pp. 273–274.

Stone, Jeffrey C.: 'Robert Gordon of Straloch: cartographer or chorographer?' in *Northern Scotland* (1981) no. 4 pp. 7–22.

Strathdee, R. B.: 'Rugger in the North' in *Gordonian* (May 1929) Vol. III no. 5 pp. 237–241.

Strathdee, R. B.: 'An Athletic Cavalcade 1882–1932' in *Gordonian* (December 1932) vol. IV no. 6.

Strathdee, R. B.: 'Gordonians' Rugby Club' 1901–1914 in *Gordonian* (June 1947) vol. IX no. 5 pp. 168–170; 1919–1931 in *Gordonian* (December 1947) vol. IX no. 6 pp. 214–217; 1931–1948 in *Gordonian* (June 1948) vol. 19 no. 1 pp. 11–16.

Strathdee, R. B.: 'Prefects or Censors' in *Gordonian* (December 1948) vol. X no. 2 pp. 51–52.

Strathdee, R. B.: 'The Seals of Gordon's Hospital and College' in *Gordonian* (June 1950) vol. I no. 2 pp. 84–87 and *Gordonian* (December 1950) vol. I no. 3 pp. 180–184.

Strathdee, R. B.: 'Fort Cumberland' in *Aberdeen University Review* (Autumn 1952) vol. XXXIV no. 107 pp. 356–365.

Taylor, John M.: 'The House of Gordon' in *Gordonian* (December 1934) vol. V no. 4 p. 143 and *Gordonian* (June 1935) vol. V no. 5 pp. 190–191.

Thomson, James: 'Music in Robert Gordon's College' in *Gordonian* (May 1929) vol. III no. 5 pp. 256–257.

T.L.: '1862–1867' in *Gordonian* (June 1927) vol. III no.1 pp. 7–11.

Vance, Shona Macleod: 'Poverty and Pursuit of Learning' in *History of Universities* (2003) vol. XVIII no. 2 pp. 90–146.

Webster, C. H.: 'Cricket in Aberdeen' in *Gordonian* (May 1929) vol. III no. 5 pp. 245–248.

Welsh, David: 'Organs prior to 1820 in North-East Scotland' in *British Institute of Organ Studies Reporter* (July 2004) vol. XXVIII no. 3. pp. 14–19.

Whyte, Ian D.: 'The occupational structure of the Scottish burgh in the later 17th century' in Lynch (1987) *op. cit.* pp. 219–244.

Woodall, R. D.: 'Farming boy made good' [Peter Esslemont] in *Evening Express*, 21 June 1989.

Wyness, J. F.: 'Robert Gordon's Hospital. A Sketch of its History and Architecture' in *Gordonian* (December 1930) vol. IV no. 2 pp. 62–65.

Zirgulis, Rimantus: 'The Scottish Community in Kedainiai c. 1630–c. 1750' in Grosjean and Murdoch (2005) *op. cit.*

The following articles are unattributed (listed in chronological order):

'A Practical Science and Art School. Gordon's College, Aberdeen' in *Chambers' Journal*, 22 March 1884 pp. 183–185.

'The New Chemistry Rooms' in *Gordonian* (December 1913) vol. V no. 2.

'Omni nunc arte magistra' in *Gordonian* (March 1914) vol. V no. 3 pp. 79–80.

'The Doctor' in *Gordonian* (January 1916) no. 2 pp. 4–5.

'Thirty Years On' in *Gordonian* (June 1917) no. 5 pp. 17 ff.

'Pro Patria' in *Gordonian* (June 1920) no. 11 pp. 17–18.

'Musings of an Old Boy' [1872–81] in *Gordonian* (June 1921) vol. I no. 1 pp. 5–7.

'The College and Science' in Gordonian (December 1923) vol. I no. 6 pp. 167–169.

'Opening of the Memorial Playing Field and Pavilion' in *Gordonian* (June 1925) vol. II no. 3 pp. 78–80.

'Rise of Association Football in Aberdeen' in *Gordonian* (May 1929) vol. III no. 5 pp. 242–244.

'Who's Who in Gordonian Athletics' in *Gordonian* (May 1929) vol. III no. 5 pp. 264–267.

'Retiral of Mr. Herbert Wilson BSc' in *Gordonian* (December 1929) vol. III no. 6.

'Robert Gordon Bicentenary' in *Aberdeen Bon-Accord and Northern Pictorial,* 21 December 1929.

'The meaning of Sillerton' in *Gordonian* (June 1937) vol. VI no. 3 p. 46.

'From Robert Gordon's Library' in *Gordonian* (June 1938) vol. VI no. 5.

'Where is Sillerton' in *Gordonian* (June 1939) vol. VII no. 1. pp. 7–8.

'Principal Stewart' in *Gordonian* (June 1945) vol. IX no. 1 pp. 35–36.

'Seat of Learning in North for Two Hundred Years' in *Weekly News,* 29 June 1950.

'Great Scottish Scientists. Maria M. Ogilvie Gordon' in *Scotsman,* 11 August 2005.

E. DISSERTATIONS

Murray, David: 'Robert Gordon's Hospital and its relationship to the other Public Building of William Adam', Scott Sutherland School of Architecture, 1975.

Stone, Jeffrey C.: 'Maps of Scotland by Timothy Pont, Robert and James Gordon and Joan Blaeu. A Study in Historical Cartography', University of Aberdeen, Ph.D. Thesis, 1972.

Vance, Shona M.: 'Mortifications (Bursaries and Endowments) for Education in Aberdeen. 1593–1660 and their Implemention in the 17th Century', University of Aberdeen, Ph.D. Thesis, 2000.

INDEX

R

S

T

W